THE

PRACTICAL

REVOLUTIONARIES

Recent Titles in
Contributions to the Study of World History

The Myth of the Revolution: Hero Cults and the Institutionalization
of the Mexican State, 1920-1940
Ilene V. O'Malley

Accommodation and Resistance: The French Left, Indochina
and the Cold War, 1944-1954
Edward Rice-Maximin

Genocide and the Modern Age: Etiology and Case Studies
of Mass Death
Isidor Wallimann and Michael N. Dobkowski, editors

Because They Were Jews: A History of Antisemitism
Meyer Weinberg

Societies in Upheaval: Insurrections in France, Hungary, and Spain
in the Early Eighteenth Century
Linda Frey and Marsha Frey

THE

PRACTICAL

REVOLUTIONARIES

A New Interpretation of the French Anarchosyndicalists

BARBARA MITCHELL

Contributions to the Study of World History,
Number 5

GREENWOOD PRESS
New York • Westport, Connecticut • London

Library of Congress Cataloging-in-Publication Data

Mitchell, Barbara.
  The practical revolutionaries.

  (Contributions to the study of world history,
ISSN 0885-9159 ; no. 5)
    Bibliography: p.
    Includes index.
    1. Syndicalism—France—History.   2. Trade-unions—
France—History.   I. Title.   II. Series.
HD6684.M56   1987   335'.82'0944   86-15028
ISBN 0-313-25289-0 (lib. bdg. : alk. paper)

Library of Congress Catalog Card Number: 86-15028
ISBN: 0-313-25289-0
ISSN: 0885-9159

First published in 1987

Greenwood Press, Inc.
88 Post Road West, Westport, Connecticut 06881

Printed in the United States of America

The paper used in this book complies with the
Permanent Paper Standard issued by the National
Information Standards Organization (Z39.48-1984).

10 9 8 7 6 5 4 3 2 1

For

Melissa

Christopher, Michael, and Elizabeth

Contents

Acknowledgments

As is often the case in these matters, it was in the wee
hours of morning of the absolutely last day before deadline
when I finished working on this manuscript. In my fatigue
and exhilaration, my original thought was to skip the
acknowledgment section so as to send the bundle on its
appointed way. Why bother, I asked, since no one looks at
that part of a book anyway. Besides, generally those who
receive public acclaim are either foundations which have
provided the writer with funds--institutions that don't
need any publicity--or graduate students and other toilers,
who would have preferred money to public mention. I looked
at the disarray around me. There were my notes--those
pounds of paper so lovingly carried back and forth across
continents, and generally guarded with a paranoiac
concern--now strewn about the floor, practically
indistinguishable from the reams of computer paper trailing
out of the trash basket. The floppy disks, once treated with
reverence because they concealed within their innocuous
plastic coverings the full flower of my wisdom, were vying
for space on the desk with some pizza crusts on a paper
plate, from, was it two days ago?--and I at the word
processor STILL--while the rest of the household, and most
of the city, and perhaps half of the world was enjoying the
sleep of the nonwriter. I wondered: would I just make a dash
for the car and wait outside the post office until it
opened, or would I say just one more thing? In spite of the
hour, the opportunity to say a few more words was too
difficult to pass up. Besides, I concluded, no
self-respecting study could receive the stamp of completion
without some form of public declaration. Surveying the
pandemonium around me, I asked myself, "Who will I thank?"
And myself replied, "Who do you THINK you'll thank for this
business? YOU, that's who!"

Indeed, I'm sure that more than one person who has
finished a similar project has been tempted to say simply:
Many thanks to me, for conceiving of the ideas, for sitting
on hard library chairs, for laboring in dusty archives, for

trying to make sense of my notes, for plugging away at the
typewriter when everyone else was having fun, and for
smiling good-naturedly at those blissfully distanced souls
who ask why you don't apply your time and talents (assuming
you have any) to writing something that can be made into a
television miniseries.

For a historian, research is a solitary occupation.
We're not like our colleagues engaged in the "hard"
sciences, who are constantly drawn out of themselves by
having to measure and plot the actions of laboratory mice,
anemones, or microbes. Historians have few such outside
imperatives. Our subjects tend to lie patiently still,
obediently waiting until WE touch them. Bringing them to
life may be plain hard work, but it is a rather solitary
labor that involves us at our own pace. We shuffle through
card catalogs, peruse bibliographies, hide away in the
stacks, and take notes that are generally recognizable only
to ourselves. Finally, we sit in front of a yellow pad or a
writing machine and try to put into words some of the
fancies which, up to that point in time, have only danced
around in our own heads.

So doing history tends to have a narcissistic quality
about it, making it very reasonable to feel that one has,
indeed, "done the whole business oneself." But of course one
hasn't, because there is always a vast network of people who
provide us with the means to spend so many marvelous hours
of self-indulgence. Unfortunately, because of the
limitations of time and space, only a very few of my
supporters can be mentioned here.

First of all, I would like to express my appreciation
to the Board of Trustees of Chaffey College for having given
me a sabbatical leave so that I could spend more time with
the good men and women of the syndicalist movement whose
stories have captivated me for so many years.

There are the countless librarians, archivists, and
general book toters at the Library of Congress, the Hoover
Institution, Stanford, the Honnold Library of the Claremont
Colleges, the library at the University of California,
Riverside, the Archives Nationales and the Bibliothèque
Nationale in Paris without whose efforts my work and
everyone else's, would not be possible. A special salute is
reserved for Priscilla Fernandez, Frank Pinkerton, Ethel
Lewis, Phyllis Smith, et al. at the Chaffey College Library
for their endeavors. Though small in size, the staff is
massive in talent.

There is also a large network of friends and colleagues
who are interested in what I do. They know who they are, so
they don't need to be listed by name, and they know how much
I have relied on their encouragement. Particular mention
must be made of Arch Getty, and especially Irwin Wall of the
University of California, Riverside, and David Gordon of the
University of North Carolina, for having worked with me on
the original manuscript. In my own academic milieu,
applause goes to François Briot, who helped me with my
French, and Sid Silliman who helped me with my logic. Over

the years, my crony Marjorie Suchocki has been an invaluable sounding board for my ideas. Indeed, she has served as the sage-femme in the delivery of this work.

My warmest appreciation also goes to my friends Pierre and Geneviève Cahour and Sylvie Roger--my French Connection. Without their consideration and warmth I would be a lonely sojourner, rootless and confused. Because of them, I am always able to go home to Paris.

As always, the first shall be last. Thanks be to the family: Stan and Irene Fountain, my parents; Donald, Eric, and Matthew, my sons; and Helga and Janet, their wives. A stupendous bravo is reserved for Van, my husband. All have diligently tried not to draw attention to the fact that the stews haven't been salted nor the socks mended while this work has been in progress. They have behaved quite bravely and rather cheerfully during my long mental and physical absences. Of course, over the years, they have all grown accustomed to seeing me with my nose in a book. Only this time, the book was mine.

1. An Introduction to the Movement and Its Critics

The story is told that in the closing moments of Gertrude Stein's life, she roused from unconsciousness, turned to the distraught Alice B. Toklas by her side, and asked: "What is the answer?" Receiving no reply from her unhappy companion, Stein continued: "In that case, what is the question?"(1)

Analyses of French revolutionary syndicalism have usually been formulated on the basis of the wrong questions posed of the movement. Until recently, therefore, historians and political analysts have tended to dismiss syndicalism as a movement whose influence was either negative or nil. "A cause without rebels," grumbles Peter Stearns; a movement "paralyzed outside the realm of theory," unable to generate among the French workers a revolutionary commitment to match its radical rhetoric.(2) The chasm existing between word and deed, between leaders and masses, according to the consensus, was evidenced in syndicalism's failure to put its theory into revolutionary practice on the eve of World War I. Unable to make a revolution, unionism was thrust into collaboration with the bourgeois government, thereby becoming more deeply embedded in the mire of conservatism and reformism. Syndicalism's inherent weakness was finally revealed when the supporters of the Third International withdrew from the Confédération Générale du Travail (CGT) in 1921. Bereft of its radical members, the CGT then moved further to the right as bureaucrats and white collar workers began to swell its ranks once more.(3)

Currently, treatment of the movement is being aided by the social historians, armed with new methodological tools, who are studying the phenomena of mass violence and strike activity. Increasingly, everything from incidences, intensity, quantity of strikes, and the numbers involved, to personal data on the strikers is being plotted, tabulated, and ranked.(4) Local and regional profiles, as well as occupational analyses, are being compiled.(5) The collection and ordering of this information is invaluable for providing hitherto untapped sources out of which to construct new interpretations.

The purpose of this study of French anarchosyndicalism from its inception to World War I is not to effect a thoroughgoing revision of the movement, nor to test new methodologies. The evidence brought to bear has been gathered largely from the public writings of those people who were involved directly in the labor movement. In that sense, the study falls clearly within the bounds of traditional intellectual history. The methodological approach is instrumentalist. It is based on the formulation of four questions and the answers syndicalists themselves provided to the problems encompassed in these queries. The questions? Two are traditional; two have not been fully explored. How did revolutionary syndicalists define direct action? What in their view constituted the <u>patrie</u>? How should the union organizations deal with two vital elements in society: peasants and women? The answers to these four questions are meant to provide the means to construct an image of French unionism beyond the traditional interpretations of the movement and to fill a lacunae in the history of the French left. It is further hoped that these responses will open other vistas for the formulation of new questions.

MARXIST ECONOMIC CATEGORIES AND BEYOND

To generate right answers, one must frame the right questions. For decades those questions asked about French anarchosyndicalism have been influenced by Marx's attitudes toward Proudhon, Bakunin, and their anarchist disciples in the International Workingmen's Association (IWA), known as the First International.(6) Analysts have generally regarded syndicalism as utopian, a premodern phenomenon, an aberration of socialism, and/or a catchall for the dissident elements from the First International. These assumptions tend to form the questioning paradigm in all analyses by Marxist and non-Marxist alike.

A premodern phenomenon: hypotheses and interpretations abound! Most of them lead to the assumption that syndicalism was an inherently inferior movement. Within the context of early nineteenth-century presuppositions about the linear quality of social evolution on which Marx based his synthesis, "premodern" (Rousseau's noble savage notwithstanding) connotes "primitive" and "backward." In a chapter dealing with "Marxism, Anarchism, Syndicalism," George Lichtheim articulates the traditional Marxist interpretation when he characterizes syndicalism as being composed of the anarchist remnants of the Paris Commune and the followers of the Proudhonist tradition of nonpolitical trade unions. These two groups embodied tendencies that Marx and Engels considered "expressions of backwardness and immaturity" that would disappear with the emergence of a modern industrial proletariat.(7)

It is easy to see that questioning based on the application of the dialectic, and on the Marxian theory of superstructure reflecting class structure, results in certain specific conclusions regarding the nature of union organization. French society remained persistently rural.

Peasants, Marx had declared, were incapable of developing social consciousness. The first generation of peasants who moved to the city provided no better medium for the growth of socialism, particularly in France, where workers migrated back and forth between city and country. The commitment to radicalism by this first generation of industrial workers would be sporadic at best. The real spur to unionism came from the artisans. Suffering from status-anxiety, facing economic deprivation, this last generation of city craftsmen moved beyond the milieu of workshop individualism, organizing collectively to stave off the intrusion of the machine and the peasant hordes moving into the factories.(8) But the efforts of this group were doomed from the start. The wheels of capitalism rolled on, inexorably grinding artisans and peasantry alike into industrial proletariat.

The conclusions drawn from this class-based analysis tend to highlight the uniqueness of French unionism. To analysts like Stearns, revolutionary syndicalism was regarded as transitory, immature, and embarrassingly backward when compared with the German and English trade union movements, which early aligned with leftist parties. To others, like George Woodcock, the persistence of the individualistic strains inherent among peasants and artisans explains the reason for the anarchist coloration of syndicalism.(9)

The Marxian inheritance is apparent in the work of many non-Marxist historians, such as Peter Stearns. While Stearns' work is valuable for the light it sheds upon the nature of French protest, nevertheless his conclusions reflect the author's apparent tendency to equate syndicalism with industrial immaturity. A comparison of strikes led by socialists and syndicalists, according to Stearns, indicates the presence of an overriding similarity between the two in terms of strike objectives and methods used. For Stearns the phenomenon of "premodern" syndicalists engaging in the same "modern" form of protest as French socialists presents a problem to be solved. The answer he finds is that either all French workers were conservative, or that most French workers "paid little heed to the long-range goals of syndicalism."(10) Preferring to opt for the latter interpretation, Stearns places the blame on syndicalism itself. French unionism, he states, "was not attuned to the industrial age, and French workers, though moderate, were."(11) Ultimately, concludes Stearns, the French worker entered the age of modern unionism with the industrialization of the economy, leaving syndicalism wallowing in a preindustrial mire.

The methodological approach of analyzing forms of protest was used by Stearns to test how closely the workers reflected the philosophy of the union leaders. This same methodology, developed to a greater sophistication, has been applied more widely by others, such as the Tillys and Edward Shorter. "Modern" forms of labor protest are union disciplined and directed toward gaining new rights. "Premodern" protest, on the other hand, includes such forms as food riots and wanton destruction of property typical of jacqueries. It is characterized by spontaneous explosions: short-lived, intensely violent, individualistic, and reflective of a society not yet grouped and disciplined by the machine.(12) The use of modern-premodern categories of protest is a useful one for social scientists attempting to deal with a collectively mute proletarian class. This approach also offers a useful tool to plot the course of industrialization: when protest activity moves beyond the bread-riot stage to that of organized strikes, it follows that the economy is entering the phase of industrial maturity.

Generally, the hypothesis of equating strike activity to industrialism holds true for Germany and England because of the more direct correlation evident in these two countries between economic and political centralization and the growth of nationally organized unionism. Such a methodology is not necessarily so well-suited to France, however, which perhaps accounts for the proliferation of regional studies on worker protest. One such study, a work by Michael Hanagan on organization and strike activity in the Stephanois, highlights the different tempo of industrialization. He notes that in many industries, certain functions continued to be carried on by artisans, but within a factory setting. While his study supports the traditional class-based view that artisans were the leaders of the labor movement, Hanagan also emphasizes the fact that it was the skilled workers who provided the catalyst for the mass protests of the industrial proletariat.(13) These data lead to two conclusions. One is that if the French economy was not neatly stratified, neither was French unionism. Further, until a better understanding is gained of the relationship between the artisans and the industrial proletariat, the tendency to characterize syndicalism as being preindustrial, and to dismiss it as premodern, is no longer valid.

CONFUSION REGARDING THE IDEOLOGICAL INHERITANCE

If analyses of revolutionary syndicalism are complicated by persistent stereotypes of the socioeconomic order, interpretations of the movement are also hampered by the prevalence of similarly erroneous presumptions regarding the ideological content and heritage of unionism. Again, Marx's attitudes toward the French radicals have tended to influence the questioning process. Was the movement utopian? A shelter for the libertarians cast out of the First International? The anarchist word-made-flesh? If one looks at the syndicalist movement through the Marxian perspective, then French unionism was hopelessly utopian. Based on the twin strains of Bakuninism and Proudhonianism, syndicalist ideology could only produce a feeble organization, neither grounded in reality, nor able to survive the industrial process. Proudhon's tenets, resting on antipolitical action and mutualism, held no practical reality for workers after the advent of universal male suffrage. Bakunin's idea of creative violence might appeal to ignorant peasants. But a proletariat capable of working collectively toward its own emancipation within the context of a party structure, must dismiss as sheer romantic nonsense Bakunin's call for terror by the deed.

The antipolitical and antitechnological tendencies of syndicalism were anachronistic in an industrializing, centralizing, modern society: "Pathological" and "reactionary," according to Lichtheim.(14) Marxist socialism was based on scientific analyses of the past and present; it was future-oriented. French syndicalism, on the other hand, looked neither to the realities of the present nor to the possibilities of the future. Based only on nostalgic longing for a golden age by artisans and peasants, the movement was destined to disappear.

Thus the "otherness" of syndicalism was early established, and "difference" has often had a pejorative connotation, particularly with respect to the concepts of syndicalists and socialists regarding the proper route to revolution. Syndicalism preached revolution, the critics charge, but its "economic" rather than "political" approach was negative: antidemocratic, antipolitical, antirational, and antimodern. Marxist socialism's revolutionary goal, however, was pursued by positive action and practical reform. With its notions of direct action, particularly that of sabotage and general strike, syndicalism was nihilistic. Socialists sought change by orderly collective activity. One was productive, seeking a society based on economic justice. The other, according to some, was counterproductive, and degenerated into fascism.(15)

The difference between socialists and syndicalists, historians have often noted, was early established, and was based on the differences between Marx's ideas and those of Bakunin and Proudhon. For libertarian George Woodcock, those differences that led to the 1872 schism in the IWA were based on inherent personality conflicts between Marx and Bakunin:

> Marx was authoritarian, Bakunin a libertarian; Marx was a centralist, Bakunin a federalist; Marx advocated political action for the workers and planned to conquer the state; Bakunin opposed political action and sought to destroy the state; Marx stood for what we now call nationalization of the means of production; Bakunin stood for workers' control.(16)

Differences over basic principles rather than of personality, according to Lichtheim, caused the tensions between French socialists and syndicalists. The reason for the schism between these two wings of the French left, he maintains, was the disagreement over the questions of ouvriérisme, that is, workers' control of the class struggle without the aid of intellectuals, and opposition to parliamentary action--two distinct tenets of Proudhonian philosophy.(17)

What of the contribution of Proudhon's thought to revolutionary syndicalism? This has been a topic of exploration by some analysts.(18) Generally, the consensus is that Proudhon was the ideological grandfather of French unionism. Certainly to syndicalists themselves, the movement was directly related to Proudhon in its critique of existing society, its vision of a new order, and its advocacy of the methods to be used to bring about unionist goals. Syndicalism's position regarding the state and the political structure and its support of direct action as a means to revolution was directly linked to Proudhon's ideas on anarchism and federalism. The leading light of the bourses du travail, Fernand Pelloutier, declared that syndicalism was the realization of "the federative principles formulated by Proudhon and Bakunin."(19) Syndicalist Hubert Lagardelle conceded that direct action echoed Proudhon's assertion that "each class must develop its own organs of emancipation."(20) Syndicalists had a clearer concept of Proudhonian philosophy than did others, it seems. Yet much of the reigning controversy regarding syndicalist thought stems from a confusion over Proudhon's philosophy and the inability of modern historians to place Proudhon on the traditional spectrum of political left and right. Woodcock, for instance, entitled his chapter on Proudhon "The Man of Paradox." Lichtheim simply dismissed Proudhonian philosophy as being muddled and simplistic.(21)

The following discussion of syndicalism's attitudes toward the state, toward direct action, and toward women and peasants does take note of the Proudhonian inheritance of syndicalism. .But what emerges in this study is that while Proudhon's ideas influenced the early trade unionists, his philosophy came to have little bearing on syndicalist actions as unionism matured. Actually, Proudhon's theories had more in common with the guiding philosophy of the right--of employer-sponsored labor organizations and Catholic syndicalism--than of the left. In fact, the underlying presumption of this presentation is that French syndicalism was not the direct translation of any single intellectual system. As with Marxism, its ideological inheritance was based on a synthesis of the concepts generated by the Enlightenment and the French Revolution. Just as the theorists of revolution were in accord concerning the vision of a new society, although disagreeing violently over the means by which to prepare for it, so too were syndicalists in agreement with Marxists over the goals of socialism. Unionists disagreed with socialists only over the manner in which the revolution should be directed in France. They affirmed the notion of the class struggle and the belief that the proletariat was the only class that could bring about permanent revolution.

The confusion regarding where to place Proudhon on the political spectrum holds true for the syndicalists. By

positing a new vision of society, the syndicalists were
revolutionary. But since the object of their wrath was the
paraphernalia of the modern world--liberalism, capitalism,
democracy, and state centralization--revolutionary
syndicalists have been deemed reactionaries in disguise.
The problem with most analyses has been the tendency to
posit "reform," in this case defined as working for better
material conditions for labor, as the antithesis to
"revolution." Stearns, for instance, assumes that because
syndicalists participated in bread-and-butter demands, the
movement failed to live up to its revolutionary posture. In
that sense, anarchosyndicalism was nothing more than a
French version of American Gomperism. Robert Goetz-Girey,
however, rightly declares that "the idea of reform would
always be one of the poles of the syndical movement."(22)
Félicien Challaye points out the naïveté of drawing too
sharply a distinction between reformist and revolutionary
elements within syndicalism. Reformism, he notes, was
always an animating spirit of revolutionary syndicalism
because syndicalists were never partisans of an
all-or-nothing approach.(23)

      This study will go beyond the observations of both
Goetz-Girey and Challaye in demonstrating that economic
reforms were never perceived by syndicalists as part of a
polarity, but were always regarded as a way station to
revolution. This being the case, then political analysts
must look beyond the traditional definitions of reform and
revolution when assessing the radical content of French
unionism. They will also have to shed the classical notions
that political action is narrowly encompassed in
parliamentary and electoral activity.

GUIDED BY PRACTICAL NECESSITY

      Once the qualitative differences between socialism and
syndicalism are revealed to be less vast than were formerly
held, then some of the questions traditionally posed of the
movement elicit different answers. Was syndicalism
antimodern in its philosophy and approach, trying vainly to
resurrect a long-past golden age? If one uses as a
criterion for measuring modern tendencies the acceptance of
industrialism as a practical means to bring about greater
well-being for all, then syndicalists were as modern in
their outlook as the Marxian socialists. Fernand Pelloutier
said the machine in no way debased that which in England
"they call the standard of life."(24) Even Stearns admits
that syndicalists did not dwell on what he believed were
"the anti-industrial implications of their doctrine."(25)
Syndicalists, Pelloutier charged, wanted to carry out the
revolution by means of progressively eliminating "capitalist
forms of association, production, and consumption, and
replacing them with corresponding communist forms."(26)
      Was syndicalism the ideological product of anarchist
dissidents from the International? For anarchosyndicalists
the movement was not part of an ongoing heresy. Syndicalist

Emile Pouget stated that the movement was "no more than the logical following" of the First International.(27) Was syndicalism an aberration of socialism? Certainly syndicalists never perceived themselves as different. Holding strongly to the notion of class conflict, those who spoke for the unions regarded their mission as a necessary crusade to rescue socialism from the malaise into which it had fallen as the result of having spent too much time doing battle in the electoral arena.

Lastly, one must inquire if this crusading impulse was not utopian in character. Once the traditional stereotypes have been shed concerning the movement, new questions can be posed of syndicalism. The conclusion drawn, which is the central thesis of this study, is that there is very little of a utopian nature about syndicalism, that it was a very pragmatic movement in theory and practice. Syndicalist philosophy was in constant evolution, a synthesis of past theories practically applied to the needs of the times. It was not the ideological manifestation of French national character, but rather the natural response to the French milieu. There was no single ideological mentor, little written protocol, and no intellectual priesthood to serve as guardian of the sacred flame. It was no more compounded exclusively from the theories of Marx, Bakunin, or Proudhon, than it was the metaphysical inspiration of Blanqui or Sorel.

In fact, it is not the intent of this study to examine syndicalism from the vantage point of the thought of the syndicalist intellectuals such as Edouard Berth, Hubert Lagardelle, or Georges Sorel. The theories of the "Sorelian Syndicalists" have been ably explored by Jules Levey in a 1967 Ph.D. dissertation. Sorel's philosophy has been brilliantly examined by Professor John Stanley in a recently published book.(28) Rather, perhaps reflective of the ouvriérisme of the syndicalists themselves, this study seeks to explore the revolutionary syndicalist movement in light of the ideas expressed by those men and women associated with unionism who contributed articles to the working-class press and arguments at the trade-union congresses. What emerges from this approach is the conclusion that the ideas of the lesser known working-class representatives had as much weight in determining the policies of the bourses and the CGT as did the theories of the well-known leaders, such as Fernand Pelloutier, Georges Yvetot, Alphonse Merrheim, Victor Griffuelhes, Emile Pouget, Georges Dumoulin, and Léon Jouhaux. While the latter are more often quoted in the succeeding text, and are certainly regarded as the major spokesmen of the syndicalist movement, the respective philosophies of these men who frequently argued among themselves, were often sharply divergent on important issues. The only point of consensus among them was that the social revolution must occur in order to bring into being a just society, and that unionism was the means to achieve that end. Beyond that commitment, syndicalist leaders shared little common philosophy. Indeed, philosophy had little to do with French anarchosyndicalism: theory was always the adjunct to practice. The movement always worked within those limits prescribed by the social, economic, and political imperatives.

Certainly the development of the working-class movement was influenced by the economic order. From 1871 to 1914 France continued to be a major force, enjoying second place as a world colonial power and a third-place position in Europe in industrial terms. Yet, during the period coinciding with the growth of syndicalism, France's place of importance in Europe and the world diminished, partly due to global factors, but mostly as a result of inherent economic defects in France.

There was the rural nature of the country, compounded by the persistence of small landholdings and subsistence agriculture. In 1896, after twenty-two years of agricultural depression, 44.9 percent of the French population was still employed in agriculture.(29) Many of the surplus producers, particularly those engaged in viniculture and mulberry cultivation, had lost their crops to disease. Others, such as grain farmers, had suffered major setbacks as a result of competition from the United States and other countries. In the face of these disasters, subsistence farming looked even more attractive to large numbers of rural landowners.(30) This penchant for subsistence agriculture, combined with the price depression, meant that tenant farmers, smallholders, and large landowners lacked the needed surplus to modernize or add acreage. The agricultural depression also meant that farmers had little available cash to buy the goods produced by the industrial sector. Potential consumption was further reduced as a result of the slow growth in population in the years before World War I. Population stagnation was the result of a host of factors: poor diet, minimal health care, wretched living conditions, and a very high infant mortality rate, a problem compounded by the widespread practice of employing wet nurses, who passed along diseases and malnutrition to their charges.(31)

Of course the greatest contribution to the sluggish economy in France lay with the business sector. Used to serving local or regional needs, the majority of businesses were family owned, managed, and financed. The typical French businessman thought in terms of thrift and low overhead, keeping production costs minimal so he could reinvest his profits. Self-financing was cheaper and safer. From 1896 to 1913, 1.6 billion francs of the 2.5 billion invested annually in French businesses was supplied by the owner.(32) Banking facilities tended to be localized also, so vast amounts of money were not available for investment. Without sufficient capital there were neither incentives nor resources for expansion. Artisanal labor and luxury goods production continued to dominate the business sector at the expense of industrialization. While France remained second to none in its production of luxury goods, such a system offered few incentives for expansion. Artisanal work units were static, with scant interest in or capital for modernization. This is why in 1904 the traditional

industries of textile, clothing, and leather still employed
the bulk of French workers. And of that number, 68 percent
of those employed were women earning minimal wages.(33)
     Economic recovery began after 1896. This upturn was
due largely to three factors: increased investment of
domestic capital, the rise of farm income with the advent of
protectionist legislation, and the spread of electrification
and railroads. These factors provided the dynamics for a
series of local and regional industrial revolutions. In
turn, these catalysts stimulated urbanization and population
concentration, the growth of newer industries, such as
metallurgy, and the increase in the number of workers
employed in the industrial sector. By 1911, 45 percent of
industrial workers worked in factories employing over fifty
workers.(34)
     Industrialization brought changes in the condition of
the working class. Per capita income rose; living standards
improved; and life expectancy increased. Changes were
manifested in employer-employee relationships. Larger
industrial units had required greater investment, so
employers were sometimes more reluctant to lay off their
workers. Other industrialists practiced a form of
paternalism, providing workers with company medical care and
factory housing. This seemingly better treatment brought to
the individual worker a greater sense of job security.
     But the industrial revolution did not follow the same
pattern in France as it did in other western countries.
Although per capita incomes increased, wide divergences in
wages continued to exist among various occupational groups,
in different regions, and between the sexes. A few years
were added to life expectancy, but mortality rates
fluctuated wildly by department and even by Parisian
arrondissement. Large investments might make the
industrialist a little more protective of his workers, but
it also gave him more incentive to call upon the government
to use force in putting down workers' demonstrations. The
increase in the large factory unit neither destroyed the
artisanal class, nor did much to elevate the technological
expertise of the unskilled factory worker. Some large-scale
newer industries, such as the manufacture of automobiles,
for instance, employed artisanal labor.(35) The rest of
those working in the larger factories continued to be little
more than machine tenders.
     What the industrial revolution brought to France was a
change in scope, if not in scale. From 1871 to 1914 factory
production increased, but regional variations were
heightened; class differences were amplified; and the
economy stayed localized and decentralized. The pace of
change quickened, but the micro-unit of production remained
the norm in both the industrial and the agrarian sectors.
Thus, French society consisted of an economic mosaic in
which industrialization occurred rapidly in some places,
sluggishly in others, and not at all in other locales. The
social order, like the economic order, was also in a state
of transition. Peasants were becoming proletarians,
artisans were moving into industry, unskilled workers were

becoming skilled. If France was a socioeconomic mosaic the
labor movement, reflecting that milieu, had to embody within
itself all the different patterns and paces of industrial
evolution. Given that reality, syndicalism had to be
inclusionary rather than exclusionary. As will be
demonstrated, the movement sought to provide a large
theoretical and organizational umbrella under which could
huddle Frenchmen of every stripe: Positivists, socialists,
cooperationists, liberals, anarchists, Marxists, mutualists,
unionists, conservatives, Catholics, atheists, nudists, and
vegetarians.(36)

Pragmatism, then, was syndicalism's guiding force. The
confederal structure of the CGT, for instance, was perfectly
suited to the needs of the diverse society. The bourses
were grouped geographically, the unions by occupation.
These units made up the horizontal structure that took
account of philosophical differences and provided an outlet
for the varied demands of the assorted trades adhering to
the Confederation. These groups were represented in the
CGT, the vertical structure of which allowed the different
organizations to maintain their distinction and total
autonomy, while still being affiliated to a central body in
the interest of building working-class unity, solidarity,
and strength. The CGT was a practical structure in which to
carry out the class struggle. That reality, rather than any
felt need to remain consistent with anarchist philosophy,
served as the impetus for maintaining a confederal
organization.

Syndicalism's stand on party politics also had little
to do with philosophy. The CGT's emphasis on direct action,
as opposed to parliamentary inaction, may have squared
ideologically with Proudhon. But philosophy was less an
imperative than was the practical need to survive. To do
that syndicalism had to overcome the atomism of the
socioeconomic order. It also had to thwart the politicians
of the Third Republic and stave off the political socialists
who wished to turn the unions into recruiting adjuncts of
the party. Common sense influenced the antipartisan stand
of anarchosyndicalism. The Third Republic inspired loyalty
only insofar as it was the unlovely benefactor of the
Revolution of 1789. Outside of that inheritance, the
Republic had little else to endear it to its people. The
guiding political force was a mass of shifting and falling
coalitions. The French people smarted under the numerous
political scandals and crises: the attempted takeover by
General McMahon, the exposé of wholesale government
corruption over the construction of the Panama Canal, the
malfeasance and numerous cover-ups over the Dreyfus
affair.(37) The political structure of the Third Republic
was scarcely adequate to carry on the workers' revolution.
Lacking a trustworthy electoral medium, the leaders of the
working class could only fall back upon themselves.

Revolutionary syndicalism, therefore, was a movement
based on practical action, designed to appeal to a diverse
work force united only in its realization of individual
suffering and a desire for immediate material reform. As

such, syndicalism emphasized less a future apocalypse than
it demanded that the present world be made more habitable.
To achieve these goals, it directed itself toward organizing
the workers and prodding them along the path toward a just
order, all the while burrowing from within the capitalist
regime by gaining reforms. The French syndicalist movement,
this study concludes, was consciously designed to be an
instrument of practical revolution.

A RHYTHM OF REPRESSION AND ENCOURAGEMENT

Because syndicalism was so clearly the product of the
French milieu, a brief historical overview tracing the
contributing factors in the development of the union
movement is helpful.(38) The modern working-class movement
began with the passage of the 1884 legislation (the
Waldeck-Rousseau Law) giving workers the right to associate
in defense of their professional interests. Neither
working-class action nor labor organizations began in 1884,
however. The compagnonnages of journeymen dated from the
fifteenth century. These organizations, formed within the
guild structure, were generally devoted to providing mutual
aid for their members. But they also directed strikes and
boycotts in defense of their economic interests.(39)
When when all citizens were given the right to combine
freely in 1790, workers quickly took advantage of the law by
organizing into trade unions. When a multitude of strikes
ensued, employers demanded protection against this "new
tyranny." The government obliged with the passage of the Le
Chapelier law in 1791, forbidding all combinations for the
purpose of changing existing labor conditions. As a result,
workers turned either to organizing legal "friendly
societies" or to illegal underground activity: the formation
of sociétés de résistance by which workers could protect
themselves against the rapaciousness of the employers. Over
the succeeding decades, the more prosperous craftsmen, such
as the typographers, often defied government regulations and
organized.(40)
Proscriptions against workers' organizations continued
until the Second Empire, when the right to strike and form
associations was granted by Napoleon III. As a result of
this new freedom, organizational activity escalated, as did
offensive strike action for higher wages and shorter hours.
Chambres Syndicales Ouvrières, later known as syndicats,
were formed in the older industries and in those
occupations, such as metallurgy, that had never been
organized. In addition, French workers participated in the
creation of the International Workingmen's Association in
London in 1864. The bulk of delegates from the French
section, which came to be the largest national section in
the First International, were Proudhonists who supported
workers' activity in the economic realm through the
formation of unions, cooperatives, and mutual banks, rather
than through party activity. As anarchists, they placed
great emphasis on spontaneous action, voluntarism,

federalism, and ouvriérisme, thereby putting them in direct opposition to the Marxist program of collectivism, electoral activity, and the centralization of both the International and the state.

At home the syndicalists' position was always tenuous, as the French government acted to stamp out any hints of radicalism existing within the movement. Government repression of the workers reached a crescendo as a result of the belief that the Commune was directly inspired by members of the First International. Tens of thousands, the bulk of whom were neither unionists nor Internationalists, were executed, transported, or imprisoned.

The massacre of the Communards changed completely the nature of the working-class movement and socialism. On the one hand, as David Stafford notes, the subsequent failure of the violence of 1871 to bring on the social revolution served to discredit for many the Blanquist notion of a coup de main. On the other, government repression of the Commune destroyed confidence in the Proudhonist notion, dear to the hearts of many French workers, that emancipation would occur through peaceful evolution. Most important, the Commune threw the nascent syndicalist movement into a temporary eclipse. With most of the French militants either dead or in exile, unionism was forced into a period of moderation. In the post-1871 twilight, working-class restraint became the keynote, and workers' cooperatives and mutuals the panacea.(41)

The feebleness of the working-class movement was evident in the proceedings of the first national workers' congress held in Paris in 1876. The right of assembly was still illegal, so this group of delegates met as private citizens. The distinctly working-class character of the movement was enunciated. So too was the distrust of politicians ("theoretical men") and party action. The delegates condemned socialist theories as being "bourgeois utopian." But they also rejected strikes for creating "civil wars among workers." The bourgeois press lauded the delegates for their moderation.(42)

The next two decades were pivotal in the formation of revolutionary syndicalism. Worker unrest was spurred during the depression years. This was also a time of vacillating attitudes toward the workers, of severe government repression of all forms of protest between 1875 and 1878, and of overtures by the "opportunist" governmental leaders between 1879 and 1884 aimed at welding an alliance with the working class in order to bolster the Republic. This attempt at détente saw the passage of legislation designed to woo the workers. The government granted amnesty to the Communards and passed the 1884 law allowing workers to organize. Of course, Radical Party Opportunism was not radicalism. As L. Goyard noted in 1911, the Waldeck-Rousseau Law was designed more "to recognize those organizations politically [rather than] professionally," and was not intended to give the workers full freedom of association and action.(43) What the government could give, it could also take away. Faced with strikes, unemployment, and threats from Boulangists, radicals, and anarchists, the government plunged into another round of repression between 1883 and 1886 that included the use of troops against striking workers.

GUESDISTS, BROUSSISTS, AND ALLEMANISTS

Economic fluctuations and government vacillation were not the only impediments to the growth of unionism. More problematical was the ideological sectarianism persisting among those seeking unity. The collectivist-federalist debate that helped kill the IWA was only one aspect in the bitter struggle being waged among Blanquists, Bakuninists, positivists, mutualists, cooperationists, and radicals within the workers' organizations.

The paralysis caused by clashing philosophies begged for the emergence of a powerful leader. Marxist disciple Jules Guesde surfaced at the Third Workers' Congress, held in Marseille in 1879, as the one to lead the unionists from their sectarian wilderness.(44) The red posters adorning the walls of the Folies-Bergères, where the delegates were meeting, offered slogans for everyone: "the Earth to the Peasant, the Tool to the Worker, Work for all--Science; Peace; Union; Justice."(45) But the resolutions adopted by the delegates, proclaiming equality between the sexes and supporting collectivization of the soil, were clearly Guesdist in their inspiration. Having gained the working-class tribunal, Guesde sought to organize socialism in France and wed labor to it. His task would not be an easy one.

By the Fourth Workers' Congress, held in Le Havre in 1880, a new leaven was introduced. The Communards had been amnestied, and some of the militants were in attendance. The delegates ranged from anarchists and collectivists on the left to the more timorous on the right who feared radicalism. The left united to push through a program that was an admixture of the theories of Marx and Bakunin. The moderate syndicalists, those who remained committed to mutualism and cooperation, left the congress and formed their own organization, which ultimately died in indifference after only two congresses.(46)

If apathy was the fatal ingredient among the moderates, passion was the tragic flaw of the radicals. In 1881 delegates met at Reims. Arguments broke out over everything: from adopting a program, to placing blame for the poor showing of socialist candidates in the 1881 elections. In the melee, Paul Brousse and his lieutenants grabbed the spotlight from Jules Guesde.(47) The congress threw out the Guesdist proposal, adopted the previous year, sanctioning tight party control over elections, and adopted Brousse's newspaper as the official organ of the organization.

At the next congress, held in Saint-Etienne in 1882, Guesde was only a voice crying in the wind. In the interim between the two congresses, he had campaigned steadily for a tightly organized and disciplined Socialist Party. The setting was ripe for schism, which came swiftly. When all of Guesde's resolutions were rejected, he and his followers left the hall. Sighing good riddance to Guesdist authoritarianism, the Broussists then voted to exclude this group from the party. They further agreed to form themselves into a new political party favoring a federalist structure and "possibilist" action. Brousse had declared himself in favor of seeking immediate reforms by splitting socialist demands, he stated, "into what is possible."(48) With their antagonists purged, the possibilists were able to hold an orderly convention in 1883. Delegates did little more than change the name of their group to the Fédération des Travailleurs Socialistes (FTS) in an attempt to attract all factions. The Guesdist minority, rejecting possibilist reformism, organized itself into the Parti Ouvrier (PO, later the POF). Meeting in Roubaix the following year (1884), they declared themselves a party committed to Marxist orthodoxy, and pledged to carry the class war into the political domain by winning elections.(49)

Despite the initial victory, the power of the Broussist FTS was clearly on the wane. During the next few years the party leaders devoted the bulk of their energies to winning local elections. As part of their political offensive, they also supported the creation of a central bourse du travail in Paris, with annexes in all the departments. Despite some modest success in the 1887 elections to the Paris Municipal Council, internal factionalism was growing. Challenging the Broussists were the more radical representatives of the working class, led by printer and former Communard Jean Allemane, who castigated the possibilists for their alleged obsession with politics. Political infighting halted briefly during the Boulanger crisis of 1888, as all factions within the FTS agreed to support the Republic against the dictator. But schism was a foregone conclusion.

In the months before the 1890 convention, the disciples of Allemane had carried on a vigorous offensive in the newspapers against possibilist opportunism, charging the Broussists with having sold out to the bourgeoisie in the interest of political expediency. The propaganda campaign against Brousse served to attract the more radical elements to the Allemanist side, but it was not strong enough to put Allemane at the head of the party. At the next national congress of the FTS, the Allemanist "rebels" were expelled. Without its revolutionary element, the Broussist-dominated FTS moved further to the right. Four years later the party held its last real congress in Tours.

The year 1890 also saw the convening of the Guesdist PO, their first congress in six years. The meeting was short and uneventful, with the delegates doing little more than agreeing to demonstrate on May Day. During those years the major activity of the Guesdists had been carried on within the Fédération Nationale Syndicaliste (FNS, then FS). In 1886 a national congress of unions had been convened at Lyon for the express purpose of establishing a federation of trade unions. This "union of unions" was seen as being necessary to build working-class unity and to provide a socialist counterorganization to the Radical-dominated Union des Chambres Syndicales. The FNS was the creation of representatives from all philosophical schools, but it very quickly became "a hotbed of Guesdisme." (50)

By now radicalism was also firmly ensconced in the newly organized Parti Ouvrier Socialiste Révolutionnaire (POSR), an Allemanist political creation. In 1891 the POSR met in Paris. Delegates to this first convention agreed to undertake aggressive action to win the agrarian proletariat to socialism and the eight-hour day for workers. The delegates also warmly applauded the use of the general strike, which they suggested might be the tactic to precipitate the socialist revolution, and committed the new party to unionism rather than to electioneering. Members were urged to join a union and to create one where none existed.

Allemanists were united in their belief that political action was only a means of propaganda designed to achieve "a rigorously revolutionary" end.(51) The two Guesdist organizations--the FNS (now the FS) and the PO, on the other hand--remained clearly committed to political action, albeit with a slight deviation. In 1888 the FS had met at Bordeaux-Le Bouscat. The most surprising aspect of the congress was the adoption of the principle of the general strike, rather than the conquest of political power, as the means by which to make the revolution. The notion of the general strike had been a bone of contention within the IWA and was supported by French anarchists. This deviation from Marxist orthodoxy must have been with the approval of Guesde, who was not in attendance. Engels would later complain to Paul Lafargue during a walk through Hyde Park that Guesde's support of the principle of the general strike was "an absurdity" and a hangover from his anarchist days.(52) It was a case of temporary absurdity, however, because at the next congress of the FNS, held in Calais in 1890, the Guesdist majority accorded only qualified support to the principle: maintaining that a general strike of miners alone would be effective. The question of the general strike was clearly becoming another schism-producing issue to the leftist-oriented unionists.

At their Lyon congress in 1891, the delegates to the PO concerned themselves mainly with national political issues in preparation for the forthcoming elections. But dissension was brewing in the wings. When the FS met that same year, the Guesdist majority found itself confronted by a growing number of union representatives who were converted to the principle of the general strike, which the Guesdists now completely rejected as an illusory form of action that would deflect energy from the revolution. But the groundswell of support for the tactic could not be denied. When the fifth congress of the FS convened in Marseille in 1892, the supporters of the general strike were ready. Over Guesdist objections, and after a sterling defense by then socialist journalist Aristide Briand, the principle of a universal general strike as a viable instrument of combat was adopted by the FS.(53) Having lost the vote, the Guesdists lost interest in the labor federation and turned their full attention to their political party.

Meanwhile, other groups of socialists were also in the process of organizing. Blanquists rallied around Communard Edouard Vaillant. Their platform, a reflection of Vaillant's discipleship of both Proudhon and Blanqui, was based on the doctrine of double autonomy: independent economic action by the unions and independent action by the parties. In 1898 this group adopted the name Parti Socialiste Révolutionnaire (PSR). There were also the Independents, formed first as a cadre of socialist deputies in 1886. This faction, among whom Alexandre Millerand and Jean Jaurès were the leading lights, became the most important socialist group in parliament. But the Independents were hampered because there was no unity of philosophy among its members.(54) Of greater significance to the left in 1892 was the organization of the Fédération des Bourses du Travail (FBT).

THE FBT AND THE CGT CHALLENGE

Since 1886, when the first bourses were opened under the aegis of the FTS, numerous bourses had sprouted forth in the provinces. These bourses reflected both new and old forms of organization. As with the compagnonnages, the bourses served as employment bureaus and fraternal organizations, providing itinerant workers with clean beds, baths, and suppers. They were also cultural centers in that they compiled libraries and offered vocational classes for the local unions. The bourses also demonstrated the effects of positivist philosophy in that the members committed themselves to the task of compiling statistics on such things as the variances in the cost of living, wage rates, and job availability. Acting in this capacity, the bourses generally received municipal support in the way of cash subventions or rooms in the mairies from which to operate. In addition, the bourses quickly became the chief center for organizing trade unions. These unions were usually affiliated by profession. Under the sheltering umbrella of the local bourses, however, the unions tended to take on a more regional characteristic, organizing into federations, with the federations subsequently forming into the FBT.(55)

Despite the mutualist activity and government support of the bourses, the FBT clearly demonstrated a radical cast. The thirteen bourse delegates who met at Saint-Etienne in 1892 included Blanquists, Allemanists and non-Guesdist members of the FS who supported the principle of the general strike. The object of the meeting was to group workers in a national organization of bourse federations to serve as a rival to the PO-controlled FS. But another result of this meeting was the convening in 1894 of a national confederal congress of unions, groups, federations, and bourses in Nantes open to all.(56)

The show of unity was also intended to provide the
means by which to launch an offensive against party control
of labor. In an attempt to stave off a possible purge of
Guesdist influence, the PO convened its congress in the same
city, meeting ahead of the general convention. The
Guesdists expected to impress the laborites with the
efficacy of political action. In 1893, mostly because of
the Panama scandals and the decomposition of Boulangism,
over fifty socialists had been elected to parliament. The
congress opened with a cordial salute to the socialist
deputies, adopted an agrarian program, and changed the
party's name to the Parti Ouvrier Français (POF) in order to
enunciate the political and economic aspects of socialist
action. The delegates then soundly rejected the principle
of the general strike as being utopian and unrealizable and
one that would bring reaction and reprisals, ruin unionism,
and divide city and country workers.

The delegates to the larger confederal congress met the
following day amid great tumult and confusion. After two
days of intense debate on the issue of the general strike,
cloture was finally voted. The next day the resolution
favoring the general strike won by 65 to 37. The minority
then convoked a separate meeting of the FS and declared
itself an autonomous organ. Its actions were only a show of
bravado since the Guesdist labor group had suffered
irreparable division, with one faction dependent on the POF
and the other clearly under the influence of the FBT.
Thereafter the FS limped along as an appendage to the POF
until its final convention in 1898.

By contrast, in the spring of 1895 the FBT held a
successful congress at Nîmes. Fernand Pelloutier, a former
Radical-turned-Guesdist, had been converted to anarchism
because of his preference for federalist principles of
organization and because anarchism emphasized the individual
in opposition to the centralized state.(57) A brilliant
organizer and theoretician, Pelloutier was elected secretary
of the Federal Committee of the FBT. The major source of
conflict within the congress was over the question of where
to house the directing body of the organization: in Paris or
the provinces. The issue seemed to be one reflecting the
longstanding fears of provincials against Parisian
domination since arguments were all based on the issue of
federalism versus central control. But more pointedly at
issue was the fact that the bulk of Guesdist influence lay
in the provinces while, in Paris, the bourse was run by
anarchists and Allemanists. Central direction would
neutralize Guesdist direction in those bourses under their
control. Pelloutier voted with the majority in favor of
establishing a permanent office in Paris, thereby setting
aside, at least temporarily, his commitment to the
federalist principles of anarchism in favor of political
expediency.

Although the FBT was a strong organization,
particularly under Pelloutier's leadership, another
organization ultimately came to encompass the FBT. With all
factions still jockeying for control, another national

congress was convened in Limoges in 1895. Included in the delegations were bourse leaders, those of the FS who supported the general strike, and militants from the POSR, now in eclipse, including Allemane himself. The time had come, delegates agreed, to organize a stronger national committee in order to coordinate labor activities. The new organization took the name of Confédération Générale du Travail (CGT).(58) Its task was to serve as a kind of clearing house of labor activity between syndicats and bourses on the local, regional, and national levels. The CGT would be housed in Paris, but would hold congresses in various parts of the country. Delegates to the administrative council and to the congresses were to be elected by the individual organizations. The duties of the national council were to carry on propaganda and coordinate strikes. More important, every bourse, local union, and trade federation adhering to the Confederation, regardless of the number of members in its organization, would have one vote. Despite the scope of its charge, for several years the CGT remained a shadow organization. The real link between the various corporate groups continued to be the bourses and the FBT.

During the years coinciding with Pelloutier's leadership, the FBT was able to stave off both CGT and Guesdist domination. At the Tours congress in 1896, Pelloutier successfully held out once more against the proposal to rotate the Federation's headquarters annually. In 1897 another Guesdist-inspired foray was defeated. The general strike was upheld, and a resolution was passed disclaiming political action and declaring that the issue would never again be raised. Victorious finally against the party socialists, the FBT was less successful in the battle against being subsumed into the CGT.

From the outset, the FBT intended to dominate the CGT, just as the POF had controlled the FS. Pelloutier's refusal to attend the first three congresses of the Confederation was an indication of how unimportant he regarded that organization to be.(59) The Federation even snatched a page from the Guesdists' book by convening its own congresses in the same city, with delegates meeting immediately before the opening of the CGT conventions in order to marshal their forces. At the first few congresses, the more financially solvent FBT was able to dictate successfully to the underfinanced CGT on questions involving the role of the bourses in the Confederation.(60) Thus, for a few years at least, the FBT remained officially independent, united to the CGT by little more than a mutual commitment to carry out the work of social revolution, particularly through the use of the general strike, and by its desire to dominate the infant organization.

TOWARD SOCIALIST PARTY UNITY

By 1898 not even the POF seemed to be a threat to the FBT. Guesdists had spent much time in 1892 discussing the problems of centralization versus local autonomy. One resolution gave the wayward unionists a stern rebuke. Those rejecting the commitment to political struggle were wrong; political activity was indispensable. The POF further urged its members to join the unions and declared that it was the workers' duty to adhere to the POF. At Montluçon in 1898, the party leaders again called for unity within the left. The Dreyfus affair had once more split the groups. Allemanists, Broussists, and independent socialists vigorously supported Dreyfus. Guesde and Vaillant were claiming that the Dreyfus affair was not part of the workers' struggle and should be ignored. In response to the controversy, delegates at Montluçon also called for the formation of a central committee in which all the socialist factions would be equally represented.

The following year (1899) President Faure died. Paul Déroulède attempted to stage another Eighteenth Brumaire. Fearful of a monarchist plot, the socialist factions within the party joined together in a Comité d'Entente. A congress of unity was held in Paris in April 1899. Delegates pledged to maintain cordial relations with all groups. In June Waldeck-Rousseau was charged with forming a cabinet of "Republican Defense." Seated together in the new cabinet were socialist Alexandre Millerand and General Gaston de Galliffet, the latter associated with the repression of 1871. Millerand's decision to enter the government sundered the flimsy Comité d'Entente.

When the political socialists again gathered at Epernay in 1899, Millerandism was the order of the day.(61) After a debate lasting two days and two nights, the meeting ended with little more accomplished than a pledge to convoke another congress to discuss the question of unity. Shortly thereafter, a General Congress of Socialist Organizations of France was convened in Paris. The delegates called for "Entente and international actions of workers, political and economic organizations, [and] for the conquest of the means of production and exchange."(62) Fusion would be achieved by membership in a single organization, offering equal representation to parties, unions, and cooperatives. Both political and economic action would be deemed effective methods of achieving revolution.

Although the question of the direction of the socialist party was settled, the issue of ministerial participation aroused violence and deep emotions among the delegates. After all sides filled the room with angry charges, the vote was taken. The resolution that was passed, however, was a model of avoidance. It stated that the nature of the class struggle allowed no entry of socialists into a bourgeois government, although circumstances might arise to cause the party to redefine its position.

It was now imperative to take a position that would attract labor to the political fold, having sidestepped the question of Millerandism. After listening to Briand and others defend the principle of the general strike, the delegates agreed almost unanimously that all means of action--economic activity, electoral and revolutionary action, boycotts, and the general strike--must be employed in the struggle by the socialist party. Peace reigned momentarily within the party's ranks. However, the government's actions in the ensuing strikes at Châlon-sur-Saône split the ranks of the political socialists. In 1900 the Guesdist POF met in their eighth congress at Ivry-sur-Seine. Their principal bid for labor's support was in the form of an acerbic condemnation both of police brutality and of the alleged betrayal of the French workers by the deputies. They closed by forcefully rejecting ministerial collaboration. When the Congrès Général des Organisations Socialistes Françaises convened in Paris later that year, the meeting began with squabbles over the question of mandates, and closed with fistfights on the floor. It would be five years before a final socialist unity would prevail.

SYNDICALIST ACCORD AT AMIENS

At the very moment socialists were trying to stop the shattering of their political force, the syndicalists were moving toward greater accord. The FBT congress in 1900 firmly rejected adherence to the socialist party and again agreed to remain aloof from any political involvement and organizationally separate from the CGT.(63)

In 1901 Pelloutier died. At the FBT congress in Nice that year, delegates concurred that keeping the organizations separate was not in the interest of building working-class unity. When the FBT met in Algeria the following year, the delegates sanctioned all but total fusion with the CGT. The CGT met four days later at Montpellier and adopted the principle of unity. Unions entering the CGT must adhere to both their industrial federation and a bourse or local union, and they would have to support the officially sanctioned newspaper, La Voix du Peuple. The CGT would be comprised of two autonomous sections: that of the industrial and professional federations and isolated unions and that of the federation of bourses. Each section would be directed by a committee and would collect its own dues. Congresses would be convened every two years. Between congresses a Confederal Committee, composed of the committees of both sections, would be in charge of daily affairs. The single-unit voting provisions were upheld; the question of proportional representation was overwhelmingly rejected 392 to 76. To the libertarians of the CGT, the French political structure was based on indirect democracy. The one unit-one vote system they adopted seemed to offer the greatest protection to individual workers even within the smallest unions.

With détente in the blueprint stage, the CGT was presented with another problem that had arisen as a result of the unification effort: the confrontation with the reformists within the Confederation. Reformism had always been regarded as the bête noire of radical unionism, but the term had come to encompass a variety of definitions. In the early years of syndicalism, "reformists" consisted of the more conservative artisanal elements who believed that capitalism should be preserved in a humanized form through the electoral process and through the pacific forms of direct action such as mutualism and cooperation. These reformists supported Republican and later Socialist Party candidates, and they tended to regard the Republic as a patriarchal force that could be called upon to broker the conflicting demands of labor and the bosses. This group of reformists, epitomized in the person of Auguste Keufer, remained a marginal, although articulate element, within syndicalism.

To the left of this group was another, equally branded as reformists by the more radical labor activists. These were the members of some of the larger federations—particularly metallurgy, printing, and tobacco—who were committed to practical activism, including strikes, to achieve labor reforms. But they tended to eschew what they considered to be the more violent forms of direct action, such as sabotage, and they dismissed as chimerical the use of the general strike. This group's slogan was caution; they found comfort in numbers, hence their penchant for organization and for distributing some of their eggs in the socialists' basket. To achieve that end, they worked within the CGT for détente with the party socialists and engaged in battles to overturn the single-unit voting system in the Confederation. Only through proportional representation could the giant federations exercise power commensurate with their organizational wealth and numbers. Only with the exercise of that power would radical strength, usually centered in the smallest unions and bourses, be diffused

Also tagged as reformists, as we have witnessed, were those syndicalists who believed that workers should participate in the political sphere to the same degree as they were involved in activity in the economic realm. The most dangerous element among the "party socialists" were the Guesdists, who went beyond merely soliciting working-class support for leftist candidates. Guesdists wanted to turn the unions into recruiting organs subservient to the Socialist Party. For syndicalists this was the most pernicious brand of reformism because it would have placed the workers' destinies in the hands of politicians.

At the Bourges congress of the CGT in 1904, those reformists representing the larger federations waged another frontal assault to achieve proportional representation, and were defeated 825 to 369. The trouncing was not surprising since the reformists were trying to gain victory while operating within a system that was designed to insure their defeat! But by the next congress of the CGT, held in Amiens in 1906, conditions had changed. The more powerful unions were marshaling their forces; disruption was threatening at the very time the party socialists were reveling in their victory of unity. In April 1905 they had met in Paris. All factions had agreed to fuse into a single party, the Section Française de l'Internationale Ouvrière (SFIO). The political socialists were now crooking a beckoning finger at the unions to join them.

The discussion at Amiens opened with the Guesdist delegate Renard of the textile federation making another bid for the Confederal Committee to endorse unity with the socialists. The object, he declared, was to work for the triumph of "reformist principles of the workers," which, translated, meant adherence to the SFIO. His suggestion was soundly rejected by 736 to 34. Then Auguste Keufer of the printers' union demanded that the CGT not become "the instrument of anarchist and antiparliamentary agitation" and that the Confederation immediately establish relations with the political parties.(64)

In answering the reformists' challenge, the majority reaffirmed the CGT's nonpartisan and "legalistic" position, adopted at their founding congress in 1895. They were constituted as a body to group themselves outside of all political schools, their resolution declared, in order to rally the conscious workers in the struggle to bring about the disappearance of the wage system and capitalist exploitation. Involvement in political sectarianism, the argument continued, would only deflect the workers from their objective, which was social transformation. The resolution against Guesdism and reformism was overwhelmingly accepted 834 to 8. It came to be called the "Charter of Amiens," equal in magnitude to the Magna Carta, syndicalists said, because it was designed to pave the way for achieving working-class unity.

The Charter of Amiens was a practical document serving a multitude of purposes. It spoke to the ideological preferences of the anarchists and libertarians by further stating that all workers had the liberty of conscience to pursue whatever political objective they desired, as long as this activity was carried on outside the context of the Confederation's congresses. The document further recognized a fact of life apparent to all: if the French workers were going to unite successfully, fusion would have to take place under a broad enough umbrella to accommodate without too much discomfort members from every school. All would be welcomed, as long as they did not bring their political prejudices into the congress hall.

The resolution also took the wind out of the reformists' sails. It became the raison d'être for not having to debate the thorny issue of affiliation with the political socialists, whose unification had been achieved only at the cost of much bloodshed and recrimination. The Charter further allowed the anarchist elements to take the offensive since the commitment to work outside the parameters of partisan sects seemed implicitly, at least, to sanction direct and personal workers' action in the economic realm. The anarchosyndicalist element, not content to rest on its laurels, further proposed that antimilitarist-antipatriotic propaganda be carried on. A weak majority agreed. But another motion, calling for the establishment of a commission to undertake propaganda supporting the eight-hour day and the principle of the general strike, was unanimously approved. In another show of radical strength, a motion was carried to suspend temporarily relations between the CGT and the Second International, since the latter organization had refused to consider a motion at the 1905 Amsterdam congress calling for support of the general strike, the eight-hour day, and antimilitarism. At the CGT's congress two years later, the reformist bid for proportional representation was finally laid to rest by a vote of 716 to 379. Now the syndicalists could get on with the task of organization.

In the CGT the leftist labor movement had a proper organization to carry on the class war. Its guiding philosophy was based on mass trade unionism, independent of church or patrons, working by direct action within the bourses and syndicats to overthrow bourgeois capitalism and put in its place a new society based on industrial, rather than parliamentary organization. The Confederation's operating principles were supple enough to attract individuals of every leftist shading, and its organizational structure was capable of mediating the demands of any labor organization: large trade federations or unskilled workers; peasants or artisanal groups. Delegates to the Amiens congress believed they had swept away the last barriers to building a powerful labor confederation into which the working class could gather. But as René Garmy so aptly phrases it, the CGT became "not a fortress in which one masses, but a hallway through which one passes."(65) Yet as industrialization progressed, that hallway served as a necessary shelter into which the militants could either escape or regroup, and down which the recently initiated could travel on their way to gaining revolutionary consciousness. Even if anarchosyndicalism never became the battering ram of revolution its founding fathers intended it to be, the movement nevertheless left an indelible mark on the history of France and its working class.

NOTES

1. Stein's final words are transcribed "officially" in Norman and Betty Donaldson, How Did They Die? (New York, 1980), p. 349.

2. Peter Stearns, Revolutionary Syndicalism and French Labor: A Cause Without Rebels (New Brunswick, 1971), p. 102. Stearns concedes that the only positive aspect of syndicalism was its negative effect. "Insofar as it frightened workers away from the unions it not only held French union membership down," he states, "but reduced its chances of controlling spontaneous protests" (p. 94.) The negative aspects of syndicalism are emphasized by friends and foes alike. J. W. Scott claims that syndicalism was "the failure of the socialist idea to prove its fitness for power," and declares that the movement constituted a confession that socialism was unable "to do what it set out to do--namely, run a state." Syndicalism and Philosophic

Realism (London, 1919), p. 1. Jean Montreuil calls syndicalism "a deaf aspiration toward an order where the worker no longer will be isolated and mistaken." Histoire du mouvement ouvrier en France (Paris, 1947), p. 531.

3. E. Drexel Godfrey, Jr., Fate of the Non-Communist Left (New York, 1955), p. 24. Writing in 1920 against Jouhaux and Merrheim, Lenin outlined the specific charges that would remain the themes of indictment against anarchosyndicalism. He charged that Jouhaux and other leaders of the Confederal Committee had betrayed the working class by joining the government of national defense, by criticizing unjustly the Russian Revolution, and by collaborating with the bourgeois state. Reported in Georges Lefranc, Le syndicalisme en France (Paris, 1957), pp. 57-60. Stearns maintains that the increased membership occurring after 1906 resulted in more moderates entering syndicalism. Bernard Moss refutes this charge, noting that the new recruits, having come in on the crest of heightened strike activity, tended to be more radical. The Origins of the French Labor Movement (Berkeley, 1976), p. 152.

4. See Michelle Perrot, Les ouvriers en grève, France 1871-90, 2 vols. (Paris, 1974); Edward Shorter and Charles Tilly, Strikes in France 1930-1968 (Cambridge, Mass., 1974); Charles, Louise, and Richard Tilly, The Rebellious Century (Cambridge, Mass., 1975).

5. Michael P. Hanagan, The Logic of Solidarity: Artisans and Industrial Workers in Three French Towns 1871-1914 (Urbana, Il., 1980); Joan W. Scott, The Glassworkers of Carmaux (Cambridge, Massachusetts, 1974); Rolande Trempé, Les mineurs de Carmaux, 1848-1914 (Paris, 1971). Local and regional studies have always been of interest to the French, and are too numerous even for a sampling here.

6. David Stafford, historian of the possibilists, notes that work on his subject has also suffered from "the dead weight of Marxist historiography." Stafford points out that histories of the socialist movement have stressed the Marxian inheritance, so analysts have generally tended to pay little attention to the nonorthodox groups, such as the possibilists. From Anarchism to Reformism: A Study of the Political Activities of Paul Brousse Within the First International and the French Socialist Movement, 1870-90 (Toronto, 1971), p. 5.

7. See for quotes two works of George Lichtheim: Marxism (New York, 1965), p. 222; and A Short History of Socialism (New York, 1971), p. 289.

8. For an exposition of the artisanal basis of syndicalism see the work of Moss, The Origins of the French Labor Movement.

9. For a history of anarchism see the following: Jean
Maitron, _Histoire du mouvement anarchiste en France
1880-1914_ (Paris, 1955); James Joll, _The Anarchists_ (New
York, 1964); George Woodcock, _Anarchism: A History of
Libertarian Ideas and Movements_ (Cleveland, 1962). Woodcock
defines the relationship between anarchism and syndicalism
in a chapter entitled: "Syndicalism, the Industrial
Expression of Anarchism," in Leonard I. Krimerman and Lewis
Perry, eds., _Patterns of Anarchy_ (Garden City, 1966), pp.
38-42.

10. Stearns, _Revolutionary Syndicalism and French
Labor_, p. 36.

11. Ibid., p. 102.

12. See particularly the work of the Tillys, _The
Rebellious Century_, and of Shorter and Tilly, _Strikes in
France_.

13. Hanagan, _The Logic of Solidarity_, pp. 11-12.

14. Lichtheim, _A Short History_, p. 289.

15. Frederick F. Ridley, _Revolutionary Syndicalism in
France_ (Cambridge, England, 1970), p. 230. See also Paul
Mazgaj, _The Action Française and Revolutionary Syndicalism_
(Chapel Hill, N.C., 1979).

16. Woodcock, _Anarchism_, p. 171.

17. Lichtheim, _Marxism_, p. 226.

18. Annie Kriegel, "Le syndicalisme révolutionnaire et
Proudhon," _Le pain et les roses_ (Paris, 1968); Lucien
Febvre, _Une question d'influence: Proudhon et le
syndicalisme contemporain_ (Paris, 1919); E[douard] Berth,
"Le centenaire de Proudhon," _Le Mouvement Socialiste_ (1 Jan.
1909): 49-55. All generally agree that syndicalism was a
direct-line translation of Proudhon's ideas.

19. Fernand Pelloutier, _Histoire des bourses du
travail_ (Paris, 1971), p. 262. A biographical overview of
some syndicalists mentioned in each chapter is listed
alphabetically following the notes.

20. Hubert Lagardelle, et al., _Syndicalisme et
socialisme_ (Paris, 1908), p. 47.

21. Woodcock, _Anarchism_, pp. 106-144; Lichtheim, _A
Short History_, p. 289.

22. Robert Goetz-Girey, _La pensée syndicale française:
Militants et théoriciens_ (Paris, 1948), p. 29.

23. Félicien Challaye, _Syndicalisme révolutionnaire et

syndicalisme réformiste (Paris, 1909), p. 38.

24. Pelloutier, Histoire des bourses du travail, p. 258.

25. Stearns, Revolutionary Syndicalism and French Labor, p. 105.

26. Pelloutier, Histoire des bourses du travail, p. 249.

27. Pouget quoted in Challaye, Syndicalisme révolutionnaire, p. 12.

28. Jules Levey, "The Sorelian Syndicalists: Edouard Berth, Georges Valois, and Hubert Lagardelle" (Ph.D. Dissertation, Columbia University, 1967); John Stanley, The Sociology of Virtue: The Political and Social Theories of Georges Sorel (Berkeley, 1981).

29. For concise discussions of the French economy, see the following: Clive Trebilcock, The Industrialization of the Continental Powers 1780-1914 (London, 1981), pp. 135-204; Tom Kemp, Economic Forces in French History (London, 1971), pp. 217-298; Roger Price, An Economic History of Modern France 1730-1914 (New York, 1981). France's position as a world power is treated by Kemp, p. 222. Statistics are listed on p. 168 in Price.

30. See Georges Dupeux, French Society 1789-1970, Peter Wait, trans. (London, 1976), who states that the 1884 census showed that 50 percent of French agricultural land consisted of parcels of twenty hectares or less, supporting 97 percent of the rural population. (P. 109). See also Kemp, Economic Forces in French History, p. 233; and Price, An Economic History of Modern France, p. 226.

31. Ibid., pp. 202-208.

32. Ibid., pp. 149, 234. David Landes describes this practice quite graphically as "small firms drowning in their own liquidity." "French Business and the Businessman: A Social and Cultural Analysis," in E. M. Earl, ed., Modern France (Princeton, 1951), p. 339.

33. Price, An Economic History of Modern France, p. 236.

34. Ibid.

35. Kemp, Economic Forces in French History, p. 276.

36. In attempting to explain which groups supported birth-control campaigns, Francis Ronsin notes the inchoate quality of leftist thought, and concludes that the different

doctrines within socialism were not inherently contradictory. This was why, Ronsin explains, it was possible "to be at the same time syndicalist, socialist, cooperator, and Christian." La grève des ventres: Propagande néo-malthusienne et baisse de la natalité en France 19(me)-20(me) siècles (Paris, 1980), p. 165.

37. For a background on the political climate of the period see D. W. Brogan, The Development of Modern France, 1870-1939 (London, 1940); and Roger M. Soltau, French Parties and Politics 1871-1921 (New York, 1965).

38. The literature on the formation of socialism and syndicalism is vast. A few of the works specifically dealing with syndicalism include some of the following: André May, Les origines du syndicalisme révolutionnaire (Paris, 1913); Val R. Lorwin, The French Labor Movement (Cambridge, Mass., 1954); Georges Weill, Histoire du mouvement social en France (Paris, 1924); Edouard Dolléans, Histoire du mouvement ouvrier, 3 vols. (Paris, 1967); Léon Blum, Les congrès ouvriers et socialistes français, 2 vols. (Paris, 1901); Confédération Générale du Travail, La confédération générale du travail et le mouvement syndical (Paris, 1925) [hereafter cited as La CGT et le mouvement syndical]; Marjorie Ruth Clark, A History of the French Labor Movement (1910-1928) (Berkeley, 1930). Already noted are the works by Ridley, Moss, and Stearns.

39. On the compagnonnages consult the following: E. Martin Saint-Léon, Le compagnonnage (Paris, 1901); Emile Coornaert, Les compagnonnages en France du moyen age à nos jours (Paris, 1966).

40. For the early years, see Rudolph Rocker, Anarcho-Syndicalism: Theory and Practice (London, 1938), pp. 66-67; and André Marchal, Le mouvement syndical en France (Paris, 1945), p. 10; Léon de Seilhac, Les congrès ouvriers en France de 1876 à 1897 (Paris, 1899), pp. 1-14.

41. Stafford, From Anarchism to Reformism, p. 20; Ridley, Revolutionary Syndicalism in France, p. 63.

42. Quotes appear in Blum, Les congrès ouvriers, pp. 7 and 14.

43. L. Goyard, La crise du petit commerce et le syndicalisme (Paris, 1911), p. 15.

44. On Guesde see Claude Willard, Le mouvement socialiste en France 1893-1905: Les guesdistes (Paris, 1965).

45. Quote appears in Blum, Les congrès ouvriers, vol. 1, p. 36 (their emphasis).

46. On the early workers' congresses see ibid., pp.

32-71 of vol. 1; pp. 210-238 in Weil, Histoire du mouvement social; de Seilhac, Les congrès ouvriers en France.

47. See Stafford's work From Anarchism to Reformism; and Blum, Les congrès ouvriers, pp. 128-131.

48. Brousse quoted by Stafford, From Anarchism to Reformism, pp. 175-176.

49. See pp. 218-248 in Weil, Histoire du mouvement social.

50. For quote see René Garmy, Histoire du mouvement syndical en France (Paris, 1933), vol. 1, p. 147.

51. Blum, Les congrès ouvriers, vol. 2, pp. 128-130; see p. 129 for quote. See Ridley, Revolutionary Syndicalism in France, pp. 63-67. For an overview of the congresses from 1886-1914, see Robert Brécy, Le mouvement syndical en France 1871-1921: Essai bibliographique (Paris, 1963), pp. 17-83.

52. See bottom of p. 20 in ibid. for the Sunday conversation in May, 1890, between Engels and Lafargue.

53. For the development of the tactic of the general strike by Briand and Pelloutier see Jacques Julliard, Fernand Pelloutier et les origines du syndicalisme d'action directe (Paris, 1971).

54. For a brief overview of the political situation see Ridley, Revolutionary Syndicalism in France, p. 48.

55. Fernand Pelloutier, Histoire des bourses du travail. In the F(7) series at the AN there is a circular from the Minister of the Interior dated 8 Dec. 1894 to prefects regarding the bourses du travail, in which he assured the prefects were primarily employment agencies. He expected the bourses to create no problems because they had neither legal nor actual autonomy. Discussion of politics, religion, or even economics in general were forbidden by the terms of their charters. He advised the prefects that they were authorized to close the bourses if these organizations strayed from their original purpose.

56. Blum, Les congrès ouvriers, vol. 2, pp. 132-157. La CGT et le mouvement syndical, pp. 26-37.

57. On Pelloutier's anarchism see his Histoire des bourses du travail, pp. 87-90, 98.

58. For the beginnings of the CGT to 1899 see the following: Blum, Les congrès ouvriers, vol. 2, pp. 159-172; May, Les origines du syndicalisme révolutionnaire, pp. 94-108, Lefranc, Le syndicalisme en France, pp. 64-70.

59. Brécy, Le mouvement syndical en France, p. 37.

60. The CGT's liaison with the FBT was a happy one for the Confederation since, in 1895, the CGT had 85 centimes in its treasury and 47.65 francs in debts. See La CGT et le mouvement syndical, p. 40.

61. Blum, Les congrès ouvriers, vol. 2, pp. 173-185, for the party machinations from 1899 to 1900.

62. See p. 178 in ibid. for quote.

63. For activity within the FBT and the CGT from 1900 to Amiens see the following: Brécy, Le mouvement syndical en France, pp. 51-64; Blum, Les congrès ouvriers, vol. 2, pp. 187-191; Ridley, Revolutionary Syndicalism in France, pp. 67-76; Lefranc, Le syndicalisme en France, pp. 71-84, 125-146; May, Les origines du syndicalisme révolutionnaire, pp. 109-114, 120-135; La CGT et le mouvement syndical, pp. 73-85.

64. On the Amiens congress see ibid., pp. 95-99; Brécy, Le mouvement syndical en France, pp. 63-68. The quotes of Renard and Keufer appear in ibid., p. 64.

65. Garmy, Histoire du mouvement syndical, vol. 1, p. 159.

PERSONS CITED

The biographical material used here comes from a single source: Jean Maitron, Dictionnaire biographique du mouvement ouvrier français, vols. 10-15 (Paris, 1964). Unfortunately, Maitron does not list information on every person cited. The reason for including this material is to give the reader a brief background on some of the working-class spokesmen and spokeswomen. Biographical information is confined to those who were specifically syndicalists.

Allemane, Jean (1843-1920), was born in the Haute-Garonne. The son of a wine seller, he left for Paris to learn the trade of typographer. He was imprisoned for his strike activity, and ultimately deported for his participation in the Commune. After being amnestied, he joined a cooperative and then the PO. In 1890 he formed his own party, and served in parliament for five years, although he regarded electoral activity as nothing more than a vehicle for propaganda. He was a supporter of the general strike and antimilitarism. He was a member of the CGT, and after 1905, of the SFIO. After 1910 he retired from party affairs. He supported the party's stand in World War I, but was a sympathizer of the newly formed Communist Party in 1920.

Dumoulin, Georges (1877-1963), was born at Pas-de-Calais and died in Lille. His father worked as a peddlar, his mother

as a tile cutter. Georges left school when he was eight to
work as a crop picker with his father. At the age of eleven
he was working in a sugar beet factory, and later in a coal
mine. He attended school with the help of the bourse. He
became involved in unionism as a result of the coal miners'
strike at Courrières. He became a Guesdist, but broke with
the POF after returning from his army duty. He was fired,
jailed, and later exiled from Belgium, where he had fled to
escape persecution for his union activity. In 1906 he was
Secretary of the Young Syndicalist Miners. He subsequently
moved to Paris, where he again supported himself by doing
odd jobs. After 1910 he was given a permanent position as
CGT treasurer. In 1911 he was sentenced to thirteen months
in prison for his antimilitarist activities. He was
mobilized into the army on 4 Aug. 1914. Dumoulin's war
activities are discussed in a later chapter of this work.
After the war he joined the SFIO, but did not participate in
the disputes of that organization. In 1931 he returned to
the CGT. After World War II he was sentenced to death for
his support of Vichy during the war. He went into hiding,
working as a farmhand in a small village in the Eure until
1951, when his sentence was remanded and his miners' pension
reinstated. He returned to the Nord and converted to
Catholicism.

Griffuelhes, [Jean] Victor (1874-1922), was born in the
Lot-et-Garonne. He was from a poor family, and left school
at fourteen to apprentice as a shoemaker. After his
military's service he moved to Paris and for a time became
active in socialist politics, finally abandoning politics
for unionism. Within the CGT he supported the move away
from craft unionism to industrial unionism. He was a
remarkable organizer, directing the campaign for the
eight-hour day and against the reformists within the CGT.
He also personally directed several strikes, many of which
would have foundered without his direction. He served
numerous prison terms. His irascible nature earned him more
foes than friends. His enemies were finally able to
undermine Griffuelhes' reputation by claiming he had
misappropriated CGT funds. Griffuelhes resigned as CGT
secretary and limited his activities to journalism
thereafter. He supported the war effort, perhaps because of
his long-standing hatred of the Germans. He was also an
admirer of the Russian revolution.

Jouhaux, Léon (1879-1954), was born and died in Paris. A
member of a working-class family with a history of
radicalism, Jouhaux apprenticed in numerous trades, finally
becoming a match worker. He continued his education by
reading in the library. At sixteen he was involved in his
first strike. After his army service, he returned to match
making and militancy. He was imprisoned and fired for his
radicalism. Until hired by the CGT, Jouhaux stayed alive by
working at odd jobs. He was elected secretary of the
Confederation as a compromise candidate, revolutionary
enough for the left, but not enough to frighten away the

reformists. His actions at the start of and during the
First World War are discussed in the text. Jouhaux was
imprisoned by Vichy during World War II. He remained
General Secretary of the CGT until 1947. In 1951 he
received the Nobel Peace Prize.

Keufer, Auguste (1851-1924), was born in the Haut-Rhin. He
was orphaned and raised by the Brothers of the Christian
Doctrine. He became a compositor, moved to Paris, and
married. Keufer's attraction to positivism gave his ideas
on unionism a highly moral quality. He was the first
treasurer of the CGT, and carried on numerous battles
advocating the reformist position against the anarchists.
He supported the government of national defense in 1914.
Keufer was the guiding light of the Fédération du Livre,
serving as its general secretary from 1884 to 1920.

Lagardelle, Hubert (1875-1958), was born of a middle-class
Toulousean family. He was a socialist journalist and an
advocate of syndicalism. He supported the government during
World War I and Vichy during World War II, and was
subsequently sentenced to prison for collaboration.

Merrheim, Alphonse (1871-1925), came from a working-class
family. He left school at the age of ten to work as a
soapmaker. This was the first of numerous apprenticeships.
He joined the POF, leaving the party because of the violence
of the May Day 1890 demonstrations. He created a
coppersmithing union in 1891, and was instrumental in
getting his union fused into the Federation of
Metallurgists. At Paris he was shocked by the demagoguery
and immorality of many of the militants, although he had
spent six days in jail for adultery in 1897. At Amiens he
opposed joining the politicians, but rejected
antimilitarism. He participated in numerous strikes,
directing many of them between 1905 and 1910. He was honest
and a hard worker. He built solid friendships, such as with
Griffuelhes, with whom he frequently disagreed, and with
Monatte, with whom he launched La Vie Ouvrière. He approved
of Jouhaux's actions during the July Crisis, but was one of
the first to criticize the policy of Union sacrée. He
remained as interim secretary of the CGT during the German
offensive while the rest of the Confederal Committee went to
Bordeaux with the government. By the end of 1914 he was
working with Trotsky and Martov; by 1915 he was leading
peace demonstrations. His actions earned him great
opprobrium. He was tagged as a German agent, and never went
anywhere without being accompanied by two large dogs. He
attended the Zimmerwald conference, and was able to get his
more moderate proposal passed over Lenin's. By the end of
that year he had returned to the center, not wishing to see
the syndicalists split. After a violent critique of Jouhaux
in 1918, he voted and remained with the majority.

Pelloutier, Fernand (1867-1901), was the son of a postal
worker, raised in Saint-Nazaire. He was rejected for a

baccalaureate degree because he was more involved in fantasies than in schoolwork. He supported Aristide Briande's election as a Radical, then joined the POF, leaving the party when the Guesdists rejected the notion of the general strike. By 1892, when he settled permanently in Paris, he had become an anarchist, although he spoke out against anarchist terrorism. By this time he was ill from lupus and in financial difficulty. Jean Jaurès obtained a position for Pelloutier in the Labor Office, an appointment that brought bitter charges of government cooptation against Pelloutier in the 1900 FBT congress.

Pouget, Emile (1860- ?), was born in the department of the Aveyron of a middle-class family. He migrated to Paris, participating eventually in the creation of the Textile Workers' Union. By then he was an anarchist and committed to antimilitarism. He served three years in prison for his participation as a leader in an 1883 meeting of unemployed workers. During the years of anarchist terrorism, Pouget served as bourse secretary in Algeria. He published Père Peinard, collaborated with Sébastien Faure on several libertarian journals, and in 1900 became editor of La Voix du Peuple. Pouget's appearance was described as "ironic to the point of looking almost acerbic, philosophical." He spent another two months in prison in 1908 for his strike activity. In 1909 he married and retired to the provinces. He supported the government during World War I.

Yvetot, Georges (1868-1942), was the son of a policeman. Born in Paris, he was orphaned at an early age. He became a typographer. He was an anarchist and antimilitarist, and opposed the political socialists' involvement in unionism. From 1902 to 1918 Yvetot was second in command in the CGT. He was extremely authoritarian, earning the nickname "Bulldog." He and the equally stubborn Griffuelhes clashed frequently. Yvetot was arrested numerous times for his radical activities, serving a combined total of several years in prison. He resigned from the CGT in opposition to the politics of the Union sacrée. During most of the war he worked as a typographer and directed the National Association of War Orphans. In 1918 he leaned toward the CGT minority. Between the wars he worked as a proofreader, and was involved with unionism on a local level. He was a pacifist during World War II.

2. The Question of Direct Action: Action in the Economic Realm

As evidenced in the preceding chapter dealing with the historical development of the syndicalist movement, the most compelling characteristic of revolutionary syndicalism, and that which sets it apart from political socialism, was its advocacy of direct action. Not through parliamentary proceedings and the sheer weight of electoral numbers would the worker realize emancipation, syndicalists preached. Rather, this liberation could only occur through individual and collective action carried out in the economic realm.

As defined by syndicalists, direct action came to include a host of activities, ranging from union membership, to the use of sabotage, to participation in cooperatives and strikes--particularly the general strike. This definition of direct action resulted in the development of an ideology designed to attract militants of every philosophical stripe, from Proudhonists to Marxists. Direct action was a way to build union membership by pressing for labor reform and by offering the means, both large and small, by which workers could carry out a revolutionary act. The theory and practice of direct action, therefore, served as a vehicle for welding together disparate groups of militants and workers, thereby heightening the development of class consciousness. The idea of direct action was also a practical response to contemporary conditions: an unstable parliamentary structure, a labor force in the process of change, a revolutionary tradition that elevated the ideal of a highly centralized state, and a leftist movement continually torn apart by organizational schism.

Given such prosaic means and ends, why has there been so much misunderstanding and criticism by past and present observers of syndicalism's emphasis on direct action? To many critics direct action was narrowly synonymous with a coup de main or terror by the deed. To syndicalists, however, direct action was any action carried on by the worker against the bourgeois state or capitalist profits. The social revolution would be thoroughgoing and cataclysmic in the change produced. But the primary message of syndicalism was that revolution would be achieved incrementally, with partial expropriation leading inexorably to total expropriation.

AN APPEAL TO ALL PHILOSOPHICAL SCHOOLS

One of the most obvious ways to work for revolution was to entice the timid masses to join the unions. The benefits to be derived from association fill the literature. The union is defined as a shelter, a legal entity, and the natural aspiration of mankind. Also popular is the theme that direct action is a natural and ethical act, sanctioned by history, and the only effective means to integral emancipation.

The naturalness of direct action and of association was a constant theme. Emile Pouget noted that because unions were spontaneous groupings organized on the economic terrain, workers could realize within the syndical fold a sense of identity transcending philosophy, politics, or religion. The syndicat was "the school of the will," he asserted, "wherein the individual lost nothing of his personality as he did in the democratic milieu."(1) Birds and animals recognized "the need to organize in order to face the exigencies of life," declared shoemaker Henri Dret at the regional meeting of the Auxerre bourse in 1907. Workers needed to do the same. In association they would become more than a collection of individuals. The syndicat was not merely "Pierre, Louis, or Jacques separately," concluded Dret, "but Pierre, Louis, Jacques . . . all together."(2)

Rather than being a mere bastion, a static doctrine, or an entity constructed for the moment, the union, syndicalists constantly proclaimed, was a living, evolving organism moving outside the temporal domain. Unionism was not a dogma nor a party doctrine, stated socialist historian Paul Louis; it was "socialism in action" and the only truly dynamic means by which society could be transformed.(3) Unionism was a momentous force, "forms of energy," according to Monsieur Larrivière of the lithographers' union in a 1901 article. Such energy, he contended, was strong enough to combat "the inertia which comes from egoism."(4)

In addition to being living energy, syndicalism also transcended time. Emile Pouget concluded that the union was "the organic cell of society," constituting "a double blow: present and future."(5) Workers at the 1900 congress of the CGT agreed on the organic character of unionism and concurred with the assessment of Joseph Braun of the metallurgy union. Future society could only be organized by the syndicats, he asserted, because these associations were "the embryos of future social organization."(6)

The rhetoric urging workers to direct action through syndicalism was designed to compress individual men and women into a new class: vital, dynamic, capturing within itself past and future. Propaganda was phrased in such a

way as to appeal to the artisanal elite, who believed in the
superiority of their position in society and in the work
force. But the message was also intended to instill in the
unskilled worker a sense of community and a feeling that he
and his comrades had been tagged by destiny to be the new
heroes of the world. Syndicalist propaganda was also
realistically contrived to appeal to workers of every
philosophical hue.

The educational value of syndicalism was lauded,
thereby casting its appeal to those attracted by the works
of Auguste Comte. Writing in Le Libertaire in 1903,
Georges Yvetot reminded his readers that it was in the
unions and bourses that workers could realize the benefits
of association by first airing their grievances, and then
studying the means to equalize the conditions of each
individual to the betterment of all.(7) In a little book
of "opinions," militant anarchist Dr. Marc Pierrot praised
the educational aspect of syndicalism. Through propaganda
the exploited worker would "arrive at the exact knowledge of
[his] misery and servitude." This enlightenment would not be
imposed from above, however. In the unions, anarchist
Pierrot declared, "education is accomplished by example and
by contagion."(8)

The emphasis on the educational aspects of direct
action was favored by the more cautious elements within the
working class. But syndicalist propaganda was also designed
to appeal to the radicals, such as the followers of Blanqui,
who were impatient with empirical and reasoned approaches to
improving the conditions of the working class. Blanqui's
doctrine of revolution held that a small, well-trained cadre
would carry out a violent coup de main that would be the
revolution. Many syndicalists espoused this line in their
apparent preference for audacious minorities over large
masses of unionized workers. Certainly one might conclude
that this expressed preference for a small revolutionary
elite was only a case of making a virtue of necessity. To a
large degree this was true. As previously noted, union
membership was always small relative to the work force in
France. Nevertheless, early syndicalist literature is
replete with praise for the superiority of small numbers in
the work of revolution.(9)

In his history of the bourses du travail, Fernand
Pelloutier warned that if the number of union members grew
too large, syndicalism would become "pacific and legal and
would violently resist any attempts at coup d'état."(10)
The equation of passivity with numbers was also voiced by
Blanquist Eugène Guérard of the railroad workers' union in
1901. Jaurès' view that the revolution must be the work of
a majority was illusory, since the majority is always inert.
We are governed by a minority, Guérard noted; capable
leaders are always a minority. Syndicalism must assemble a
minority committed to direct action and strong enough to
check the ruling elite.(11)

Anarchist rather than Blanquist notions appear to have
weighed more heavily in the construction of syndicalism's

underlying philosophy. The literature is filled with paeons
to syndicalism's spontaneity and voluntarist nature, to its
profession of libertarian ideals, and to the federalist
structure of the CGT, a form anarchists held to be the least
authoritarian. Syndicalists praised the use of direct
action as a means to heighten the individual's will to
action and thereby strengthen class solidarity. For Pouget
in 1901, direct action constituted "the soufflé of
revolution" because it transcended the narrow particularism
of individual demands.(12) CGT leaders Victor Griffuelhes
and Léon Jouhaux noted in the Encyclopédie du mouvement
syndicaliste that direct action was akin to an athlete's
training program. Through his exercise of direct action the
worker learned that "his personal activity is based on the
general action of his corporation and class."(13)
    Union membership and the use of direct action were
effective because such activity constituted a break with the
tradition of using municipal or state authorities as
intermediaries in workers' conflicts with employers. Thus,
syndicalism was hailed as a new departure in working-class
independence. Hubert Lagardelle declared that direct action
simply signified the will of the working class "to rule its
own affairs in place of representation, delegations, and
mandates of a third party intervening in [the workers']
place." There were two contrary principles, he observed:
indirect action, the principle of democracy and its
successor parliamentary socialism; and direct action, which
eliminated all intermediaries existing between the worker
and his objective.(14)
    Because syndicalism emphasized the necessity of
individual workers acting on their own behalf to bring about
a just society, the movement provided a common meeting
ground for both anarchists and Marxist socialists. But both
schools emphasized the fact that the revolution could never
be made by mere congeries of individuals, however ethical.
Instead, heightened class consciousness, the precondition
for revolution, must be gained through association.
Therefore, despite the rhetoric preaching the virtue of
small cadres, the bulk of syndicalist actions and propaganda
was directed toward advancing union membership.
    Clearly, syndicalism's greatest strength was that it
provided the means by which to weld individuals into a
united whole. A report to the 1897 CGT congress at Toulouse
declared that the union sheltered the exploited under "its
red banner."(15) Lagardelle asserted that the union was
"the prolongation of the workshop," operating to build
cohesion. In the union, he concluded,

    philosophic, religious, and political differences
    are worn away. And all that can remain is the
    force of the workers to defend their common
    interest. . . . And the moral unity that
    transforms their amorphous mass into a living
    block forms itself little by little through the

progressive development of the consciousness of their solidarity.(16)

The belief in the inherent superiority of syndicalism's organizational structure, a form particularly appealing to libertarians, was expressed by many. Dufour pointed out that the Confederal Committee of the CGT was antiauthoritarian in its role, designed to serve "only as an intermediary, as a council to assure the cohesion and simultaneity of action of the different federations that guard their autonomy thoroughly."(17) Such organizational structure did not lessen the power of the individual worker. In a 1908 propaganda brochure designed to combat jaunisme, that is employer-sponsored unionism, jeweler Arthur Danrez noted that each federation and syndicat remained autonomous. This independence allowed the worker to continue to be inspired by "a single free discipline: the practice of solidarity."(18)

Perhaps more eloquently than anyone, Pelloutier articulated how perfectly the working-class organizations were structured. Their blueprint, he noted, was the federative principle of Bakunin and Proudhon. But the system of checks and balances he described as existing within the unions appears to have been designed by Montesquieu. Unions, said Pelloutier,

> separate in power all that can be separated, define all that can be defined, distribute between different organs or functions all that has been separated and defined, leaving nothing undivided, gathering unto their administration all the conditions of publicity and control.(19)

Apparently such diffusion of power did not hamper organized labor in challenging the boss. According to a pamphlet circulated by the metalworkers' federation, in confrontations between employees and employers, the bosses would come to a clearer understanding of who were friends and foes "by clairvoyant means" rather than "by force."(20)

TO ECLIPSE NO ONE'S PLACE IN THE SUN

Despite assertions of syndicalism's antiauthoritarian nature, not all anarchists were convinced that the CGT would not succumb to the temptation of emphasizing organizational might at the expense of individual rights. Discussions on the value of association were always carried on to the accompaniment of a militant chorus who feared that organizational success would destroy the voluntarist nature and activist spirit of revolutionary syndicalism. In a 1908 article in La Guerre Sociale, a contributor attacked the CGT for the lackluster turnout on May Day. The organization was emphasizing recruitment at the expense of action, the critic

charged.   Adopting   such   priorities was dangerous, for the
more the Confederation added to its battalions, "the more it
will   be   timid   and   reformist."   Revolutions,   the   writer
pointed   out,   "are   made   only with passion, enthusiasm, and
audacity."(21)
     Radical anarchist fears were also expressed in articles
in Le Libertaire, which ran, ironically, during the precise
point   in   time   when   the   CGT   was   seeking   adherents and
anarchists were looking for legitimacy. In a 1900 issue,
Max Pèlerin pointed out that syndicalism's goal of defending
workers'   interests, particularly with regard to salary, was
nonessential to anarchists, who recognized neither wages nor
authority. Furthermore, to be effective in their   struggle,
the   unions   had   to   work   toward   realizing   a   sense   of
permanency. Despite what syndicalist leaders proclaimed,
the   desire   for   permanence   would   give   unions   civil
personalities,   interests,   properties,   and   regulations
needing to be defended. The very act of being constituted
by law forced the unions to become part of the legal power
structure. As such, according to union typographer Pèlerin,
syndicalism and anarchism constituted negations of each
other.(22)
     Responding to Pèlerin's negativism, other libertarians
praised the compatibility between anarchism and unionism.
Conceding that unionism's reformist and expedient goals were
"paltry," Pierre   Comont   nevertheless   suggested   that
anarchist militancy alone would save the worker from being
duped by "socialist, étatiste politicians."(23) In another
article,   F. Richard   concluded   that   unionism   did   not
constitute   a   refutation   of   libertarian   ideals. Rather,
concluded Richard, himself a member of two unions, "To be an
anarchist   is   to   carry   on   the   campaign   against social
inequalities."   Therefore,   syndicalism was a valid means to
anarchist ends.(24) The integrity of that goal, Antoine
Antignac later warned, would only be assured as long as the
unions became centers "reuniting the proletarian forces,
grouping   them   against bourgeois disorder, stifling no one,
and allowing each idea its place in the sun."(25)
     For all the pronouncements lauding the ideals of
libertarianism or in support of Proudhon's juste milieu and
the apocalyptic vision of Blanqui and Marx, syndicalist
leaders constantly stressed the movement's utter lack of
utopianism and the preeminently   practical   nature   of
revolutionary syndicalism's goals. Syndicalism, Lagardelle
declared, is "devoid of all utopianism in the sense that it

subordinates   its   triumph   entirely   to   an   ensemble   of
preexisting conditions, and while waiting [for   the   social
revolution], it plays a renovating role in the world."(27)
The   program   syndicalists   followed   consisted   of   struggling
for   better   pay,   fewer   hours,   and   improved   working
conditions.   In 1921, when the CGT was in the throes of the
attack upon it by the proponents of the Third International,
the Confederation's leadership still stressed the   pragmatic
nature of the movement.   Syndicalism, they said, was merely

> the defense of professional interests.   It is   the
> only basis of workers' actions.   It is not because
> he   adheres   to a political system, a philosophic
> doctrine, a social theory that the worker has come
> to the syndicat.   It is because he wants   to   join
> with   his   comrades   into   a collective force that
> would permit him to oppose successfully   patronal
> exploitation and to improve his lot.(28)

REFORMIST AND REPUBLICAN HESITATION

Despite this ongoing rejection of philosophy as a motive
force   in   the   syndicalist   movement,   the   influence   of
anarchism cannot be denied. For the   most   part,   anarchism
provided the leaven giving form and substance to the program
of   direct   action,   particularly   in   the   adoption   of   the
principle of the general strike and sabotage as part of   the
militants'   revolutionary   arsenal.   The   influx   of
libertarians to unionism   further   strengthened   syndicalist
resolve to remain aloof from politics and independent of the
Socialist   Party.   Certainly the anarchist specter hovering
over unionism helped to generate within the middle   class   a
fear   of   the movement that went well beyond the force of its
members.
Criticism of anarchosyndicalism and its professed brand
of direct action came both from reformists within   and   from
the party socialists and bourgeois republicans from without.
The   impractical   nature   of   union   activism   was   noted by
historian Edouard Dolléans in 1906.   Syndicalists'   emphasis
on   strikes smacked of a new religiosity. Their attempt "to
concentrate all   socialism   in   the   drama   of   the   general
strike,"   he   chided,   was   akin to the people of the Middle
Ages believing in the millennium.(29)
A constant criticism was that   syndicalism   had   fallen
under   the   spell   of   a   small cadre of evil geniuses.   The
doctrine   of   "eternal   negation"   of   syndicalism,   taunted
Célestin Bouglé, was "simplistic and violent." It frightened
away   the   mass   of workers, concluded this "fellow traveler"
of   reform   syndicalism,   so   "a   noisy   minority"   could
rule.(30) Reformist Louis Meyer claimed that a violent
minority was organizing "goon squads" to beat up workers who
refused to take   part   in   street   demonstrations.(31)   In
1910,   the   year   following Meyer's treatise concerning "the
crisis   of   syndicalism,"   Auguste   Keufer   suggested   that

syndicalist emphasis on violence was merely a cover-up to
the reality of the impotence of the Confederation's
leadership. These radical militants had failed to translate
theory into practice. At two particularly violent strikes,
they had been in such disarray they were ineffective in
directing the strikes. In the struggle to suppress
employment bureaus, a campaign costing over two million
francs, Keufer alleged, little results had been achieved.
This sorry state was due to the fact that anarchists who had
taken over the unions, were in Keufer's words, "diehards"
and "products of the university."(32)

That same year, Radical-Socialist Gaston Gros echoed
the notion that violence was the wish of a small cadre
within the unions who dreamed of a "syndicalisme du
théâtre." The syndicalist majority must seek détente with
the Radical-Socialist Party in order to pursue "the noble
ideal of social regeneration."(33) Socialists of other
persuasions had their own plans for unionism. In 1911
Guesdist deputies Henri Ghesquière and Adéodat Compère-Morel
noted on the floor of the Chamber that syndicalism had
become too dangerous to ignore. Their speeches, punctuated
by applause from the left, praised "syndicalism of accord."
The tactics of "guerre à outrance" being carried on against
employers by the CGT denied the spirit of negotiation, a
necessary adjunct to the use of strikes. Taking up the
theme, Compère-Morel asserted that strikes should be
regarded by the working class as "the last arm" of their
struggle because they were too dangerous and were not in the
workers' interest. Children going hungry or workers eating
in soup kitchens were victims of a movement that was content
to sacrifice means to ends. Rather, concluded
Compère-Morel, syndicalism must rely on parliament as the
instrument of reform, for the eventual capture of the state,
and the ultimate expropriation of capitalism.(34)

The idea that syndicalist leaders were exploiting the
workers was also the theme of a British observer of French
syndicalism in 1912. Sir Arthur Clay noted that the CGT
used strikes to intimidate the middle class and familiarize
workers with the idea of the general strike even when there
was little hope that the strike would produce immediate
tangible results. Syndicalism's strength, concluded Clay,
lay only

> in its direct appeal to the primitive instincts of
> mankind . . . many of the men to whom the
> appeal is made have but little knowledge or
> experience of life outside their immediate
> surroundings, they are not given to reflection,
> and they are therefore at the mercy of
> glib-tongued agitators who assure them that they
> can never hope in their own lifetime to obtain
> their "rights" by constitutional methods of
> reform.(35)

TOWARD THE GENERAL STRIKE

To critics, direct action was naive, impractical, idealistic, and a tactic that placed workers in serious jeopardy, either through loss of salary or from adverse public opinion. Strikes hampered the steady progress toward working-class reform. Direct action also frightened workers away from union membership. Despite the critics, as time went on, representatives to union congresses and contributors to the working-class press professed increasing acceptance of all forms of direct action, particularly for the general strike. These professions of support were backed up by solid evidence of a leftist swing within the working class itself: from the movement of some reformist unions, such as the miners, into the radical camp, to the sharp rise of militant leadership within the federations and unions, to the increasing willingness of the rank and file to resort to violent confrontations to press their demands.(36) The theory and practice of direct action did not develop in a vacuum. They were an integral part of the evolution of the trade union movement in France.

Strikes were not a modern invention. But with the exception of a period between 1878 and 1882, years which served as a catalyst to the passage of the Waldeck-Rousseau Law, most strike activity in France had had only a limited effect in gaining satisfaction of workers' demands. Government repression was a factor. So too was the economic climate. "In times of crisis, the strike is a mediocre instrument," notes Michelle Perrot in her masterful study of strikes in France. The years of highest unemployment were also the years in which strike activity received its highest check.(37) Workers' élan was easily broken by the gravity of the economic situation and by the fact that high unemployment provided employers with a ready pool of scabs. Another factor contributing to the limited success of strikes during the early years of unionism, according to Perrot, was that most demonstrations were simply explosions of discontent, carried on outside of any organizational pattern. Between 1871 and 1890, approximately 72 percent of the conflicts escaped syndicalist direction.(38) But as syndicalism grew, so did strike activity and union involvement in labor demonstrations.

Why was syndicalism so slow to direct workers' demands during this period? Partly this was a reflection of the essential hesitancy of workers and their leaders to resort to violence. In part, syndicalism's weakness was due to its own internal factionalism and the struggle between trade unionism and political socialism. Yet, in surveying the speeches of delegates to trade expositions and workers' congresses, Michelle Perrot denotes an evolution in thinking regarding strikes. The tendency evidenced in workers' meetings during the 1870's was to condemn the strike as "a scourge": illegal, expensive, and unpatriotic. Said delegate Vonnois of Marseille at the 1876 Paris conference:

"If we wish to see our industrialism conserve its renown and the rank it has always occupied in Europe," he stated, then workers must reject the use of strikes.(39)

During the 1880's, Perrot records, a change occurred. In many of the unions, economic crisis brought a general decline of up to one-half of the membership. Apparently many who dropped from the ranks wanted to follow the more conventional forms of economic activity, such as establishing cooperatives. In many organizations, only the activists and the more militant young members remained. The falling away of the more conservative members had its effect: from 1888 to 1893, according to Perrot, syndicalism "was carried to new heights." The effect of this surge in syndicalist activity was the increase in successful strike action and the election of socialist deputies in 1893.(40)

Neither workers' militancy, nor the use of the general strike was new. What was novel about the concept was the assertion that the general strike was to be either the precursor of revolution or the revolution itself. This notion was encompassed in a resolution at the FNS congress in 1888. Partial strikes were only "a means of agitation and organization," Said excavation worker Boulé, the general strike "would make the social capitalist edifice turn somersaults."(41) Thus, as Perrot points out, "the experience of the generalized strike preceded the theory of the general strike; the spectacle of the power of the strike provoked reflection on its possibilities."(42) Those seeking to lead the burgeoning trade union movement would have been deficient in leadership qualities if they had failed to seize upon the idea of the general strike as a primary weapon in their revolutionary arsenal.

The adoption of the general strike as the ultimate expression of the anarchosyndicalist movement involved more than turning the reality of general strike into a theory of revolution. The device of the general strike seemed to be practically suited to all facets of syndicalism. This is perhaps why the principle came to be exclusively identified with radical unionism. For one thing, the use of the strike appeared to be in keeping with the Law of 1884. Speaking in 1892, Briand assured workers that the strike was an action of "legal revolution." "That which you cannot obtain by persuasion, obtain by force--not by violent force, by barricades and bullets, but by legal force, . . . through a sit-down strike."(43)

Furthermore, the introduction of resolutions on the general strike in the early labor congresses, as previously noted, was a conscious political move aimed at purging Broussists and Guesdists from positions of power. The Bordeaux delegates in 1888 were not just being transported on a wave of revolutionary rhetoric when they called for adoption of the general strike; they were also seeking to rid the FNS of its possibilists. The same device was used to purge Guesdists from the FNS and the FBT by those who rejected electoral activity as the means to revolution.

Finally, once these "political" elements were gone, it became necessary for union leaders to find a means of uniting the residue of workers who now comprised the syndicalist movement. The principle of the general strike appealed to the more militant Blanquists, Bakuninists, and anarchists within unionism.

It is not surprising that initially the idea of the general strike had as many interpretations as interpreters. When Briand introduced the resolution at the Nantes congress, delegates were more confused about it than adverse to the idea. Perhaps Briand himself was intentionally vague concerning the specific nature and consequences of that which he was proposing. For him the general strike was to be "a family, a flag, . . . a fusillade" to overcome workers' egoism and provide a direct assault on capitalism. The immediate response to Briand's proposal indicates the eclectic nature of the early syndicalist movement. Jules Magré of Toulon was supportive, calling the general strike "a revolutionary moment which must follow." Precision instrument maker Rémy Bes voiced fears that a general strike would be premature on the grounds that the proletariat was not organized. Bourse activist Beaupérin's only concern was that the strike should be spontaneous. Dijonnaise bookbinder Adolphe Raymond believed that the employment of direct action was a useful instrument of propaganda, while watchmaker Etienne Pedron was suspicious because the idea seemed to him to be in the nature of a political debate. And militant Guesdist Félix Lavigne dismissed the notion as a utopian scheme and one that was clearly illegal.(44)

In 1897, with the Guesdists purged, delegates to the Toulouse congress of the CGT were less confused about the idea of the general strike and more committed to accepting it as a means of class action to gain workers' demands.(45) By the 1900 congress, delegates were more enthusiastic about the proposal, if no more agreed as to what the strike was and what it could achieve. Edouard Briat, representing precision toolmakers of Paris, wholeheartedly applauded the idea for its practical nature. For years unions had been uncertain about the efficacy of partial strikes. This was because the majority of workers were generally cool to such walkouts. After a few weeks the militant minority was forced to seek work elsewhere, leaving the politically indifferent gaining seniority in the factories. A general strike, lasting only a few days, however, would enlist more supporters to the revolutionary cause. Furthermore, continued Briat, the nonviolent nature of a general strike was another practical feature. Many men might be hesitant about taking a gun and making revolution in the streets; or they would be dissuaded from such activity by their wives' fears. But in a general strike, particularly a sit-down strike, Briat concluded, "it is the worker who remains in his own place, putting outside the law the employer who wants to force him to leave."(46)

Most of Briat's confrères supported him in his endorsement. Delegate Bourchet of the leatherworkers' union was chauvinistic in his defense. Speaking to those who believed that a general strike could succeed only if it were part of an international movement, Bourchet, a noted debater, assured the delegates that French workers had nothing to fear by initiating the strike. During the French Revolution, ideas that ultimately came to prevail were thrown into the world. The society of well-being and freedom installed as a result of a revolution made on economic terrain would provide an example once again for the world's workers to follow. Bourchet's speech was so stirring that the delegates voiced enthusiastic support for the general strike, agreeing not only to its efficacy, but also calling for its immediacy!(47)

Few had any fanciful illusions about the effects of direct action in general or of the general strike in particular. More often the practical results to be obtained by these measures were stressed. Writing in 1901, metallurgist Paul Delesalle declared that the general strike was "a new form of revolution more in keeping with the modern industrial regime."(48) To Griffuelhes direct action was infinitely practical because it was incremental: it was the daily exercise of the workers' efforts until the final end of general strike and social revolution occurred.(49)

Generally, syndicalists emphasized that strike action was a practical right sanctioned by law, ethics, and history. In 1900 Delesalle pointed out that capitalists sought to discourage workers' activity by claiming that strikes were useless in the face of the law of supply and demand. But capitalists themselves resorted to similar methods when they claimed they had a right to deny employment to those who did not produce enough. If strikes could be carried on by employers, he contended, the right to strike must be equally extended to employees.(50) Direct action was also a right authorized by French history. A contributor to La Voix du Peuple declared that the general strike was merely "the putting to practice on the economic terrain the article of the Declaration of the Rights of Man which says that when members of the social body are oppressed . . . insurrection would be the most holy of obligations for every one."(51) Such insurrection need not be a violent occasion. Direct action, said Paul Louis, "does not necessarily signify a coup de force, premeditated violence, brutal suppression, effusion of blood, pillage, and destruction. It is not the romantic revolution." Direct action could take many forms, Louis concluded, "from boycott to general strike, from pacific demonstrations to refusing to pay taxes."[52]

SABOTAGE AND OTHER "BENIGN" FORMS OF DIRECT ACTION

"Practical" and "pacific" seem scarcely appropriate words to define the use of sabotage. Along with the general strike, sabotage appears to have been among the more violent aspects of direct action supported by syndicalists. At the 1898 CGT congress at Rennes, the theoretician and leading proponent of the tactic, Emile Pouget, suggested that sabotage was a bourgeois rather than a proletarian invention. "The deliberate adulteration of food and the construction of wretched slums" were two examples of bourgeois sabotage.(53) Naturally the reformists rejected such violent methods. Keufer condemned the practice as "a system lacking in morality, courage, and dignity."(54) Proponents of such action believed to the contrary, that sabotage was a simple means for the worker to act in his own defense and on his own initiative.

Far from being a necessarily violent act, many considered sabotage an alternative to violence. Sabotage was to be directed solely against the capitalists' profits, insisted Yvetot in 1914, rather than against the life or health of another person. The particular milieu and the creativity of the individual worker dictated the means to be employed. Charcutiers could leave salt out of the pâtés; wine stewards might leave casks open for the wine to evaporate. Restaurant workers could give larger portions and be careless with the butter, Pouget suggested.(55) When the boss forced workers to use shoddy material and workmanship in order to increase profits, former Blanquist Victor Griffuelhes suggested that workers could sabotage capitalist designs by working with integrity to produce a perfect product.(56)

Sabotage did not produce nebulous results, as critics charged. Dufour noted in 1913 that the complexity of industry meant that a small act could have enormous consequences.(57) By constant application of creative methods of sabotage, declared Henri Dret at a bourse conference at Auxerre, "the employer will see his benefits diminishing, and he will conclude by understanding that in the excess of work resides his own diminished profits."(58)

Sabotage campaigns were successful because they operated on both the employers and the consumers. In their bid for a six-day work week, novelty and confectionary store workers displayed signs saying that Sunday customers would be badly served. Parisian cobblers warned that shoes brought in on Sundays would be damaged rather than repaired. Hairdressers campaigning for shorter hours announced that any client who had the audacity to keep workers beyond eight o'clock in the evening "would be scalped."(59) The use of "benign sabotage" was the impetus to legislation providing for Monday closings for hairdressers. In this instance, Yvetot concluded in 1914, the use of sabotage proved to be more effective than "four years of beautiful discourse at the tribune of parliament."(60)

Because of the felt need to woo the less militant workers, the more traditional, less aggressive methods of working-class activity were suggested. Although Marxists had rejected the formation of mutuals and cooperatives as being utopian, syndicalists accepted these organizations as valid under certain circumstances. Participation in cooperatives might encourage "egotistical preoccupations" and acquisitive tendencies associated with the bourgeoisie, noted Pelloutier.(61) But as long as members retained their qualities "of convinced militants and not shopkeepers," declared Jouhaux in his report to the 1912 CGT congress, cooperatives represented a valid form of direct action.(62)

Always the practical nature of cooperation was stressed. At a 1910 conference of bourses of Toulouse, A. Danrez reminded his confrères that cooperation served not only to suppress "parasitic intermediaries," it also brought money into the unions' coffers. Profits from the coops, rather than membership dues, could be used to carry on the struggle against capitalism, Danrez pointed out.(63) That same year, Etienne Tabard also praised the pragmatic nature of this form of direct action, noting that during strikes, products furnished by the cooperatives at reduced prices would be used in the communal soup kitchens run by the unions.(64)

Newer forms of direct action were called for.(65) An important campaign was carried on by reform syndicalists in support of the use of the union label as a form of direct action preferable to sabotage or boycott. Introduced by Keufer in 1883, the use of the label was a form of direct action having widespread appeal.(66) One supporter, who signed himself "D.S. Typo" in La Voix du Peuple, praised the use of the union mark as an excellent propaganda device. Goods produced under the label were better products because they were made by union workers. By using the label, the public would know that the best workers were organized. On the other hand, boycotts meant unemployment and sabotage harmed the workers, who as consumers had to buy damaged goods. The future of syndicalism, concluded the contributor, rested on such offensive actions as using the label, and not on defensive actions such as strikes.(67)

The introduction of the use of the union label by the reformists was intended to attract the more moderate workers to unionism and diffuse some of the radical strength within the CGT. Yet, a number of the more revolutionary members of syndicalism also praised the many advantages afforded by using the label. In 1902 Pouget ridiculed those bourgeoisie who said that the use of the syndicalist mark constituted an illegal restraint of trade. Sheer nonsense, jeered Pouget. If that were the case, the government would have to banish all advertisements from the newspapers.(68) Hairdresser Alexandre Luquet was more direct: using the label "strikes our hated adversaries in the cash register," he cheered. As such, it was an effective revolutionary act!(69)

To leaders of syndicalism every act, every union campaign to achieve any economic gain, was a successful battle in the class war. Direct action was defined as strikes, boycotts, and using the label. It also referred to a host of other activities: agitation for regulation of apprentices and in support of minimum wages, shorter hours, enforcement of factory safety legislation, equal pay for equal work, suppression of piecework, or of work in convents, prisons, and military garrisons. Direct action included reporting strike activity as well as incidences of suicides and deaths from starvation.(70) It was evident in campaigns conducted against worker-supported retirement legislation, forcible arbitration contracts, or the use of dangerous substances in factories.(71) All these activities constituted "the improvements which are necessary for the working class to march toward its emancipation," declared delegate Cleuet at the CGT congress in Le Havre.(72)

Most syndicalists agreed with Lagardelle that this revolution would take place incrementally, as "the natural conclusion of a long series of preparatory acts" by a working class "long educated and patiently organized."(73) Partial strikes were necessary skirmishes leading to the main event. Even if checked, exclaimed Pouget, the failure of a partial strike left in the heart of the vanquished worker a desire for vindication. Feelings of revenge were necessary attributes to the development of class consciousness and the will to action.(74) Every failure served as a deposit in the memory bank of the working class to be drawn upon when the general strike was at hand.

All gains, all actions were revolutionary. Economic reforms were to be achieved by the workers themselves by direct action. These efforts increased workers' sense of solidarity. Reforms increased the well-being of the working class, while constituting a partial expropriation of capitalist profits.(75) In unionists' minds, therefore, the dividing line between reformist and revolutionary activity was an artificially imposed one.

REFORM IS REVOLUTIONARY

Indeed, much of the literature of revolutionary syndicalism was directed to the task of explaining that reforms, defined as economic gains achieved by direct action at the expense of capitalist profit, were revolutionary acts. One cannot classify "direct action as being the theory of revolutionary syndicalism and reformism as being against it," declared militant socialist and syndicalist Eugène Fournière. All public demonstrations were instances of direct action and hence, revolutionary.(76) A survey of the reform campaigns carried on in the working-class press reveals how thoroughly syndicalists regarded reform and revolution as being synonymous. In 1905 typographer Louis Niel pointed out that with over 700,000 workers unemployed, a shorter workday would reduce joblessness and result in higher wages. Increased wages would benefit labor and serve as a drain on capitalist profits.(77)

In a lengthy piece in La Voix du Peuple, Pouget took

Auguste Keufer to task for claiming that revolutionaries sought to perpetuate working class misery by heartlessly rejecting all labor reforms. Such assertions were patently false, countered Pouget. "Reforms prepare the revolution; well-being engenders well-being . . . the miserable slave who lives under an implacable yoke of bondage is incapable of desiring liberty; . . . with starvation, anemia, empty stomachs, it is impossible to make an effort." Revolutionary syndicalists were far more practical than reformists credited them with being. Who preferred working twelve hours to working eight? Who would rather earn twenty-five sous per day instead of ten francs? No worker Pouget had ever met! No unionist opposed reform. When real ones came along, he declared, we take them--even from our enemies. Yet revolutionaries were wise enough to know that such benefits did not result from the capitalists' fondness for labor. Reforms occurred because the capitalists could not do otherwise. "There is no antagonism between reformists and revolutionaries," concluded Pouget, except that which was generated by politicians "who try to profit from our divisions and sow discord in the labor organizations."(78)

In another article written the same year, Pouget returned to the theme that reform and revolution were not at opposite poles. Keufer had again charged that to be a revolutionary was "to refuse to submit to inevitable contingencies." This was absurd, said Pouget. The revolutionary is not a Don Quixote charging imaginary windmills. Rather he is "a conscious man who wants to transform the actual social milieu and who knows that the best means of preparing and hastening this transformation is daily to force amelioration of the condition of the life of the masses and to increase [workers'] knowledge." That was why syndicalism's struggle rested on double principles: reform and revolution. Revolutionaries are not enamored with "le beau geste," nor do they have an inordinate desire to engage in violence, Pouget continued. They were as dedicated as political socialists to seeking partial reforms. Why not? Whenever parliament passed workers' legislation it was only because such reforms had either been demanded or already largely conquered by the unions. The government was only submitting to the obvious and the inevitable. That reformists failed to see the practical nature of the revolutionaries surprised Pouget. Reformists were astonished, for instance, when revolutionaries negotiated with their employers. But "The boss is not a myth," reminded Pouget; "we must thus take account of him--despite the fact that we are in a struggle against him." He may be the enemy, but he was a real enemy. Therefore, the unions could not afford to ignore him. The only real reformists," concluded Pouget, "are the revolutionaries."(79)

Not even anarchists were partisans of all-or-nothing. In 1902 Sébastien Faure's Le Libertaire carried responses to questions posed of leading libertarians. One question asked

for opinions on the best means to hasten the establishment
of future society. Although many respondents suggested
education as the sole means, and some like Louise Michel
dismissed reforms as useless, a few others accepted the idea
that improvements were necessary to the social revolution.
Partial reform, said Urbain Gohier, even if mediocre,
expanded however slightly the workers' means of action and
helped to dramatize the evils in present-day society.
Indeed, any means--"apostolic, pacific, or
philosophic"--were acceptable "to propagating the idea of
justice."(80)
        In another series exploring the nature of socialism and
anarchism, the editor himself undertook to explain that not
even anarchists were immune to responding to contingencies.
For Faure revolution and evolution were part of the same
process. The anarchist was neither "an evolutionary
antirevolutionary nor a revolutionary antievolutionary."

> He knows that Evolution and Revolution are
> conjoined [Faure declared], that the one precedes
> and the other follows, that the first prepares and
> the second accomplishes, that slow is the one and
> prompt is the other, that there is between the
> former and the latter the same relation as between
> the effect and the cause, as between the newborn
> and the ascendant.(81)

Evolution and revolution are not two contradictory facts,
concluded Faure: "In different times and in special
circumstances, [the two represent] a series of facts and
ideas, indissoluble and inseparable."(82)
        To revolutionaries, then, there were two kinds of
reformism: direct action carried out on the economic terrain
by the workers themselves and legislative activity carried
on by politicians for electoral gains. To pursue reform by
the first means, said Delesalle in 1902, guaranteed workers'
independence. But seeking reforms from the state by means
of electoral activity could only make labor subservient to
the middle class controlling the state.(83)
        Syndicalism's stance regarding electoral activity was
originally dictated by the need to survive in the face of
murderous political sectarianism and the fear of Guesdist
domination. As a result, the 1906 Charter of Amiens was
designed to be labor's magna carta of freedom from partisan
disagreement. The continuing aversion to electoral politics
stemmed from a host of other practical imperatives. To
become involved in party activity, syndicalists believed,
would dilute labor's effectiveness in the struggle for
integral emancipation.
        Electoral activity tended to temper revolutionary
commitment, was the conclusion of Griffuelhes in 1911, after
an extensive tour of France. Among the miners in
Pas-de-Calais, he noted, the union was merely a "recruiter
of electoral votes" and "the springboard" to political
office. In Lyon and Grenoble partisan politics had ravaged

the workers' movement. Syndical action and party action were incompatible, he reasoned, for wherever politics was strong, unionism was weak. To maintain its vitality the working-class movement must exercise itself without any limits and remain isolated from "the capriciousness of central authority and the interest of a heterogeneous electoral clientele."(84)

In a 1902 article, Emile Pouget outlined how the infiltration of political elements into the unions created discord. Unionists want to achieve their own social emancipation, while

> political adherents need the intervention of an exterior agent—state or municipal—to resolve conflicts and establish relations between capitalism and labor, and effect the social transformation. To do that, [politicians] must be preoccupied with their agents, in sympathy with them. Then the union mirrors politics and is lost to political action.

This kind of political action, Pouget concluded, taught workers only how to vote, not how to become conscious of their situation.(85)

Electoral activity was seen as being disruptive because it also created a conflict between means and ends. Speaking at the 1900 congress of the CGT, Parisian teamster Henri Gérard noted the irrelevance of political government in the social revolution. "It's not that the form of government can influence economic conditions; isn't it the reverse, [he queried] that economic conditions influence the form of government? We're not making a revolution with the goal of changing the government." Therefore one could not hope to use electoral means to effect an economic transformation.(86)

Another criticism was that partisan activity hampered the development of class solidarity. A party was heterogeneous, but a class was the creation of the economic milieu and represented men at the same stage of development. The Socialist Party was without "a single common economic thread [to] maintain its cohesion." As a mélange of social elements resting on an ideological base "without material support," the party was unable to represent the real strength of the working class. Powerless, the party sought to become part of official society and thereby had lost its revolutionary élan, concluded Lagardelle. "The class struggle transforms itself into class collaboration, socialist opposition into ministerial socialism, the state of war into the state of peace. This has made such a chaos of consciousness that one would have to construe it as the twilight of socialism."(87)

Workers must guard against falling into a similar slumber. Partisan activity dulled the proletariat into a false lethargy. The electoral battle occurred only every

four   years.   In the interim, concluded André Saulière in a
1913 study on the general strike, the voter trusted   in   his
deputy and dosed "in a limitless confidence on the effect of
his   vote."(88) Political   parties may   have been created to
represent the workers, as Jean Grave pointed out   in   1906.
But they had too quickly become mired in political reformism
and   more devoted to preserving their legal status and their
huge   treasuries.(89)   Party   politics   also   corrupted   the
politician.   In the beginning "you have a revolutionary as a
deputy," asserted Briat in response to Millerandism.   At the
end   of   four   years,   however,   the   militant has become "a
perfect reactionary."(90)
        Electioneering   did   not   lead   to   revolution,   was
syndicalism's message.   Industrialism had   rendered party
politics   impotent: only   working-class   pressure   was
sufficient   to force parliament to pass labor reforms.   Thus
the political body, noted La Voix du Peuple, had become
nothing   more   than   "a chamber of registration" to workers'
direct   action.(91) Above all, partisan activity was   aimed
primarily   at   winning   elections,   while   syndicalism   was
committed to revolution.   The union's goal was to take from
the   boss   his   function   within   the   workshop,   concluded
Lagardelle.   Syndicalism's aim was to take   from   the   state
its function in society.(92)

THE PRAGMATISM OF DIRECT ACTION IN THE ECONOMIC REALM

        The abundant literature on these forms of direct action
leads   to   some interesting conclusions regarding the nature
of the French workers' movement.   When   one   examines   the
rhetoric   and   practice of direct action from the context of
the   syndicalists'   definition   of   this   activity,   it   is
apparent   that   the   emphasis   on   direct   action   was aimed
practically at the initial goal of recruiting union   members
and raising class consciousness.   As such, the principle was
designed   to   appeal   to a specific population, possessing a
particular historical tradition, at   a   distinct   stage   of
social and economic development.
        Syndical   organization   was   narrowly   proscribed   by
government legislation.   The working   class   was   relatively
passive because of purges of militant workers in the wake of
1871.   It   was a class consistent only in the fact that its
members were in a highly transitional state.   Artisans   were
moving professionally.   Peasants were moving geographically:
flocking   to   urban   centers   to   work   in   the   burgeoning
industries.   Little   class   consciousness   could   exist   among
this   fragmented   population.   The peasant-worker was barely
literate.(93) The   better-educated   artisanal   element   was
wedded   to   a   variety of philosophical schools.   Illiteracy
and ideological sectarianism ensured the   slow   growth   of
working-class unity.
        The   workplace   too   was   composed   of   a   myriad   of
conflicting and competing entities, going beyond the   simple
categories   of   male   and   female   worker,   artisan   and

proletariat. The occupational community unionism sought to
address was comprised of all types: from the worker in the
small provincial factory with some degree of corporate and
local identification, to the peasant "bird of passage"
alienated from his comrades and his natal village. There
were those whose fortunes were rising as a result of
industrialization, and others employed in trades which for
centuries had ranked among the professional elite, now
teetering on the brink of technological obsolescence. The
organizational life of the worker was equally varied. There
were federations with long rosters of committed dues-paying
members, and small locals with shadow bureaucracies, meeting
in bare rooms grudgingly provided by the local town
councils. There were members of corporations who
traditionally had used the tactics of carefully planned,
concerted job action; while there were other groups, never
given to patience, accustomed to quick, often violent
demonstrations in order to cow the bosses into submission.
To appeal to this diverse population, syndicalists had to be
able to speak to the multitudes without falling into the
mire of banality. Direct action was the lingua franca of a
fragmented population and the way to give viability and
expression to the culture of revolution.

     The call for direct action in the economic realm was
designed to attract both conservatives and radicals to
unionism. Direct action was labor's natural right. The
industrial revolution had brought into being a new condition
of existence. Economics had spawned the development of
large industry and had dictated the growth of unionism and
the development of class consciousness, syndicalists
preached. The new man produced by the changing economic
milieu was the one directed "to proclaiming the necessity of
imminent well-being," declared a union supporter in 1906,
and to preparing citizens "to break all the obstacles by the
most effective and prompt means."(94) The use of direct
action, enlisted in the service of removing barriers to the
realization of immediate material reform, had a realistic
appeal to all workers, skilled and unskilled.

     Also practical was the fact that direct action, so
defined, provided a multiple route to revolution. It
encompassed all forms of working-class participation, from
joining a study circle to joining in the general strike.
Such a broad gamut of activity might appeal to timid
peasants and artisans, as well as those steeped in a
tradition of violence. Every impulse for action was served.
Buying union-made products or joining a consumers'
cooperative was a revolutionary activity the passive worker
could feel comfortable performing. Yet, as defined by
unionists, all forms of direct action were deemed legal and
ethically justifiable.

     Even that which has generally been regarded as the
epitome of violence, the general strike, was cast in such a
way as to appeal to the most diverse elements within the
work force. By participating in the general strike, the

artisan could take pleasure in the feelings of security generated by the idea of corporate action by all workers. This effort, infinitely superior to bombs and barricades, would be the social revolution initiating a new society infused with the ethics of the workshop.

The dramatic nature of the general strike further appealed to both the submissive and the fatalistic, the skilled worker facing an uncertain future, as well as the unskilled worker threatening and threatened by the future. Sir Arthur Clay's charge that direct action played upon the primitive instincts is not without validity. Rather than serving as a criticism of the movement, this method suggests one of syndicalism's basic strengths. It addressed the primal needs of those workers who were unionism's potential recruits.

The summons to direct action was not generally symbolic or utopian, however. The call to revolution was almost always framed in the most pragmatic of terms. Edouard Berth might speak of the general strike as Marx's "grand battle" of life and death, God's judgment, or Hegel's world spirit realizing itself.(95) Georges Sorel might praise the symbolic nature of the general strike. But to syndicalists, Sorel and other intellectuals were "fanatics."(96) Their assertion that the general strike was intended to have an apocalyptic goal, held out to the workers like the promise of heavenly wings and halos, was a total misreading of syndicalism's meaning. The tactic of the general strike was never intended to be a myth. It was as much of a reality as any other form of direct action, but one inchoate in form, and therefore unlimited in its possibilities. By not concretizing the definition of the general strike, radicals and reformists could sharply disagree among themselves as to its definition, yet still unite over the common goal of revolution.

In sum, few working-class leaders thought or spoke in cosmic terms. Fewer still had any grand illusions about the nature of the revolution they were attempting to launch. A 1921 report presented to the Lille congress of the CGT proved to be another strong assertion of unionism's pragmatism.

> We do not believe in the apocalypse [the report noted], nor can we tell our followers that capitalism is foundering when everything demonstrates to the contrary. We do not want to trick workers into thinking the road is easy and the end is in their hands. We would rather point out to the proletariat the difficulty of its task.(97)

The task at hand was revolution. Direct action through efforts to gain reforms was the means to attain that end. Such means were also practical responses to reality. Labor reforms swelled the ranks of unionism with new converts and fellow travelers, thereby heightening class consciousness by

building solidarity. Reforms also increased the well-being
of   the   workers.   Material   benefits   were   regarded   as
incremental stages of the   revolution.   Each   gain   chipped
away   at   capitalism's   treasure   chest   and transferred the
chips to the working class. Ultimately,   it   was believed,
the   treasure   would   belong to the producers instead of the
exploiters.
       Direct   action   was also a practical means of achieving
adherence to unionism by those with differing   philosophies.
The   emphasis   on   action   appealed   to Blanquists and
anarchists.   The devotion to data-gathering and the   support
of   revolution   through   reform appealed to   positivists.
Syndicalism's   antiministerial   pronouncements might   even
appeal   to   Guesdists.   Anarchists   were   attracted   by the
relative lack of organizational structure within unionism,
which was in itself not so much the result of ideological
preference as it was a simple response to the fact that
union   membership   was   always   modest in scale. Anarchists
supported the CGT's unit voting policy and were attracted to
the nonautoritarian structure of the Confederation, which as
Pouget pointed out, was not

> an   organ of direction, but of coordination. . . .
> here   there   is cohesion and not centralization,
> impulsion   and   not   direction.   Federalism   is
> supreme,   and   at   every   degree,   the   different
> organisms--individual, syndical, Federational,   or
> the Bourses du travail--are all autonomous.(98)

In the CGT, power remained diffused.   The Confederation's
role,   observed   Jouhaux, was not to manipulate strikes, but
"to second them [and] call for national solidarity." The CGT
did not determine if strikes were to be "violent or pacific
in   [their]   demonstration,"   Jouhaux   concluded.   That
determination   was   based   on   necessity   and   attendant
conditions.(99)
       The   idea   of direct action appealed to Proudhonist and
Marxist prescriptions concerning the idea of the working
class   carrying out its own revolution. The common practice
in France had been to use the offices of the state to
mediate   disputes   between   labor   and   the   bosses.   This
tradition,   syndicalists   believed,   not   only   dulled   the
individual's   ability   to act on his own behalf, it also
further enhanced the power of the centralized state.   Only
through the worker's individual and collective effort could
he commit himself to the goal of emancipation, develop
feelings   of   solidarity,   effect   partial   expropriation of
capitalism's   wealth,   raise his own and his   comrades'
immediate state of well-being, and prepare for the day when
the final blow would make the social revolution. While some
followers of Proudhon may have been in agreement with their
mentor's abhorrence of strikes, others no doubt believed, as
Annie Kriegel has noted, that the strike was only an
extension of Proudhon's theories concerning the necessity

for economic war.(100) The syndicat seemed to parallel
Proudhon's mutuals, wherein individuality was maintained and
the worker laboring for his own well-being, furthered the
well-being of all. Action within this most primary social
unit would produce revolution through devolution. The new
order, to be based on the union, appeared to be in
accordance with Proudhon's anarchist vision.

The definition of direct action as encompassing
everything but partisanal activity was infinitely practical.
The aversion to politics assured independence from leftist
parties and diminished the possibilities of schism within
the labor movement. It appealed to the politically
sophisticated worker, frustrated by government vacillation
toward labor or exasperated by the circuitous development of
the Socialist Party. It also sought to give reassurance to
the newly arrived, unskilled worker confused regarding the
nature of the milieu in which he found himself. To the
politically naive, the process by which electoral choice was
translated into who would be seated in the Chamber must have
seemed to be a mystery as unfathomable as the church's
preachings on the doctrine of transubstantiation. In
syndicalism there was neither electoral uncertainty nor
party labels.

Further, the definition of direct action as economic
activity allowed union members to exercise an unheard-of
freedom in the electoral realm. It is true that while the
CGT remained officially aloof from partisan stands, the
working-class press often carried articles counseling
workers to withhold their support of a specific candidate or
to abstain in a particular election. Syndicalists
understood that electoral abstention was often more
effective than participation in influencing a political
outcome. An individual or collective act of abstention in
the voting booth was regarded as being as acceptable a form
of direct action as boycotting a particular employer or a
nonunion product.

The Charter of Amiens emancipated the political
conscience of the individual; it did not outlaw individual
political action. The Charter merely meant that union
membership was not dependent on party affiliation. In fact,
association was not dependent on much of anything except the
will to belong. For syndicalists, noted Jouhaux, direct
action was "aparliamentary," not antiparliamentary.(101)
Syndicalism was not antipolitical; it just took a dim view
of party politics. That distinction is a necessary one. It
helps to explain the fact that so many working-class leaders
were also politically engaged. In spite of this political
activism--or more practically, because of it--the CGT itself
took no official position in electoral contests. Such
neutrality notwithstanding, syndicalists were nevertheless
aware that pressure in the economic realm produced reaction
and responses in the parliamentary realm. Thus, as Edward
Shorter and Charles Tilly explain in their study of Strikes
in France 1830-1968, direct action was utterly
political.(102) Socialists used political activity to

achieve economic reform; syndicalists were committed to
using economic activity to bring about reform of the state
and the workplace. But for syndicalists, the union rather
than the party constituted the primary locus of workers'
political power.

As conceived by syndicalism, party socialism was
divisive and exclusionary. Direct action, so defined, was
simple and direct. It constituted a return to the idea of
Rousseau's world of the social contract, wherein individual
will was the primary force in denoting the general will.
With direct action there were no intermediaries between
immediate act and immediate consequence. The worker as
subject acted directly to better the material conditions of
his existence. His actions produced a chain reaction. A
multitude of quantitative changes would ultimately work to
produce a vast qualitative change that would be the social
revolution.

As defined by syndicalism, direct action was also
intended to be ahistorical. It was a way to wean workers
away from their faith in the Republic of Jacobin centralism.
This was not an easy task. Many workers, such as Auguste
Keufer, were tenacious in their support of the Third
Republic. Said Keufer in 1909, "I place the Republic above
all forms of government, even above ignorant universal
suffrage and the mistakes that it can commit."(103) To the
revolutionaries, however, the Republic and the political
system supporting it, in the hands of the bourgeoisie, was
repressive, exploitative, and based on competition and
inequality. The series of shocks from the repression of the
Communards, and from Boulangism, the Panama scandal, and the
Dreyfus affair, demonstrated that both state and system were
inept and corrupt. While much of their rhetoric was aimed
at assuring workers that the economic revolution was to be
an extension of the political revolution of 1789,
syndicalists nevertheless remembered that the efforts of the
preceding revolution had also been devoted to erasing all
forms of corporate identity, from feudalism to unionism. To
be a republican patriot was to be nonassociated. Thus, the
notion of direct action through unionism, which was itself a
critique of the state, was a practical means of overturning
Jacobin ideas of nonassociation and maintaining a
revolutionary posture.

What inspired syndicalism's practical thrust? For the
most part, pragmatism was dictated by the need to survive.
The Waldeck-Rousseau Law had stated that workers could form
associations only for the defense of their professional
interests. In the early years, therefore, syndicalist
leaders stressed the pursuit of bread-and-butter issues over
the loftier goal of workers' emancipation. Syndicalism's
pragmatism was meant to be a magnet to union membership. At
the 1900 Paris congress, porcelain worker Edouard Treich
emphasized the fact that the members, particularly from the
provinces, demanded of their leaders a clear-cut and
achievable program.

If you want us to follow you [he reminded them],
be practical, indicate the formulaes, indicate the
fashion under which you will operate, and do not
blame the provincials for being colder than you,
and above all, more practical. Have confidence in
them also; they not only ask to follow you, but on
the condition that you give them proof, that
having indicated that you wish to be followed, and
of the end you wish to attain, that you are
sufficiently strong enough to hold on to the power
that you are seeking.(104)

Were the methods of syndicalism a success? Strike
activity increased, as did other forms of direct action.
Union membership rose, as did union involvement in directing
strikes. Immediate reforms were forthcoming; workers'
consciousness was also raised.(105) Granted, the growth of
unionism was always connected to the sway of the economic
pendulum; but the practical nature of revolutionary
syndicalism allowed unionists to attempt to take advantage
of every economic situation. Inflations and depressions
produced working-class discontent and raised union
membership. Economic upturns, on the other hand, brought
wage increases, thereby providing the greater cushion of
well-being needed to sustain workers during walkouts.(106)
Union membership was always linked with strike activity, and
each influenced the other dialectically. In turn,
syndicalist strength and working-class militancy were able
to force legislators to take notice of labor's demands.
    Direct action, in terms of its political effects, was
also successful, because it allowed syndicalists to
articulate a consistent program of action and clearly
defined goals, even in the face of working-class apathy,
discouragement, or confusion. Further, by positioning
itself on the extreme left, syndicalism was able to serve
both as a radical point of reference for the Socialist Party
deputies involved in the game of political compromise and as
a constant reminder to them of the power of their
working-class constituents. Syndicalism's reliance on
direct action provided unionists with the means of affecting
the political decision-making process without being
chastened by it. The commitment to steer clear of the
shoals of internal political sectarianism was also in
evidence after World War I. The autonomy of the CGT was
maintained against those who wished to subvert the union
organizations to the nationalist and political aims of the
leaders of the Third International. If direct action were
to be defined narrowly as remaining independent of political
sects and parties, then the road followed by revolutionary
syndicalism can be deemed both consistent and a success.

NOTES

1. Pouget in Robert Goetz-Girey, La pensée syndicale francaise: militants et théoriciens (Paris, 1948), p. 57; and in V[ictor] Griffuelhes, et al., Syndicat et syndicalisme (Paris, n.d.), p. 7.

2. Bourse Régionale du Travail. Compte rendu du congrès régional corporatif (Auxerre, 1907), p. 23.

3. Paul Louis, Le syndicalisme contre l'état (Paris, 1910), p. 4. The idea that syndicalism was "rescuing" Marxism and/or socialism is strongly articulated in the literature. Griffuelhes told delegates to the 1907 International congress held at Paris that syndicalism seemed to be "carrying socialism toward a renaissance." Reported in Hubert Lagardelle, et al., Syndicalisme et socialisme (Paris, 1908), p. 3. The same idea was expressed by delegate Klemczynski at the 1912 meeting of the CGT. He said that syndicalism was "of pure essence Marxist, and a regeneration, a renaissance of socialism." Quoted in XVIII(e) congrès national corporatif (XII(e) de la C.G.T.) . . . Compte rendu des travaux (Le Havre, 1912), p. 113.

4. La Voix du Peuple, 28 July 1901.

5. Pouget in Robert Goetz-Girey, La pensée syndicale, p. 57.

6. XI(e) congrès national corporatif (V(e) de la confédération générale du travail . . .) (Paris, 1900), pp. 116-117.

7. Le Libertaire, 18 Jan. 1903.

8. Marc Pierrot in Griffuelhes, et al., Syndicat et syndicalisme, p. 8.

9. The literature is full of discussions on the effectiveness of the small cadre of unionized workers. Louis Meyer noted that the use of direct action actually swelled the unions' effectiveness by keeping "society in a constant disorganization." La crise du syndicalisme (Paris, 1909), p. 12. Shoemaker Bernard Capjuzan redefined the nature of beneficial membership in 1900. The French tremperament was moved to action only when it could count on numerical strength, so membership was important. But the recruits to the CGT must be those possessing a "militant commitment" to the cause. XI(e) congrès [Paris, 1900], pp. 113-114. Others noted that syndicalism's strength lay in the distribution of membership as well as in the degree of commitment. In 1913, for instance, 80 percent of the

workers in the critical industries of baking, building, electrical, and industrial trades were purportedly unionized. Dufour, Le syndicalisme et la prochaine révolution (Paris, 1913), p. 142. The theme of the union as a guiding force was noted by Raymond Joran, who wrote that unionized workers were "skeletons around which the masses congregate during a conflict." But when the crisis passed, "the effects are like snow in the sun." L'organisation syndicale dans l'industrie du bâtiment (Paris, 1914), p. 98. The foes of unionism were not lulled by the diminished membership. Joseph Guérin cautioned that "To evaluate numerically is to evaluate superficially. There are other things more powerful than number. A minority of men of action, disciplined and deciding to have recourse to violence is stronger than men of peace." Le syndicalisme et la propriété (Paris, n. d.), p. 22.

10. Fernand Pelloutier, Histoire des bourses du travail (Paris, 1902), p. 91.

11. La Voix du Peuple, 8 Sept. 1901.

12. Ibid., 24 Feb. 1901.

13. Victor Griffuelhes, Léon Jouhaux, eds., Encyclopédie du mouvement syndicaliste (Paris, 1912), pp. 14-15.

14. Lagardelle, et al., Syndicalisme et socialisme, p. 44.

15. IX(e) congrès de la fédération nationale des bourses du travail . . . Compte rendu des travaux du congrès (Toulouse, 1897), p. 33.

16. Lagardelle, quoted in Sylvain Humbert, Le mouvement syndical (Paris, 1912), p. 82.

17. Dufour, Syndicalisme et la prochaine révolution, p. 154.

18. Arthur Danrez, Vérités syndicales (Paris, 1908), p. 15. This red-bound book on "syndicalism's truths" is similar to the format later used by Chairman Mao. Peter Stearns contends there were "lost opportunities in strikes" because there were not enough union leaders to go around. Revolutionary Syndicalism and French Labor: A Cause Without Rebels (New Brunswick, 1971) p. 74. However the small bureaucracy was in keeping with libertarian desires. And a small number of permanent officials represented an important savings for a chronically poor organization.

19. Pelloutier, Histoire des bourses, p. 262.

20. Noted in Griffuelhes, et al., Syndicat et

syndicalisme, p. 7.

21. La Guerre Sociale, 6 May 1908.

22. Le Libertaire, 4 Mar. 1900.

23. Ibid., 5 Aug. 1900. André May recaps Georges Sorel's argument as to why anarchists entered the unions. He concludes that anarchists tired of hearing "the same grandeloquent maledictions hurled against capitalism, and wanted to find a way to conduct themselves in really revolutionary action." Anarchists believed the syndicats were instruments of social revolution. Les origines du syndicalisme révolutionnaire (Paris, 1913), p. 102.

24. Le Libertaire, 11 May 1902.

25. Ibid., 29 Mar. 1902.

26. Ibid., 2 Sept. 1906.

27. Lagardelle, et al., Syndicalisme et socialisme, p. 8.

28. Confédération Générale du Travail, La crise du syndicalisme et l'action de la C.G.T. (Lille, 1921), p. 8.

29. Edouard Dolléans, Le caractère religieux du socialisme (Paris, 1906), pp. 2, 4, 22, 23 for quoted material.

30. C[élestin] Bouglé, Syndicalisme et démocratie (Paris, 1908), pp. 90-91, 200-201.

31. Meyer, Crise du syndicalisme, pp. 36, 42.

32. Auguste Keufer, La crise syndicaliste (Aurillac, 1910), p. 17 for quote.

33. Gaston Gros, Le contrat collectif et le syndicalisme (Paris, 1910), pp. 42-43 for quotes.

34. [Henri] Ghesquière, [Adéodat] Compère-Morel, L'action syndicale (Lille, 1911), pp. 22, 29 for quotes. Commenting on the political rhetoric of the socialists, Alphonse Merrheim noted that whenever Ghesquière or Compère-Morel spoke, it was not to defend the working class, but to safeguard municipal elections for the Socialist Party. XVIII(e) congrès [Le Havre, 1912], p. 132.

35. Arthur Clay, Syndicalism and Labour (London, 1912), p. 107.

36. Judith F. Stone, The Search for Social Peace:

Reform Legislation in France 1890-1914 (New York, 1984), pp. 84-85.

37. Michelle Perrot, Les ouvriers en grève, France 1871-1890, 2 vols. (Paris, 1974), vol. 1, pp. 71, 150. Stearns draws opposite conclusions from Perrot, noting that from 1910 to 1914, French workers enjoyed a rise in real wages, while Perrot maintains that 1910-1913 were years of high inflation and lowered real wages. The prosperity, according to Stearns, tended to temper workers' radicalism. Stearns, Revolutionary Syndicalism and French Labor, p. 79.

38. Perrot, Les ouvriers en grève, vol. 2, pp. 424-425.

39. Ibid., vol. 2, pp. 440-443. Quote appears on bottom of p. 443.

40. Ibid., vol. 2, pp. 435-438. Quote appears on p. 438.

41. Ibid., vol. 2, pp. 496-497.

42. Ibid., vol. 2, p. 499.

43. Aristide Briand quoted in Jacques Julliard, Fernand Pelloutier et les origines du syndicalisme d'action directe (Paris, 1971), p. 63. His italics.

44. Humbert, pp. 23-31 for a discussion of the general strike at the Nantes congress. See 6(me) congrès nationale des syndicats de France. Compte rendu des travaux du congrès . . . (Nantes, 1894), pp. 24-40.

45. IX(e) congrès [Toulouse, 1897], pp. 110-116.

46. XI(e) congrès [Paris, 1900], pp. 106-124.

47. Ibid., pp. 107-108.

48. Paul Delesalle, L'action syndicale et les anarchistes (Paris, 1901), pp. 7-8.

49. Griffuelhes, quoted in André Marchal, Le mouvement syndical en France (Paris, 1945), p. 39.

50. Paul Delesalle, La grève (Paris, 1900), pp. 11-13.

51. La Voix du Peuple, 5 July 1903.

52. Louis, Syndicalisme contre l'état, p. 224.

53. Pouget quoted in Rudolph Rocker, Anarcho-Syndicalism: Theory and Practice (London, 1938), p. 127.

54. Keufer quoted in Goetz-Girey, La pensée syndicale, p. 223.

55. La Voix du Peuple, 1 May 1905; Jules Cazalis, Syndicalisme ouvrier et évolution sociale (Paris, 1925), p. 70.

56. Griffuelhes quoted in J[acques] Rennes, Syndicalisme français (Paris 1948), p. 134.

57. Dufour, Syndicalisme et la prochaine révolution, p. 138.

58. Congrès régional corporatif [Auxerre, 1907], p. 15.

59. La Voix du Peuple, 14 July 1901, 15 Dec. 1901. Quote appears in first issue cited.

60. Ibid., 4 Jan. 1914.

61. Pelloutier, Histoire des bourses du travail, p. 79.

62. XVIII(e) congrès [Le Havre, 1912], p. 69.

63. La Voix du Peuple, 4 Dec. 1910.

64. Ibid., 30 Jan. 1910.

65. Syndicalist newspapers urged workers to learn Esperanto, a language purportedly easy to learn. A common language among the world's proletariat, many believed, would heighten class solidarity and better prepare the ground for the general strike. Further, proponents suggested what they believed was the practical immediate consequences of speaking Esperanto: during periods of high unemployment in one country, workers could easily emigrate to other nations where work was abundant. Le Libertaire, 30 Apr. 905; La Voix du Peuple, 13 Jan. 1901, 23 Feb. 1902, 10 Sept. 1905, 5 Dec. 1909.

66. Albert Choppé, Le label (Paris, 1908), p. 240. See also Confédération Générale du Travail, La confédération générale du travail et le mouvement syndical (Paris, 1925), pp. 65-66.

67. Series appears in La Voix du Peuple, 14 Apr. 1901, 28 Apr. 1901, 12 May 1901, 16 June 1901.

68. Ibid., 7 Sept. 1902.

69.   Ibid., 4 May 1902.

70.   The newspaper Le Libertaire, edited by Sébastien Faure, often carried accounts of all the suicides and deaths by starvation in order to heighten consciousness of the corruption and lack of humanity intrinsic to the bourgeois regime.

71.   The CGT opposed the retirement legislation because workers were required to contribute. Their opposition reflected their constituents' antipathy toward the measure, since over three-quarters of the workers considered the plan a swindle and refused to join. Georges Dupeux, French Society 1789-1970, Peter Wait, trans. (London, 1976), p. 177.

72.   XVIII(e) congrès [Le Havre, 1912], p. 124.

73.   Lagardelle quoted in Cazalis, Syndicalisme ouvrier, p. 82.

74.   Pouget quoted in Pierre Paraf, Les formes actuelles du syndicalisme en France (Paris, 1923), p. 50. Paul Delesalle was less convinced of the efficacy of the partial strike. He noted that while immediate gains might be forthcoming in a partial strike, the costs of any reforms ultimately would be passed along to the working-class consumer. La grève, pp. 14-15.

75.   Jouhaux noted that reform must be considered "not only by the immediate realization that it will bring about, but by the transforming ends [they] carry within [themselves]." Quoted in Maxime Leroy, Les techniques nouvelles du syndicalisme (Paris, 1921), p. 146.

76.   Eugène Fournière quoted in Griffuelhes and Jouhaux, eds., Encyclopédie du mouvement syndicaliste, p. 16.

77.   La Voix du Peuple, 26 Mar. 1905.

78.   Ibid., 5 Apr. 1903.

79.   Ibid., 16 Aug. 1903.

80.   Articles ran in subsequent issues of Le Libertaire beginning 21 Nov. 1903 and ending on 1 Jan. 1904. Urbain Gohier's and Louise Michel's responses appear in the first number.

81.   Ibid., 13 Sept. 1903.

82.   Ibid., 27 Sept. 1903.

83. Paul Delesalle, Les deux méthodes du syndicalisme (Paris, 1903), pp. 2-5.

84. Victor Griffuelhes, Voyage révolutionnaire (Paris, 1911); see particularly pp. 9, 22-23, 58. Former Guesdist Léon Robert criticized an officer of one bourse for running in the 1910 election because union comrades, reflecting "all colors of the political rainbow," might be driven off at the example of a bourse official seeking public office. Voix du Peuple, 11 Sept. 1910.

85. Ibid., 15 June 1902.

86. XI(e) congrès [Paris, 1900], p. 118.

87. See Humbert, Le mouvement syndical, p. 81; Lagardelle, et al., Syndicalisme et socialisme, quotes on pp. 38, 45.

88. André Saulière, La grève générale: De Robert Owen à la doctrine syndicaliste (Bordeaux, 1913), p. 177.

89. La Guerre Sociale, 19 Dec. 1906.

90. XI(e) congrès [Paris, 1900], p. 122. Even Aristide Briand, defender of the notion of the general strike in 1892, cooled to the idea once he was elected to the government. On the eve of his entry into the Chamber, Briand told his constituents that he was seeking a politics of détente for all citizens because "there is no prosperity in strikes." Reported in Georges Michon, La préparation à la guerre: La Loi de Trois Ans 1910-1914 (Paris, 1935), p. 10.

91. La Voix du Peuple, 1 May 1902. The notion that government was impotent was expressed by E. Anthony, who noted that in 1899, 84 strikes were declared to force employers to abide by existing legislation regarding accidents at work. Laws were obviously "dead letters" because the government was unable to enforce them. Ibid., 27 Jan. 1901.

92. Lagardelle in Cazalis, Syndicalisme ouvrier, p. 49.

93. Dupeaux, French Society, pp. 12, 155-162 notes that 1872-1911 were years of rural exodus of the young to the towns and cities. A letter from some bootmakers to the 1880 regional workers' congress in Bordeaux noted that most workers could not read: thus, illiteracy was one reason for their indifference to organization, they maintained. Congrès ouvrier régional de Bordeaux . . . (Bordeaux, 1880), p. 9.

94. La Voix du Peuple, 14 Oct. 1906.

95. Berth quoted in Humbert, Le mouvement syndical, p. 46.

96. Paul Delesalle, Les deux méthodes du syndicalisme, p. 15.

97. Noted in C.G.T., La crise du syndicalisme, p. 44.

98. Pouget in Roger Picard, Le mouvement syndical durant la guerre (Paris, 1928), p. 31.

99. Léon Jouhaux, Le syndicalisme français contre la guerre (Paris, 1913), p. 19.

100. Annie Kriegel, "Le syndicalisme révolutionnaire et Proudhon," Le pain et les roses (Paris, 1968), p. 49.

101. Jouhaux, Le syndicalisme français contre la guerre (Paris, 1913), p. 32 (his emphasis).

102. Edward Shorter and Charles Tilly, Strikes in France 1830-1968 (Cambridge, 1974), p. 193.

103. La Voix du Peuple, 4 July 1909.

104. XI(e) congrès [Paris, 1900], p. 113.

105. Louis, Syndicalisme contre l'état, p. 230.

106. Shorter and Tilly, Strikes in France, pp. 102, 145.

PERSONS CITED

Antignac, Antoine (1864-1930), born in the Corrèze of a poor family. Began his career as a militant in the POF, then joined the bourse. He was befriended by Sébastien Faure and worked on several papers. He was often arrested for his militant anarchist activities, particularly when important persons came to Paris. Married, with a family.

Beaupérin, Pierre (?-?), a shoemaker and secretary of the Rennes bourse. Involved in the founding of the CGT.

Bes, Rémy (1872-?), born in the Cantal. He was a precision instrument maker and treasurer of his union. He was mobilized in 1914 to a war plant. From 1916 to the armistice, he participated on a committee to reestablish international relations.

Boulé (?-?), a woodcutter from the Nièvre. Noted for making "cerebral revolution" in his unions during the 1890s. He joined the excavation workers in Paris. He supported the principle of the general strike at the FNS meeting in 1888. He was also involved in the CGT.

Bourchet, A. (1869-?), was an officer in the leatherworkers' federation. A Blanquist, he was a remarkable debater and often spoke in support of the general strike at CGT congresses. In 1916 he participated in the minority action against the war, but abandoned that position until after the armistice, when he then sided with Marty and others involved in the Black Sea mutiny.

Braun, Joseph (?-?), a mechanic, married, with two children. He was an Allemanist and became a secretary in the metallurgists' federation. He belonged to a compagnonnage, and was a member of the general strike committee.

Briat, Edouard (1864-1948), cooperator, syndicalist, and socialist. In 1895 he was instrumental in founding a cooperative of precision toolmakers. Participated in CGT congresses.

Capjuzan, Bernard (1855-1912), born in the Basses-Pyrénées, died in Paris. A shoemaker, member of the shoemakers' federation and of the Paris bourse. He supported the Guesdists as opposed to the possibilists. Attended the 1899 meeting of the International. Capjuzan edited numerous labor journals and supported the principle of the general strike.

Cleuet, Auguste (1876-1956), born in the Nord and died in Paris. Worked in a bank after his military service. He was involved with the unity movement within socialism while also involved in unionism. As secretary of the Amiens bourse, he was active in gaining legislation outlawing night work for bakers. He was also involved with cooperatives. He was mobilized during the war.

Danrez, Arthur (?-?), diamond worker and militant in the Federation of the Jura. In 1908 he joined the SFIO. That year he was fired from his post as assistant to the socialist mayor of his town for putting up anti-Clemenceau posters. He pursued political, cooperative, and syndicalist action simultaneously. He supported Jouhaux and the majority during the war.

Delesalle, Maurice Paul (1870-1948), born in the Seine-et-Oise, and died in Paris. His mother was a seamstress, his father a machinist. Studied at night school to become an industrial draftsman and toolmaker. Moved to Paris, where he became active in anarchist and socialist groups. He became an officer in the FBT and the CGT. He was always on the left: supporting the general strike, agitating for the eight-hour day, and opposing reformists.

He was instrumental in drafting the Amiens charter. He worked for a time on Jean Grave's Temps Nouveaux, and was arrested in 1907 for his protest against the government's use of troops in the Midi. In 1908, with the help of a friend, Delesalle opened his own bookstore and resigned from the CGT. His shop became a foyer for leftist intellectuals. He collaborated with many people in publishing syndicalist literature. He supported Jouhaux in 1914, but later joined the Communist Party.

Dret, Henri (1875-1941), born in the Dordogne, died in the Seine-et-Oise. A shoemaker who became secretary general of his federation, he was very active in the CGT and organized many farmworkers' unions in 1906. He was involved in a demonstration against the firing on striking farmworkers at Draveil in 1908, and had his right arm amputated as a result of wounds sustained there. He was listed on the Carnet B, but rallied with the majority in 1914. He was an early member of the POF, then went through an anarchist phase, returning to party socialism later in his life.

Faure, Auguste Sébastien (1858-1942), born in the Loire, died in the Charente-Inférieure. Born of middle-class parentage, he was educated by the Jesuits, served in the military, and lived in England for a time. He returned to France and moved from Catholicism to socialism. Married and divorced. Under Elisée Réclus' influence, he became an anarchist. He was sentenced to twenty years of hard labor in 1895 for his terrorist activities, but was subsequently granted full amnesty. He was a pacifist during World War I.

Fournière, Eugène (1857-1914), born at Paris of working-class parents; died in the Seine. At the age of eleven he became an apprentice to his jeweler uncle in Paris. He continued his education by reading at the Bibliothèque Nationale. He was first attracted to Guesdism, then Millerandism. He joined the SFIO in 1905 and remained a party faithful to his death. He was subsequently elected a Municipal Councilor in Paris, and then a deputy from the Aisne in 1898. He was attracted to socialism rather than syndicalism.

Gérard, Henri (?-?), lived in Paris. He represented Parisian teamsters at the CGT congresses, and was a member of the Committee of the General Strike.

Gohier, Urbain (1862-1951), born in Versailles (Seine-et-Oise) and died in the Cher. He obtained a degree in law. He was involved with antimilitarism and was sentenced to prison for his activities. He collaborated on Le Libertaire. During World War II he supported the Vichy government.

Grave, Jean (1854-1939), born in the Puy-de-Dôme, died in the Loiret. His father moved the family to Paris, where

Jean was educated in a Catholic school. He apprenticed as a mechanic at the age of twelve, then learned the shoemaking trade. After his military service, he became involved in political activity and anarchism. Thereafter he concentrated his efforts on spreading the anarchist message through his paper, the Temps Nouveaux. He was an antimilitarist, although he publicly rallied to the Union sacrée during the war. He was twice condemned for his antigovernmental activity: once for his protest against the shootings at Fourmies in 1891, and later for charges of anarchist terrorism. He was acquitted each time.

Guérard, Eugène (?-?), a reformist and secretary general of the railroad workers.

Klemczynski, Ernest (1876-1930), born in the Oise, died in the Jura. Father was a railroad station master. Ernest became a draftsman for a railroad company and was one of those who later formed a union. He was also a political socialist. He attended the CGT congresses, wrote for numerous working-class newspapers, and was an untiring propagandist for socialism. He supported the First World War and remained with the minority SFIO after the schism.

Lavigne, Félix (1851-1930), born and died in Bordeaux. He collaborated in the creation of the first bourse at Bordeaux. He was a Guesdist, participated in the International, and argued against the general strike at Nantes. He was part of the Guesdist cadre to leave that meeting, and he participated in unionism thereafter on a local level. He was an important member of the SFIO until the schism in 1920. Married, with two children.

Luquet, Alexandre (1874-1930), born in the Cher, but came to Paris as a small child. He was a hairdresser who became part of the first rank of the CGT, although he never broke his link to the Socialist Party. He was opposed to proportional representation, and remained with the syndicalist majority after World War I.

Magré, Jules (?-?), lived in Toulon, and was a bourse member.

Meyer, Louis (?-?), lived in Paris. Delegate to numerous CGT congresses.

Michel, Louise (1830-1905), born in the Haute-Marne, died in the Bouches-du-Rhône. Militant Communard who was jailed and exiled for her militancy. After her amnesty she devoted her time to anarchism and conducting demonstrations supporting striking workers.

Niel, Louis (1872-1952), born in the provinces, died in Corsica. Café worker, then typographer at Montpellier. Served in the military. He was an anarchist, syndicalist, and officer in the bourse. He was a force in getting the FBT to join the CGT. He was also involved with organizing farmworkers. He became a reformist in reaction to Yvetot's antimilitarism. He was elected general secretary of the CGT in 1909, but left that post after a strike of postal workers was checked in the wake of Niel's call for a general strike. He became a proofreader, and later joined the SFIO. After that he served as an agent for the Society of Dramatic Authors and Composers and worked in the mayor's office.

Pédron, Etienne (?-?), born 1849 in the Loire-Inférieure. An artisan clockmaker and employed in the mayor's office, he was a pioneer of socialism in the Marne. He spent more time propagandizing than working, although he had a large family to support. He was involved in agitation among farmworkers and helped draft the agrarian program of the POF. He was a vivid orator and organized socialist theatrical troops, writing part of their repertoire.

Pierrot, Marc (1871-1950), born in the Nièvre, died at Paris. From his days as a medical student he was interested in anarchism and revolutionary syndicalism.

Raymond, Adolphe (?-?), born in the Allier in 1843. He was a bookbinder and militant syndicalist. He was involved in numerous areas in spreading the syndicalist message among the miners. In 1901 he became the secretary of the Dijon bourse.

Robert, Léon (?-?), originally from the Pas-de-Calais. Involved in syndicalism in its earliest stages, representing gas employees and printers in the 1900 CGT congress. He was on the committee of La Voix du Peuple and directed the CGT in 1908 when secretaries Griffuelhes, Yvetot, and Pouget were arrested.

Tabard, Etienne (?-?), lived in Paris. He represented numerous congresses of the CGT. He was a secretary of the male store workers' union and a member of the general strike committee.

Torton, Léon (?-?), a hairdresser, born in 1884. Sentenced to prison in 1906 for putting up placards. The next year he was jailed when police found explosives in his home. He was jailed again for hitting a police commissioner during a demonstration of railroad workers. In 1911 he received another prison sentence for his antimilitarist activities.

Treich, Edouard (1860-1929), born in Limoges, died in Bordeaux. He was a porcelain worker and secretary of a bourse. Supported the general strike as long as it was identified with the social revolution. He was also a militant political socialist and was a candidate in numerous elections. Treich served as a delegate to numerous union congresses.

3. The Question of Direct Action: The Syndicalist As Moralist

Direct action in the economic realm, as noted in the preceding chapter, was defined by syndicalists as any activity carried on outside the parliamentary sphere by the workers themselves. Such action could encompass a variety of deeds, from joining a union, to purchasing union-made goods, to leaving corks out of wine casks. But since the ultimate goal of revolutionary syndicalism was the construction of a just universe, the battle was unmistakably a moral one. That which the proletariat was seeking to overturn was a society based on competition, inequality, and exploitation by a corrupt class, the bourgeoisie. In the factories the capitalist denigrated the worker by forcing him to endure inhuman surroundings. His usurpation of the product of the working man's labor was a villainous theft. In the chamber halls the middle class manipulated a government constituted solely for the preservation of wealth stolen from the producers. The means to revolution, however, must practically reflect ends. Demoralized workers could not wage a moral struggle to bring into existence a just society. Justice could not be achieved realistically through immoral acts. Therefore, as further defined by syndicalism, direct action included a host of rather prosaic activities designed to raise the moral as well as the material well-being of the working class. The dialogue on morality suggested activities covering a broad gamut: from protecting the family unit to preserving the workers' health. But a large degree of syndicalist efforts were directed toward achieving three specific reforms: education, temperance, and birth control.

Perhaps in no other area does syndicalist thinking follow Proudhon's dictates so closely as it does concerning his conclusions regarding the nature of man and society. Indeed, as Annie Kriegel has noted, the labor movement was infused with Proudhonian ideas on morality.(1) For Proudhon, work was equated with man's existence and defined him as human. Work was a basic ethical standard and a social necessity. Labor was the only way for man to transcend his "undisciplined egoism" and voluntarily fulfill his mission to bring into existence a new moral order.(2)

Therefore, the dignity of human labor had to be preserved from capitalist exploitation as it existed in the workshop and in the government. In the literature dealing with direct action in the preceding chapter, variations of Proudhon's ideas on morality provide a strong underlying theme. Producers associating and acting within the unions developed a consciousness of their individual and collective misery. They were moved to struggle for their own emancipation. Direct action intensified the virtues of the working class. Proletarian morality was to provide the basis of the new society. The rhetoric of revolutionary syndicalism is full of these ethical postulates.

Also common in the literature is the portrayal of those institutions aimed at corrupting the worker and his family. For anarchists, in keeping with Proudhon's aversion to government, the political system and its processes constituted the ultimate evil. To Antoine Antignac, syndicalism's task was to liberate the individual, "muzzled by authority" and immobilized by the snares of a false morality that "prevented his heart from beating with altruism."(3) Most heinous of the social crimes was the degradation of the individual and the family. The capitalist had "destroyed the balance between supply and demand [and had] created wage earners and misery," exclaimed a 1902 propaganda pamphlet published by the FBT. Because of the capitalists, "the family life of the workers and the small employer is only an historical memory."(4)

To such theorists, the capitalist-created state fortified the "bouge immonde" [filthy hovel] that was present society.(5) For others, that hovel was more tangible. It was the factory and the life industrialism imposed on workers. An article appearing in an 1888 publication of the FBT outlined "the profoundly immoral" conditions of industry. Comrades worked in buildings defectively constructed and badly ventilated. They breathed noxious gases, were exposed to dangerous materials and machines, and labored long hours.(6) Even if the physical surroundings were improved, workers would still be at a disadvantage, for industrialism had altered the nature of labor itself.

Work was now intensified. The laborer was chained to a machine that moved at an accelerated pace, noted a contributor to La Voix du Peuple. He no longer had time to talk to his neighbor or look at the sky. The machine's demands, compounded by the long hours of work, created great "cerebral exhaustion."(7) Fatigue demoralized: it was the largest cause of premature birth among women and alcoholism among men. A 1906 report to the CGT stressed the fact that overwork "reduces the human being to the vegetative position of beast of burden, hinders the blossoming of [the worker's] feelings, and prohibits him from creating an interior of love and thought."(8) Greater leisure was needed to expand the intellectual, moral, and political life of the worker. Delegates to the 1898 CGT congress at Rennes heard a report on the benefits to be derived from a weekly repose. A shorter work week would give the laborer a chance "to rest his fatigued limbs, quiet his agitated nerves, calm his over-excited intelligence, and revive his diminished strength." Fewer working hours would also allow him the opportunity to be a social creature. With a day of rest the worker could "fulfill his rights of citizenship" and take "pleasure at being a living, thinking, playing man."(9) All workers had "the right to enjoy the social riches" of retirement, noted a 1901 report to the CGT.(10) But long labor meant that at the age of fifty the worker was deformed and broken.(11)

Workers had the moral right to realize a better life: social law must conform to moral law was the theme. But the immoral capitalists cared little for the social interests of the workers, noted Fernand and Maurice Pelloutier. The contemporary worker labored one hour longer each day than had the worker of the Middle Ages. But the growing number of intermediary agents existing between production and consumption had increased the cost of living. Inflation meant that even with longer hours of labor, the worker realized a lower real wage than his medieval counterpart, the authors charged. Besides being forced to endure the degrading conditions in the workshop, the proletariat had to suffer the indignity of living in dirty tenements with stinking latrines on each floor, crowded together on tiny streets polluted by fumes from factories, in neighborhoods that bred crime.(12)

How did the bourgeoisie respond to its immoral creation? When confronted with the unsavory conditions in the factories, the government insisted that capitalists were possessed of sufficient "sentiments of humanity to take the necessary measures to protect the life and health of the worker."(13) Such "humane sentiments" did nothing to improve the inhuman conditions, however. If the bourgeoisie felt any flicker of humanity within it, it generally responded with philanthropy, such as sponsoring "les soupes populaires." The "moral work" of bourgeois-sponsored soup kitchens, warned Henri Couthier in 1899, was really "calculated to maintain the actual social order with its vices and defects" and to debase workers further by making them as dependent on charity as some were on alcohol.(14)

If the middle class was unable to correct the abuses it inflicted upon the workers, it was the proletarians themselves, acting through the unions, who must labor to maintain the moral worth necessary to regenerate the world. Syndicalist literature is filled with assurances that each one was equal to the task. The May Day speech of a Toulouse deputy at the Paris bourse in 1901 outlined the workers' mission. The time had come, he said, when labor could "Regenerate this world of errors and illusions, so that in working, one can live not as a convict, but as a free man."(15) The new hero of world revolution was the working man. In him, Lagardelle declared,

are revived the eternal elements of the culture:
the sense of dignity, the taste for liberty, the
spirit of independence, sacrifice, and struggle.
Beyond that lies all the ruins of bourgeois
decadence, [the worker] remains the depositor of
sublime sentiments supporting the world, and he
remains the great heroic leader of
civilization.(16)

SYNDICALIST HEROISM AGAINST BOURGEOIS DECADENCE

Working-class virtue preserved in unionism was the way
for the innate morality of the proletariat to be augmented
and refined. In a 1912 speech to the CGT, André Chalopin of
the teachers' union outlined the virtues of the syndicalist.

To be a syndicalist, [he declared] is to have a
heart of ardent love for the working class, of
that working class without which society would be
nothing and which society too often
misunderstands; it is to feel a shudder, an
anguish, when one sees unrolling the black
cortege of the strike; it is to feel a sudden
respect for workers who, often by the simple
act of solidarity, come to the aid of some
comrades [demoralized] by long privations and
condemned to misery.(17)

Workers possessed qualities the bourgeoisie lacked.
They were to be the new moral force in the world. But the
social revolution also required the assistance of the
unions. According to Louis Niel, syndicalism provoked

the best of moral sentiments in grouping workers
for the strggle against the common evil. It
proves to them the dangers of isolation,
impotence, and egoism; the impossibility of
individualism of the bourgeois kind; and develops
in them the indispensable sentiment of solidarity
without which all social life would be
Utopian.(18)

Unionism was synonymous with morality, noted one writer,
since man is moral only because he is social.(19)
Unions were to aid in the ethical task of directing the
development of class consciousness. They were also to
provide moral direction. Workers had been accustomed to
receiving moral guidance within the workshops and labor
associations.(20) Guilds had always concerned themselves
with the ethics of their members. The compagnonnages were
deeply involved in the moral health of their brethren.
Those who did bad work were excluded from the organizations.
All members were governed by a strict moral code: they must

pay their debts, they must not drink to get drunk, swear, or
abuse a confidence. Even after they were outlawed in 1791,
the compagnonnages continued to exert a strong force on
labor throughout the Second Empire. Thus, it was natural
that the bourses and the syndicats would carry on many of
the same traditions, since it is likely that many
"companions" became union members during the early stages of
anarchosyndicalism.(21)

The unions would also direct the individual worker in
carrying out the moral work of revolution. Action through
association, confirmed Lagardelle,

> instructs the working class in its formation of
> combat. [The proletariat] is the only class which
> can, by the conditions of its life and its
> affirmations of conscience, renew the world, but
> on the condition that it remains alienated from
> bourgeois society. It takes the producers in
> their own cadres . . . and it organizes their
> revolt against personal authority; . . . it
> gives body finally to the specific ideas of the
> proletariat.(22)

The labor union was "a school of heroism." Strikes
constituted "A certain indice of the moral elevation of the
masses." May Day exercises were demonstrations of the moral
renewal of the workers in the face of government
repression.(23)

The workers' ethical struggle received the sanction
even of Christ and the early church fathers, according to
the keynote speaker at a 1905 conference of the Union des
Syndicats. "The moral beauties of life" had been "harvested
by misery and vice," proclaimed Abbé Vral. But workers had
the "right and power to make a personal and untiring effort
to ameliorate and transform their present social conditions
without waiting for God to replace this effort by a
miracle." Moreover, direct action was equivalent to the
position taken by the early church fathers, who had decried
riches and materialism, noted Vral. St. Ambrose had
professed that "Riches beyond measure, by whatever title and
whatever means they have been acquired, always carry with
them a principle of injustice and inhumanity." St. Bernard
had even cried out in the middle of a sermon that "Interest
is theft." Christ too had declared that he had come so that
all men "would be living each day more abundantly." The way
to fulfill Christ's promise and defend workers' interests,
declared the cleric, was to join the "red syndicats." Take
care, capitalists, warned the Abbé, for the worker is now
literate and organized. He is fighting gambling and
alcoholism, as he was fighting capitalism. Surely Christ's
ethical kingdom was at hand: and it would have a reddish
cast.(24)

If not founded on Christianity, the future would surely
be based on the ethics of the workshop. The social order of
the future would rest "not on authority, but on exchange;

not on domination, but on reciprocity; not on sovereignty, but on the social contract," noted a CGT resolution in 1919.(25) It would be a society of abundance, based on a ten-hour week and two-month paid vacations, prophesized Armand Champion.(26) In the new moral universe even former capitalists would work, for work would be "an indispensable gymnastic to corporate health," carried on for the good of all.(27) In a word, the future would see established an altruistic society, according to anarchist Rieutor. Since it would be a libertarian universe, there would be no need of morality.(28)

MORAL ACTIVITY DESIGNED FOR ALL

In preparation for that future, syndicalists offered a host of suggestions. To many the course to moral uplift and social revolution lay in the development of a clean mind and a healthy body. Personal hygiene, diet, couture provided the key. A contributor to Le Libertaire, Adrien, believed that vegetarianism was a means of helping "the ensemble of the social movement" along the path toward morality and good health.(29) Another agreed with feminists that women should throw away their corsets ("instruments of torture") and adopt the same dress as that worn by female bicyclists. Women must not, however, wear culottes, exclaimed the writer, because this costume made women look like "ridiculous monsters."(30)

In a 1902 article, Louis Niel exhorted workers to make their bodies "an instrument as adept as possible for translating orders of the spirit." Frequent bathing, both in summer and winter, was the key to good health, he continued. Workers should demand free public baths in each commune, and take advantage of those installed in union halls and in the bourses. Furthermore, working-class families should enjoy the outdoors as much as possible. Breathing fresh air and communing with nature would help workers to think more clearly. Above all, men should stay away from alcohol. The money saved through abstinence could be spent on baths and practicing hygiene.

Women must also change their personal habits, particularly in the matter of nursing their children. "I know that some women, hoping to preserve their figures, give their babies to wet nurses," said Niel. Such practices "violate[d] all natural and psychological laws" and produced children afflicted with rickets and scrofula, "incapable later of all action." Comrades must strive to rid themselves of their faults, concluded Niel. "Let's work to develop our muscles and our biceps; and you, women, nurse your kids if you want to have men; we will have great need of them in the next Revolution."(31)

The avoidance of numerous pitfalls was the way to moral uplift. A contributor to La Voix du Peuple condemned spectator sports as a scourge to morality. "Work is totally debased by sports, by the ring, and by boxing. In place of

going to one's union, instead of organizing for liberty or
work, [workers] go to the theatres in the evening, reveling
in and being brutalized by watching champions in the arena."
Sports, like alcohol, the writer warned, served as
"dissolvants" upon the workers' morality.(32) Pettiness
was another disruptive factor to moral elevation. It is
natural to think that one is the best, lectured M. Gastel in
La Voix du Peuple. But vanity is exclusionary and must be
avoided. One brother must never criticize another, and must
always defend all unionists against adversity. In this way,
"sentiments of moral solidarity" could be advanced.(33)

     Union discipline was "the best guardian against
capital," according to anarchist Constant Martin.(34) Some
workers, however, complained that syndicalism was too
vigilant in its campaign against immorality. A 1904
contributor to Le Libertaire, signed "Francis," criticized
the "workers' mentality" demonstrated at the Bourges
congress of the CGT. At that meeting delegates had upheld
the proscription of a group of Versailles hairdressers from
bourse membership, based on the charge that they were
"pornographers" for having held a conference on voluntary
procreation. The crime of lèse-pudeur [an affront to
modesty] with which the coiffeuses were charged had
apparently made them morally unfit to unionize.
Syndicalists could hardly break the chains of capitalism,
scoffed Francis, when they were "still entwined in the
chains of [their own] ignorance." The confrères would do
well to recall the words of Anatole France, who stated that
"ignorance is the worst kind of servitude, and morality is
only another less dangerous form.(35)

     Fernand Pelloutier envisioned a more esteemed function
for the bourses as a way to elevate the workers' mentality.
The bourses performed numerous services for workers, he
noted, from offering courses, to providing placement and
shelter for traveling workers, to compiling data on
fluctuations in employment and living costs. The bourses
not only exercised "a material influence" on the conditions
of labor, concluded Pelloutier, they also had exerted "a
moral influence on the direction of the socialist
movement."(36)

     Syndicalist organization was aimed at producing a new
aristocracy, observed Félicien Challaye: workers cultivated
by lectures, discussions, action, would become an elite of
strong individuals capable of administering and
governing.(37) But to achieve this end, workers must be
educated to the task under the direction of the bourses, the
unions, and the popular universities.

EDUCATION AS A FORM OF DIRECT ACTION

     The idea that education was necessary to the moral
development of the workers was a common theme in syndicalist
literature. Often the goal was perceived as being
revolutionary in nature. Only through self-learning could

workers "assure themselves by themselves of their emancipation," observed Paul Delesalle.(38) To anarchosyndicalists, who believed that social revolution could occur only through individual perfection, intellectual development was a necessary revolutionary action preceding social reorganization.(39) Clearly, education was regarded as another form of direct action: a precondition for carrying out the revolution and a necessity for directing future society. Workers must be sufficiently knowledgeable to administer the new state themselves, was the conclusion of a Parisian group, "or at least control the devoted intellectuals who will consent to assume the responsibility."(40)

Frequently working-class leaders looked to the more practical aspects of education. Workers must be taught the means by which to battle personally against the high cost of living. The fight against inflation, noted a 1912 CGT report, could be accomplished through abstention from drinking, gambling, unnecessary spending, and by carefully adhering to a budget.(41) Additionally, noted E. Barré at this same congress, education was a more acceptable means of distraction for the workers, being infinitely superior to sitting around in cabarets, singing "stupid songs" and listening to "inept recitals that often morally poison" those who hear them.(42)

The fact that workers seemed to prefer moral poison to intellectual uplift was the result of an immoral social and economic system that had saddled the proletariat with inferior educational facilities. As children of the poor, workers had been taken out of school at an early age in order to contribute to their families' support. As workers, they had been forced to terminate their primary school careers at twelve or thirteen in order to begin their apprenticeships.(43) What little education they had received had been "adapted to the needs of conservative capitalists," noted delegates to the 1908 congress of the FBT.(44) This was why workers had long demanded that useful, free, secular, and compulsory instruction be made available to children.(45) Many syndicalists called for union-sponsored vocational training, believing that even the trade schools were tainted by capitalism. Delegate Lauche of the mechanics' union observed at the 1898 Rennes congress that the public school education currently being offered apprentices was designed to make them "afraid of the boss."(46) These gross educational deficiencies, explained Paul Delesalle, inspired in workers a desire to know and receive instruction. No wonder the <u>bourse</u> libraries, although admittedly sparse, were well-attended by men and women, even at the end of ten or twelve hours in the factories. Technical and scientific works, as well as books by Darwin, Marx, Guesde, Zola, France, Lamennais, and Rousseau were "read with avidity," declared Delesalle. Their tattered covers attested to their use!(47)

Working-class leaders suggested a host of other means by which to circumvent bourgeois teaching and gain a moral

education. Workers' study groups were important. So too
was attendance at union-sponsored theatres, night courses,
popular soirées, and recitals. Another important vehicle to
workers' intellectual emancipation was the popular
university.

Although a history of the movement has yet to be
written, the universités populaires were interesting
phenomena in early twentieth-century France.(48) These
universities, established in Paris and the provinces
beginning in 1899, were often founded under the aegis of
local industry, banks, or municipal authorities. Most of
the lecturers were local teachers and professors, although
at L'Union Mouffetard in Paris, members of the printers'
union taught many of the classes. Despite the bourgeois
coloration of these people's universities, they were
vigorously supported by the syndicalist movement. In
numerous instances, universities were initiated by the local
bourses or cooperatives. Often the bourses supported the
institutions financially, either by direct monetary
contributions or by providing the classes with a meeting
place. Syndicalists had practical as well as idealistic
motives for supporting the universities: since so many
members were workers, such support was a means to introduce
the working class to the union hall and, thus, build
membership.

In most cases, the universities were expressly designed
to meet the needs of a working-class population.(49) La
Fraternelle was housed in "the most populous" quarter in
Paris. At Rouen the university met in an exclusively
working-class district. In Marseille meetings were held in
brasseries and cafés, places where workers would normally
congregate, throughout all the quarters on a rotating basis.
Members of Le Contrat Social met in a wine cellar, although
the secretary, a temperance advocate, admitted that the
university was seeking another meeting hall.

The curricula of the popular universities, unlike that
of the bourses and the unions, which were
vocational-oriented, emphasized a broader liberal arts
approach. At Annecy lecture topics ranged from researching
paternity to a discussion of Fourier. The university at
Vincennes took its members on visits to the gas works. At
Marseille auditors went on promenades to local factories and
historical monuments. In Clermont-Ferrand there were
botanical excursions throughout the summer. At Montpellier
lectures covered such subjects as the Commune, strikes, and
unionism. But since workers there allegedly had "a taste
for music and a true ear," musicales were frequently staged.
Throughout the provinces, conversational German seemed to be
a popular course.

So too were subjects appealing to women, since women
students were often the mainstay of these universities. At
Rouen controversial subjects, such as feminism, were
discussed at least once a month. The Bar-le-Duc université
populaire offered lectures on clothes-making and child care.
Daytime classes at the Montmartre UP were dismissed at the

hour coinciding with the children's release from school. In
the industrial town of Le Cateau, one-third of the active
members of that university were women and girls. The
university of Saintes offered coeducational classes. This
radical approach, boasted the secretary of the organization,
would serve "to redirect the Catholic mentality of
separating the sexes" and teach boys "to respect their
female friends." At Montpellier the secretary proudly
proclaimed that antialcohol posters hung everywhere. That
UP planned to open a temperance café in the future;
meanwhile only beer was served on the premises.

Workers apparently responded to the appeals made in
their behalf. The membership of Bar-le-Duc was composed of
400 families of workers and minor employees. The thirty
bourgeois members there paid higher dues. Membership in the
Alais university was more middle class: of the forty or
fifty regular auditors, most were artisans, small-business
men, or employees. The recording secretary noted, however,
that the purely working-class element was beginning to
attend. The regular members at Montpellier were classed as
being socialists. The stated goal of that university was to
contact "the real people" and shun the bourgeoisie. The
leaders of the Besançon UP sought to place workers in
contact with intellectuals, so its activity was very high,
with over twenty-two conferences offered every week.

The work of the universities was not easy. Those with
knowledge to impart were not always eager to do so gratis.
Some teachers, according to Delesalle, had difficulty
dealing with "the rude logic of the workers."(50) Others
had problems making a shift in pedagogical techniques:
different teaching methods had to be employed on tired
workers than one was accustomed to using on children forced
to attend school.(51) Politics also appear to have been a
danger to the longevity of the universities. Many of the
UP's took their cue from the CGT's Charter of Amiens and
forbade all discussion of politics. At Bar-le-Duc, for
instance, no newspapers were allowed in the reading room,
and members were admonished against making political
propaganda. In their UP, noted the recording secretary, the
Declaration of the Rights of Man (with appropriate
modification regarding the passage on private property) was
the only political program supported by the membership.
Admittedly, some members were disappointed in the neutral
stand taken by their UP's, asserting that political
arguments were a normal and sought-after stimulant after a
long day's labor.(52)

Working-class apathy was another problem. Workers
might enjoy the facilities and programs offered by the
Angers university, noted its secretary M. Mercier. But few
stepped forward to assist in running the operation. "Ah!
In the cabarets, before a bottle of white wine," the
comrades were quick to speak of revolution, he mourned. But
when it came to doing anything more than talking, the
workers "had not a speck of energy." "Workers," he pleaded,
"I have only the evening . . . to occupy myself with all

humanitarian things which are of my heart." Surely others might help in this important crusade. The dearth of worker members at Calais failed to discourage that university's director.(53) "If we succeed," he said, "we will know that we have had a hand in the development of the humanity of tomorrow, which we want to be healthy and intelligent."(54)

THE VIRTUES OF "SALUBRIOUS REVOLT"

Safeguarding the workers' mental and physical health was regarded as a practical necessity. Syndicalist leaders knew that workers could accomplish nothing if their brains were besotted and their physical well-being impaired because of alcoholism. Thus, one of the most vigorous moralistic campaigns carried on by anarchosyndicalism was aimed at leading workers to sobriety. Published statistics devoted to pointing out the depths of French impropriety were common in the working-class literature.(55) The Pelloutiers noted that alcoholism was "the characteristic of our age." The consumption of alcohol in the department of the Seine, for example, had increased by 13 1/2 liters per person per year, with workers consuming more liquor than the other two classes. Particularly dangerous, they concluded, was the absinthe cult that had taken hold of the nation.(56) In a 1905 study Auguste Besse lauded syndicalism's efforts to combat alcoholism, since by that year, France was leading the world in the number of alcoholics.(57)

What was the cause of drunkenness? Syndicalists laid the blame at the doorstep of industrial capitalism. The 1898 report at the first full-scale working-class discussion on alcoholism noted that drunkenness increased proportionally to the heightened intensity of capitalism. Mechanization had made the worker "a prolongation, a spoke in the industrial wheel." Industrial organization also discouraged the stimulation of technical intelligence, thereby weakening the worker's professional knowledge, his faculties for judgment, and his moral sense.(58)

The physical and mental brutalization of the workers was an overriding theme in the CGT's campaign for an eight-hour day. Long hours were physically and morally harmful, members declared, and led to alcoholism and tuberculosis.(59) Piecework was another culprit. According to Raymond Joran, workers were forced to overproduce in order to maintain their wage levels. In response to these "unnatural forces," workers turned to drink.(60) Alcoholism, concluded typographer Emile Girault, was due to "fatigue, work, boredom, sadness, and the need for diversion after long days passed in the capitalist prison."(61)

It was natural for a worker to seek a stimulant, particularly if that stimulant was his cheapest form of nourishment. In 1902 D. Sieruin noted in an article on alcoholism that drunkenness was highest in those trades which required a greater expenditure of strength, but where wages were the lowest. Needing to compensate for his loss of energy, the worker turned to cheap liquor, which was less expensive than food.(62) Why was this so? The Pelloutiers blamed inflation caused by competition. The exploited worker, with insufficient wages to eat properly, could gain temporary strength with cheap liquor.(63) "Meat and wine are expensive," noted the 1898 Rennes report, "and you know with what rarity they appear on our tables. Alcohol replaces them for a great many workers."(64) Additionally, declared one writer, drinking was a means to distract the worker from the tawdriness, the overcrowding, and the loneliness of his circumstances.(65) Alcohol, concluded the Pelloutiers, "is not the cause but the effect of misery."(66)

Alcoholism was also the result of bourgeois machinations aimed at subverting the workers' struggle for emancipation. The entry on "Alcoholism" in the Encyclopédie du mouvement syndicaliste, written by Dr. Paul-Maurice Legrain, warned workers that the capitalists used liquor to turn them into "dupes." Drinking debilitated the body, diminished muscular energy, decreased life expectancy, and produced senility.(67) "Alcoholism is the surest agent of the capitalist bourgeois in that it atrophies the conscience and reduces the force of resistance of the proletariat," stated a resolution at the Rennes congress.(68) It also filled asylums full of alcoholics and hospitals full of "rachitic, scrofulous, epileptic" children, "unfortunate fruits of alcoholic fathers." The report continued:

> Here we are, people who profess that fathers of the family have no right to impose on their children this or that confessional religion, this or that philosophical concept. Yet here we are accepting the right to condemn to intellectual death and physical suffering the descendants struck by [the fathers'] vices and miserable passions.(69)

It was not with "an army of degenerates" or "inveterate drunks, whose brains were pickled and whose bodies were atrophied by alcohol," that the new society would be built, warned A. Amonot. Rather, that "noble task" was to be reserved "to workers united, grouped syndically, to men conscious of their rights and obligations, to healthy and robust workers possessing all the moral and physical elements indispensable to combat.(70) "History shows us that the greatest revolutionaries were nearly all water drinkers," professed anarchosyndicalist Fernand-Paul in Le Libertaire. "Let the bourgeoisie wallow in their orgies and insobriety. We will go on with our social renewal," he stated. But that work would require comrades who could become vigorous, robust men, consciously capable of "salubrious revolt."(71)

The struggle to become sober revolutionaries would not

be an easy one, since capitalists used alcohol to retain their power over the proletariat. A 1904 article in Revue Vinicole had warned the middle class of the dangers of passing antialcohol legislation. If the cafés were closed, the writer declared, workers would soon be "breaking from the workshops, red flag in hand, shouting the 'Carmagnole' in the streets." Responding to this observation, La Voix du Peuple agreed with the vintners. "Alcohol, like religion, was a good way to keep workers under the capitalist stranglehold," the editor noted. There was little danger that the government would try too hard to control the scourge, the article concluded, because the leaders of the Third Republic were well aware of the beneficial political effects to be obtained from working-class alcoholism.(72)

For A. Bruckère, writing in La Guerre Sociale, alcoholism was clearly the tool of the government. "Alcohol kills the revolution first; it kills the man next," he charged. The government would never do anything about the problem because it was composed of petty bourgeoisie, masons, "savings-bank clientele," and Russian sympathizers. These parasites were men who "fraud in wine and starve the vintner, who fraud in alcohol and brutalize the worker, who fraud in milk and poison the child." There were one-half million alcohol-dependent people in France, Bruckère concluded. "What electoral strength!"(73) The corrupt Roman empire had provided the people with bread and circuses. The Third Republic gave the masses cheap liquor and patriotic displays. Noting in La Voix du Peuple that the bars were "in full swing" on Bastille Day in 1902, A. Levy wryly applauded the café owners. It was these "bistro poisoners, monopolists of alcohol and patriotism, and entertainers of the people," Levy charged, on whom the government depended to preserve itself in office.(74)

Because of the government's need for a debauched public, the conclusion was that the passage of antialcohol legislation was only a smokescreen. A 1900 piece in La Voix du Peuple noted that the government chose not to check alcoholism because it used insobriety as a means to control workers at home and people in the colonies. Alcohol helped to squelch any ideas of revolt among the colonial people, the editor charged. Only Algeria had effectively protested against French imperialism, and that was because its Muslim population did not drink.(75) Nor could the government "reform manners by taxes," declared A. Bourchet. The government had increased the alcohol tax, so that liquor would become prohibitive to the poor. Instead, it was making "more money on vice."(76)

All the laws in the world were useless: alcoholism would end with the integral emancipation of the worker, concluded those who wrote about the disease. But once again, syndicalists preached that the revolution must be practical and incremental. If alcoholism directly paralleled the intensity of capitalist exploitation, then the first step toward diminishing the disease was to improve the workers' resistance. To that end, unionism must fight for better material conditions, increased moral authority, and greater intellectual power. If alcoholism was worse among lower paid workers, observed Joseph Blanchard, secretary-general of the Nantes bourse, then the remedy was to fight for higher wages.(77)

Fewer working hours would also be an effective reform in the war against alcoholism. Employers always argued that shorter hours would only give workers more time to spend in the cafés. This was a false assumption. The remedy to alcoholism could be found in the suppression of human misery and workers' exploitation, declared Secretary Bourchet of the leatherworkers' union in 1901. The capitalists must assure the workers of

> greater well-being, security in their work, less fear for the future; do not tear away from the workers; homes the woman, [who is] moral educator of the child; see that the worker has a comfortable environment, open to all joys; thanks to a remunerative salary, you will also see fewer miserables seeeking to forget their troubles and to lose their reason in "the green fairy [absinthe]."(78)

If the work of moral liberation must be the work of the proletarians themselves, then militants must become "mortal enemies of strong drink" and "propagandists of temperance," declared the Rennes resolution on alcoholism.(79) Apparently, attempting to induce temperance among the militants was not an easy task. The formulation of the Rennes resolution was negotiated over a rocky road. Many delegates were opposed even to the idea of discussing alcoholism. Metallurgist Braun demanded to know if the meeting was a workers' congress or a health conference. Another delegate enthusiastically suggested that a syndicalist absinth be bottled!(80) At the Bourges congress in 1904, when the question of alcoholism was again on the agenda, a reporter for La Voix du Peuple noted that in his survey of a particular restaurant frequented by congressional delegates, only seven of the nine seated at one table were drinking water.(81)

Such reluctance to stop drinking was apparent in the fact that in 1906 a workers' temperance group, L'Association des Travailleurs Antialcooliques, housed at the Paris bourse, was formed. Three years later, according to E. Quillent of the umbrella and cane makers' union, membership in the group numbered only 300.(82) Since it was apparent that workers were not leaping in great numbers onto the teetotalers' bandwagon, L. Saufrignon urged temperance advocates to direct their efforts to the young. "Don't waste time among the drunks," he charged. Instead, concentrate on impressing the next generation of workers that temperance would assure them of their morality and

their health.   Only   then   would   they   become   good
militants.(83)

THE STRUGGLE TO SAVE THE FAMILY FROM CAPITALIST ASSAULTS

The need to provide for the future of the workers'
children and to safeguard the family was another moral
preoccupation of the working-class leaders. In keeping with
Proudhon's notion that the family was the ethical core of
society, syndicalists praised familial virtues and sought
means by which to keep the family safe from bourgeois
corruption. Liberalism was atomistic and bred social
disorganization. Industrialism produced large cities in
which workers existed with no point of social reference.
Capitalism was a greedy Moloch that devoured women and
children and destroyed the proletarian family. The family
is "the embryo of humanity," and the familial foyer "an
emblem of liberty," declared Etienne Bellot in La Voix du
Peuple. But in actual society, distorted by capitalism,
brothers were competitors, husband and wife enemies.
Marriage contracted out of considerations other than love
were acts of prostitution. The true family, possible only
under socialism, must be the symbol of the human
species.(84)
Anarchists also stressed the fact that the most basic
human sentiments and relationships were deprecated as a
result of the existing social milieu. As currently
constituted, the family was an unnatural grouping based on
economic domination. Love was "the sentiment debased by
marriage." Marriage was "the immoral mercantilism" that had
invented the family. The family was "a mechanism of
intrigue, hypocrisy, immorality," charged anarchist Pierre
Comont.(85) One of the most hideous aspects of the
traditional family was that it perpetuated the idea of
paternal authority. Because of its patriarchal nature, the
family was the best "support of the government and the prop
of the past," according to Sainte-Andréa. As absolute
master of his children's thoughts, the father instilled in
his children feelings of passive obedience, thereby
unwittingly raising his sons for the barracks and for
electoral servitude.(86) Male authority was the fruit of a
usurpation confirmed over time through the weakness of the
victims, asserted André Girard in 1885. This authority
produced timidity, mediocrity of the spirit, and a general
weakening of morality in wives and children. Working-class
fathers must come to understand the "illegitimacy" of what
they had always considered to be their right, Girard
concluded.(87) Libertarians preached that the family must
be reconstituted on the basis of sexual harmony, noted
"Vulgus" in 1905. But such harmony was dependent on a
social milieu free of all moral servitude, this libertarian
proclaimed.(88)
For anarchists and syndicalists the family could

survive only in a well-ordered future society free of economic and psychological exploitation. For the pragmatic syndicalists the preservation of the family depended upon reforms in the present. Parents must be free to continue the task of educating the young. Mothers must join together to regenerate the world, declared A. Bouvard in 1900. Only when mothers had taught their children that all men are brothers and that "the soil of every country [was] lighted by the same sun" would peace prevail.(89) Because of their importance as purveyors of morality, women should be allowed to remain at home. But if this arrangement were not possible,, declared a contributor, Paul Chanvin, to the Information Ouvrière et Sociale in 1918, then legislation must assure women of a decent work environment so they would be equal to the task of devoting their evening hours to educating their children.(90)

Fathers must also be allowed sufficient time to spend with their families. A weekly repose, noted an 1898 CGT resolution, would give the working-class father time to enjoy the pleasures of being surrounded by his loving family. Delegates further agreed that unless the father had more time, he could not adequately oversee the education of his children, "follow their progress, direct their young intellects, and provoke in them the development of impartial feelings and generous passions."(91)

Preservation of the family also required that children be properly educated. Syndicalists constantly stressed the important role of the bourses and unions in aiding parents to educate the young. Children should be prevented from working until they reached the age of sixteen, declared the Bulletin Officiel in 1887. This most crucial period when children's strength and intelligence were developing should be reserved for education.(92) Delegate Chosle suggested at the 1912 Le Havre congress that the bourses should take an active role in educating the young. Nurseries could be established where the young proletarians would learn revolutionary songs "they could understand." The bourses could organize summer camps and physical education programs so the young would develop "good physiques, muscles, and grace." Good technical education must also be provided, stated Chosle, in order to turn the children of the proletariat into useful workers rather than into "arrivistes, wash-outs, pedants, or unhappy déclassés."(93)

Most important to a child's well-being was an adequate apprenticeship. Apprentice training currently was in the hands of the middle class; delegates to the Rennes congress agreed that the unions must take full control in determining the number of apprentices.(94) The future of the child depended upon his or her ability to support himself or herself by means of a useful trade. Not to provide him or her with adequate training would be immoral.(95) Regulation of apprentices further ensured that the young worker would not flood into the labor market and continue to depress the father's wages.

THE SABOTAGE OF LIVING MATTER

Trying to survive "the iron law of wages" also served as the inspiration for a moral crusade undertaken in support of "Neo-Malthusianism." "The fecundity of the working class is the ultimate resource of the ruling oligarchy," asserted the Pelloutiers. The poor continued to increase their numbers, while the rich--fearful of morcellation and in the face of rising inflation--silently practiced birth control.[96] The danger of working-class proliferation was noted in a report given at the Bourges congress of the CGT by one of the leading proponents of Neo-Malthusianism, anarchist Paul Robin. Too many children created a drain on the family's already strained resources. Numerous births contributed to unemployment. A large pool of jobless, whose ranks were swelled by the young, ensured that employers need not listen to union demands. Further, unemployed youths often became apaches or, worse, soldiers. To prevent this fate, Robin urged workers to stop reproducing. The "sabotage" of their own "living matter," he noted, would assure a better standard of living for all and make communism not a utopia, but a fact. "Workers," exhorted Louis Grandidier in 1910, "if you wish to put an end to patronal exploitation, end your lapinisme! Make fewer children."(97)

That birth control was another form of direct action was the message of other syndicalists. Neo-Malthusianism, said Roy of the textile workers, was the "grèves des ventres."(98) "If the workers do not wish to tighten their belts to the larger profit of the boss," declared Gustave Cauvin in La Voix du Peuple, then they must stop producing like animals. Workers' suffering could only be a check on revolution. Pauperization of the masses was not a vehicle of revolution because the miserable only became "the clientele of bistros and the army of the jaune." No wonder the ruling class struggles so violently against Neo-Malthusianism, Cauvin concluded.(99)

While the CGT did not officially sanction Neo-Malthusianism, as Francis Ronsin notes in her study of birth control and depopulation in France, it did give its unofficial support.(100) The Confederation often passed out birth control devices, provided information, and issued numerous tracts on the subject.(101) One such pamphlet circulated by the CGT was entitled Syndicalisme et néo-malthusianisme. A high birth rate among workers served as a check on unionism, declared the authors of the brochure. Sometimes pauperization of the worker did increase working-class militancy. But more often, effective class action was diluted because of the laborer's concern for his family. Even while suffering under the capitalist lash, a worker feared joining the union because it might jeopardize his job and his family's survival. With too many mouths to feed, the worker could not spare even a few centimes to support the _syndicat_. His commitment to a strike was diminished by the reality that his children were going to go hungry. Thus, the authors conceded, the limiting of families was a revolutionary act. Fewer children would allow workers to think only of the class struggle. The use of birth control, the pamphlet concluded, would bring into being "a generation to tumble the edifice of hideous capitalism."(102)

For syndicalists, birth control was a means by which to assure the advent of a new socialist future. It was also regarded as a way to improve conditions in the present by redressing the social balance that had been skewed by capitalist greed. The earth was capable of supporting twenty times more people, observed D. Sieruin in _La Voix du Peuple_ in 1902. If society were organized properly an equilibrium between production and consumption would exist. There would be no need for workers then to restrain their families, since each man would consume the equivalent of his own production. But in contemporary society, profit was drained away by the capitalist, so the worker was left with only one-third of his production. The result was that workers had to limit further their consumption. By being so prolific, Sieruin conceded, French workers were "the authors of their own misery." The only way to arrest the plummeting spiral was by practicing self-restraint: workers must no longer abandon themselves "like beasts to their procreative faculties."(103)

Birth control and abortion were regarded by libertarians as a necessary adjunct to free union. Neo-Malthusianism was also the means by which women could control their bodies and thereby express their individualism. Numerous articles appeared in the anarchist press praising birth control as a revolutionary act and suggesting home remedies to prevent pregnancy.(104) Women were "martyrs of a gutless society," proclaimed Suzanne Carruette in 1900, because of their procreative abilities. Women must demand the right to abstain from having children. Would the right to control their own bodies mean that women would never choose to have children, as so many critics charged? Not at all, concluded Carruette. For in an equitable society, maternity would be willingly accepted by women as "a promise of future joy."(105) A contributor to _La Guerre Sociale_ supported birth control as an alternative to abortion. The writer cited the fact that six abortionists had been recently arrested in the Nord. One of them had admitted to performing between two and three abortions weekly for the past fifteen years.(106) "God blesses numerous families, but he doesn't feed them," quipped Gustave Hervé in 1911.(107)

For Neo-Malthusians, limiting families through sexual restraint or with birth control devices was a moral act directed against bourgeois corruption. As might be expected, the campaign for birth control, although vigorous, did not convert everyone. In 1908 house painter Paul Guiraud complained that although the "disciples of Malthus"

were to be found in small numbers among the proletariat, the
upper classes practiced birth control to a great
extent.(108) The adoption of the resolution supporting
Neo-Malthusian propaganda at the 1909 meeting of the
leatherworkers' union was not unanimous. Shoemaker Jean
Rougerie insisted that the matter was one of individual
conscience, and that resolutions supporting birth control
would alienate some workers from the union.(109)

Nor were all anarchosyndicalists in accord. Paul Robin
and Sébastien Faure praised birth contol as the means to
effect "a peaceful revolution." Yet another leading
anarchist, Elisée Réclus, charged that the practice would
produce an elite who would ultimately reject libertarian
ideals.(110) In 1906 the French population registered a
decline.(111) Le Libertaire published a warning that year
of the dangers of birth control practices. Specifically the
writer, signed "Populo," cited the inherent danger in
abortion as the means to ward off the specter of starvation.
The effects of abortion on women was a serious matter.
Furthermore, declared Populo, even if abortion methods were
perfected and readily available, the workers' lot would not
improve. If the capitalists could not exploit the cheap
labor of French youths, they would simply import Chinese.
Then the older generation of French workers, with no
children to turn to in their declining years, would suffer
even further deprivation.(112)

The fears of the effects of depopulation following in
the wake of large-scale adoption of birth control practices
were expressed by Gustave Hervé in a series of articles
begun, ironically, in the weeks immediately preceding the
July crisis in 1914. Hervé, who had been "condemned to
years in a cage" for his radical views, confessed that he
still supported the principle of free love. But he urged
moderation in the use of birth control: the working class
should not stop reproducing, but should bear only as many
children as had one's parents. Total abstinence would
denude France of her population, so that by the year 2112,
Hervé predicted, the French would be extinct. Depopulation
of France would not help labor's cause because foreign
workers would be imported, becoming passive tools of
capitalism. Further, noted the former "sans-patrie," who
had made a pest of himself in the meetings of the Second
International by his antipatriotic harangues, racial suicide
would be a blow to world progress. France was "la patrie
révolutionnaire" and the only "foyer of intellectual liberty
and of humanity in the world at the present time." The
proletariat claimed it was the class that carried "within
itself the future." But the future, Hervé reminded his
readers, lay with the young: it is "the children who will
continue you, who prolong you, who battle at your side for
your ideal of social justice and human fraternity. You're
for the future? Show me your children!"(113)

MORAL AND ECONOMIC ACTIONS . . . THE ONLY PATH TO REVOLUTION

The goal of revolutionary syndicalism was Proudhonian in its basic moral vision: the salvation of civilization by the total elimination of a debauched and useless class. The proletariat would achieve this revolution because it represented the superior virtues inherent in being producers and creators. If the goals appeared to be idealistic in their grander revolutionary vision, the means--always inseparable from the end to syndicalists--were infinitely practical. Direct action in the moral and economic realms offered an open-ended spectrum of activity by which each individual could become both initiator of the revolution and an initiate in the new society syndicalism was calling into being.

Most important, as the new moral force in the world, the worker must be ethically pure. That was an enormous responsibility, particularly for the unskilled worker only recently arrived from the countryside. He was hardly the stuff of which world revolutionaries are made! Therefore the means provided by syndicalism to achieve the moral revolution were as simple as they were practical. Workers must associate in unions in order to struggle for reforms, however small. Every reform helped the worker to regain his dignity and build class consciousness, all the while chipping away at the bulwark of bourgeois evil: egoism, competition, and materialism. The worker could also stop eating meat or watching sporting events. He could bathe more often and spend Sundays with his family in the park. He could stay out of the bistros, or at least drink only wine, thereby enhancing the material well-being of his peasant comrades engaged in viniculture. Every mouthful less that he drank constituted a minor revolutionary act. He could compensate for his inadequate education by reading in bourse libraries, upgrading his technical skills in union-sponsored classes, or by listening to evening lectures on socialism and classical Greece at the people's universities. He could practice birth control, so that the fewer children he brought into the world would be assured of a better existence. As potential revolutionaries, they too must be strong and healthy.

One might wonder if the new moral universe founded on proletarian virtue, as conceived by the syndicalists, was not merely a recasting of bourgeois society: a French translation of Samuel Smiles. Clearly, insofar as the syndicalists themselves were concerned, direct action was designed to overthrow bourgeois society, not move workers into it. Syndicalism's aim was to carry out a revolution within the narrow limits prescribed by the government, without doing damage to the individual's ethical prescripts, and among a profoundly heterogeneous society: one that was localistic, particularistic, and individualistic. It was also a traditional society in a state of transition. But rapid change had not bred anomie. Rather, the culture was composed of a rich, varied, and abundant organizational life. As James Madison had so aptly pointed out, the presence of a multiplicity of factions hindered the development of mass group loyalties. The Frenchman was fiercely devoted to his family, his commune, his quarter--and beyond that, to the overarching symbol bequeathed him by the bourgeois culture: the patrie of the Revolution.

In the face of these difficulties, what syndicalists were seeking to achieve was a permanent revolution, having as its goal the implementation of a totally just and democratic society. To accomplish that, syndicalism would have to do more than build class consciousness; it would have to create a countering paradigm--virtually another culture--autonomous and distinct from existing society, embodying within it new means of thought and action. This new culture would have to express the needs of its constituency, all the while changing completely the way individuals thought about themselves and one another. In other words, syndicalism was directed toward a thoroughgoing revamping of the social and moral relations governing society and the individual. But if this mass movement was to be democratic and truly revolutionary, it could not be dictated or imposed from above.

Sorel's observation that syndicalism was bent on creating a substitute form of allegiance was correct; only he misunderstood that syndicalists were much too practical to waste time with intellectual abstractions. The "cult of violence" would not have rallied the masses: the prospect of such immorality would have horrified most and scared the rest to death. There was nothing about direct action that was intended to be metaphorical or mythical. Syndicalist leaders understood human nature too well, knowing that the average Frenchman would prefer to doze in the safety of mythical abstractions while someone else did the world's labor. If revolution was to be the work of the producing class, the workers' actions had to be concrete and real, not cultic or symbolic.

Direct action in the economic and the moral realm was the means by which each worker might become both a participant and a director of social change. It provided the means by which the basic unit in society, the individual, could willingly carry out a collective revolutionary activity to benefit all. A solitary act against capitalist profits or toward increasing the worker's moral health, no matter how incidental or seemingly inconsequential, created a bond of allegiance among the workers that transcended family, religion, locality, patriotism, and social status. So direct action constituted a form of apprenticeship by which the individual worker learned the métier of revolution.

Given the reality of French society, that revolution would have to be episodic rather than linear, with each unit moving along at a different pace. Sometimes there would be perceptible gains; but most often the results of the separate acts would be neither measurable nor immediate. But the goal would be achieved because the means to the end were achievable. What revolutionary syndicalism was attempting to do was to carry out by moral action a thoroughgoing democratic revolution: perhaps the first and only such attempt the world has ever seen.

NOTES

1. Annie Kriegel, "Le syndicalisme révolutionnaire et Proudhon, Le pain et les roses (Paris, 1968). Kriegel does concede some differences between Proudhon and the majority of the syndicalists, however. Proudhon was opposed to the idea of birth control and abortion, while the bourses, she notes, were "principle foyers of neo-Malthusian propaganda." (pp. 34-35).

2. James Joll, The Anarchists (New York, 1964). See particularly pp. 66-69 on Proudhon's attitudes about the moral value of work and the nature of man.

3. Le Libertaire, 22 Mar. 1903.

4. Fédération des bourses du travail de France et des colonies, Brochure de propagande syndicale (Paris, 1902), p. 18.

5. Louis Grandidier in Le Libertaire, 19 Aug. 1900.

6. "Partie non-officielle: Hygiène et sécurité du travail," Bulletin Officiel de la Bourse du Travail 83 (26 Aug. 1888): 1-2.

7. La Voix du Peuple, 18 Dec. 1904. Apparently a high degree of personal freedom was customary in French factories and workshops. Michael Hanagan quotes the observation of an English metalworker on the characteristics he found among his French counterparts in 1904.

> In the workshop [in France] there is much more freedom than, I believe, exists in English factories. Discipline is by no means of a cast iron character. If Maurice or Jules have a sudden idea which they wish to communicate to Henri at the other end of the shop, they go at once, without looking around to see where the foreman is, or pretending to go on business. A good quarter of an hour is lost each morning in shaking hands and passing salutations with comrades in all parts of the factory. To omit the handshake or the "salut comarades" [sic] is a serious breach of manners. In most workshops in France smoking is allowed . . . provided there is no deliberate

wasting of time or shirking of work, the workman
has the utmost freedom in the workshop, and any
attempt to limit this freedom is resented as
deeply as an attack on the economic position of
wages and hours.

The Logic of Solidarity: Artisans and Industrial Workers in
Three French Towns 1871-1914 (Urbana, Ill., 1980), pp.
11-12.

8. Confédération Générale du Travail, Rapports des
comités et des commissions pour l'exercise 1904-06 (Paris,
1906), pp. 12-13.

9. Report of the XI(e) congrès [Rennes, 1898] in
Confédération Générale du Travail, La confédération générale
du travail et le mouvement syndical (Paris, 1925), p. 69.
[Hereafter cited as La CGT et le mouvement syndical.]

10. Report at the XII(e) congress [Lyon, 1901],
quoted in ibid., p. 80.

11. Armand Champion, Propos syndicalistes et
révolutionnaires (Paris, 1911), p. 11.

12. Fernand and Maurice Pelloutier, La vie ouvrière
en France (Paris, 1900), pp. 19, 228-230.

13. Bulletin Officiel, p. 2.

14. Le Libertaire, 1 Jan. 1899.

15. Raymond Leygue quoted at a public conference
celebrating May Day 1901. Printed in poster form by G.
Berthoumier.

16. Lagardelle quoted in Jean Taboreau, Le sophisme
antipatriotique (Paris, 1912), p. 34.

17. XVIII(e) congrès national corporatif (XII(e)
de la CGT) . . . Compte rendu des travaux (Le Havre, 1912),
p. 39.

18. Louis Niel quoted in Taboreau, Le sophisme, p.
13.

19. B. Jacob, Devoirs (conférences de morale
individuelle et de morale sociale) (Paris, 1910), pp. 2, 99.
The moral quality of joining the union was a favorite theme.
Charles Janey professed that syndicalism had evolved from
"the cries for moral order." Evolution de l'idée syndicale
(Toulouse, 1904), p. 8.

20. Georges F. Renard and G. Weulersse. Margaret
Richards, trans. Life and Work in Modern Europe

Fifteenth to Eighteenth Centuries (New York, 1968), p. 193.

21. Pelloutier frequented the compagnonnages and Griffuelhes was a member of the Ardent Corporation of Shoemakers and Bootmakers. Reported by Emile Coornaert, Les compagnonnages en France du moyen âge à nos jours (Paris, 1966), p. 22.

22. Hubert Lagardelle et al., Syndicalisme et socialisme (Paris, 1908), p. 4.

23. Lagardelle quoted in Tabareau, Le sophisme; Jouhaux quoted in V. Griffuelhes and L. Jouhaux, eds., Encyclopédie du mouvement syndicaliste (Paris, 1912), p. 8; in Maurice Dommanget, Histoire du Premier Mai (Paris, 1953), p. 60.

24. Abbé André Vral, Les pages de l'ouvrier (Paris, 1905), pp. 6, 7, 10, 11, 15, 17, 21.

25. Resolution at the XIV(e) congress [Lyon, 1919). Quoted in Maxime Leroy, Les techniques nouvelles du syndicalisme (Paris, 1921), p. 110.

26. Champion, Propos syndicalistes et révolutionnaires, pp. 9-11.

27. La Voix du Peuple, 24 June 1906.

28. Le Libertaire, 8 Sept. 1901.

29. Adrien in ibid., 24 Aug. 1901.

30. R. Vertpré in ibid., 30 Sept. 1900.

31. La Voix du Peuple, 12 Jan. 1902.

32. Ibid., 25 Dec. 1913.

33. Ibid., 12 Jan. 1902.

34. Le Libertaire, 4 Dec. 1896.

35. Ibid., 24 Sept. 1904.

36. Fernand Pelloutier, L'histoire des bourses du travail (Paris, 1900), p. 247 for quote.

37. Félicien Challaye, Syndicalisme révolutionnaire et syndicalisme réformiste (Paris, 1909), p. 33.

38. Paul Delesalle, Les bourses du travail et la C.G.T. (Paris, n.d.), p. 27.

39. Sébastien Faure in Le Libertaire, 4 Oct. 1903.

40. La Voix du Peuple, 5 May 1901.

41. Report on "La vie chère," at the XVIII(e) congress [Le Havre, 1912], in La CGT et le mouvement syndical, p. 124.

42. La Voix du Peuple, 23 Dec. 1900.

43. Delesalle, Les bourses du travail, p. 27.

44. XVI(e) congress [Marseille, 1908], quoted in La CGT et le mouvement syndical, p. 107.

45. Congrès ouvrier régional de Bordeaux . . . (Bordeaux, 1880), p. 15.

46. X(e) congrès national corporatif (IV(e) de la confédération générale du travail) . . . Compte rendu des travaux du congrès (Rennes, 1898), p. 188.

47. Delesalle, Les bourses du travail, pp. 28–29.

48. See the following works: Université populaire: Histoire de douze ans (1898–1910), preface by Gabriel Eailles (Paris, 1910); Charles Guieysse, Les universités populaires et le mouvement ouvrier (Paris, n. d.); and Les universités populaires 1900–1901, 2 vols. (Paris, n. d.). Volume one of this latter work deals with reports from the UP's in Paris and the suburbs, catalogued first by arrondissement, then listed alphabetically for suburban organizations. Volume two lists in alphabetical order reports from the provincial UP's. The study of the UP's noted in this chapter comes from the latter two-volume work unless otherwise noted.

49. Guieysse notes that the Parisian universities tended to involve themselves in more mundane things, such as campaigning against the use of harmful substances in the factories and demonstrating support for Russian radical students living in Paris. Ibid., pp. 30, 70. E. Barré, however, indicated that the program at the Paris university was a little lighter. At the 12 February 1901 soirée, he announced, one guest would recite poetry and another would discuss the crimes of Napoleon. La Voix du Peuple, 23 Dec. 1900. Of course, others disagreed on the virtues to be derived from attending the UP's. Anarchist Charles Malato wondered if anyone seriously believed that the revolution would be undertaken because the proletariat had read the classics. Le Libertaire, 24 Sept. 1904.

50. Delesalle, Les bourses du travail, p. 31.

51. Guieysse, Les universités populaires, p. 6.

52.   Ibid., pp. 4, 16.

53.   Quotes appear in ibid., pp. 8-10.

54.   Ledoux in ibid., p. 32.

55.   See the article by P. E. Prestwich on the linkage between middle-class reformers and working-class groups involved in the temperance campaign. "French Workers and the Temperance Movement," International Review of Social History 25 (1980):   35-52.

56.   Fernand and Maurice Pelloutier, La vie ouvrière, pp. 312-316 on alcholism. See also P. E. Prestwich, "Temperance in France: The Curious Case of Absinthe." Historical Reflections 6 (Winter 1979): 301-319 for a discussion of the battle to outlaw absinth consumption waged by temperance advocates.

57.   Auguste Besse, Education sociale. Les lois sociales et le syndicalisme (Paris et Cahors, 1908), p. 20.

58.   X(e) congrès [Rennes, 1898], pp. 353-360 for the report on alcoholism. The program articulated at this congress remained an integral part of the CGT's official policy on alcoholism. Workers must educate themselves and one another against the evils of drink. They must organize cooperatives in order to keep "the capitalists' patent poison" off the market. But these were only anodynes. Until the social revolution was achieved, workers should demand that the production, regulation, and sale of alcohol be placed under the administration of a commission composed of doctors, chemists, hygienists, and workers.

59.   Rapports des comités, pp. 12-13. Long hours and alcoholism contributed to higher incidences of tuberculosis, charged Gustave Cauvin.

60.   Raymond Joran, L'organisation syndicale dans l'industrie du bâtiment (Paris, 1914), p. 210.

61.   La Voix du Peuple, 14 Feb. 1902.

62.   Ibid., 14 Sept. 1902.

63.   Fernand and Maurice Pelloutier, La vie ouvrière, p. 321.

64.   X(e) congrès [Rennes, 1898], p. 355. It might be noted that the French and their government made a distinction between "natural" alcohol, such as beer, cider, and wine (the latter termed a "natural and hygienic" drink), and "industrial" alcohol, which was made from grains, beets, or molasses. Prestwich, "French Workers and the Temperance Movement," p. 35.

65. D. Sieruin in La Voix du Peuple, 14 Sept. 1902.

66. Fernand and Maurice Pelloutier, La vie ouvrière, p. 314.

67. Dr. [Paul-Maurice] Legrain, "Alcoolisme," Encyclopédie du mouvement syndicaliste, pp. 60-64.

68. Reported in J. B. Sévérat, Le mouvement syndical, vol. 7 of Encyclopédie socialiste, syndicale, et coopérative de l'internationale ouvrière 1912-1913 (Paris, 1912-1913), p. 246.

69. X(e) congrès [Rennes, 1898], pp. 356-357.

70. La Voix du Peuple, 17 Oct. 1909.

71. Le Libertaire, 1 Nov. 1902.

72. La Voix du Peuple, 4 Dec. 1904.

73. La Guerre Sociale, 1 July 1908.

74. La Voix du Peuple, 20 July 1902.

75. Ibid., 16 Dec. 1900. Jean Foré declared that cafés flourished in spite of the laws regulating drunkenness. Why? Because the legislators themselves were the bistros' most frequent users. Le Libertaire, 7 May 1904.

76. La Voix du Peuple, 6 Jan. 1901.

77. X(e) congrès [Rennes, 1898], p. 149.

78. La Voix du Peuple, 6 Jan 1901.

79. X(e) congrès [Rennes, 1898], p. 356.

80. Ibid., pp. 147-148.

81. La Voix du Peuple, 9 Oct. 1904.

82. Griffuelhes and Jouhaux, eds., Encyclopédie du mouvement syndicaliste, p. 64.

83. La Voix du Peuple, 23 Oct. 1910.

84. Ibid., 6 Dec. 1901.

85. Le Libertaire, 28 Mar. 1896.

86. Ibid., 21 Oct. 1901.

87.   Ibid., 21 Dec. 1885.

88.   Ibid., 27 Aug. 1905.

89.   La Voix du Peuple, 23 Dec. 1900; 6 Jan. 1901.

90.   P. Chanvin in Information Ouvrière et Sociale, 7 Mar. 1918.

91.   Resolution at the X(e) congress [Rennes, 1898], quoted in La CGT et le mouvement syndical, p. 69.

92.   Bulletin Officiel, pp. 2-3.

93.   XVIII(e) congrès [Le Havre, 1912], pp. 66-67 for discussion; quote on pp. 20-21.

94.   Noted in a discussion of the X(e) congrès [Rennes, 1898], pp. 66-67.

95.   Even during the war, when the work force was being decimated, the unions called for longer mandatory schooling and apprenticeships. Dumoulin felt this was necessary because the war had demoralized the working class. Education must counter "the bad habits, errors, corruptions" now prevalent among the proletariat, he insisted. Information Ouvrière et Sociale, 24 (Mar. 1918). Mme. Brunschwieg agreed that better technical, intellectual, and moral training was necessary because the younger generation would have to fend for itself in a world in which so many fathers had been sacrificed. Ibid., 7 Apr. 1918.

96.   Fernand and Maurice Pelloutier, La vie ouvrière, p. 19. Duveau notes that during the Second Empire the better paid workers wanted fewer children, and that workers in large industries were more prolific than those in the ateliers. He attributes this fact either to boredom, or an optimistic faith in capitalism. Georges Duveau, La vie ouvrière en France sous le Second Empire (Paris, 1946), p. 433.

97.   Paul Robin quoted by Louis Grandidier in La Voix du Peuple, 4 Dec. 1910. Workers in their congresses also discussed the need for birth control as an aid to revolution.

98.   Roy at the Sixième congrès de la fédération nationale des cuirs et peaux (Paris, 1909), p. 84.

99.   La Voix du Peuple, 13 Oct. 1912.

100.   Birth control was a departure from both Marx and Proudhon, Ronsin notes. Lenin also opposed it, saying that Neo-Malthusianism would retard the class best prepared to make the revolution. A large proportion of members of the

Neo-Malthusian Group of Auxerre in 1914 were listed as workers. Of these, a high majority were syndicalists and antimilitarists. Usually those unions with a high Guesdist orientation were opposed to birth control, probably because of their Marxian orthodoxy. See Francis Ronsin, La grève des ventres: Propaganda néo-malthusienne et baisse de la natalité en France, 19(me)-20(me) siècles (Paris, 1980), pp. 171-173; membership list on pp. 112-115. Ronsin also notes that many neo-Malthusians extolled the virtues of the x-ray for painless sterilization. P. 53.

101. Kriegel, Le pain et les roses, p. 34.

102. "La Commission," Syndicalisme et néo-malthusianisme (Lille, 1911), pp. 2, 4 for quotes.

103. La Voix du Peuple, 21 Sept. 1902.

104. See for example Le Libertaire, 2 Dec. 1900.

105. Ibid., 22 Apr. 1900.

106. La Guerre Sociale, 20 May 1908.

107. Ibid., 12 Apr. 1911.

108. La Voix du Peuple, 13 Sept. 1908.

109. Jean Rougerie in Compte rendu du septième congrès national de la féedération nationale des cuirs et peaux (Paris, 1911), p. 12.

110. Marie Fleming, The Anarchist Way to Socialism: Elisée Réclus and Nineteenth-Century European Anarchism (London, 1979), p. 231.

111. Paul Louis, Histoire de la classe ouvrière en France de la révolution à nos jours (Paris, 1927), p. 179. See also Joseph J. Spengler, France Faces Depopulation (Durham, 1938).

112. Le Libertaire, 30 Dec. 1905.

113. Hervé in La Guerre Sociale, 17, 24 June 1914; 1, 15, 22, 28 July 1914.

PERSONS CITED

Adrien [Georges Darien] (1862-1921), a romantic revolutionary and extreme antimilitarist who believed that "only war alone could kill militarism completely."

Bellot, Etienne (?-?), born in Marseille in 1865. A carpenter by trade, but a journalist by avocation. His mother was the daughter of a wealthy man, but Bellot preferred the life of a radical. He was a militant socialist.

Blanchard, Joseph (1860-1927), born at Nantes. He taught carpentry at the municipal school. Attended numerous congresses of the FBT, the CGT, and socialist parties. Supported the general strike but also helped mediate employee disputes to a settlement. A candidate in numerous elections.

Bouvard, A (?-?), an artificial-flower maker, Mademoiselle Bouvard attended the 1900 CGT congress and wrote articles for socialist and syndicalist papers.

Bruckère, A (?-?), militant of the Seine, collaborator on La Guerre Sociale from 1907 to the war.

Chalopin, André (?-?), born in the Aube. Secretary of a teachers' union from 1919 to the war. He was a voice of moderation on antimilitarism, claiming that the Sou du soldat was really a vehicle for solidarity rather than antipatriotism. He was mobilized in 1914 and killed in the first weeks of the war.

Champion, Armand (?-?), shoemaker, socialist revolutionary, bourse secretary of Blois (Loir-et-Cher).

Chanvin, Paul (1865-1938), born in Paris; died in Draveil. Chanvin's role in syndicalism was slight until 1914. He was secretary of the building workers federation from 1915 to 1921. He supported the Union sacrée. After losing his position in the federation as a result of the 1921 schism, Chanvin left Paris. His declining years were unhappy ones.

Girard, André (1860-1942), born and died in Bordeaux. He worked in the office of the prefect until it was discovered he was an anarchist. After being fired he worked as a proofreader, joining that union in 1902. He contributed to numerous papers. He advocated Neo-Malthusianism. When the war came, he had reservations about supporting the Union sacrée. After the war he joined the CGTU.

Girault, Emile (1871-1933), born at Paris of a radical family. He was a splendid orator, speaking at many conferences. He was a typographer and an anarchist. His oratory and his politics earned him numerous prison sentences. He was on the Carnet B and closely watched by the police. He supported the Russian Revolution, and after the war became an anarchocommunist in opposition to anarchist individualism.

Grandidier, Louis (1873-1931), a libertarian who exhorted his colleagues to leave their anarchist ivory towers and join the unions. He was sentenced to prison for his

antimilitarist   activities.   He   was a bourse secretary and
worked on numerous papers until 1921.

Guiraud, Paul (?-?), painter from Bordeaux.   Member   of   the
FBT and of the SFIO.

Lauche (1872-1920), born in the Landes. He was   a   mechanic
who, at   the   age   of   thirteen,   had to support his family
following his father's death. At the age   of   eighteen   he
moved   to   Paris.   Lauche joined   the   POSR   and   became a
syndicalist and secretary of his union.   He was in the
reformist camp in 1906. He was active in a cooperative and
in the SFIO after its organization. Lauche was elected   to
the Chamber and supported the Government of National Defense
during the war.

Malato   de   Cornet,   Charles   (1857-1938),   born   in   the
Meurthe-et-Moselle;   died   at   Paris.   He   accompanied   his
Communard father into exile in New Caledonia.   Charles was a
militant   anarchist,   who   worked   as   a   proofreader   and
publicist.   He collaborated on numerous newspapers and wrote
works on anarchism. He supported the defense of France   in
1914.

Martin, Constant (1839-1906), born in the Basses-Alpes, died
in   Paris.   Blanquist,   then   anarchist   involved   in   the
Commune.   After   his   amnesty   from   deportation,   he
collaborated with Pouget on anarchist journals.   He was
sentenced to twenty years of forced labor because of his
terrorist activities. He fled to London, and in 1896 he was
acquitted.

Quillent, E. (?-?), at several congresses of the CGT and
FBT.

Rougerie, Jean (1869-1931), born in the Haute-Vienne. He
was a vigorous propagandist for syndicalism. He served in
several directing posts in the bourse, cooperatives, and the
shoemakers' union.   He joined the SFIO, and was regarded as
an orator who was listened to when he spoke. He was elected
a municipal councilor for Limoges before and after the war.
He opposed the Union sacrée and Jouhaux in 1915.

4. The Woman Question: The Legacy

In 1866, a full twenty years before the first stirrings of revolutionary syndicalism, and before the industrial revolution had changed the social structure in France, women already comprised 30 percent of the work force.(1) How well did syndicalism respond to women's presence in the labor force? If the syndicalist movement was directed, as it professed itself to be, toward creating a new culture of revolution, the needs of the female proletariat could not be ignored.

Yet, some recent studies of women and the French left have concluded that the tensions between the sexes were not attenuated to any perceptible degree by unionism, and that revolutionary syndicalism followed the model of socialism. Both allegedly did little more than pay lip service to the need to include women in their progress toward socialist revolution. Marilyn Boxer's work notes that political socialists subordinated the question of women's rights to the need to garner electoral support. Hence, their capitulation to political expediency resulted in a step backward for women.(2) Madeleine Guilbert concludes from her study of women and syndicalism before 1914 that women's membership in the unions remained weak relative to their presence in the labor force, and their participation in trade union congresses and strikes was feeble. The primary failure, Guilbert charges, was due to the political orientation of the syndicalist movement. More "preoccupied with agitation than with immediate reforms," syndicalists did not concede first priority to the cause of "the most disinherited [and] least conscious," the woman workers.(3) Michelle Perrot concurs that the workers' movement only slowly became conscious of women because the different currents of syndicalism were too concerned with other things to view women's emancipation favorably.(4)

This work leads to an opposite conclusion. In answer to both Guilbert and Perrot, this study argues that because revolution was defined by syndicalists as incremental, then immediate reform for all workers was a necessary step toward revolution. More important, it was the preoccupation with internal and external forces threatening unionism that forced anarchosyndicalists to shed the dead weight of the past and deal with the reality of women's presence in the work force. And, although party socialists did abandon women's rights issues in order to build their electoral constituencies, as Boxer points out, this study contends that the opposite occurred within syndicalism. As a result of its commitment to serve as a valid agent of working-class interest, and out of the need to build unionism, French syndicalism moved beyond the paternalistic and antifeminist attitudes inherited from the past to address practically the needs of laboring women.

To evaluate fully the syndicalist response to women, it is necessary to explore the milieu in which the workers' attitudes toward women in the work force were formed. To that degree, one must review the historical presence of women in France, both as an economic factor and as a social being. It is also important to examine the philosophical framework that defined attitudes toward women in France, since discussions in the early workers' congresses often tended to reflect the ideological inheritance of the Utopian Socialists, Marx, and Proudhon. Indeed, some recent analysts, such as Jean Maitron, have concluded that the latter's ideas on the woman question provided syndicalism with its antifeminist stance.(5) This work suggests, however, that philosophy came to play a minor part in syndicalist attitudes regarding women. Far more important to the shaping of workers' ideas were the practical issues formulated in response to a host of variables, including the reaction to such outside threats as the degree to which women constituted a dangerously competitive presence in a particular trade, and the reaction from socialists, feminists, and independent syndicalists. Also formative in syndicalism's response were the internal pressures that produced spasmodic waves of schism during the early years of unionism and remained a threatening force throughout the first quarter of the twentieth century.

THE ROOTS OF ECONOMIC AND SOCIAL EXPLOITATION

The advent of large-scale industry in France did not create a new need for women in the work force. Women were employed in a variety of trades throughout the Middle Ages. Some professions were exclusively set aside for women; others were mixed corporations in which men and women worked together. Many women were employed in trades unregulated by the guilds.(6) With the beginning of cottage industry, much of the work carried on by urban artisans came to be the exclusive domain of the peasantry. The extent of peasant involvement in the clothmaking industry, for instance, was noted in the memoirs of an eighteenth-century intendant of Languedoc, who marveled at the fact that there was not a single peasant worker "who does not have in his home a trade . . . which occupies him . . . when the work of the field is absent; his wife and children card, thread, and prepare the wool chiefly during the winter."(7) The penetration of industrial labor into the countryside in the seventeenth and eighteenth centuries was accompanied by an increase in the female labor force.(8) Women became an integral part of family industry. The extent to which women participated in home manufacturing partially explains the ease with which large industry in the nineteenth century was able to recruit females.(9)

The gross exploitation of women was not something unique to nineteenth-century capitalism. In all ages women were restricted in the exercise of their trades. In the Middle Ages, for instance, although women might be admitted to the regulated corporations, male preponderance was as solidly established in the professions as it was in family life. In many trades women could not advance to the position of master. In others, although a woman might inherit the mastership, the members of the corporation could severely limit the exercise of her rights.(10) Economic regulations passed by the guilds, in the form of increasingly expensive masterpieces and elevated fees, further tended to prevent women from succeeding to that position.(11)

Exclusion from the head of the corporation was not the only professional inhibition suffered by women. In many mixed corporations work was strictly apportioned on the basis of sex. In numerous workshops women were often assigned the more laborious or monotonous tasks. Women fared little better in the home manufactories, since they had to divide their day between completing their household chores and participating in the family labor process.(12)

With the harnessing of steam to production, the more elementary operations generally performed by women in the home became the most receptive to early mechanization. The use of machinery also meant that work was physically less laborious. As a result, women and children were drawn into the factories and into performing functions hitherto reserved exclusively for men.(13) The early factories to which women and children were called were both badly lighted and vented. The machinery was often so poorly adapted that industrial labor was dangerous in the extreme. Because the work that women performed was so simple, female laborers could be easily replaced. The tenuous nature of their employment made women accept more readily than men the meanest tasks, the crudest conditions, and, of course, the lowest wages.(14)

The great disparity in wages existing between men and women was one of the worst abuses women had to bear, not only in the nineteenth-century factories, but in the shops of preindustrial France. At the end of the fourteenth century, women earned three-fourths of the wages paid men. The development of cottage industry brought women flooding into the labor market. The oversupply of their labor increased the sexual wage gap. With industrialism, the employment of women and children at one-half the wages of men became for the factory owner, according to Madeleine

Guilbert, "the means par excellence of reducing the cost of
fabrication,   or   compensating   for the high price of
machinery."(15) Women's need to work and their tendency to
do so under any conditions guaranteed that their own wages
would remain low. Their labor also contributed to the wage
depression that would spread to the entire labor force.
This reality earned for female workers the wrath of the
majority of working men from the mid-ninetenth century
onward.(16)

     In addition to the changes their labor wrought in the
economic life of French society, women's wholesale
participation in industrial growth brought into being a new
kind of working woman. Now, women's working environment was
the workshop or factory rather than the foyer.

A WEB OF WEAKNESSES

     Ironically, during the first half of the nineteenth
century, when large numbers of women were being funneled
into factories, writers on the phenomenon of industrial
combination raised no call to improve women's working
conditions.   Nor did they express much concern over the
implications to French society from the fact that women now
had to leave their homes in order to work.(17) It was not
until the second half of the nineteenth century, with the
development of working-class organizations, that the woman
questions--that is, the question of working women--received
a hearing.   Labor's initial response, however, was colored
by those preconceptions of women that were the dismal
inheritance of Salic law, the patriarchal tradition of
feudalism, and the misogyny of the Civil Code.   The effect
of these combined forces had served to deny women their
civil and economic rights, and to define them legally as
"eternal minors."(18)

     By the end of the Old Regime, women's position in civil
society had assumed a character that no amount of battering
in the following century could effectively erase.   Women
were   forbidden   in   most   cases to exercise any civil
functions. Because of their presumed "natural modesty and
shame," women were not allowed to be in the company of an
assembly of men.   When a woman married, the father's
tutelage right passed to her husband. Within the family
circle the woman exercised no juridic function, not even
over her children, whose legal responsibility she did not
share with her husband.   Cohabitation was her primary
obligation, and she could be forced by law to return to her
marital bed. Fidelity was the husband's moral right.   If
the wife was found guilty of adultery, she could be placed
in a monastery and be subject to the loss even of her
personal property.(19)

     With women defined historically as a legal cypher it is
not   surprising that little attention was paid to their
education until the seventeenth century. Under the aegis of
the church, several schools for young women were opened in

France. Some of these educational establishments provided vocational training for poor girls needing to earn a living.(20) Others, such as St. Cyr, catered to the educational needs of the daughters of the aristocracy.(21) Regardless of the social background of the student, the curricula of the schools of this century and the next, according to Gustave Fagniez, were based on the same premises: "the mistrust of feminine nature, the preoccupation with warning against zeal, of always keeping the girls occupied, always protecting them against the temptations of idleness, . . . and to keep their place."(22) The end product of such an educational system was the ideal woman who, irrespective of class, "spins, confines herself to her husband, holds her tongue, believes, and obeys."(23)

In the seventeenth century the woman question received a brief hearing by some of the leading lights of French society. Their feminism was inspired by the permeation of Cartesian logic and the rise of a school of Neoplatonism. More practical, seventeenth-century feminism was a response to the very real influence women were exercising on society from the salons of Paris. From Descartes came the notion that men and women were born with the same innate ideas, thereby implying that the sexes were morally and physically equal. The Neoplatonists, with their cult of love, assigned a valued place to the "womanly" virtues of imagination, sentiment, intuition, and a desire for peace. To these thinkers, women's qualities were important commodities, necessary to a future world of peace and harmony.(24)

Such a movement, claiming women's right to free choice and proclaiming the equality of the sexes, seemed to be aimed at the destruction of the social hierarchy.(25) The response to the threat engendered by the feminist writings of the préciosité is valuable for the insight it offers into just how deeply entrenched were the attitudes toward women, and how persistently these attitudes were to remain as common themes in the succeeding centuries.

Opposing any change in women's social role, the seventeenth-century antifeminists fell back upon the traditional Eve theme. Women were composed of "a web of weaknesses" requiring numerous restraints, chief of which was "the salutary yoke" of marriage.(26) The antifeminists glorified marriage and the family, not only as a way for women to achieve social worth and eternal salvation, but as the only sure means by which to preserve and strengthen the nation. As "a little kingdom" the family was a component of the larger kingdom. When the individual family was well-ruled, "the others could not be disordered." Marriage, said one seventeenth-century antifeminist,

fills cities with citizens . . . kingdoms with subjects. . . . It is this which puts laborers in the country, judges in the tribunal, priests in churches and soldiers in armies. . . . [It makes] arts and sciences flourish, sustains commerce;

which makes society subsist, and to which one owes
most of one's good laws. [Without marriage] the
world would be a cavern of brigands.(27)

Concludes Carolyn Lougee on the subject: "the antifeminists'
social vision was paternalistic; society was a family writ
large, a web of private ties by which all persons were
interdependent and through which alone individuals could
develop."(28)

THE DEMAND FOR LIBERTY, EQUALITY, FRATERNITY

     Swaddled thus in the ideal of the family, the woman
question rested for yet another century, until it was
revived by the philosophes. In calling for the rule of
reason and the establishment of a just society based on the
prescripts of natural law, the philosophers of the
Enlightenment began to analyze the place of women in
eighteenth-century France. Diderot regretted that women
were treated as "imbecilic children." D'Alembert noted that
women's subservient position was the result of their
inferior education. In his Persian Letters Montesquieu
espoused the belief that the two sexes were created equal,
but men had usurped authority by exploiting women's
weaknesses.(29)
     Although united in their hatred of the existing regime,
the philosophes were not in complete accord on the subject
of women. Countering Montesquieu's feminism, Rousseau
asserted that because women were weak and fragile in
intelligence, they had invented love in order to gain
precedence over men. In Emile he set forth the belief that
women were only children; in his Discourse on Inequality,
Rousseau said that women were made for men's pleasure and
for their use. Women were obliged "to love and honor them,
raise the young, care for them, counsel them, make their
lives agreeable and sweet."(30)
     With the beginning of the Revolution in 1789, active
elements of political feminism began to appear. Some of the
Cahiers de doléances carried pleas calling for the right of
women to have a deliberative voice in the political forums
of the land.(31) In 1789 a petition to the king asked that
women be given equality--even in the pulpit!(32) French
feminist Olympe de Gouges submitted to the Assembly a
"Declaration of the Rights of Women" in which she declared
that women possessed natural rights equally with men. Those
rights extended even to the privilege of their entering any
trade or profession based on their capability. Further, if
women had the right "to mount the scaffold," she asserted
prophetically, they must have the equal right "to mount the
tribune."(33)
     Despite the fact that women's equality was supported by
such male worthies as Sieyès, Fouchet, and Condorcet, and
that women's participation in the Revolution was lauded by
all segments of the political community, little permanent

gain was achieved for women, save for a slight revision of the existing divorce laws.(34) For all the professions of "liberty, equality, fraternity" generated by the revolutionaries, the centuries' long attitudes toward women continued to remain safely barricaded against the onslaughts of those who demanded the erection of a new society built on sexual equality. Indeed, the antifeminist tradition is enshrined in the language of one pamphlet distributed during the Revolution. It cavalierly proclaimed:

> Civil and political liberty is of no use to women and should therefore be kept from them. Since they . . . are born to be dependent from the cradle to the grave, they have been endowed only with private virtues. . . . A woman is acceptable only in the context of her father's or husband's household. She needs to know nothing of what goes on outside beyond what they may see fit to tell her.(35)

Even before the Revolution had merged into the Empire, the woman's movement had lost most of its male supporters. The government abolished women's political clubs, checked their revolutionary ardor, and sent them back to the condition of their former legal estate.(36) This enforced retreat became a rout with the accession of Napoleon to the throne of France. The Civil Code drafted in 1804 not only reflected the prejudices of the codifiers of Roman law, it also bore the traces of the misogyny of the Emperor, who once remarked to his colleagues that "What is not French is to give authority to women. They have enough of it."(37) Reflecting its Napoleonic inspiration, the Code reasserted the principle of the family as a moral person and the male as supreme in the family and society.

A MECHANICAL PIVOT

For all its failure to bring about the reign of liberty, at least for women, the Revolution of 1789 did inspire numerous social theorists in the following century to scrutinize society seeking the roots of oppression that also hindered sound progress. In the process of their analyses, the theorists assigned to women a heightened role in the establishment of a just and equal society for all.

In 1824 the Exposition de la doctrine was published by Saint-Simon. In this document he outlined an ideology of liberation for women that became a source of renewed inspiration for French feminists. Although the Count was interested more in furthering the cause of the transformation of society as a whole, he expressed the belief nevertheless that the liberation of women was a natural outgrowth of the evolution of society. For Saint-Simon the age of militarism, characterized by individualism, was on the wane. This age was to be

succeeded by the reign of peace and love, based on the
principle of association and marked by the entry of two
groups who had been sacrificed by the military age: the
industrial workers, because of their productive capacity,
and women, because of their abundance of sympathy.(38)
Saint-Simonianism was carried to the point of absurdity by
his disciple "Père" Enfantin, who undertook an unsuccessful
search for a "female messiah," and was ultimately imprisoned
for immorality.(39) Yet Saint-Simonianism in general gave "a
vigorous élan to the feminist movement," as Marguerite
Thibert points out, because the Count and his followers
raised anew the question of sexual equality and depicted
women as moral saviors of civilization.(40)

If much of Saint-Simonianism culminated in mysticism,
the program of another Utopian Socialist, Charles Fourier,
was infinitely more practical. In his Théorie des quatre
mouvements et des destinées générales published in 1808,
Fourier expressed the view that women's present position of
servitude was a hangover from the barbaric past. He further
suggested that women's subjugation in economic life was a
danger to society as a whole because it brutalized both
sexes: the man because he alone bore the full responsibility
of supporting his family, and the woman because her
industrial servitude led her to prostitution.

To remedy the "trickery" being perpetrated on both
sexes, and to restore society, Fourier proposed for women,
among other things, universal education, full freedom of
choice in the selection of a spouse, and the right to work
at equal pay. The principle of equal pay for equal work was
one which Fourier regarded as a fundamental right. The only
free woman was the one who lived by her own labor. Further,
the extension of all privileges to women was the general
principle of all social progress, for women's liberation,
Fourier declared, was the "pivot mécanique" on which
revolved the liberation of all humanity.(41)

These Utopian Socialists gained disciples among
numerous women, many of whom established newspapers
dedicated to advancing women's civil and economic rights,
particularly the right to work. One such Utopian feminist
was Jeanne Deroin. Devoting her attention not only to
feminist issues, but also to the workers' cause, Deroin was
instrumental in founding over a hundred workers'
associations. In 1849 she formed a "red party," and was
proposed as its candidate for election before being arrested
and imprisoned for her political activities.(42)

Deroin's colleague and fellow Saint-Simonian, Pauline
Roland, was also a proponent of sexual equality. This
equality, she believed, must begin with equal education of
both sexes, and must end with changed attitudes regarding
marriage. When Pauline Roland was brought to trial for her
socialist ideas, she shocked the judges by professing that
matrimony was little more than "a state of servitude" for
the woman. Echoing Fourier, Roland wrote in 1851 that
"woman is a free being, equal to men," and must therefore
"make her life by her own work, from her own love, by her

own intelligence."(43)

Another Utopian Socialist, who has been called "a bridge between the working-class movement of unions and crafts and the socialist efforts to form a new vision of society," was Flora Tristan.(44) Saint-Simonian in her belief that working men and women were destined to claim their rights, Tristan devoted her efforts to achieving the dual goals of sexual equality and the advancement of the proletariat through the establishment of working-class associations. In accepting the Utopians' assignment to women of the role of moralizers of humanity, Tristan questioned how women could fulfill this task when they were legally subject to their husbands and economically inferior because of their small earning power. Working-class women, wrote Tristan, exist "on a little work, a little thievery, a little begging, and a lot of prostitution." In order for women to assume their place as a moral elite in society, Tristan demanded they be extended their full natural rights, including the right to political representation, the opportunity for increased academic and vocational instruction, and the chance to work in any trade. She also demanded the right for women to be paid on the basis of utility rather than on the supposition of their lesser needs.(45)

In her vision of the future, Tristan regarded feminism and socialism as being mutually dependent. But she believed that women could not hope to free themselves: they must depend on the decision of men workers to accept women as equals. This decision, Tristan supposed, would be motivated by reason and self-interest. Men would choose to work for women's freedom because they would accept the social fact that women's liberation was the prepatory step to the transformation of society. When "the last slaves still remaining in French society" were emancipated, Tristan proclaimed, the social revolution would be complete.(46)

Unfortunately for her grand vision, French working-class men were hardly reasonable about the competition from French working-class women. At the very moment Tristan was preaching sexual equality in her Workers' Union, the working-class newspaper, L'Atelier, published from 1840 to 1850, was expressing in print what male workers were noting in the workshops. It was not mechanization, but the feminization of industry that was the greatest danger to the worker and his family. To halt this blight, workers' associations must try to keep women out of the trades.(47) In regarding the liberation of workers and women as inseparable and the requisite to the liberation of all humanity, Tristan was following the dictates of Saint-Simon. But in attempting to implement the simultaneous liberation of the two, Tristan's philosophy prefigured the same dilemma upon whose horns the leaders of the later workers' movement would be launched.

HOUSEWIFE OR COURTESAN

The activities of these early nineteenth-century feminists are important to the later workers' movement for still another reason: the reaction they provoked in Pierre Joseph Proudhon.(48) It would be a simple matter to dismiss Proudhon's attitudes toward women, as does Marguerite Thibert, as being a mere case of "natural antifeminism," an articulation of "the peasant attached to patriarchal custom, the tradition of the farmer in all his tendencies." There was much of the aura of "the peasant soldier" about Proudhon, to be sure.(49) But his ideas were more than just a reflection of childhood heredity. Inspired with the notion of social change as a result of having read Fourier, Proudhon was initially attracted to the ideas of all the Utopians. He had even been an admirer for a time of Flora Tristan and her project of forming workers' associations.(50) But after the briefest of honeymoons, Proudhon discovered Hegel. Thus, much of his subsequent work is a curious mélange that both incorporates and refutes Utopian teachings.

Along with Fourier, Proudhon recognized that man's passions were the root cause of social malaise. But he quickly came to believe that the Utopian's goal of changing man's institutions in order to deflect his passions was superficial and did not touch the heart of the matter--man himself. "Man is by nature a sinner," he wrote. "That is to say not essentially a wrongdoer but rather wrongly made," so that more than a simple reordering of society was necessary to change man.(51) It was only through the moral reform of man himself, individually, voluntarily, and within the context of the smallest natural unit of society, the family, that human society could be purified. Later Proudhon would reveal the importance of the family to his metaphysic when he would proclaim: "Point de famille, point de cité, point de république."(52)

With the image of the family as the basis of society's restoration continually before him in his writings and in his thinking, it was natural that Proudhon would turn his attention to the cosmic glue binding the family, that is, to the relationship existing between men and women. By the time of his second major work in 1846, Proudhon's discovery of Hegel had gone a long way toward unseating the theories of the Utopians from the throne of his metaphysics. In the Système des contradictions économiques, ou philosophie de la misère, written as an attempt to investigate the economic basis of contemporary society, Proudhon devoted some portion of the work to applying his understanding of the dialectic to an analysis of the relationship between the sexes. The Utopians' tenet of sexual equality was false, he decided. Woman could not be identically equal to man. Rather, she was man's complement, not his resemblance. To the Saint-Simonians the sexual relationship was man and woman. For Proudhon, however, that relationship was the result of a

process that occurred through the conjugal union between man
and woman as subject-object. Outside of this relationship
woman had no social identity and hence, no social worth.
Thus, woman could be "a housewife or a prostitute"--she
could assume no middle identity.(53)

It was this pronouncement, repeated against the
candidacy of Jeanne Deroin for the legislature in 1849,
which Proudhon continued to enunciate, refine, and embellish
throughout the remainder of his life.(54) His theories were
not so much an attack on women as they were an attempt to
overturn the wrongheaded notions of the Utopians,
particularly in their Enfantine phase, whose theories
constituted for Proudhon a danger to the course of human
progress. It was "the sects of the epoch, Icariens,
humanitarians, Saint-Simonians, phalanstériens," as well as
the assortment of "bohemian artists and littérateurs" who
attacked the institution of the family as being only a word,
a convention, with no absolute value, and led them to
espouse divorce and free love.(55) It was their obsession
with the equality of the sexes that had been carried to its
most absurd point with the Deroin candidacy. Further, it
was the bankruptcy of their philosophy, Proudhon believed,
that had been partly responsible for the failure of the 1848
revolution, a revolution that had defeated them all.

Returning again to his theme of the failure of Utopian
ideas in response to two well-directed attacks made upon his
Justice by women followers of George Sand, Proudhon wrote La
pornocratie, ou les femmes dans les temps modernes.(56) This
book was the culmination of all his ideas on marriage, the
family, and the pernicious effect of Utopian Socialist ideas
on society. The events over the preceding thirty-five years,
culminating in "the national prostitution" that was the
Second Empire, were an indication to Proudhon that society
had lost its virility and was now experiencing a fatal
decline. This national malaise was the result of the
continual absorption by the sects with extremist democracy
and its notions of sexual equality. The idea of equality of
the sexes, declared Proudhon, was a "sophism" attributed "to
all epochs of fatigue, of exhaustion, above all, of
oppression and exploitation; when the mass of males have
been transformed into beasts of burden, when iniquity
renders work less lucrative, life difficult, marriage
perilous, the generation onerous, the family
impossible."(57)

Women's dearth of moral energy was well-known, he
continued, and accounted for a variety of unattractive
feminine attributes. Women are given to tears, for
instance, "which are as touching as a doll," but hardly
denotes the behavior of "a lion or a man."(58) Woman is an
idealist, possessed of a kind of "intuitive and divining
spirit" that takes the place of "reason and conviction."(59)
She has a greater penchant for lasciviousness, and thus
struggles less than man against the inclination toward
animality.(60) Because women were so frail, to allow them to
enter the political arena would be to feminize further a

society already in danger because of its lack of masculine virtue. And when social emasculation, or "pornocratie" occurred, Proudhon cautioned, "then marriage is dishonored by interest; the law of succession is regarded as a spoliation; the family abandoned for the State. Everyone is thrown onto the State. Liberty is disowned. Justice is no longer; it is weakened in the soul."(61)

To halt this decay, Proudhon advocated a return to "the law of the sexes" upon which depended "the family, . . . the order of society, and the constitution of all humanity."(62) For Proudhon the sexual law could be found only in "monogamous and indissoluble" marriage, an institution in which man is tempered by woman.(63) Only through the conjugal union would woman recover her dignity and man develop his "individuality, character, and heroism" and regenerate society.(64) In marriage the spouses became "the representative of divinity" in their completion of each other in a kind of divine dialectic held together by Justice: Proudhon's imminent force moving through history and society and working to elevate humanity.(65) The Utopian Socialists had said that woman was the mechanical pivot upon which rested the perfection of humanity and the freedom of society. To Proudhon that was a false equality, for it was only as long as neither pole--that is, strength-beauty, politics-art, right-ideal, subject-object, man-woman--gained the ascendancy that true equality, and hence Justice, could prevail.

Although his theories seem today to be little more than a paean to the traditional antifeminist belief in the natural inferiority of woman, for Proudhon his man-woman synthesis was not inequality but the epitome of justice incarnate. "The ancients had personified justice by the idea of God," points out Thibert. But Proudhon symbolized its fullest manifestation in the conjugal couple.(66) Man and wife represented a Hegelian synthesis in which were eliminated the deficiencies of each; the process of their conjugal relationship was one that completed and perfected each. For Proudhon, this was a perfect unity: man represents authority, woman liberty. Masculine force was tempered by feminine beauty. The man rules; the woman obeys. Equality is derived by the tension of opposites. Woman loves man, and he reciprocates that love, so that each sex is equivalent in the love that unites them. In terms of social destiny, Proudhon believed that a complete equality likewise prevailed. To man was given the realm of public life and social labor. To the woman was assigned the private realm, the familial foyer.(67)

PROUDHON VERSUS MARX

In analyzing Proudhon's attempt to use Hegelian dialectics to explain what he believed to be the root of France's decay, it becomes apparent that the object of his wrath was not so much women and feminism as the whole body of Utopian Socialism. But by applying the tenets of German idealism to the social situation in France, Proudhon was rejecting the more enlightened ideas of the Utopian feminists and providing a solid philosophical sanction to centuries of French paternalism. To conclude, however, that syndicalist attitudes on the woman question were merely variations on a Proudhonian theme is misleading for a number of reasons. For one thing, these conclusions tend to focus on Proudhon's utterances on women outside of their Utopian Socialist context. For another, they fail to consider if Proudhon influenced popular sentiment or merely articulated it. Certainly Proudhon's paternalism represented the bel idéal of a large majority of French men and women, particularly when women were being forced to work outside the home. Also, Proudhon the printer belonged to a profession that by the time of his death was beginning to feel the ravages of "the feminine peril."

More important, conclusions that have hitherto been made posing a straight line between Proudhonian theory and syndicalist practice have been based on conjecture and incomplete evidence. They have not rested on an in-depth look at the position of the French left on the woman question, since such studies have only recently been undertaken. Marilyn Boxer's work deals almost exclusively with the political socialists.(68) Madeleine Guilbert's study and the following chapter of this work examine the position of revolutionary syndicalism on women laborers. Two similar conclusions are drawn from this work and that of Boxer's. One is that positivist and Marxist philosophy vied with the theories of Proudhon on a relatively equal basis in the early discussions on the woman question. Further, Boxer's work on socialism and this study on syndicalism indicate that very quickly, both groups tended to set aside theory in the interest of practical considerations.

Despite the practical thrust of syndicalism, a look at the Marxian inheritance in socialism is important to a deeper understanding of French unionism. Unlike Proudhon, Marx never devoted a whole treatise to the subject of women. But his analysis on the position of women in society, scattered throughout his works, remains relatively consistent, according to Boxer.(69) Marx's theme was that capitalism had caused the degeneration of the family and the degradation of women within the familial structure. He charged the middle class with being responsible for prostitution. Marx also claimed that the family relationship of the proletariat was superior to that of the bourgeoisie. Regardless of ideological consistency, few of Marx's pronouncements were available for popular consumption, except for the Communist Manifesto. In this widely circulated tract, Marx charged the capitalists with exploiting women and destroying the family by reducing all human relationships to a cash nexus. Social revolution would end slavery of class, of generations, and of sexes.

The philosophies of Marx and Proudhon first competed in the International Workingmen's Association. Delegates to most conferences discussed the role of women in society and in the workshops. Marxists declared that work was "a sacred right" rather than a sin from which women should be excluded. Women were necessary allies in the struggle for emancipation. They further insisted that women's exclusion from the work force was a practical way to prevent wage depression. These views always called forth shocked rejoinders from the Proudhonians. French delegates continued to insist that women had no existence outside the home. Any attempt to go beyond the familial domain would constitute a perversion of womanhood and a potential threat to the continuation of the human species.

No clear-cut decision on the woman question was forthcoming in the IWA, particularly on the notion of how to translate theory into practice. Women were admitted to membership; a woman was appointed to the General Council. Marx called for the organization of women's sections in all the trades. But in the face of Bakuninist onslaughts against his control of the International, Marx subsequently withdrew his motion. One of the last pieces of work to be concluded in the IWA was the exclusion of the American section headed by free-love advocate Victoria Woodhull. In this action Marx concurred with the majority. Woodhull and company were "bourgeois quacks," he declared, and too much involved with feminist nonsense to be useful to the furtherance of the class revolution.(70)

The ideological inheritance of Marx survived the demise of the First International and was transmitted to France by the major leaders of political socialism. Virtually everyone from Paul Brousse to Compère-Morel penned works espousing the equality of women under socialism. The most vocal proponents of feminine equality, however, were the Guesdists. In a series of tracts beginning in 1876, Jules Guesde popularized and refined Marx's theories. The year of the first tract coincided with the assembling of the first of the three congresses serving as forerunners to the establishment of permanent labor organizations. At the outset, Guesde was able to use the woman question as a lesson in capitalist exploitation and as a useful tool against the Proudhonian reactionaries among the left. The question of women's intrusion into the work force could not be divorced from the larger issue of capitalist exploitation, he insisted. Proudhon's sexual equation of "ménagère ou courtisane" was false. "If woman is forced to be a housewife, unable to subsist ouside the household," Guesde lectured, "she must necessarily be a courtesan." Women had an equal right to liberty with men. As with men, women's place was anywhere they wished it to be. The Proudhonians might extol the sanctity of the foyer, but to Guesde, the family was no longer a natural unit. It existed for the development of the husband only. In modern society, therefore, woman was a proletarian, forced to prostitute herself either on the streets or in the marriage bed.(71)

Among the political socialists, Marxian orthodoxy came increasingly to reign supreme over Proudhonian conservatism.

During the decades spanning the first workers' congresses in 1876, to the formation of the SFIO in 1905, while socialism hurdled sectarianism in an effort to build a base within the nation, socialist "feminism" became a useful tool for gaining adherents. With one-third the female population in France employed, as Boxer notes, feminism was certainly fashionable. Socialist deputies fought for protective legislation to ease the burden of the laboureuses, and used the example of women's degradation to lecture on the evils of capitalism. Socialists called for equal representation for women in the party, and punctuated their demands by placing women in highly visible positions within their political organizations.

Such women were particularly useful to Guesde in his drive to build a socialist party around Marxian orthodoxy. He enlisted socialist-feminist Paule Mink to his cause. The famous pétroleuse drew sizeable audiences wherever she went, thereby attracting large numbers of workers to the Guesdist fold. Aline Valette was another prominent and useful woman for the Guesdists. As a teacher professing equal education for women, Valette gained support for socialism among bourgeois feminists. As a factory inspector, she could appeal to working-class audiences whom she enticed by brandishing the party's call for equal participation for women in the workshops and equal pay for equal work. In recognition for her service, she was given membership in the National Council of the POF and was chosen to represent the party at meetings of the Second International.(72)

Perhaps the most vital proponent of women's equality and the Guesdist brand of socialism was Dr. Madeleine Pelletier.(73) It was a result of her powerful lobbying in socialist papers and journals and by organizing street demonstrations that the question of votes for women was finally adopted at the SFIO congress in 1906. Her plea for women's suffrage was grounded in Marxist logic: if socialists were fighting in the political arena, she argued, then women must be enfranchised in order to swell the ranks. By the time Pelletier was able to place her call, the socialists were less concerned with orthodoxy than with building political constituencies. The resolution demanding women's suffrage was never elevated beyond what Pelletier tagged "a platonic wish."(74)

The question of women's emancipation belonged to the heroic period of political socialism, when the sects were struggling for cohesion. Then the socialist message was one based on a philosophy of unity: sexual equality and integral emancipation after the revolution. With union achieved, the demand for women's liberation in the present became an embarrassment outside the inner party circles. The woman's question, as Pelletier so succinctly noted, became "a parenthesis very quickly closed" in order to return to the more vital question: that of winning elections.(75) The need to gain power in the chamber halls precluded fighting for unpopular causes, chief among which was the issue of women's equality. Because of the legacy from the past, any appeal for female suffrage could only turn away the male electorate. Practical politics rather than philosophical integrity came to define the parameters of the woman question for party socialists.

The legacy of the French past confronted socialists and syndicalists alike in their discussion of the woman question: a long tradition of patriarchy; legal, social, and economic repression; and a well-defined philosophy of antifeminism. But for syndicalists, the tradition also included the historical presence and importance of women in industry, the very real dependence on women's labor to augment the family wage, and a historical liberalism that over the centuries had been used occasionally to justify women's need for freedom. It was a mixed inheritance upon which nineteenth-century workers and working-class leaders could draw when called upon to meet the dual challenge of industrialization and feminization of the trades.

NOTES

1. Madeleine Guilbert, Les femmes et l'organisation syndicale avant 1914 (Paris, 1966), p. 14. That figure increased to 38 percent in 1911. The statistics on women in the work force would be considerably higher if the female agricultural workers were included, since until 1850, agriculture was the largest single employer of women. Another astonishing statistic is that the percentage of male to female workers, excluding agriculture, has remained a constant. In 1866, 31 women to 69 men were employed in industry. In 1968 the figure was 35 women to 65 men. Georges Dupeux, French Society 1789-1970, Peter Wait, trans. (London, 1976), pp. 17-18.

2. Marilyn Jacoby Boxer, "Socialism Faces Feminism in France: 1879-1913" (Ph.D. Dissertation: University of California, Riverside, 1975).

3. Guilbert, Les femmes et l'organisation syndicale, p. 433.

4. Michelle Perrot, Les ouvriers en grève, France 1871-1890, 2 vols. (Paris, 1974), vol. 1, p. 324.

5. Jean Maitron, "La personnalité du militant ouvrier français dans la seconde moitié du XIX(e) siècle," Le Mouvement Social 33-34 (Oct. 1960-Mar. 1961): 67-86, p. 84.

6. On the place of women in the corporations during the Middle Ages and the early modern period see Madeleine Guilbert, Les fonctions des femmes dans l'industrie (Paris, 1966), pp. 21-28. Also Gustave Fagniez, La femme et la société française dans la première moitié du XVIII(e) siècle (Paris, 1929), pp. 94-114.

7. Quoted in Guilbert, Les fonctions des femmes, p. 29.

8. Besides being involved in textile manufacturing, peasant women made a wide variety of other products, such as tools, nails, and stirrups. Patricia Branca, Women in Europe Since 1750 (London, 1978), p. 26.

9. Guilbert points out that the existence of cottage industry continued far longer in France than in other countries, particularly England, where the enclosure movements produced the great migrations to the cities well before the machines had ruined domestic industry. In France this was not the case. Rather, the development of cottage industry provided the means by which peasants could continue to own their small plots of land or add further to their property holdings. This fact, in turn, served in a circular fashion to inhibit the development of industrial combination because the peasant worker was not driven off the land into the large cities until the eighteenth and even until the nineteenth century. See Les fonctions des femmes, pp. 34-35.

10. Ibid., p. 23; Fagniez, La femme et la société française, pp. 100-102.

11. The sixteenth century onward witnessed the phenomenon of masters closing ranks and tightening up on guild regulations. George F. Renard and G. Weulersse, Life and Work in Modern Europe, Fifteenth to Eighteenth Centuries, Margaret Richards, trans. (New York, 1968). pp. 161-162.

12. Guilbert, Les fonctions des femmes, pp. 24-25, 30-31.

13. Ibid., p. 36.

14. Ibid., pp. 25, 38-39.

15. Ibid., p. 36. The extent to which women were involved in industry is recorded by Yves Lequin, who notes that in mid-nineteenth century Lyon, one of the chief attractions for marriage was the prospect of having a second income. "Rare are the young wives who could say 'housewife' or 'without profession'" he concludes. La formation de la classe ouvrière régionale, vol. 1 (Lyon, 1977), p. 206. There were other reasons than the fact that women would work for any wage offered that made them an attractive commodity in the work force. In her report on "Le travail des femmes en France," Mlle. Schirmacker notes that women were in demand because of their moral qualities, among which were those of "sweetness, patience, politeness, docility, and sobriety." Further, women neither drank nor smoked, and needed less nourishment than men, which was the reason why

they could live on a lower wage. Schirmacker's article appeared in Le Musée Social, Arthur Rousseau, ed. (Paris, 1902): 321-372. See pp. 337-338 for quote.

16. Actually, men's hostility toward women who worked for less than standard wages had a long tradition. The lower salaries accepted by women were the reason in 1675 that the master tailors of Paris protested the establishment of a guild of women dressmakers. In the strikes of 1744, weavers noted, "It is sad to see us on the streets without work, while girls are employed at the loom." See Renard and Weulersse, Life and Work in Modern Europe, p. 194.

17. Guilbert, Les fonctions des femmes, p. 40.

18. Dupeux's term of "eternal minors," French Society, p. 128.

19. See Fagniez, La femme et la société française, see the chapter on "La femme dans la famille," pp. 135-203; and Jane Cerez, La condition sociale de la femme de 1804 à l'heure présente (Paris, 1940), pp. 61-64.

20. Fagniez, La femme et la société française, pp. 30-34.

21. Carolyn C. Lougee, Le Paradis des Femmes: Women, Salons, and Social Stratification in Seventeenth-Century France (Princeton, 1976), pp. 173-174.

22. Fagniez, La femme et la société française, pp. 46-47.

23. The definition of "a good woman," according to educational theories of Archbishop François Fénelon, pedagogical director of St. Cyr. See Lougee, Le Paradis des Femmes, p. 187 for quote.

24. Ibid., pp. 15-20.

25. Francis Baumal in Le féminisme au temps de Molière (Paris, n.d.) states that eighteenth-century literature of the eighteenth century betrays the fear that women will organize in resistance to the tyranny of their fathers, tutors, and their husbands; p. 130.

26. Lougee, Le Paradis des Femmes, pp. 60-61 for quote.

27. Ibid., pp. 90-91 for quotes.

28. Ibid., p. 88.

29. Cerez, pp. 114-115. La condition sociale de la femme.

30. Rousseau quoted in ibid., p. 117.

31. Ibid., p. 68.

32. Reported in Theodore Stanton, ed., "France," The Woman Question in Europe (New York, 1884), pp. 235-236.

33. "Prophetically" because de Gouges herself was guillotined. See Louisette Blanquart, Femmes: L'Age politique (Paris, 1974), p. 16.

34. Cerez, La condition sociale de la femme, pp. 73-80.

35. "Révolution de Paris," quoted in Ann Foreman, Femininity as Alienation (London, 1977), p. 11.

36. Blanquart, Femmes: L'Age politique, p. 17.

37. Quoted in Cerez, La condition sociale de la femme, pp. 139-140. Napoleon confessed his aversion to women meddling in politics to Sophie de Condorcet. "You're right, my general," she replied, "but in a country where they cut off your head, it's natural that [women] would want to know why." Quoted in Blanquart, Femmes: L'Age politique, p. 18.

38. For a discussion of Saint-Simon's theories see Marguerite Thibert, Le féminisme dans le socialisme français de 1830 à 1850 (Paris, 1926), pp. 8-14.

39. S. Joan Moon, "Feminism and Socialism: The Utopian Synthesis of Flora Tristan," Socialist Women, European Feminism in the Nineteenth and Early Twentieth Centuries, Marilyn J. Boxer and Jean H. Quataert, eds. (New York, 1978), p. 27.

40. Thibert, Le féminisme dans le socialisme, p. 82. Saint-Simonianism had some practical aspects as well. One follower of the sect, as Minister of Public Education, sought to remedy the imperfections in the law regarding women's education. Another, a wealthy industrialist, gave money to encourage the discussion of equality of women's wages.   It was purportedly due to the efforts of Saint-Simonians that women were hired as railroad crossing guards. See ibid., p. 93. On women employed as crossing guards, see footnote on p. 239 of Stanton, The Woman Question. The author adds: "and I never see one of those sturdy women, as the train whizzes by, a baton at her shoulder, without thinking that the eccentric Saint-Simon accomplished some practical good in the world."

41. See Thibert, Le féminisme dans le socialisme, pp. 99-145 for a discussion of Fourier's feminism.

42. Blanquart, Femmes, L'Age politique, pp. 21-24.

43. Edith Thomas, Pauline Roland: Socialisme et féminisme au XIX(e) siècle (Paris, 1956), pp. 116, 124; quote on 155.

44. Moon, in Boxer and Quataert, Socialist Women, p. 19.

45. Ibid. Quote appears on p. 33. Working women's prostitution carried on to compensate for the pitifully low wages they received was commonly referred to as "the fifth quarter of the day." See Edith Thomas, The Women Incendiaries, James and Starr, trans. (New York, 1966), p. 8. This specific practice caused the Procurator of the Appeals Court of Alsace to brand factories dens of "shameless debauchery" in 1855. Quoted in Dupeux, French Society, p. 131.

46. Quoted in Boxer and Quataert, Socialist Women, p. 37.

47. Ibid., pp. 34-35.

48. On Proudhon, see George Woodcock, Pierre-Joseph Proudhon (London, 1956); Edouard Dolléans, Proudhon (Paris, 1948); K. Steven Vincent, Pierre-Joseph Proudhon and the Rise of French Republican Socialism (New York, 1984).

49. Thibert, Le féminisme dans le socialisme, p. 185.

50. George Woodcock, Anarchism: A History of Libertarian Ideas and Movements (Cleveland, 1962), p. 111.

51. Proudhon in Système des contradictions économiques ou philosophie de la misère, vol. 1, p. 356, quoted in James Joll, The Anarchists (New York, 1964), p. 67.

52. Proudhon, Carnets de P. J. Proudhon, quoted in Dolléans, Proudhon, p. 318.

53. Proudhon, Système des contradictions, quoted in Thibert, Le féminisme dans le socialisme, p. 172.

54. In her response to Proudhon's attack, Deroin declared in print on 28 Jan. 1849 that she knew of many women who "became courtesans only to escape the necessity of being housewives." Quoted by Edouard Dolléans, Féminisme et le mouvement ouvrier: George Sand (Paris, 1951), p. 5.

55. Pierre Joseph Proudhon, La pornocratie: Ou les femmes dans les temps modernes (Paris, 1875), pp. 114, 162-163.

56. Jenny d'Héricourt in La femme affranchie, and

Juliette Lamber in Les idées antiproudhoniennes sur l'amour, la femme et le mariage, noted in Thomas, The Women Incendiaries, pp. 21-26. Proudhon's remarks are in La pornocratie, p. 150. Apparently Proudhon's own household was not always harmonious. In a letter to Michelet on 15 Mar. 1860, Proudhon noted that his wife had been ailing, was having trouble sleeping, and was suffering from migraines. She had told him: "You have your ideas, and I, when you are at your work and my daughter is in class, I have nothing." Despite Proudhon's assertion to Michelet that he would rather have to deal with the passions of "combat, rage, [and] hatred," than with his wife's migraines and martyrdom, Proudhon's revelation to another friend indicates that his ideal woman was one who was "simple, obscure, retiring," appears to attest to the fact that Proudhon's confidence to Michelet was made in a weaker moment of temporary frustration. Letter to Antoine Gautier, 20 Feb. 1862, reported in Thibert, Le féminisme dans le socialisme, p. 181. See ibid., pp. 182-183 for other quotes.

57. Proudhon, La pornocratie, p. 13. His emphasis.

58. Ibid., p. 161.

59. Ibid., p. 37.

60. Ibid., p. 29.

61. Ibid., pp. 41, 266. His emphasis.

62. Ibid., p. 161.

63. Ibid., p. 19.

64. Ibid., p. 179.

65. Ibid., p. 13.

66. Thibert, Le féminisme dans le socialisme, p. 194.

67. Proudhon, La pornocratie, p. 194.

68. Although her work is concerned with party socialism, Marilyn Boxer deals with syndicalism to a certain extent, particularly with the printers' federation and the Emma Couriau affair. Boxer includes the French left in general when she concludes that the woman question remained only "a superficial accoutrement, grafted onto a socialist program concerned essentially with economic issues." The only problem with her analysis is that she takes the printers as representative of the entire syndicalist movement. "Socialism Faces Feminism in France" (Ph.D. Dissertation) and "Socialism Faces Feminism: The Failure of Synthesis in France, 1879-1914," in Socialist Women; see p. 106 for quote. The findings of Charles Sowerwine, on the

other hand, are more in agreement with my conclusions, presented first as a preliminary study to this larger work: "From Foyer to Factory: French Revolutionary Syndicalism and the Woman Question," Eighth Annual Conference of the Western Society for French History, Eugene, Oregon, October 1980. Sowerwine contends that the Couriau affair forced the CGT "to confront the problem of women's equality in the workplace from the perspective of class struggle." "Workers and Women in France Before 1914: The Debate Over the Couriau Affair," Journal of Modern History 55 (September 1983): 411-440, quote appears on p. 440.

69. Ibid., pp. 11-17. See also Paul Lafargue, La question de la femme (Paris, 1904); Jules Guesde and Paul Lafargue, Le programme du parti ouvrier (Lille, 1897); August Bebel, Women and Socialism, Meta L. Stern Hite, trans. (New York, 1910).

70. Boxer, "Socialism Faces Feminism," (Ph.D. Dissertation) pp. 38-51; quote appears on p. 50.

71. See ibid., chapter 3. Quote on p. 71.

72. See ibid., chapter 4 on the Mink-Guesde connection, and chapter 5 on Aline Valette.

73. Pelletier was originally attracted to the Guesdists because of their antiministerial stand; p. 250 in ibid. When the Guesdists became too "reformist" for the radical Dr. Pelletier, she joined Hervé's branch of the party for a time.

74. Chapter 8 in ibid. deals with Pelletier. Quote on p. 232.

75. Ibid., p. 235.

5. The Woman Question: From *Foyer* to Factory

If the party socialists, with their relatively concise and consistent body of Marxian thought concerning women, were forced to disavow their ideological inheritance in the interest of political expediency, how much more impossible it would have been for French unionists to remain faithful to the disorganized and seemingly paradoxical pronouncements of Proudhon in their bid for working-class unity. If Proudhon was the spiritual father of anarchism and the intellectual progenitor of the working-class movement in France, it was natural that some of his ideas might be initially attractive to working men as philosophical ammunition against women's competition in the trades. Of course as socialists, French workers were also exposed to the Marxist view that women's labor was the source of both their exploitation and their emancipation. In the earlier workers' congresses, discussion of the woman question often wavered between these two ideological poles. However, based on a survey of syndicalist pronouncements on the woman question in the congresses and in the working-class press, this study takes the position that as the union movement matured, philosophical precepts were quickly dethroned in favor of more practical considerations.

PROUDHON'S "EQUIVALENTS" OR MARX'S "EQUALS"

During the early years of unionism the debates on the woman question centered on three specific themes, both Marxist and Proudhonian in their orientation: the demand for equal pay, a call for the education and organization of women, and the expressed fear of familial, hence class, demoralization occasioned by the presence of so many wives and mothers in the workforce. Fundamental to these concerns were the issues of sexual equality and women's right to work.(1) In many trade union and national labor congresses, the demand for the education and unionization of women workers appears most often to have had a positive goal: to raise women's class consciousness by making them aware of their rights and, thus, no longer an easy prey to capitalist exploitation. Resolutions submitted by workers in congress suggested that a variety of agencies be charged with the task of educating women workers. The resolution of the 1879 congress proposed that women be admitted to all men's labor and political meetings and study circles. At the 1902 FBT congress, delegate Angers asked that mixed commissions be set up in each factory, composed of employers and workers, syndicated and nonsyndicated, men and women. By their participation in the work of these commissions, women would become aware of their exploitation, practiced in articulating their economic demands, and more favorably attracted to unionism.(2)

On the matter of the demoralization of society due to women's employment outside the home, delegates to the early workers' congresses voiced the fear that capitalist exploitation of women had a deleterious effect on the working-class family. The 1894 report to the Congrès National des Syndicats spoke of "the shocking consequences" of women working. It cited the 60 percent mortality rate of babies born to women in the tobacco industry and warned that women's industrial employment was conducive to abortions and sterility, the "social and moral consequences" of which were surely to be "the depopulation and disorganization of the family." The middle class was charged with attempting to destroy the family by taking away its "soul" and throwing the woman "like some beast into the factory" where she could only wind up in the hospital or on the streets.(3) Although dealing with real statistics, workers' resolutions in these early congresses often repeated the tenets of Proudhon. A typical resolution was the one adopted by the Guesdist-dominated FS at its 1888 congress, which asserted that women working was contrary "to the natural role of women in a well-organized society" and the principal cause of "the moral degradation" of women and children. To halt the decay, the resolution called for the preservation and guarantee of motherhood through the suppression of all work outside the home for women with children.(4)

Twisting like a thread throughout the early discussions of women's presence in industry was the Proudhonian theme voicing concern over the changing sexual roles that must occur when women entered the factories in large numbers. This fear was aptly expressed by Marseille typographer Jean Coulet at the inaugural meeting of the Nîmes bourse in 1893. He called for equal pay as a way to end competition. If competition from women were not halted, he declared, there would come a time when women worked and men stayed at home caring for the family--a task he reminded the assembly was "contrary to [man's] character."(5)

Ideological pronouncements were frequently used in the early congresses to buttress arguments for or against women's right to work. A woman worker, Citoyenne Laurent, noted at the founding congress of the FNS in 1886 that men's inadequate salaries brought women into the work force. But even without the demands of necessity, women must work to be independent of men. To that end, Laurent called for equal pay. She concluded her appeal by questioning the Proudhonian notion of sexual spheres:

> if we want to raise the moral level of woman, she must be equal to man. Why can't this be? Is this because nature has made woman that she must die of misery by the insufficiency of her salary? Since she gives her time and her sweat in equal pain with men, [she must have] equal salary. And then you will not fear the competition of women's work which lowers wages.(6)

Such appeals were generally countered by the more conservative workers who based their arguments on Proudhon. A typical response was that of hotel worker Louis Martino at the 1892 congress of the FS. Martino, a Guesdist in his political persuasion, was nevertheless Proudhonian in his attitudes toward women. Women were men's servants, he declared, because their natures disposed them to this function. Despite such expressions of what would be deemed today as sexual chauvinism, the resolution passed at this congress was a model of moderation. It proclaimed that for "moral and social reasons, the place of women is in the foyer and not in the shop," but reluctantly added that in the actual situation created by capitalism, women were forced to work. Therefore there must be equality of wages, an eight-hour day, the abolition of night work for women and children, and a six-week maternity leave before and after delivery.(7)

Well before the first feminist meetings in France the subject of political and civil emancipation was raised in a regional workers' congress by a male delegate. The response to his appeal was mixed. Some applauded; others agreed with another respondent, Darlas, who supported equal education for women, but who claimed that females were too immature for political emancipation. Still another received support for his Proudhonian declaration that nature had made men superior and "women should stay wives and mothers and let men carry on the political struggle." The resolution following the debate was a compromise: it called for women's civil emancipation but withheld support for their political rights.(8)

The resolution passed at the 1879 congress was the most interesting of those framed in the early congresses because it clearly represented an attempt to present a comprehensive plan to deal more realistically with the woman question. Moreover, the resolution adopted, although initially framed in Proudhonian language, represented a clear-cut victory for the Guesdists. The preamble to the resolution began in a traditional vein by saying that men and women were "equivalents in nature" [Proudhon's term], interdependent upon each other for the perpetuation of society. But the resolution then moved away from Proudhon's theory by asserting that both sexes must rule in society through the process of equal division of rights and responsibilities in both the public and private sectors. On that basis, the congress affirmed "the absolute equality [not 'equivalence'] of the two sexes." The resolution recognized that women had the same social and political rights as men, among which was the right to work based on the equal need of both sexes to be producers in order to be consumers. The resolution further avowed that since the faculty of production was equally possessed by both sexes, then the equal pay principle must be rigorously applied. Noting that prejudices restraining woman's freedom were detrimental to her emancipation, the congress declared that women must have the same liberty of action as men. Women's exercise of free choice would give them a sense of responsibility. Espousing the belief that the role one fills in society was a matter of choice, the resolution concluded by saying that woman must not be confined to a particular social sphere, but must take "the role and place [in society] her vocation will assign her."(9)

THE DOUBLE-EDGED ISSUES OF EQUAL PAY AND UNIONISM

The debates carried on in the national congresses of the individual trades followed the same lines as those of the early workers' congresses. Within the professions the call for equal pay was a constant theme. Sometimes the demand for equal wages was seen as a way to reduce women's competition; other times it was regarded as being morally just. Notable in these discussions is that more appeals were made to practical necessity than to ideology. It was only in the Fédération du Livre that the conservative theories of Proudhon stubbornly continued to hold sway.

But its history had made the printers' situation relatively unique. The printers' Proudhonian caste was reinforced by the fact that since 1861 the profession had been fighting a losing battle against the introduction of women into the trade at one-third the wages of men.(10) Then in 1909, a group of women compositors, organized under the direction of wealthy bourgeois feminist Marguerite Durand replaced union printers on strike in Nancy. This jauniste act appears to have provoked an "if-you-can't-fight-'em-join-'em" attitude among the members, and the Federation passed a resolution the following year seemingly opening its ranks to women. On the basis of this Bourdeaux resolution, Emma Couriau, who had worked as a typographer at union scale for over seventeen years, applied for membership to the union. She was refused admission and her typographer husband was expelled from the union for having "forced" his wife to work. The debate over the Couriau affair was widely publicized in the press, causing the printers to become even more defensive of their antifeminism. Smarting from both female competition and bad publicity, the printers regularly found refuge in the support of equal pay as an instrument of sexual exclusion. The unionists believed that if employers had to pay equal wages, they would hi.re men. Then women would be returned to the household where they belonged.(11)

The printers were not alone in opposing women's employment. Groups and individuals within other trades, particularly in industries where competition from women was taking a heavy toll, also believed that equal pay and sexual exclusion were synonymous. In the leather industry, a trade attracting large numbers of women workers, union members regarded the equal pay demand as a way to halt the replacement of men and preferable to forbidding women employment. Jewelers found themselves in equally dire straits due to the fact that the number of employed women had risen by over 40 percent in fewer than forty years. David, a diamond craftsman from the provinces, told delegates to their first congress in 1909 that his profession was so depressed in his area that they were going to have "to call in the Red Cross" to assist them. The resolution following the discussion of women's competition stated that since proletarian women were "condemned" to compete with men, there must be equal pay.(12)

Yet other workers, male and female, regarded the equal pay provision as a matter of simple justice. A Paris bootmaker, Saulnier, pointed out in congress that because some women preferred "a certain independence of their personalities to the familial foyer" there must be equal wages. At a national meeting of tobacco workers, a trade in which women outnumbered men by almost nine times, Madame Jacobi protested that women had always been paid "a stupid salary" under the pretext that theirs was only a supplemental income. But the woman with children bore the same expense as a male head of the family, so salaries must be equal.(13)

Competition for wages was not the sole reason for wanting to exclude women from the professions. Some printers believed that women were too placid, too docile, hence useless to unionism. "She will cry," said typographer Sergent of Paris, "but she will never think of making a movement of resistance or of seeing the means which would render this resistance possible." A woman delegate to an 1889 hatters' congress stated that women had not yet learned the principles of solidarity. Male members of the same union complained several years later that women too frequently joined employer organizations, and then when they did join workers' syndicats, they did not want to pay dues!(14)

Moral pronouncements directed against women working were a familiar theme at all the trade congresses. Baker Henri Grégoire, himself orphaned at the age of three, complained that working women contributed to human degeneration because their children were raised in the streets. A Paris compositor, Moret, in 1883 opposed the admission of women into the profession even on an equal pay basis because it was immoral and unnatural for women to work. Recalling "the beautiful words of Proudhon," Moret

solemnly noted that woman is to be "the mother, the
companion in the world of workers." Her eviction from the
workshop was the only way she could attain her dignity.(15)

The implementation of the equal pay demand was not the
only way suggested to keep women home tending to their
casseroles. Dijonnaise delegates to the 1885 printers'
congress announced that when a local publishing house
declared its intention to hire women, "the confrères left
the house." Apparently others did the same. Between 1890
and 1908, 56 recorded strikes were staged by workers
demanding the dismissal of women. Milder courses were also
suggested. A printer thought the problem of women's
competition could be solved through the process of
absorption: "each male typographer would marry a female
typographer," and then forbid his mate to work!(16) There is
no record of his idea being implemented to any major extent.

As with the equal pay issue, the question of organizing
women was another two-edged sword. Among hatmakers in 1887,
when women were rapidly replacing men as basters,
syndicalist organization was regarded as the only way to
mitigate the effects of their competition. At that year's
convention, Frédéric Favreau of Paris suggested lowering
union dues so as to attract women members. Yet other groups
believed that unionism was a positive rather than an
exclusionary device. The 1910 report to the printers'
federation warned that it was folly to chase women from the
unions. The better course would be to make allies of them.
"Convinced of our good faith and our cordial camaraderie,"
the report noted, "she will be our most precious auxiliary,
instead of serving the designs of the boss against our
interests." Lithographers in 1913 admitted women to the
federation and levied equal dues on them, not only to ensure
the stability of their membership, but to provide women
workers with a maternity fund. Secretary Gervason of the
clothing workers expressed no ulterior motives when he
called for women to unionize, except that they were
exploited worse than men and needed the protection provided
them from union membership.(17)

Throughout all the congresses, one can see evidence of
men bowing to the inevitable. Despite the entrenched
conservatism of the printers, at each one of their national
congresses some member voiced support for women in the
profession and the union. The assertion that women do not
belong in the factory was sound theoretically, stated Victor
Vandeputte in a 1911 report to the textile workers, "but in
a capitalist regime, it is an impractical thing, for capital
employment and the development of machinery industrialize
women more and more." With that view in mind, his report
called for passage of the English week, that is a 5 1/2-day
work schedule, because women had to perform "la corvée du
ménage" after their day's employment, and thus had little
time to rest or take care of their husbands. To believe
that women could be expelled from industry was "a platonic
idea," leatherworkers were warned in a 1900 report submitted
by Victor Griffuelhes. Women's employment was "a factor in

the   system   of   production"   which   no   human   law   could
prevent.(18)

THE CGT TAKES UP THE QUESTION

      The official stance of the CGT was a reflection of the
variety   of   attitudes expressed by its member unions. From
its founding, the CGT had called for equal participation of
the sexes.   But it was not until the 1898 Rennes congress
that the woman question was raised officially.   The Rennes
debate   is   interesting for the extremity of ideas expressed
and remedies suggested. The issue of equal pay was seen by
some   as   a   way   to   prevent men's replacement by women; by
others as a way to remunerate women fairly for their   labor.
By   still   others, the equal pay principle was regarded as a
means by which to keep employers from   realizing   a   profit.
The organization of women was generally conceived of as
being necessary for preventing the exploitation of both
sexes.   Only   one   delegate, bootmaker Lacaille, voiced the
belief that syndicalism was a way to exclude women from the
labor force.   His suggestion was not at all connected to the
warning of another delegate, Larsonneur of the Parisian
brushmakers' union, who noted that women in his industry,
earning 30 to 40 percent less than men, had rejected all
attempts to unionize them because they knew their employer
would only hire men if they had to pay equal salaries.
      Solutions   presented   at   Rennes also tended to revolve
around two extremes. On the one hand was the suggestion of
delegate Roche of the cab drivers' union of the Seine, that
women be given equal salary, paid maternity leaves, and that
the syndicats should seek the political and civil   equality
of women.   Needless to say, his proposal received only mild
support.   But less support was forthcoming for the
resolutions of the spokesmen of the other extreme, chief of
whom were the printers, who made their usual demands to
exclude women from the unions and the workshops. An attempt
to reflect all opinions, the resolution adopted by the
congress was a pragmatic statement. It began by repeating
Proudhon's notion that "In all milieux, we intend to
propagate the idea that men must support women," but then
conceded   that   if women must work, the equal pay formula
should be applied.(19)
      The woman question was not again addressed in the CGT
until 1900, when it received a spirited hearing as a result
of a discussion by the delegates over the slow growth of
syndicalism in general. Delegates to that Paris convention
were filled with a sense of promise that the new century
symbolized,   and confident of their value because the Paris
Exposition had attracted people from all over the world to
admire the work of the producing class. In that mood,
unionists were anxious to overcome the "nonchalance" of the
French   workers, increase union membership, and heighten the
sense of working-class solidarity. The need to build unity
was hampered, however, as long as a third of the working

class was treated as inferior by the unions themselves. Speaking on this issue was precision instrument maker Briat of Paris, who angrily accused men of perpetuating this inequity: "Haven't we always considered women inferior beings, and haven't we excluded them from the unions? We must admit women and make them understand that they are all our equals and that if they are capable of doing the same work as we, they must receive the same salary." Responding to Briat's accusation of antifeminism, the congress appointed a committee to study the question of women's right to work. The specific demands subsequently presented for delegates' approval were routine. But the preamble to the resolution reveals the workers' growing sense of impotence concerning the presence of women in industry. Although all agreed that women's employment was bad for the working class from a moral, physical, and economic point of view, the resolution began, it was not in the workers' power to change things.(20)

The addendum to the resolution's passage is also noteworthy. Accompanied by vigorous applause, Citoyenne Bouvard of the artificial-flower makers' union of Paris informed the Rennes delegates that when men make enough money, mothers "will ask for no more than to remain in the family, as certain militants desire of her." Her declaration brought the objection of railroad worker Eugène Guérard, who pointed out that women would be free only when they became the mistresses of their wages and independent from their husbands. This interjection of support stiffened Bouvard's radical resolve, for she closed her discussion by demanding to know how "the revolution that we dream of" was to be made if women did not work.(21)

After 1900 the fear of women as a competitive force was no longer an official concern voiced by the CGT. Beset with the triple task of purging the movement of all varieties of reformism, of "civilizing" the numerous anarchists who were joining the organization, and of trying to achieve unity with the FBT, the CGT allowed its interest in the woman question to wane for several years. When the organization again took up the subject, perhaps in response to the renewed interest by the socialists in treating the woman question, syndicalists were no longer concerned with how to return the wife to the fireside. Instead they were wondering how to attract her to the union halls.

At the congress of Toulouse in 1910, for instance, Comrade Amblart, representing a union of women printers in Marseille, requested admission to the CGT as an isolated union with consultative powers. For ten months, she pointed out, these women had been seeking affiliation from the typographers' and lithographers' federations. She feared the lengthy impasse would affect the viability of her group, which she said was "a syndicat on the move." More to the point, Amblart reminded her fellow workers that unionism could scarcely hope to realize its own ambitions if it continued "to thrust sticks in the spokes of the wheels" every time a group of women attempted to organize. After

giving Amblart a hearty round of applause, not only for her
rhetoric but also for the success of her union in including
within its membership the margeuses [paperfeeders] of the
trade--a feat which no group of men "more advanced in
syndicalism" had been able to accomplish--the delegates
unanimously voted to admit the Marseille group to the CGT,
not in a consultative position, but with a deliberative
voice in the organization.(22)
    In the last full congress held before the war, the
subject of women working was once more discussed, but again
peripherally to other questions. The 1912 commission report
on the conquest of the English week, which had become an
important CGT goal by this time, cited the moral impact the
reduction of hours would have on the family if women had
Saturday afternoons free. Not mentioned in the report, but
certainly evident by the later propaganda posters, was the
fact that the campaign for the English week was regarded by
the organization as a union-recruiting device for women.
To accomplish that end, another suggestion was made that the
establishment of a treasury providing women with paid
maternity leaves was an excellent way to attract mothers to
the CGT. But the graver question of work for women was
relegated to a commission for further study.(23) By the time
the next congress convened in 1919, the war had changed the
nature of the debate on the woman question.

EQUALITY, NOT FEMINISM

    Besides receiving a hearing in the labor congresses,
the question of women working was also reviewed in numerous
editions of the working-class press.(24) Although a host of
issues was raised, a sampling of the attitudes toward women
taken from a few of the papers demonstrates that the
fundamental question dealing with women's place in society
and the most effective means to achieve their liberation was
articulated in all shades of revolutionary opinion. What is
important to note is that the dialogue on the woman question
tended to move over time from the abstract to the
particular, from idealism to realism, and from a discussion
of women in a hypothetical position in society to a series
of debates revolving around questions that presuppose the
fact of women's presence in the industrial system.
    The paper Le Libertaire, published by Sébastien Faure
from 1885 to 1907, during the period when anarchists were
moving into and influencing the syndicalist movement,
devoted a great deal of space to the woman question.
Because libertarianism was posited on the theory of the
perfect equality of beings, anarchists naturally supposed
that women's emancipation was necessary for the full
development of human freedom. In the earliest years of the
paper's publication, contributors to Le Libertaire often
wrote on the subject of marriage as a major instrument of
women's psychological exploitation. Marriage was a tool of
male tyranny because it forced "a degrading tutelage" upon

women. One writer wryly noted that the only benefit to be derived from the institution was that the man was saved the price of supporting both a maid and a mistress. The danger from this exploitative relationship, the anarchists preached, was that as "the servant of love" woman was unable to express "her thoughts, her desires, her tastes, her moi." She became unconscious of the inequities of the society in which she lived and voluntarily accepted her subservient role.(25)

The first step to women's psychological emancipation, anarchists believed, occurred in free unions through which women's personality and independence could naturally blossom. The children conceived from these unions, professed Laurentine Sauvray, would carry within them "the elements of a harmonious development," thereby providing the basis for a nonauthoritarian society to evolve in which woman would be "the equal of man; relieved of all care, loved with intelligence and disinterest, . . . and in possession of a liberated brain."(26)

It is interesting to note that despite the fact that Proudhon is regarded as being the philosophical grandfather of anarchism, generally his attitudes about women were firmly disavowed by contributors to Le Libertaire. In a lengthy article published in 1899, Louis Grandidier took admirers of Proudhon to task. Proudhon had charged that women did not understand the concepts of justice and sought only to gain distinction over everyone else. He had cited as an example the fact that women would give sexual favors to the boss in return for special privileges. The example was incorrect, Grandidier charged, because when a woman did respond to the caresses of "a satyr of the atelier" it was only because she knew that if she rejected his advances, she would be thrown into the street. To believe that women were trapped in an intellectually inferior state from which they could not leave, Grandidier continued, was to follow the dictates of the church fathers who had based these conclusions on all "the nonsense of Eden." To the charge that women raised from one vice necessarily fall into another, Grandidier responded by saying that not even Proudhon took such an idea seriously. Women were not the cause of social evil, he concluded, but participants in society's transformation.(27)

After 1900, and the first feminist conferences on political emancipation, newspaper coverage increasingly turned away from discussing women as creators of society, liberated by free unions and education, to matters at hand: the feminist movement. For many contributors to the paper, the immorality of marriage became less threatening than the immorality of politics.

In a series of articles, E. Gérault charged that feminism had distorted the relations between the sexes. Women now wanted "to ape the bestiality of man," not the least of which was that "engendered by politics." Or women were seeking to enter into "a direct antagonism with men" as the means to their own development. But cooperation with men was the way women could become strong enough to combat "the harmful currents of religion, mysticism, and politics." Gérault herself seems to have gained a more liberated view of women as the series wore on. In the first issue she declared that women's best role was that of educating their children. By the fifth number she was admitting that women did not have to remain at home; they had the right to enter any profession they chose, but must unionize in order to receive equitable wages and to assist in furthering the revolution. Unless women had the chance to become animated by "a consciousness of revolt," Gérault concluded, they would never join with their companions "to storm the economic Bastille."(28)

The evils of feminism were denounced in another series in 1904 written by Henri Duchmann. Feminism, he said, was "a reactionary, conservative, and exclusivist" movement. The feminist was seeking to combat her husband, not marriage. By demanding equality, women were only antagonizing the battle of the sexes. Nelly Roussel, a member of the Groupe de la Solidarité des Femmes, responded swiftly to Duchmann's charges. Feminists were demanding economic independence only because it was the source of all other freedom, she declared. To that end, they were seeking equal pay, the right to work, control over the decision to have children, and for those who chose motherhood, a maternity wage so they might remain at home to care for their families.

Duchmann's rebuttal sought to demolish Roussel and her cause, if not by reasoned argument, then by ridicule. The feminists' plank demanding payment for maternal labor would only extend the state's power and encourage the evils of Malthusianism by the procreation of more children. Obviously it was nonsense that women would believe they could be freed from exploitation through "the lucrativeness of confinement." Roussel's "Last Response" in the succeeding issue effectively ended the antifeminist aspect of the debate. Not enough men had been educated regarding the degree of women's abuse, and feminists feared that women would be assigned the same role in future society as the one they now filled. Using Marx as a sanction for feminism, Roussel concluded her argument:

> Feminism is not the work of this or that individual. It is--as other movements of ideas--created solely by the forces of things, because it was necessary; and it will similarly disappear the day when it will become useless, that is to say, the day when woman will have conquered in the world the place she demands and which belongs to her.

Duchmann's response took an entirely different tack. Women were necessary to the revolution, he conceded, because the new society could not be built without them. But since revolutionary propaganda had tended to regard women as "a

negligible quantity," he announced he would undertake a
complete study of the woman question in order to determine
"what limits capitalist society [imposed] on her integral
development" and how her revolutionary energies might be
brought to bear in the name of social change. For the next
three issues, Duchmann played upon the traditional anarchist
themes of the immorality of marriage and the middle class,
carefully ignoring any further reference to feminism. By
the fourth issue Duchmann moved to even safer ground and
stopped tendering any further opinions on the woman
question.(29)
     In the waning years of its existence, Le Libertaire
dealt with more practical issues concerning women. One of
these was to voice opposition to the law prohibiting night
work on the grounds that it was a violation of women's right
to work. Additionally, the law would only further degrade
women because it would effectively exclude them from the
work force and turn them into "ladies of the night" in order
that they might support their children.(30)
     The last reference to women in Le Libertaire was a
sardonic piece written by G. Roussel calling again for
economic equality. All that wailing about returning women
to the foyer, she noted, treated them as if they were
"vestal virgin[s] conserving the sacred flame." Yet the
reality of women's existence was far from enviable:
employers paid them less because they were not the sole
support of their families; economic fatalities transformed
them into beasts of burden; and the infamous Code placed
them in "a state of moral inferiority." But while they were
waiting for their brains--and the new era--to evolve,
Roussel wryly concluded, women could demand equality of
suffering with men.(31)
     While not devoting as much space to the woman question
as Le Libertaire, the paper La Guerre Sociale, published by
Gustave Hervé, occasionally dealt with issues affecting
women.(32) Following its commitment to avoid theoretical
discussions, the paper's first article on women was a
plain-spoken attack on Marguerite Durand on the occasion of
Durand's appointment to the government's newly created
Women's Labor Office. Durand's feminist stance had been
relatively brief but intense. In 1900 she had been the
chief organizer of the Congres International de la Condition
et des Droits des Femmes, which had attracted delegates to
Paris from all over the world to recognize feminism
officially. Under Durand's influence the congress had
devoted as much attention to the plight of working women as
it had to the call for political and social equality. Her
daily paper, La Fronde, not only preached the natural link
existing between bourgeois feminism and female
proletarianism (the latter being those who would "make the
revolution for their bourgeois sisters"), but it was a
continual champion of the formation of female unions.
Durand herself had been instrumental in forming four unions
before 1900.(33)

Durand's middle-class background, her wealth, her connections to the government, her influence with women, all served to earn for her the undying enmity of working-class males. Carrying on the tradition, the article in La Guerre Sociale pointed out that Durand was the same one who had sent female scabs to break up the Nancy strike. She was also a woman whose credits were highly suspect, for she was "ex-director of La Fronde, ex-general of Tricoteuses de France, ex-codirectress of L'Action, former wife of Deputy Langerre, old intimate friend of Madame de Rothschild, old friend of Perivier, old friend of Viviani, old--what hasn't the woman done?" Now this woman of "remarkable intellect" but of "doubtful morality," La Guerre Sociale reminded its readers, was the predominant voice in the court of the ministry on the labor question.(34)

Although more involved with the causes of antimilitarism, by 1912 even La Guerre Sociale was making an effort to recruit women to the workers' movement. In the 21 August issue appeared the announcement that a woman's corner was going to be a regular feature of the paper, beginning with the following issue. How many times, comrades, have you tried to interest your companion in our cause, the editors queried, and have been told that "there is nothing in La Guerre Sociale for us." Aware that their "masculine preoccupations" usually had caused them to overlook the ladies, the editors intended to correct the oversight with the publication of this new column.(35) Despite the fanfare, however, the articles subsequently written by Citoyenne Fanny Clar were only vignettes, scarcely touching the issues of women's emancipation. By 1914, with the paper in financial trouble and more involved in waging war against the three-year draft law, both Clar and the column were gone.

FROM FOYER TO UNION HALL

The issues dealt with, the opinions expressed, the conclusions drawn in La Guerre Sociale and Le Libertaire tended to be the same as those reflected in the official paper of the CGT, La Voix du Peuple. Although this latter paper carried an exuberant fraternal salute to the ladies in the first issue, and the promise to give them a large space in its pages, the bulk of the early coverage by La Voix du Peuple of the woman question was confined generally to those questions affecting working women. Most of the paper's message was that unionism was the sole route to women's liberation. But ideological treatises were also few: the theme of "la femme au foyer" was advanced only once, in 1902--by a woman columnist!(36)

Occasionally the editors used their support of women's right to work and to organize less out of a concern for women than for union politics. In 1908 an editorial appeared taking "the brave typographers" of Lille to task for threatening to strike in protest over the employment of a woman with over twenty years of professional experience. Workers must realize that syndicalism was past the stage of having entrance requirements, the editors lectured, because all were exploited without distinction of age, sex, or nationality. Behind this reminder of the nature of syndicalism was a more frankly political message, however. The Fédération du Livre had consistently spearheaded the drive for proportional representation and called for political affiliation with the SFIO. The aim of the article reminding readers of the corporate nature of syndicalism was less to defend women's right to work than it was to discredit the reformist wing of the syndicalist movement. The Lille affair, readers were told, and the typographers' policy of exclusion, which was narrow and particularist in its vision, were just another example of the antediluvian tendencies inherent in reformist thinking.(37)

Thereafter the newspaper published no more important articles on the woman question until 1912, when it turned again to the plight of women as part of the paper's drive for the English week. These articles were interesting because their starting point was the acceptance of women's employment outside the home. The Saturday repose would benefit the entire family, but the campaign for the shorter week was regarded by the paper as a device to recruit women to CGT membership. Not only would the ranks of the movement be filled, but because women would accompany their husbands to meetings, union participation would also contribute to the growth of women's own intellectual freedom and social knowledge.(38)

By 1913 membership considerations and the need to gain supporters for the CGT's heightened antimilitarist campaign also spurred the paper to take more positive stands on the woman issue. That year, Georges Yvetot, writing under the name "Georges Allombre," firmly upheld women's right to work. The "stupid vanity" of some men caused them to regard women as their enemy. Such attitudes, he warned, only increased competition and exploitation of all workers. Further, he noted, if the man is a wage slave, woman is "the slave of the slave. She does not complain. She accepts, the unhappy one, this burden of unequal life, deprived of her social worth, because social and moral prejudices have made in her a deplorable mentality." Even if she were fortunate enough to remain at home, life was neither less difficult nor more gay, because even in the foyer women are reduced "to humiliating passivity." Therefore it was unjust to restrain the individual liberty of women, for whom work was the only means to a life free from dependence upon a man. If syndicalists believed that women were to be the equal of man in a communist regime, he concluded, then she must be given a place "in the ranks for conquering happiness."(39)

Bringing women to syndicalism would not be easy. Georges Dumoulin pleaded for women to overcome their admittedly justified suspicions toward union membership and

join the struggle.(40)   In 1913   Alphonse Merrheim urged men
to shed their masculine prejudices and join with women
militants in recruiting working women to the unions.(41)
     It was the Couriau affair, along with feminism, which
spurred debates in La Voix du Peuple regarding women and
syndicalism, particularly after feminist organizations took
up the woman lithographer's plight.   In numerous articles
written by school teacher Marie Guillot, a militant unionist
and feminist, the CGT was denounced as irrelevant because of
its silence on the issue of women.   Guillot warned the
unions that if women were refused a hearing within the ranks
of labor they would be forced to depend on those groups
organized by the bourgeoisie.(42)
     The responses to Guillot's series were written by
members of the Fédération du Livre.   Their arguments are
interesting because they reveal less of a Proudhonian
concern that women's natures required them to remain at home
than an abiding interest in practical economics and union
politics.   One respondent, a printer signed A. Hagmann,
outlined his union's position.   It was easy for militants
who had never suffered from the incursion of women into
their trade to call the typographers "egotists," he charged.
But he was sure that if they had to battle within their
professions the influx of women who worked for lower wages
and under any conditions, these detractors would change
their attitudes.   The printers' federation, Hagmann firmly
asserted, was a force which "must be placed at the service
of the defense of its members."   Women must either be
unionized and receive the same wages as men, or be
considered as "outside of us and forcefully against us."
     From the exigencies of practical unionism, Hagmann
concluded his letter on a Proudhonian note.   It was not
utopian to say that woman's place was in the home, he
insisted, for it is in the foyer that man receives the balm
to treat "the mortal wounds" made during the day.   But if
his companion is too tired to fulfill her "natural role as
comforter" then the husband would have to seek elsewhere for
sympathy and the family would disintegrate.   If men would
only accept as a basic truth the reality that the home was
the only place for women, they would then be forced to
demand better wages in order to support their
households.(43)
     Hagmann's article prompted a rejoinder from Emily
Couriau, who took issue with the printer's suggestion that
women be paid equally even before they joined the union.   To
do so would hamper the growth of syndicalism.(44) The
dialogue that might have continued could have proven
fascinating.   Unfortunately, Madame Couriau's answer to
Hagmann appeared in the last issue of the CGT's official
public forum to be published before the war.

A NEW GAUGE OF VICTORY

Behind all the rhetoric, what are the conclusions to be drawn regarding anarchosyndicalism's response to women workers? The most apparent is that an evolution in thinking did occur, away from exclusionism and toward a commitment to accept women into trade unions. More often than not, as has been noted, union politics rather than a primary concern for women's plight was the motivation for such enlightenment.

Outside pressures, such as the struggle against the extension of the draft law, proved to be an impetus for stepping-up the drive to welcome women into the syndicalist fold. Another important pressure was feminism, which was initially dismissed as a nonsensical battle by bourgeois women for control of political power. To revolutionary syndicalists, with their anarchist underpinnings, the vote was a worthless prize and one destined for extinction with the success of the revolution. However, the short-lived liaison between socialism and feminism, the feminist organizations' defense of Emma Couriau, and the actions of the Frondeuses forced syndicalists to regard feminism as a real and present danger.

Affinities with feminists were recognized by socialist women, who began their collaboration by sharing the same camp with their bourgeois sisters in the battle for equal pay, minimum wages, and against the regulative legislation being discussed and passed in the Chamber. From there it was only a short march to the acceptance of the similarities existing between sexual antagonism and class conflict. Even though the attempt to unite feminists from both classes broke down almost at once, socialist women never stopped brandishing the threat of a feminist alliance as a means to achieve economic justice.(45)

The perceived danger to which syndicalists responded the most acutely was that posed by Marguerite Durand and the group organized around her newspaper. Dismissed initially as "a dry fart" by the syndicalist press, she and her Frondeuses became the object of more sober considerations after the Nancy strike.(46) There were still voices being raised at workers' congresses in support of unionism for women as an innoculation against the virus of jaunisme long after Madame Durand and her Fronde had ceased to be a threat.

Less dramatic than feminism or Frondisme were the threats made to corporate and class unity by the numerous confessional or employer-sponsored unions organized in the wake of the publication of the papal encyclical letters known as Rerum Novarum in 1891, a document upholding the dignity of labor and decrying class conflict. The first mixed union was established by a Jesuit the following year for women employed in the needlecraft and clothing trades. It was based on "the familial spirit reigning between patrons and their employees" in the corporations of the Middle Ages. Yet, it seemed more in keeping with Proudhon in its demand for cooperative restaurants, municipal banks, and workshops for the unemployed.(47) Although these mixed unions never posed much of a threat to revolutionary syndicalism, having by 1912 only 40,000 members, one-fifth of whom were women, the unions organized under the porch of the Church did constitute a force with which to be reckoned.(48) The natural reticence of women to organize was overcome in these Catholic unions, where women were not berated for being evil instruments of competition, where they were comforted by the union's opposition to the class struggle and the alleged violence of direct action, and welcomed as a force for pacification between capital and labor.(49) The success of Catholic syndicalism was evidenced in the membership figures of 1912. While women affiliates to the CGT numbered only 101,000 in 1911 (a bare one-tenth that of male members), over 85,000 women, based primarily in large manufacturing centers, belonged to Catholic syndicats.(50)

Nor did these movements ignore the wives and daughters of the peasantry, for whom the laws protecting agricultural workers did not apply, and who, like their city sisters, worked the same hours as men for one-half the pay.(51) At the end of the century, the syndical movement under La Société des Agriculteurs de France (SAF) and L'Union Centrale des Syndicats des Agriculteurs de France (UCSAF), a Catholic group, began making real inroads into organizing the peasantry. This latter organization, under the guiding genius of the Catholic aristocrat the Comte de Rocquigny, made its bid to attract rural farm laborers by framing its message in the language of Proudhon, a language the rural farm laborer could understand. The UCSAF preached that the union must be "the soul of order." The peasant was praised for being "an enemy of novelty" and a zealous patriot, firmly attached to private property and the practitioner of a paternalism that would have made Proudhon envious. The family was the most important social group, ran the pronouncements, for it "unites and forms a city, the city forms a nation, the nations united form humanity." The embryo of this humanity was the father, who was the provider and thus, the leader. Not forgetting the peasant woman, in 1911 a ladies' section was formed in the UCSAF. Far from aiming at raising consciousness, however, the organizational efforts of the ladies' section were directed toward establishing mutuals for dowries and trousseaux, as well as schools to teach scientific housekeeping to women who spent their days in the fields.(52) The only future offered the peasant wife was one in which she would be remanded to the foyer, where she is "a queen" and wherein she would realize equality. In the home, the ladies were told, "all women are equal because they find there the same joys."(53)

A respectable concentration in industrial areas of women workers seeking the preservation of social peace through a détente forged between capitalism and labor posed a serious problem to the development of class consciousness. More threatening still to the success of the impending

revolution was the presence of a cadre of women in the
countryside who aspired only to be housewives! It is not
surprising, therefore, that the CGT, which from its
inception had sought to develop an acceptable philosophy to
attract agricultural workers to its cause, began after 1905
to develop a program dedicated to enlisting the aid of the
peasant women to its side.

Women's activity in strikes was another reason for
gradually recognizing women's value to syndicalism. At
their 1905 congress, for instance, printers heard from
Comrade Fraut of Belfort that the entry of women into the
unions was not so dangerous as many believed. Women
involved in strikes at Vizille and Héricourt had shown
themselves to be as courageous as men, he noted. Hatmakers
in 1912 were told that women's involvement in solidarity
strikes with men had resulted in raises for all. The 1904
report of the ceramics workers noted that a group of
unorganized decal workers had struck at Limoges. As a
result of trade union assistance, these women had organized
into a <u>syndicat</u> that now numbered two hundred. Because
women were not afraid "to throw themselves also into the
battle and share with [men] the pains and wounds of the same
combat," the president of the clothing workers' union in
1912 announced that women's presence at the congress and in
the unions represented "a new gauge of victory" and "a moral
encouragement" to all workers.(54)

Women's support of their husbands' strike activity was
also important. Their combativeness was encouraged, not
only as a way to boost their husbands' morale, but as a
gauge of the intensity of the workers' commitment to the
strike. As a result, women were applauded for picketing,
heading parades, or manning the strike office. They were
also praised for their more violent manifestations, such as
breaking into factories, lying across railroad tracks or in
front of soldiers, or as in the case of the good women of
Molières in 1890, for making a public example of a would-be
strikebreaker by pulling down his pants and spanking him on
his bare bottom.(55) The encouragement of female militancy
is not surprising. As the general strike came to be adopted
by the CGT as the primary instrument of revolution, women's
support of and participation in strikes became vital to the
success of that revolution.

What of the role of Proudhonian ideology in inspiring
syndicalism's attitudes toward women? As has been
demonstrated, Proudhon came to be cited less frequently and
then almost not at all in the press and at the congresses
than did the ideas of Marx and Guesde, Engels and Bebel.(56)
The fact that syndicalists could pragmatically abandon any
ideology that did not square with their ideas of the present
and future is evidenced by the anarchists. Although in tune
with much of Proudhon's thinking, they completely rejected
his ideas about women as being an inhibiting force to their
psychological and social emancipation. In fact, the only
group who consistently invoked Proudhon were the Christian
and independent syndicalists. Clearly, as time went on

syndicalism's pragmatic sense grew apace. The intrusion of the machine widened the gulf between the industrializing present and the artisanal past. In terms of the woman question at least, the ideal of Proudhon's little woman in the foyer no longer squared with the reality of a labor force composed of over one-third women.

Pragmatism increasingly came to rule the day over ideology. The organization of women was regarded as a practical response to a stubborn reality. Women did work in horrible conditions. Generally they were not far removed from the countryside and the tradition of cottage industry as a means to supplement the father's or husband's wages. Used to working, women tended to take whatever factory job they could get under whatever conditions were offered. This was because they were passively accustomed from preindustrial times to see job roles and lower wages as natural and to regard their time in the work force as temporary. Women did not "define their lives through their work," as Patricia Branca notes. Nor did they lose their primary identification with the family.(57) As a result, even though female workers in some industries, such as the clothing and tobacco trades, tended to be militant, most women were reluctant to participate in union activity, since that seemed nonessential to those who believed they were going to work for only a few years.(58)

Moreover, women did work for half the wages because mechanization of many operations allowed them to perform the same tasks as men had done previously without benefit of long apprenticeships and with virtually no training. Their competition did depress wages in every instance where they were able to enter the labor market in sufficient quantity. So unionism was the only way to halt the cycle of wage depression set off by women's employment. Further, working women did give birth to stillborns and rachitic babies. Children were raised in the streets. Stockings did not get mended or stews salted. In the face of this shocking reality, the traditional Frenchman's ideal household could be conjured up by both the syndicalists and the socialists to present a graphic indictment, not so much of working women, but of the bourgeoisie, whose tentacles of corruption reached even into the workers' homes.

In point of fact, syndicalism's increasing commitment to unionize women, as evidenced in its press and congresses, was motivated by a threefold purpose. It was ideologically sound, for it was the actualization of the Marxist-Guesdist assertion that the revolution would be accomplished when women were liberated. It was pragmatic, for the organization of women with its mandate that they work for union scale was a matter of practical survival. It was a revolutionary act: unionism raised women workers' class consciousness. Further, as with the implementation of the eight-hour day and the English week, unionism for women was regarded by many revolutionaries as a direct assault on the storehouses of capitalism. Was the movement successful? Not in returning women to their foyers, certainly. The

mobilization of women during the war meant that females
flooded into the work force and moved once again into jobs
traditionally reserved for men. Many may have thought that
women's working career would extend only for the duration,
but widowhood and the high postwar cost of living kept many
wives and mothers at their machines after the armistice. In
1921 there were over 250,000 more women employed in
nonagricultural professions than there had been in 1906.(59)
     That increase in employment brought between a 16 to 38
percent rise in real wages, compared with a 25 percent gain
for men. The higher wages did not occur solely through the
generosity of the capitalists, for the increase in women's
union membership and participation in strike activity served
as a catalyst to improving their working situation.(60)
Despite men's reservations, the number of organized women
tripled in France between 1900 and 1914, while worldwide the
number only doubled.(61) The war years heightened union
participation. In 1921, an unusually low year for
unionization generally, over 15 percent of the female work
force were union members--almost double the number of
1914.(62) The increase in activity at the grassroots level
spilled over into the organizational life of the unions.
Women were given more room on the executive trade councils
and at the podiums of trade congresses. These gains
registered in the postwar period resulted from a combination
of forces occasioned by war: women's persistence in wanting
to maintain their positions in industry, men's realization
that women's suffering equaled theirs, and the dramatic loss
in CGT membership due to the schism resulting from the
question of adherence to the Third International.(63) In
response to the loss of members, women became the target of
another membership drive conducted under the auspices of
Germaine Jouhaux as secretary of a newly organized
Commission on the Study of Women. The spur to the drive was
the CGT's campaign for the minimum wage, an issue designed
to attract women's attention.(64)
     More important to the increase in women's syndical
activity than immediate pressures was the ongoing evolution
in attitudes evident within syndicalism itself. This change
was apparent long before the war; the national emergency
served only as a catalyst to its finalization. In 1866 the
French delegate to the First International had insisted that
women be routed from the workshops and returned to the
foyer. In 1919 even the crusty secretary of the Fédération
du Livre, Auguste Keufer, was moved to admit before a
congress of the brotherhood that "some of the criticisms
addressed to women no longer have the same validity today"
because women's activism demonstrated that "the female
mentality had undergone an appreciable change." Therefore it
would behoove the printers to accept women into the
professions and the unions. Apparently the male mentality
had also changed, for the confrères heeded Keufer's
advice.(65)
     The commitment to carry out the revolution caused
syndicalists to take up the woman question as a means to

build union membership and revolutionary commitment. The increased numbers of women union members amplified syndicalism's strength. The pressure from the unions, in turn, was largely responsible for the passage of legislation to improve women's conditions. During the first quarter of the twentieth century, laws were adopted that reduced the work day, abolished night work, established the English week, allowed women the right to dispose of their own wages and have their own bank accounts, provided for factory inspection, safety requirements, maternity leaves, nursing furloughs, day nurseries in many factories, and even equal pay in some professions.(66) Of course, the victory was only relative. Syndicalism never did enlist even a respectable proportion of women into its ranks. Suffrage continued to be denied. The grossest vestige of sexism--the unequal salary--remained, with few exceptions, a persistent fact of life.

In the light of the demands of twentieth-century feminists, therefore, the movement must be judged a failure. But syndicalism cannot be measured solely by the yardstick of the present's social inadequacies or goals. Because syndicalists recognized the need to include women in the struggle for a just society, concrete changes in organizational attitudes and policies did occur. The woman question, however reluctantly and for whatever motives, was addressed. The worst abuses toward society's "most disinherited" began to be alleviated. In view of the reality of women's economic competition and organizational apathy, and of the centuries of intellectual, social, and legal paternalism, the success of revolutionary syndicalism as an agent of working-class interests must be measured according to the progress of the movement within its own time.

NOTES

1. See Madeleine Guilbert, Les femmes et l'organisation syndicale avant 1914 (Paris, 1966), pp. 11-17 for a discussion of the number of women moving into industry, particularly into those trades that traditionally had been reserved for men.

2. Suggestions and resolutions made at the following congresses: Séances du congrès ouvrier socialiste de France . . . (Marseille, 1879), pp. 161, 199; Dixième congrès national des bourses du travail de France et des colonies . . . (Algeria, 1902), p. 100.

3. Report on the exploitation of women in industry before the 6(e) congrès national des syndicats de France, compte rendu (Nantes, 1894), pp. 80, 122-123.

4. Fédération nationale des syndicats . . . troisième congrès national (Bordeaux, 1888), p. 14.

5.   Souvenir de l'inauguration de la nouvelle bourse du
travail (Nîmes, 1893), pp. 18-19. The notion of reciprocal
economic functions of husband and wife as producers and
consumers was expressed in the Mémoire d'un ouvrier de Paris
of Pierre Bruno, who died in 1872. Armand Audiganne, ed.
(Paris, 1875). On the woman's role, Bruno stated that each
had a division of tasks: "the husband must earn and the
woman must dispense." P. 153.

6.   Congrès national des syndicats ouvriers . . .
Compte rendu officiel [1886] (Lyon, 1887,), p. 218.

7.   Congress of the FS [Marseille, 1892] reported in
Guilbert, Les femmes et l'organisation syndicale, pp.
156-157.

8.   Congrès ouvrier régional de Bordeaux (Bordeaux,
1880), pp. 10-13, 18.

9.   Congrès ouvrier socialiste [Marseille, 1879], p.
199.

10.   Confédération Générale du Travail, La
confédération générale du travail et le mouvement syndical
(Paris, 1925), pp. 396-398 on the background of the effect
of women in the profession. Hereafter referred to as La CGT
et le mouvement syndical.

11.   Charles Sowerwine, "Workers and Women in France
Before 1914: The Debate Over the Couriau Affair," Journal of
Modern History 55 (September 1983): 411-440. Madeleine
Guilbert records Louis Couriau's response to his having been
expelled from the union. Sounding like a liberated husband,
or an untypically French one, Louis declared in his own
defense that he had not forced his wife to work. He did not
have the right to do so, he admitted. Besides, even if he
had wanted to demonstrate his authority within his own
domicile, he pointed out, his wife would not obey him
anyway, since she contended that no one had the right to
forbid her from exercising her profession, which was "a
condition of life and independence for her." Guilbert, Les
femmes et l'organisation syndicale, pp. 409-410.

12.   Discussions at the Quatrième congrès national de
la fédération nationale des cuirs et peaux [Chaumont]
(Puteaux, 1905), pp. 31-32; Compte rendu du premier congrès
national . . . des travailleurs de l'industrie de la
bijouterie-orfèvrerie-horlogerie (Paris, 1909), pp. 54, 76.
At the leatherworkers' congress in 1900, the results of an
industrial survey were published. In Fougères in 1880,
there were 5,500 workers in the shoe industry earning an
average of 5.50 francs per day. Twenty years later there
were only 1,300 men employed, earning an average of 2.50
francs. After the introduction of machinery, the number of

women employed had increased tenfold. Compte rendu du congrès national et international des ouvriers . . . employant le cuir et la peau [1900] (Paris, 1901), p. 95.

13. Cinquième congrès de la fédération nationale des cuirs et peaux [Limoges] (Paris, 1907), p. 64; Fédération nationale des ouvriers et ouvrières des tabacs. . . [1911] (Paris, 1912), pp. 75-79.

14. Compte rendu du neuvième congrès national de la fédération des travailleurs du livre [Lyon] (Paris, 1905), p. 58; Madame Feurtey in Société générale des chapeliers de France. Congrès national et international . . . (Paris, 1889), p. 15; Fédération des syndicats ouvriers de la chapellerie . . . [Chazelles-sur-Lyon] (Paris, 1906), p. 14.

15. Deuxième congrès national et troisième congrès national de la fédération nationale des travailleurs de l'alimentation . . . [Bourges] (Paris, 1904), p. 40; Moret's quote in La Typographie Française, 1886, p. 4.

16. Report to the third congress of the Fédération du Livre appeared in ibid., p. 2. Discussion of the printers reported in Patricia Branca, Women in Europe Since 1750 (London, 1978), p. 57. See Louisette Blanquart, Femmes: L'Age politique, pp. 43-44 for strike statistics.

17. Congrès corporatifs nationaux et internationaux de la chapellerie (Lyon, 1887), p. 30; Compte rendu du dixième congrès national de la fédération française des travailleurs du livre [Bordeaux, 1910] (Paris, [1910]), pp. 463-470; Compte rendu du sixième congrès national . . . (Limoges, 1913), pp. 34-36; Compte rendu officiel des travaux du sixième congrès de la fédération des travailleurs de l'habillement (Grenoble, 1906), p. 7.

18. Compte rendu du douzième congrès national ouvrier de l'industrie textile [Roubaix] (Lille, 1911), pp. 39-40; Congrès des ouvriers . . . employant le cuir et la peau [Paris, 1900], pp. 23-24.

19. X(e) congrès national corporatif (IV(e) de la confédération générale du travail . . . Compte rendu des travaux du congrès (Rennes, 1898). See pp. 174-185 for debate, pp. 312-314 for resolution. Delegates' emphasis. It should be noted that the CGT stipulated that membership was open equally to both sexes. It later passed resolutions calling for women to be allowed to vote for prud'hommes, serve as prud'femmes, and receive equal retirement pay and accident insurance benefits. Consult the following for resolutions on women's equality: 6(e) congrès national des syndicats de France. Compte rendu des travaux du congrès . . . (Nantes, 1894), p. 78; X(e) congrès [Rennes, 1898], p. 317. At the 1895 Limoges congress the delegates agreed that the CGT stood for membership of workers of both sexes.

In 1901 the Lyon congress called for equal retirement pay.
In 1908 the workers of Marseille called for no distinction
of sex regarding accident insurance. Recounted in La CGT et
le mouvement syndical, pp. 49, 80, 106. It must also be
noted that the CGT, as the central labor organization,
enforced the rulings on equality of membership. In 1902 a
Versailles section was suspended when it refused to admit a
union of women hairdressers. The suspension brought the
errant males around to accepting women and they were
subsequently readmitted. Confédération Générale du Travail,
Rapports des comités des commissions pour l'exercise
1904-1906 (Paris, [1906]), p. 44. Regional organizations
also practiced sexual equality. Members of the Toulon
bourse, for instance, voted that there would be no sexual
distinction among its members. See Compte rendu du 1(er)
congrès régional, 1904 (Toulon, 1904), p. 111.

    20. XI(e) congrès national corporatif (V(e) de la
confédération générale du travail) . . . (Paris, 1900), pp.
31-37; Briat's quote on p. 64 in ibid.

    21. For the exchange between Bouvard and Guérard see
ibid., p. 217.

    22. XVII(e) congrès national corporatif (XI(e) de
la confédération . . . [1910]) (Toulouse, 1911), pp. 54-57.

    23. For a transcription of the cover letter and
questionnaire sent out to collect data for the commission,
see J. B. Sévérat, "Le mouvement syndical," Encyclopédie
socialiste, syndicale, et coopérative de l'internationale
ouvrière, 1912-1913. Compère-Morel, dir. (Paris, n. d.), pp.
250-251. See also XVIII(e) congrès national corporatif
(XII(e) de la C.G.T) . . . Compte rendu des travaux (Le
Havre, 1910), pp. 28-29, 70-71. A further impetus to
unionization of working women was the fact that Germany was
far ahead of France in this endeavor, according to the
report of the delegate visiting from Germany who declared
that since his last visit, the Germans had enrolled over
2 1/2 million members, of whom 200,000 were women. Ibid.,
pp. 1-2. Delegates to the regional congress of bourses at
Auxerre in 1907 had other ideas on how to attract mothers to
the workers' organizations. Suggestions made on the subject
included forming a children's choir, and organizing family
festivities to lure women to membership and heighten their
sense of solidarity. Compte rendu du congrès régional
corporatif (Auxerre, 1907), pp. 5-6.

    24. Discussion of the woman question was also carried
on in pamphlets and "encyclopedias" of socialism and
syndicalism. Célestin Bouglé, author of a work on Saint-
Simon, wrote in 1907 that the notion of the man bringing
home the bacon for the wife to cook was idealistic "because
too many women have to work." Syndicalisme et démocratie
(Paris, 1908), pp. 132-137. In a letter to Paul Delesalle,

Georges Sorel discussed his idea of the function of the unions. He saw them as a means for women to achieve justice in society as well as an instrument of domestic liberation for them. He believed the power of the union could even be brought to bear upon the husband who was treating his wife "as he would not want his boss to treat him." Georges Sorel, Lettres à Paul Delesalle, 1914-1921 (Paris, 1947), p. 32. for quote.

25. Le Libertaire, See the following issues: Levar, 3 June 1897; 27 Nov. 1897; Antoine Antignac is in the 26 Aug. and 23 Sept. 1900 issues.

26. Ibid., 1 Feb. 1896 for quote. For additional discussion on the liberating value of free love, see the commentators in the following editions of the same paper: P. Comont, 28 Mar. 1896; 12 June 1898; Suzanne Carruette in 22 Apr. 1900; Sainte-Andréa in 11 Nov. 1900; Vulgus in 27 Aug. 1905; Pollo in 3 Sept. 1905. Anarchists who preached free unions were also aware that even in such a state the woman would be the one to "pay" if she became pregnant. Therefore, the paper often gave advice on birth control methods. See 2 Dec. 1900 issue for example.

27. Ibid., 17 Sept. 1899.

28. Ibid., see the following issues: 19 Oct. 1901; 16, 30 Nov. 1901; 7, 13, 21, 18 Dec. 1901; 12 Jan 1902.

29. Ibid., see the following issues: 30 Jan. 1904; 6, 13, 27 Feb. 1904; 5, 19 Mar. 1904; 2 Apr. 1904; 4 June 1904; 10 July 1904; 20 Aug. 1904; 17 Sept. 1904;

30. Félicie Numietska in ibid., 8 July 1906.

31. Ibid., 30 Dec. 1906.

32. Hervé's feminism was certainly a mixed bag. On the one hand, he was present at a banquet of the third arrondissement, following the Revolution of 1848, at which Pauline Roland was in attendance. There he offered a toast "on the reintegration of women into society." Edith Thomas, Pauline Roland. Socialisme et féminisme au XIX(e) siècle (Paris, 1956), p. 116. On the other hand, he was offended by Dr. Madeleine Pelletier's mannish clothes and haircut. See Marilyn Jacoby Boxer, "Socialism Faces Feminism in France: 1879-1913" (Ph.D. Dissertation, University of California, Riverside, 1975), p. 251.

33. For background on Marguerite Durand, consult Charles Sowerwine, "Le groupe féministe socialiste 1899-1902," Le Mouvement Social, 90 (Jan. 1975): 87-120.

34. La Guerre Sociale, 30 Jan. 1907.

35.   Ibid., 21 Aug. 1912.

36.   La Voix du Peuple: A. Bouvard, 1 Dec. 1900;
Fernand Goth, 18 Jan. 1903; D. Sieruin, 31 Aug. 1902.

37.   Ibid., 11 Oct. 1908.

38.   Ibid., 28 Apr. 1912.

39.   Ibid., 21 Dec. 1913.

40.   Ibid., 8 June 1914.

41.   At a meeting on 11 Nov. 1913 of the Comité des
Fédérations, reported in ibid., 25 Jan. 1914.

42.   Ibid., 4 , 11, 16, 25 Jan. 1914; 1, 9 Feb. 1904;
30 Mar. 1914.

43.   Ibid., Fernand Mammale, 30 Mar. 1914; A. Hagmann,
28 June 1914. Author's emphasis.

44.   Ibid., 13 July 1914.

45.   See for a discussion of the socialist-feminist
alliance: Sowerwine, "Le groupe féministe socialiste
1899-1902."

46.   Le Libertaire, 4 Dec. 1898.

47.   Auguste Pawlowski, Les syndicats féminins et les
syndicats mixtes en France (Paris, 1912), pp. 19-21, 38.

48.   Ibid., p. 99.

49.   O. Jean, Le syndicalisme, son origine, son
organisation, son rôle social (Paris, 1913). See
particularly pp. 101-108 concerning the bylaws of the
Syndicats Libres Féminins de Grenoble, which takes Catholic
social doctrine as its guide, condemns class struggle and
direct action, seeks to establish détante between capitalism
and labor, a just salary, and acknowledges the right to
strike only when three-quarters of the members consent to
such action, and only if the strike is to achieve attainable
ends.

50.   Sévérat, Encyclopédie socialiste, pp. 42, 298-300.

51.   Michel Augé-Laribé, Le problème agraire du
socialisme (Paris, 1907), p. 268. See also the report on
the exploitation of women to the 6(me) congrès [Nantes,
1894], p. 102.

52.   For a discussion of the development of the peasant
unions see Louis Prugnaud, Les étapes du syndicalisme

agricole en France (Paris, 1957); and Adrien Toussaint, L'union centrale des syndicats agricoles (Paris, 1920). See the following pages in Toussaint: pp. 147-148 for the goals of the Section des Dames de L'Union Centrale; p. 91 on the women's section, pp. 113-116, 125; p. 116 for quote on family. See also for the speech of President Delelande before th VII(e) congrès national des syndicats agricoles (Paris, 1909), pp. 34-44.

53. Report by Madame la Comtesse de Keranfleck-Kernizne on teaching housekeeping. She had founded such a school for peasant women in Brittany. See pp. 301-304 in ibid. Catholic syndicalists believed in educating the young females to be perfect housewives. An article entitled "What Will We Do with Our Daughters?" appeared in the Catholic syndicalist newspaper Travailleur de la Terre on 15 Feb. 1906. The answer was to provide girls with good elementary instruction, where they would learn to do laundry, cover buttons, make blouses, tailor all their own clothes, bake bread, dispense medicine, and practically understand that a dress of cotton would wear better than a dress of silk. The perfect young lady would also be taught how to cultivate a garden, love flowers, and even be provided, as secondary instruction, piano and drawing lessons, according to her character.

54. See Blanquart, Femmes: L'Age politique, pp. 42-46 for a list of strikes in which women were involved. Specific references to women's participation in strikes by union delegates can be found in Guilbert, Les femmes et l'organisation syndicale, pp. 60, 73, 115, 138.

55. Michelle Perrot, Les ouvriers en grève, France 1871-1890, 2 vols. (Paris, 1974), vol. 1, pp. 318-329, vol. 2, pp. 504-512 for women and strikes.

56. It must be noted here that Proudhonian antifeminist pronouncements did not end entirely. The most vigorous antifeminist diatribe appeared in 1909, in Le Mouvement Socialist, in an analysis written by Edouard Berth of a book on Proudhon by Gustave Droz. That year was the occasion of Proudhon's centenary. Berth took issue with Droz's statement that Proudhon's antifeminism seemed "a little too forced, exaggerated, nearly false." Berth insisted that the present-day disorganization of the family, the rise of divorce, and prostitution were proof that Proudhon's philosophy was correct. "Le centenaire de Proudhon," Le Mouvement Socialiste (Jan. 1909): 49-55. Droz's quote appears on p. 52. Annie Kriegel makes much of Proudhon's influence on the syndicalist movement in "Le syndicalisme révolutionnaire et Proudhon," Le pain et les roses (Paris, 1968), pp. 33-50. If that is so, there is certainly no evidence that Proudhon's centenary produced any other attempt by contributors to the working-class press to link Proudhon's ideology with the justification to return

women to the home. Berth's article is unique in this
respect. But then Berth's career as a syndicalist and
Sorelian is suspect, since he ultimately joined the Action
Française. See pp. 248-388 in Guilbert, Les femmes et
l'organisation syndicale for a survey of all articles
relating to women in the working-class press.

57. Branca, Women in Europe, pp. 45-46. Branca
declares that employers "would have welcomed a more stable
female labour force and would have increased wage levels to
attain it--if the device would have worked. Few women were
ready to oblige. Whatever the mixture of pleasure and shock
that new urban jobs offered, there was no desire to enjoy or
suffer it permanently." Quote appears on p. 45.

58. Guilbert, Les femmes et l'organisation syndicale,
pp. 186-187 for her statement that women's militancy was
restricted to particular trades.

59. Madeleine Guilbert, Les fonctions des femmes dans
l'industrie (Paris, 1966), p. 63. See also for background:
Paul Louis, Histoire de la classe ouvrière en France de la
révolution à nos jours (Paris, 1927); Yves Merlin, Les
conflits collectifs de travail pendant la guerre 1914-1918
(Paris, 1928).

60. See Guilbert, Les fonctions des femmes, p. 54 on
strike activity. Also pp. 38-43 in Merlin, Les conflits
collectifs for statistics on the rise of salaries.

61. Guilbert, Les fonctions des femmes, p. 64.

62. Ibid., p. 64; Blanquart, Femmes: L'Age politique,
p. 31.

63. XIV(e) congrès de la C.G.T. (Lyons, 1919), pp.
302-309 for a report on women and syndicalism. Also
noteworthy is the attack by Madame Chevenard on the failure
of the CGT in not calling upon women for the moral strength
needed to resist participation in the war, pp. 304-309.

64. Germaine Jouhaux, Rapports sur les conditions de
travail au point de vue féminin (Paris, 1926).

65. Keufer's speech appears in Guilbert, Les fonctions
des femmes, pp. 64-65.

66. See ibid., pp. 54-60 for legislation passed
regarding women's working conditions. Also see Marcel
Frois, La santé et le travail des femmes pendant la guerre
(Paris, n. d.); Branca, Women in Europe, pp. 168-169; and
James F. McMillan, Housewife or Harlot (New York, 1981),
chs. VII, VIII, pp. 131-157.

PERSONS CITED

Chevenard, Jeanne (1876-1944), born at Lyon, executed by the Resistance at Venissieux (Rhône). She worked as an embroiderer. After her second marriage, she and her husband opened an embroidery shop in Lyon, but the pair had to declare bankruptcy in 1913. Later she became a propagandist for the CGT.

Coulet, Jean (1865-?), born in Marseille. A typographer and Guesdist. Attended FBT and CGT congresses. Organized May Day demonstrations in 1890 and 1891 in his area. Authored a book on socialism in Marseille.

Favreau, Frédéric (?-?), employed in a gas factory at Nantes in 1876. Secretary of the local bourse in 1911.

Grégoire, Henri (1871-1952), born at Creuse. Orphaned at the age of three, went to school to the age of ten, then apprenticed to a baker. He later moved to Paris and became secretary of the bakers' union in that city. He was also involved in setting up a cooperative bakery in 1904.

Guillot, Marie (1880-1934), born in the Saône-et-Loire, died in the Rhone. Her father, a journalier in agriculture, died when she was young. Her mother supported the family as a laundress. Marie graduated from college and became a teacher, although she always remained attracted to the plight of the farmworkers. She founded numerous unions after 1911, even in the face of official reprimands from her superiors. She was an effective speaker, praised for her clear voice and her short, but pointed statements.

Jacobi, Madame (?-?), she represented the tobacco workers' federation at the 1902 CGT congress and wrote for La Voix du Peuple. In 1901 she was a delegate to the London peace conference.

Lacaille, Ernest (1862-?), born at Nancy. He was a member of the bootmakers' union, and secretary of the Federation of Unions of the Meurthe-et-Moselle. He headed an employment bureau run by the unions. He participated in CGT congresses and founded a UP in Nancy. In 1901, assisted by Griffuelhes, he organized an enormous strike of shoeworkers. He also edited several working-class newspapers.

Laurent, Citoyenne (?-?), in 1882 she was at the Congres Ouvrier at Saint-Etienne. Helped found a POF chapter in Roanne and an FNS group in Lyon. She presented a detailed report on the status of working women at the 1886 FNS congress.

Martino, Louis (1862-?), born in Marseille. He was a hotel worker, Guesdist, militant syndicalist, and participant in several CGT congresses. He organized May Day demonstrations in 1890. Two years later he was elected to the Municipal Council at Marseille.

Saulnier (?-?), lived in Paris. He represented Parisian shoemakers at the 1901 CGT congress.

Sergent (?-?), a typographer and delegate to numerous CGT congresses. He was described as a self-assured speaker. In 1908 he led a group of typographers in a twenty-four-hour strike in protest against the shootings at Villeneuve-Saint-Georges. But when the movement was checked, he lost some of his authority within the antireformist wing of the Fédération du Livre. He was mobilized in 1914, and died the following year of an undisclosed illness.

Vandeputte, Victor (1875-?), born in the Nord. He was a weaver who took an active part in the strikes beginning in 1910. He founded a bourse in his hometown in 1909, and became its secretary the following year. He also published L'Union Syndicale.

6. The Peasant Question: Grounding the Rural Offensive

Syndicalism's goal was to weld all workers into conscious revolutionaries. As demonstrated in the preceding chapter, leaders of the movement came to realize that the revolution must include women. Those involved in directing the CGT were able to abandon centuries of antifeminist attitudes and move toward recognizing women as equally exploited comrades. The increase of women's union activity and the labor reforms legislated with the help of syndicalist pressures indicate a modest success in moving toward syndicalism's revolutionary goal.

Modest too were syndicalist gains in enlisting the support of a more numerous and equally important segment of French society, the peasantry. Practical reality dictated that unionism's revolutionary progress depended upon the growth of its numbers. But the large peasant population presented very real dangers to the industrial workers. Peasant sons continued to flock to the cities, swelling the labor force and driving wages down. Those youths who remained on the land provided the recruits for the army, which increasingly came to be used against striking workers. In addition, greater peasant profits meant higher living costs and lower real wages for the urban workers who depended upon farmers for their daily bread. Yet, without their being able to draw freely on the farmers' storehouses, syndicalists knew that the general strike, hence the revolution, was doomed from the start. Achieving détente with the peasantry was an important syndicalist goal.

But this union could only be realized after hurtling numerous obstacles. There was the problem of the peasantry itself, whose parochialism and conservatism threatened any lasting accord developing between town and country. Peasant suspicions were exacerbated by syndicalism's underlying Marxist caste and its insistence that the revolution would result in the transition from a system of private property to one of collective ownership. Such an eventuality was rejected by the large property holders as well as by the bulk of poor farmers grubbing out a meager living on their tiny parcel of land. Also problematical was the fact that the movement's antielectoral stance prevented syndicalists from competing effectively in the political arena with groups of the right and left who were also vying for the peasants' allegiance. The conclusion to be drawn from this study is that in the years before the war, the syndicalist rural offensive was able to make only minimal and sporadic gains in the countryside.(1) The peasant question remained essentially a paradox for political and economic socialists alike. It was only on the issue of antimilitarism that syndicalists were truly able to bridge the gap existing between industrial workers and the rural population.

"LA GRANDE ASSEMBLEE DES RURAUX"

That such a bridge was necessary was clearly recognized by syndicalist leaders because of the agrarian nature of France. Further, the lessons of the past had not been wasted on the left, who knew that the large peasant bloc had been instrumental in bringing about the defeat of the Commune. In 1871 the Communards had sought to educate the rural worker to the fact that the differences between town and country were fictitious. In a circulated appeal to the peasantry, the Parisians pointed out that each group of workers labored long and hard to survive; each was in "the thrall of poverty"; city workers and country workers both wanted to enjoy the fruits of their labor. But the Communards' demand of "The Land for the Peasant, the Tool for the Worker, Work for All" was not strong enough to overcome the entrenched suspicion harbored by provincials against the capital. The peasantry cast its support with what it believed to be the legitimate Versailles government.(2)

Working-class spokesmen also knew that the Third Republic continued to endure at the sufferance of the large country element. "The republic will be a peasants' republic or it will cease to exist," declared Jules Ferry in 1884.(3) The pattern of small ownership set during the Middle Ages was accelerated by the French Revolution, which saw the breakup of large estates and the abolition of primogeniture.(4) Morcellation of land ensured that the peasantry would not develop into anything representing a solid bloc. Their only common aspiration was to own land or increase their holdings; the only common ideal was that which extolled agrarian origins and peasant virtues.

What evolved in France was not a single peasant society, as Georges Dupeux notes, but rather "a mosaic of agricultural zones whose level of economic development differed--as did the degree of social and political development."(5) Seemingly occupying the top of the socioeconomic scale were the one out of two peasant families who owned their own land. Below these were the métayers, or sharecroppers, who constituted about one-fifth of the landless agrarian population in the 1880's. Laboureurs were those who owned some land and a plough, and rented other acreage. Domestiques de ferme were laborers permanently hired by a specific farmer or housed on a single estate. They received a small wage and the use of sufficient land on which to raise their own food supply. Below these were the journaliers, the landless, often migratory day laborers.

Within this agrarian world, status was not necessarily assigned on the basis of land ownership. Laboureurs working the larger leaseholds tended to be more efficient and more prosperous than the smallholder. Often they came to constitute a kind of peasant bourgeoisie. Smallholders often preferred to spend their capital to increase their landholdings rather than to invest in machinery. In such instances, métayers had an advantage over these small proprietors who preferred to sacrifice productivity for ownership. Journaliers were regarded as being on the bottom of the economic ladder because they owned no land and worked for wages. But many of the peasants who did own land, or even rented out some of their holdings to others, were themselves forced, either occasionally or regularly, to work for others in order to augment their incomes.(6) Clearly, the fashioning of a socioeconomic yardstick to assess the peasant "class" was an impossible task. This fact caused great consternation among the socialists and revolutionary syndicalists.

The lack of social or economic homogeneity was a deterrent in welding together a conscious political bloc. Critics often complained that the peasants were apathetic, grasping, materialistic clods. Marx had said their social proclivities made them akin to a sack of potatoes. Friedrich Engels was disgusted by the fact that they were narrow-minded, politically blind, ignorant "of everything that lies outside the village," in short, of "unmanageable stupidity."(7) Isolation and illiteracy worked against the development of a political consensus. Approximately one-third of the peasant population in 1886 could neither read nor write.(8) A primitive transportation network heightened provincialism.(9) Insularity helped perpetuate a suspicion, not only of urban politicians, but of people from other villages.(10) Local leaders could and did manipulate peasant votes. The parochialism of the country also served to make party labels and philosophies useless. Left-wing parishes, for instance, supported candidates from the right if they were "hometown boys." Or conservative areas voted left in order to spite a candidate from a neighboring village.(11) Generally, local issues took precedence over national ones. The author of a guidebook stated in 1873 that to the man in the country, the government was something "given to mischief-making, hard on little people, that demands taxes, prevents contraband, and dwells in Paris."(12)

Despite the peasantry's general disregard for the political state, politicians of the Third Republic were persistent in seeking the peasants' support. The Republic's electoral laws and the population distribution gave the peasants great electoral strength. Half of the political districts for the Chamber of Deputies was predominantly rural. Chosen by departmental electoral colleges dominated by village-based electors, the Senate came to be called "La grande assemblée des ruraux."(13) In response to the economic plight of its rural constituencies, parliament passed numerous agricultural relief laws, the capstone of which was the tariff legislation of 1892, the Méline tariff, which included agriculture in its protective cloak.(14) After the passage of the 1884 law legalizing associations, radicals sought to buttress the Republic further by organizing a network of peasant cooperatives throughout the country, strengthened by parliamentary subsidies. These groups were organized on the national level into the Fédération Nationale de la Mutualité et de la Coopération Agricoles (FNMCA).(15)

OVERTURES FROM THE RIGHT

Government blandishments of the peasantry were a definite obstacle to syndicalist efforts to organize the rural worker. Equally formidable was the evolution of a "syndicalisme des ducs," organized under the aegis of large landowners embued with the doctrines of Social Catholicism. The motives of the right were both high-minded and practical: on the one hand, to preserve the integrity of the peasantry; on the other, to insulate the rural elements against the twin viruses of republicanism and socialism.(16) As noted in the preceding chapter, these rightist-sponsored organizations were formidable competitors with syndicalism for the allegiance of the rural population of both sexes. Also as noted, their success was not accidental. Rather, it was because the leaders of the movement spoke to the total needs of the rural worker. These groups formed cooperatives to buy machinery and fertilizer, offered agricultural instruction, and assisted farmers in selling their crops. The unions established insurance, retirement, and mutual credit organizations. They also provided "moral services." As instruments of pacification and progress, the unions' task was to bring about social preservation and integration in the face of republican and socialist-threatened chaos. The Revolution had destroyed the older corporate structure. Republicanism, a product of the Revolution, was aimed at bringing all existing institutions under state domination. The Republic was an enemy of the Church, and the nation's secularism promoted thuggery.(17) Republicanism had fostered individualism, which in turn had encouraged capitalism. This economic system, declared Hyacinthe de Gailhard-Bancel, deputy-president of the Syndicats Agricoles, was an "idolatry of the golden calf." Further, capitalism had contributed to the growth of the city at the expense of the farm. Cities drained away the most precious rural resource, the sons and daughters, who fled the fields seeking the regular work and higher wages offered by industry. The attraction for material security was the reason for socialism's strength. But the socialists' promise of state assistance, warned de Gailhard-Bancel, was only "an allurement to attract the simple and the naive, and to earn for socialism a fabled legend."(18)

The peasant's patrie was in danger. The nation's salvation lay in the encouragement of peasant virtue and the preservation of agriculture, "the greatest moral, material, and social force in the country," according to de Gailhard-Bancel. The country furnished the largest number of soldiers, and the most robust. The rural population produced the raw materials for industry, he noted, and provided consumers for its products. The country also produced people of noble virtue: fiercely devoted to the love of freedom and to their homes, their natal village, their patois, their fields, and their cross.(19) Those country virtues must be spread throughout the land.(20) Catholic syndicalists urged the organization of agrarian unions in which all members of the farming community would be joined.(21) The program espoused by the Travailleur de la Terre, a rightist farm journal, was typical. Farmers and peasants must seek "to combat egoism and parochial ideas," it declared. Only through syndicalist efforts could the rural elements then serve as intermediaries between the public authority and the commercial interests.(22) In place of the anarchy of individualism and capitalism would be the "patrimonial syndicalism" of the farm unions. In place of godless republicanism and socialism would be the agrarian unions, the aim of which was the preservation of social peace. "God gives the victory to armed men who will fight," declared President Delelande at the Seventh National Congress of Farm Unions in 1909. Men of the fields must join together in union and remain "faithful to the emblem of fire that decorated the buckle of Jeanne."(23)

The program of agrarian unionism carried out by both Republicans and ducs was based on their desire to preserve the agrarian structure of small-property holders as it existed in France. For Radicals, this group of small independent farmers constituted a presious source of votes. To large landowners, the continuation of smallholders, as Gordon Wright has noted, provided both "a shelter against collectivism" and "a built-in supply of supplementary labor in many areas." To the right, these unions were useful organizations for combating class warfare by reinforcing the peasantry's traditional conservatism.(24) Further, as Elie Coulet noted in his 1898 doctoral dissertation, large landowners received the major material benefits from the unions because they were able to receive "better deals" for selling their products or borrowing money.(25) Radicals and conservatives, united by self-interest, supported the continuation of smallholdings. Their stance harmonized perfectly with the aspirations of the small peasant proprietors, whose numbers were increasing, according to

official statistics published in 1882 and 1892.(26) Firmly
in the mainstream on the peasant question, the right
represented a formidable opponent to political and economic
socialists alike.

THE PARADOX OF CONCENTRATION FOR SOCIALISM

Equally important to the formulation by the left of a
successful peasant program was the socialists' need to deal
with the implications revealed by the statistics. Data
indicating the multiplication of smallholdings were in sharp
contrast to socialist theory. Based on the analysis of
Marx, socialists had held that concentration in industry and
agriculture was a necessary precondition to the socialist
revolution. The smallholder was doomed to suffer the same
fate as the rest of the petty bourgeoisie, Marx asserted,
for the industrial revolution also provided the machinery to
bring about agricultural concentration. Where the peasant
continued to exist, Marx pointed out, it was only because he
was owner, capitalist, and worker combined. He could sell
his products at the actual cost of production, thereby
surrendering both rent and profit and living only on the
"wages" he paid himself. Although the peasant survived "by
superhuman labor and subhuman life," that existence was
tenuous. Marx apparently shed no tears of sympathy for the
smallholder's impending demise, for the system of petty
ownership, he declared, was "the most primitive and
irrational form of exploitation." Such a system was bound to
produce "a class of barbarians," living "outside of society,
subject to all the imperfections of primitive social forms
and to all the evil and all the misery of a civilized
country."(27) History decreed that this anamoly would be
ground out of existence. "It is not necessary that we
abolish it," Marx declared in the Manifesto. "The
development of industry has already abolished it and every
day abolishes it more." The revolution would see the
expropriation of all private property, land included. In
place of private exploitation, there would be collective
cultivation of the soil "in accordance with a common plan"
by means of "industrial armies." With agriculture and
manufacturing industries combined, concluded Marx, the
antagonism between town and country would come to an
end.(28)
Throughout the 1860's and 1870's, socialists generally
favored Marx's dicta on collectivism and nationalization of
the soil. The Marxist position supporting expropriation of
private landholdings won an early victory in the IWA against
the Proudhonists, who asserted that the preservation of
smallholdings was necessary to personal freedom.(29) In the
early congresses of the French left, the commitment to
Marxian orthodoxy on the subject of the peasantry was also
used to separate Marxist sheep from anarchist goats. The
Guesdist-dominated 1879 Marseille congress declared support
for the expropriation of peasant property.(30) In a pamphlet

published before 1880, Guesde insisted on the superiority of large cultivation and of the eventual victory of large property over smallholdings. Delegates to the Socialist Workers' Congress in 1880 upheld their earlier position on private property. While there could be no emancipation without the workers being in possession of raw materials and the instruments of their labor, the resolution declared, individual ownership was incompatible with the actual state of industrial and agrarian progress, and would only continue economic inequality. The sole remedy, delegates concluded, was collective rather than individual ownership of the means of production.(31) Insofar as the Guesdists were concerned, the peasant was destined to suffer and disappear. Any attempt to mitigate his sufferings was futile, according to Guesde. Reforms gained would remain only as dead letters in a capitalist regime.(32)

By 1884 Guesde's position on reforms in general and on the peasantry specifically had considerably softened. Ironically, the change was largely the result of having to confront the dilemma posed by the rigorous application of Marx's pronouncements, particularly since they were now a minority within the French left. In their first congress in 1884, the PO committed itself to Marxist teachings on carrying the class war into the political arena. But strict adherence to orthodoxy on the peasant question seemed to fly in the face of Marxist pronouncements on the need to win elections. Confronted with a choice between two apparent extremes, delegates opted for engaging in electoral battles rather than waging war on peasant property. On the peasant question, the Guesdists adopted an equivocal, hence politically expedient, stand. The resolution called for gradual collectivization of land and a program of agrarian reform. The reform measures included the call for expropriation of large-property holders, an issue always dear to peasant hearts, the suppression of the land tax, and free distribution of fertilizer and seed.(33)

Between the Roubaix congress and 1892, Guesdists ignored the peasant question, concentrating their energies instead on attempting to control the labor organizations and directing the FNS. By 1892, however, a series of events converged to bring the issue of the peasantry again into focus. Publication of the 1892 statistics confirmed what had been suggested in the previous data of 1882: that Marx had erred in his prediction concerning the demise of the smallholder. Because the PO was a party grounded on Marxist ideology, it was incumbent upon the Guesdists to rescue Marx in the face of allegedly damning evidence that seemed to refute the scientific nature of Marxist socialism.

Equally threatening to the continued survival of the Marxist party were the numerous socialist groups contending with the Guesdists for supremacy. The rival FBT, formed in 1892, and the bourses were particularly vocal in championing the needs of the peasantry. There were a number of reasons to explain the peasant orientation of the bourses. Many of their members were anarchists of the Bakuninist persuasion, who had assimilated their mentor's teachings on the revolutionary tendencies inherent in the peasantry.(34) The organization's interest in the agricultural population was also strongly reflective of Fernand Pelloutier's concern for the agrarian worker after he returned from a sojourn in Brittany in 1891.(35) The rural orientation of the bourses was also the logical outcome of their organizational structure. Constituted on the basis of geography rather than on profession, the bourses naturally grouped together industrial and agrarian workers. Further, those bourses located in heavily rural areas had an overtly agrarian caste.(36) An additional threat, outside of the anarchist-shaded FBT, was the newly organized POSR, which was aggressively involved in the campaign to bring peasants to socialism.

The losing battle for union control appears to have heightened the Guesdists' commitment to seek victory in the political arena. Socialists had captured many towns and a few important industrial centers in the municipal elections of 1892.(37) A general election was slated for 1893. The possibility of electoral success on a national scale and the waning influence with the unions dictated a change in tactics--one that would not ignore the industrial workers, but would also court the political favors of the peasantry. Suffering as they were from twenty years of depression, the farmers would welcome some recognition of their problems and would warm to the socialists' commitment to work for rural reform.

SOCIALIST POPULISM: A ROUTE TO ELECTORAL VICTORY

A few days after the Marseille congress of the FS closed, the PO held its convention in the same city. Delegates received the agrarian program drafted by Guesde and Lafargue, which appeared to have multiple aims. It was designed to take the wind from the sails of organizations such as the FBT and the POSR, and from socialists like Jean Jaurès, who had long campaigned on a platform of agrarian reform.(38) The program was also aimed at garnering peasant support at the polls the following year. A decent showing in the elections would discredit the anarchist elements within the FS, the FBT, and the POSR, and bring the unions safely into the sphere of political domination. The emphasis on electoral activity rather than on class warfare against private property would also help to overcome the problem posed by following Marxism too literally. The agrarian program submitted at Marseille constituted an important weapon in the battle against the syndicalists.

The inspiration for the party's program, noted Lafargue in the preamble to the resolution, was the realization that centralization in the agrarian domain was not occurring to the same degree as in the industrial realm. French farmers remained in possession of the soil. The artisans' loss of ownership of the means of production had caused that group's

decline into the ranks of the proletariat.   The anarchists
might wish to see misery intensified as the precondition for
social   transformation,   Lafargue   stated pointedly, but the
Socialist Party--the workers' party--was   dedicated   to   the
reconciliation, not the separation, of the producer from his
work.   The agrarian worker had the same right to the party's
protection   as   did   the   industrial   proletariat,   Lafargue
explained.   Therefore, the party, acting   in   the   peasants'
name,   was   calling   for   a   program   of   reform   to assist
métayers, journaliers, and   small   proprietors   during   the
capitalist   phase.   The resolution introduced demands for a
minimum wage, retirement benefits supported by a tax on   the
revenues   of large proprietors, the creation of cooperatives
for   buying   fertilizers   and   selling   farm   products,   and
indemnities   to   sharecroppers   and   farmers for the surplus
value of their property.   Other items of the program   called
for   prohibition   against   the   alienation   of common lands,
communal purchase of farm machinery, and   the   leasing   of
communal lands to landless families.(39)
    At the next party congress, held at Nantes in 1894, the
agrarian   program introduced at Marseille, and now including
a provision supporting smallholdings, was formally   adopted.
The   state of things characterized by peasant proprietorship
was only temporary, the resolution warned.   Workers would be
free "only when they are   in   possession   of   the   means   of
production,"   which   could   be   realized   solely   "under   a
collective or social form." But the smallholders could   rest
easy, at least for the time being.   Noted Lafargue:

>   The small field is the tool of the peasant as the
>   plane is to the carpenter and the scalpel   is   to
>   the surgeon.   The peasant, carpenter, and surgeon
>   exploit no one with their instruments of   labor;
>   thus   [they   should]   not   fear   seeing   [these
>   instruments]   taken   away by a socialist revolu-
>   tion,   whose   mission   is   to   expropriate   the
>   expropriators   who   have taken the   land from the
>   laborers and the machines from the workers.

Only   against   the   large capitalist proprietor, the enemy of
the peasant, the resolution declared, would the party direct
its efforts.(40)
    The publication of the POF's agrarian   program   brought
angry   recriminations   against   the   Guesdists   by those who
charged that French socialism was abandoning Marx, if not by
commission, at   least   by   omission.   In   the   vanguard   of
criticism   was   Friedrich   Engels, who publicly disavowed the
French   party's   stand.   Protecting   the   property   of   the
peasant   was not safeguarding his liberty, said Engels, only
the special form of his servitude.   French socialists, he
claimed,   were futilely trying to maintain a state of things
destined to disappear.(41)
    In   answer   to   the   charge   that   the   socialists   had
forgotten   their   Marx, Guesde declared that the critics had
apparently overlooked another of Marx's dictates: that   the

earth shall not be given to one to the detriment of the other. It was the duty of the Socialist Party to put workers in possession of the instruments of production, which in the peasant's case, were his fields.(42) The party's program was not a deviation from orthodoxy, Lafargue insisted in 1893. Socialists had merely asserted that the party would do nothing to accelerate the ruin of the peasantry during the transitional phase.(43)

Socialism's resolution of the peasant question was aimed at bringing the peasantry to socialism. Although it might sustain the existence of smallholders, concluded Jaurès in 1877, socialist support of agrarian reform would not prevent the revolution from occurring. Rather, reforms would help instill in the peasantry "the socialist spirit," which in turn would prepare them for "a more ulterior and more profound transformation."(44) Marx's prognosis of capitalist concentration was not in error, Jaurès was still insisting in 1897. Increasing morcellation was only consigning more peasants to the misery induced by intensive cultivation. Peasant independence was being destroyed by mortgages and taxes, he noted. Increasingly the small proprietor was being dominated by large industrial property: sugar refineries, giant milling companies, and the powerful middlemen who controlled the Paris markets. By a fashion more complex than formerly believed, the agricultural domain was passing to collectivism. The revolution was inevitable. Reforms gained by the socialists would assist the peasantry during the harsh process of social transformation.(45)

In their attempt to walk a tightrope between wooing the vote of the peasant smallholder on the one hand, and remaining true to Marx's original pronouncements on the other, the French political socialists developed a position on the peasant question having at its core the recognition that the party must serve as the vehicle for raising the class consciousness of the peasant population. The slow pace of capitalist expansion into the agrarian realm had left the peasants' insularity relatively untouched. The only means by which the peasants' social isolation might be overcome was through party-sponsored reforms. These reform measures might sustain the peasantry in its private ownership, but only temporarily. Ultimately the forces of historical necessity and inevitability would hold sway. Agrarian property, like industrial property, would then move from individual to collective ownership, and from individual to collective exploitation. The political socialists' response to the peasant question was a successful one. It squared nicely with Marx; placed the blame for rural disorder where it belonged--with the capitalists; and emphasized the humanitarian aspects of the Socialist Party in wanting to mitigate the peasants' plight.

The adoption of the agrarian program, like the change in the party's name to the POF, was carefully designed by the Guesdists to gain control of the left. The tactic failed. The Nantes congress witnessed the official rupture between the economic and political wings of the French left, but the split paved the way for the eventual unification of the socialist factions in 1905. The peasant proved to be a vehicle by which unity could be achieved, Marxist philosophy clarified, and the strength of the Socialist Party and its electoral representation in parliament increased. More important, at least insofar as this study is concerned, is the fact that the political socialists' adoption of a program aimed at gaining peasant support became an important force in defining for revolutionary syndicalists the parameters for their subsequent discussion of the peasant question.

THE LIBERTARIANS' RESPONSE

The difficulty of grounding the rural offensive on a solid ideological base was most immediately apparent among the libertarians. Anarchists were the first to concern themselves with the peasant question, and the problems they encountered were the same ultimately faced by the syndicalist organizations. Early anarchist tracts demonstrated a clear ambivalence in attitude toward the peasantry. The lack of consensus within anarchist populism was largely because the doctrine was based on the mixture of ideas drawn from Bakunin, Kropotkin, and Proudhon. On the one hand, the content of the anarchist message revealed the traditional contempt held by the city sophisticate for the simple-minded boor, steeped in superstition and unable to lift a finger to alter his condition. Conversely, other libertarians expressed a genuine concern for peasants who deserved a better life and who also had the power to change the course of the social revolution. More important was the question of who would be the carriers of the revolution. Some libertarians agreed with Bakunin that the peasantry was a revolutionary "elect." Others believed that the country was only tinder to be ignited by a spark from the urban proletariat. The antithetical visions of the anarchists are best exampled by the pronouncements of two among their rank: Peter Kropotkin and Elisée Réclus.

In his Conquest of Bread, Kropotkin agreed that peasants were deeply exploited. But he also characterized the peasantry as "ignorant tools of reaction" with the power to starve the revolutionary strongholds into submission. Technological developments, however, were increasing the workers' capacity to carry out the revolution irrespective of the peasants' moral or material support. Advances made in chemistry meant that greater crop yields could be gained on smaller plots. The development of steam power allowed for the construction of vast networks of temperature-controlled greenhouses. In these "kitchen gardens under glass," [Kropotkin's emphasis] the worker could grow all the food he needed without enormous expenditures of human energy and with virtually no need for expertise in farming. "Happy crowds of workers" would spend part of their labor growing their own food. They would regard this time as "hours of recreation . . . spent in beautiful gardens." Armed with the means to provide for his own material existence, the worker could anticipate the day when anarchist communes would be declared in towns and cities. Soon the peasants, inspired by the workers' solidarity, would join with their urban comrades and "march together in the conquest of the high joys of knowledge and artistic creation."(46)

For Kropotkin, the revolution would be initiated by the proletariat. For Elisée Réclus, it must emanate from the land. To the peasant, Réclus declared, nothing was more sacred than his labor and the cultivation of the soil he loved. His land was a bastion against the forces of industrialism and urbanization that had thrown millions into the category of wage slavery and spawned a leviathan state. Now "soi-disant travailleurs" from the city were preaching a new order based on expropriation and collectivization. But the peasant would be little better under this system, Réclus avowed, than was the serf on the feudal manor. The future offered by these étatistes was a society based on a hideous egalitarianism wherein horses, machines, and men would be treated equally. The farm would be "run like a factory, where the machine governs all." "They will take the fields and harvests from you," Réclus warned, and "harness you to some iron machine, smoking and strident, and enveloped in carbon smoke, you will have to balance your arms on a piston 16,000 or 12,000 times a day. That's what they call agriculture."

To avoid such a destiny, said Réclus, the peasant must guard his land, for it belongs to him, his wife, and his beloved children. He must then associate with his companions on the land, join commune to commune, and affiliate with the disinherited of the city. In solidarity they would be an invincible army of liberty against the forces of the state.(47)

Réclus' theories, based on the Proudhonian acceptance of the possession of private property as a necessary hedge against capitalists and the state, were less widely held among the anarchists than one would expect. In fact, the majority of libertarians preached the hard message of expropriation. In an 1896 article in Le Libertaire, Antoine Antignac warned his peasant "brothers in misery and ignorance" that what they called private property was a sham. "The land is not for those who cultivate it," he declared. What anarchists wanted was a common culture, mechanized to increase production, so there would be riches for all.(48)

For anarchists, the peasants' attachment to private property was the product of an obsolete mentality and a hangover from feudalism, sustained by medieval clerics and lords and encouraged by present-day liberals and now, socialists. The mission of anarchism was to rescue the rural population from its intellectual backwardness and bring the peasants into the anarchist dawn of individual liberty and freedom from the forces of government and private property.

Because peasants were raised outside the social and political centers of the city, noted anarchist Fernand-Paul in Le Libertaire, they continued to cling to their land like "crabs on a rock." A modern feudalism existed in the countryside, resting heavily on the peasant, whose brain, "encrusted with prejudices and mystic beliefs," opened slowly to enlightened ideas. Peasants were "divided by the jealousy which is the sentiment of property and by envy, which is merely the instinct of theft," noted Fernand-Paul. This captivity, encouraged and cultivated by the priest and the seigneur, produced a lethargy that killed in the peasant any desire for a good life and gave him the idea that urban workers were nothing more than brigands coming to expropriate his goods. Peasants must become aware that their small parcels could not be cultivated efficiently; that marginal farming produced only starvation rations.

Anarchists possessing "a larger vision," Fernand-Paul declared, must help peasants realize that only when the land was placed in common and cultivated collectively would the earth yield sufficient fruits for all. Anarchists must also assure the peasant that he had nothing to fear in a libertarian society that existed without laws or government.(49)

Libertarians played upon the theme that the peasant lived under a modern form of serfdom from which he was unable to wrench free. He had become "a resigned slave," noted a contributor to Le Libertaire in 1896. How long would it take, the writer asked, before this landless peasant, "this good and devoted Jacques" would gain consciousness of his exploitation and lift himself "from the nothingness where [he] remains inert."(50)

The feudal lords of yesterday, who had kept the peasant in ignorance, had been replaced by modern-day liberals and socialists. In the years 1904-1905 anarchist Georges Paul penned several articles in Le Libertaire using economic analysis to prove this charge. Nonpossessors were being duped by the bourgeois political parties. Uneducated and unconscious, the landless peasants acted by reason of a priori ideas against their own interests. Liberal economists argued that the possession of private property stimulated the farmer to work harder to increase his family's well-being. That notion was a myth. The peasant, unable to work any harder, only piled up debts, usually to village usurers, who charged high interest because of the scarcity of capital in the countryside.

With the introduction of machinery, unemployment increased. Poverty diminished the buying power of the consumer, which in turn redounded on the farmer, who then had to cut back his production. Democratic palliatives were useless against this entrenched problem, asserted Paul. So too were the blandishments of the socialist opportunists. Because of electoral considerations, socialists no longer spoke of nationalization. Instead they offered "vague reforms to lure peasants into believing in the chimera of the renaissance of property, and to the city worker the hope of a slice of the bourgeois government's cake." These were false promises. Only the end of a system of private property and the establishment of a society in which free people worked for a common prosperity would serve to liberate city and country worker alike from the vicious circle in which they were currently ensnared, Paul concluded.(51)

For anarchists, the definition of the peasant question rested largely on the supposition that farmers possessed an innate will to violence that had been anesthetized by clerics, landlords, and politicians. Anarchist tactics were aimed at enunciating the division of property holdings between the large landowners on the one hand, and the landless or pettyholders on the other. By playing on the theme of the have's versus the have-not's, anarchists hoped to ignite within the peasantry the determination to overthrow the forces exploiting them. Because the object of their propaganda was the group who possessed little or nothing, anarchists, like socialists, could preach the joys of collective ownership. For revolutionary syndicalists, the issue was far more complex.

NOTES

1. In his study of the radicalization of the countryside, Philippe Gratton confirms these conclusions, further noting that syndicalism made its greatest strides in those areas where agricultural production was taking on the characteristics of industrial production--such as among those working in the vineyards of the Midi. Les luttes des classes dans les campagnes (Paris, 1971), p. 404.

2. "Appeal of the Paris Commune to the Peasantry in 1871," reported in Neil Hunter, Peasantry and Crisis in France (London, 1938), pp. 282-285.

3. Jules Ferry, quoted in Gordon Wright, Rural Revolution in France: The Peasantry in the Twentieth Century (Stanford, 1964), p. 13.

4. Michel Augé-Laribé, among others, lays the cause of morcellation on the Revolution. In 1923, he says, there were still numerous large holdings in England of 50,000 to 500,000 hectares. In France at the same date, less than a dozen owned property of more than 1,000 hectares. About 100,000 proprietors owned 50 to 500 hectares; 700,000 middle proprietors owned 10 to 40 hectares, and 4 1/2 million Frenchmen owned 10 hectares. Le paysan français apres la guerre (Paris, 1923), p. 16. Gordon Wright, on the other hand, claims that it is a "myth" that the French peasantry became landowners as a result of the Revolution. Rural Revolution in France, p. 3. So too does Folke Dovring, who calls it "an historical mistake" to state that the

Revolution even abolished feudalism. He says this mistake is due to the fact that "the makers of the revolution, who belonged to an age when the confusion was frequent between legal terminology and social reality" failed to make the proper distinctions. Land and Labor in Europe in the 20(th) Century: A Comparative Survey of Recent Agrarian History (The Hague, 1960), p. 139. The myth of the effect of the Revolution on land ownership patterns was prevalent throughout the nineteenth century. Delegate to the Second International, Dupire, warned that peasants in France were opposed to collectivism. "Deprived so long of his liberty under feudalism" was why the peasant in France was so attached to private property. Quoted in Alexandre Klein, Les théories agraires du collectivisme (Paris, 1906), p. 27. Of course, it is tremendously difficult to present a true statistical picture of the French agrarian situation, as Wright explains. The statistics are rife with inconsistencies. Categories change from one survey to the next, often without adequate explanation. In his introduction, Wright declares, "almost any generalization about the peasantry becomes partially false as soon as it is formulated," and he urges social scientists to "avoid the quicksands of the peasant problem." Rural Revolution in France, pp. 13, 211, and p. v of preface for quote.

5. Georges Dupeux, French Society 1789-1970, Peter Wait, trans. (London, 1976), p. 118.

6. Ibid., pp. 111-112. For background on peasant life during the period cited, see Georges F. Renard and G. Weulersse, Life and Work in Modern Europe, Fifteenth to Eighteenth Centuries, Margaret Richards, trans. (New York, 1968). Eugen Weber talks about the kind of peasant hierarchy existing during this period, noting that in some districts, vast distinctions were made between those who owned the land and those who rented. Those on the upper echelon of the hierarchy would have considered it "a derogation to marry outside their 'caste'" Peasants Into Frenchmen: The Modernization of Rural France 1870-1914 (Stanford, 1976), p. 245.

7. Engels in Wright, Rural Revolution in France, pp. 10-11.

8. Ibid., p. 10.

9. Weber, Peasants into Frenchmen, p. 269.

10. Gordon Wright discusses this suspicion caused by insularity. He relates that the mayor of a rural commune whose population had drastically declined over the preceding seventy years responded to the suggestion that his commune fuse together with an adjoining one, the chief town of which was two miles distant; the mayor's reply was "We want nothing to do with foreigners!" This occurred in 1950.

Rural Revolution in France, p. 15.

11. Weber, Peasants into Frenchmen, p. 261.

12. Ibid., p. 243.

13. Wright points out that there were 20,000 communes with a population of fewer than 1,500 during the Third Republic. Each commune had one senatorial elector, while Paris, with its population of 3 million by 1914, had only 30. Rural Revolution in France, p. 213 for statistics; p. 14 for quote.

14. Ibid., pp. 15-18.

15. Ibid., pp. 19-21.   See also Yves Tavernier, Le syndicalisme paysan, FNSEA, CNJA (Paris, 1969).

16. See Chapter 5 of this work. For a discussion of the meetings to 1913 of one of these groups see André Courtin, Les congrès nationaux des syndicats agricoles (Paris, 1920).

17. H[yacinthe] de Gailhard-Bancel, Quinze années d'action syndicale (Paris, 1900), pp. 2, 18, 43-48. Adrien Toussaint reports that unions sponsored the collective' sale of wheat in 1902. In 1900, he records, over 1,000 unions were associated with the UCSAF, L'union centrale des syndicats agricoles (Paris, 1920), p. 59. President Delelande in his speech before the VII(e) congrès nationale des syndicats agricoles at Nancy in 1909 declared that their organizations, unlike the industrial syndicalist-sponsored unions, which aimed at class war, were designed to bring "order against anarchy" and "social peace" between proprietors and workers (Paris, [1909]), pp. 38-39. De Gailhard-Bancel noted an example of the secular lawlessness abroad in the land by citing an incident that occurred in the commune of Gigor (Crest) in 1887. There, six or seven of the local "bums" harassed over one hundred faithful unionists, returning from assisting at mass, by interrupting their hymn-singing procession with cries of "Long live the Republic," and "Stop playing music in the streets." Quinze années, p. 245.

18. Ibid., pp. 106, 163.

19. Ibid., pp. 76, 241.

20. President Delelande's message before the 1911 meeting of the Union des Syndicats; reported in Toussaint, L'union centrale des syndicats agricoles, pp. 6-8.

21. These farm unions were vertical organizations of all those engaged in farming in a particular community, from the large landowners to the day workers. The argument given

for mixed unions was that they were meant to bring about harmony between capital and labor, but many charged that the unions were really organized to benefit the large landowner rather than the small. Nevertheless, delegate Cheysson at the 1904 Congrès National de Syndicats Agricoles said that mixed unions were never easily accepted because many proprietors refused to believe their workers capable of discussing wages. Reported in R. E. Matillon, Les syndicats ouvriers dans l'agriculture (Paris, 1903), pp. 308-309.

22. Travailleur de la Terre, 15 Oct. 1905.

23. Delelande at the VII congrès [Nancy, 1909], p. 46.

24. Wright, Rural Revolution in France, p. 22. Apparently the goal of keeping the smallholder alive as a hedge against collectivism was not masked. Le Trésor de Rocque, president of the UCSAF, de Rocquigny, and Robert de la Sizeranne--all leaders of the right-wing movements--had publicly declared that small private property represented a "solid" and "impregnable" bastion of social conservatism. Reported in Michel Augé-Laribé, La grande ou petite propriété (Paris, 1902), p. 143.

25. Elie Coulet, Le mouvement syndicale et cooperatif dans l'agriculture (Paris, 1898).

26. See ibid., p. 62 for statistics.

27. Capital, III, ii, pp. 404, 411; quoted by Augé-Laribé, Grande ou petite, pp. 118, 125. See for the evolution of Marx's theories on the agrarian question Edouard Escarra, Nationalisation du sol et socialisme (Etude d'histoire des doctrines économiques) (Paris, 1904).

28. The Communist Manifesto, reproduced in Marx and Engels: Basic Writings on Politics and Philosophy, Lewis S. Feuer, ed. (Garden City, 1959), p. 28. Later Engels declared that socialists must explain to the peasant that his situation was hopeless and that capitalism would overtake his small property "as a train overtakes a wheelbarrow." Quoted in Klein, Les théories agraires p. 112.

29. Ibid, pp. 14, 18, 129-140. See also Aimé Berthod P.-J. Proudhon et la propriété, un socialisme pour les paysans (Paris, 1910).

30. Klein, Les théories agraires, p. 30.

31. Augé-Laribé, Grande ou petite, pp. 126-127.

32. Frederick F. Ridley, Revolutionary Syndicalism in France (Cambridge, Mass., 1970), pp. 53-54.

33. Noted in Klein, Les théories agraires pp. 32-33.
See also Gratton, Les luttes des classes, pp. 34-45 for
Guesdists' response.

34. Amédée Dunois reported that the propaganda
campaign in the countryside was begun by anarchists in 1890.
Victor Griffuelhes and Léon Jouhaux, eds., Encyclopédie du
mouvement syndicaliste, (Paris, 1912), p. 32. Philippe
Gratton notes that until 1900 the bourses were the real
initiators of syndicalism in the countryside. "Mouvement et
physionomie des grèves agricoles en France de 1890 à 1935,"
Le Mouvement Social 71 (Apr.-June 1970): 3-38, p. 32.

35. Jacques Julliard, Fernand Pelloutier et les
origines du syndicalisme d'action directe (Paris, 1971), pp.
45-46. Julliard says that Pelloutier agreed with Bakunin
that the worker was not the "elect" and wanted to have a
closer liaison between industrial and rural elements.
Pelloutier noted that the FBT sponsored the establishment of
bourses in Narbonne, Carcassonne, and Montpellier in order
to wage an offensive against the rightist unions. Farmers
owning more than ten hectares were excluded from membership.
Fernand Pelloutier, Histoire des bourses du travail (Paris,
1902), pp. 206, 213. The FBT declared itself dedicated "To
understanding and propagating the actions of the bourses du
travail in industrial and rural centers." Sylvain Humbert,
Le mouvement syndical (Paris, 1912), p. 32.

36. R. E. Matillon notes that the first rural workers
to become militants were those who were the earliest
affected by industrialization. During the 1890's, when the
use of oil fuel reduced the demand for charcoal by
one-third, the woodcutters struck. By the end of the
decade, the woodcutters had gained a great deal of influence
in these rural bourses. But as the survivors of the
industry began to receive higher wages, militancy declined.
Then the bourses began including farmworkers in their
membership campaigns. See Les syndicats ouvriers, pp.
9-10, 22-24, 46-47.

37. The new "rural tactics" adopted by French
socialists in 1892, notes Klein, were clearly aimed at the
1893 elections, Les théories agraires, p. 36. Elie Coulet
notes that in preparation for their 1892 congress, the
socialists sent circulars to all rural communes inquiring
into their needs. This information would provide them with
the basis for their agrarian program and for forming
agrarian unions under the aegis of the party. Le mouvement
syndical et coopératif, p. 68. See also Augé-Laribé, Grande
ou petite, p. 128.

38. In 1877 Jaurès declared that the only way to
develop social consciousness in the peasantry was for
militants to work for improvement of rural conditions.

Klein, Les théories agraires, pp. 110-111.

39.   Reported   in   ibid.,   pp. 42-43.   See   also   Jean
Bourdeau,   L'evolution   du   socialisme   (Paris,   1901)   for
further   discussion   on   the   socialist   party   in   France   and   the
peasant   question.

40.   Discussed in Augé-Laribé,   Grande   ou   petite,   p.
128.

41.   Engels   quoted in ibid.,,   pp. 130-132.   Engels used
numerous occasions to rail against the heretical stand taken
by the French.   In 1894 he adamantly declared in Neue Zeit
that   "We cannot tolerate in our party, groups of capitalist
interests."   By   definition   that   meant   small   or   large
landowners   and   those   who   raised animals.   In 1894 Engels
further declared: "Our French friends are the only ones in
the socialist world trying to eternalize, not only the small
proprietor,   but   the   farmer   who   exploits foreign labor."
Quoted in Georges Pélissonnier, Etude sur le socialisme
agraire en France (Dijon, 1902), pp. 65, 71.

42.   Guesde in Bourdeau, L'évolution du socialisme, p.
315.   It is interesting to note the change in Guesde's
thinking   from   his   previous   rigidly Marxist   stand   by
comparing the 1892 statement with one he had made in 1879.
Then he had declared that "the soil could not belong to some
people to the detriment of others."   The subtle nuances
between these two statements represent   radically   opposite
poles   of   thought.   The 1879 statement appears in David
Mitrany,   Marx Against   the Peasant: A Study in Social
Dogmatism (Chapel Hill, 1957) p. 19.

43.   Lafargue   in   Bourdeau,   L'évolution du socialisme,
pp. 316-317.

44.   Jaurès   in   Klein,   Les   théories   agraires,   pp.
110-111.

45.   Jaurès in Augé-Laribé, Grande ou petite, pp. 139-
140.

46.   Peter Kropotkin, The Conquest of Bread (New York,
1972),   pp. 210-229   for his chapter on agriculture, and pp.
226-229 for quotes.

47.   Elisée Réclus, A mon frère, le paysan (Saint-
Josseten-Noode, n.d.), pp. 49, 53, 55-56 for quotes and
pertinent data. His italics.

48.   Le Libertaire, 6 June 1896.

49.   Ibid., 11 Jan. 1903.

50.   Ibid., 15 Feb. 1896.

51.   Ibid., 10 July 1904, 3 Sept. 1904, 5 Nov. 1905.

PERSONS CITED

Paul, Georges (?-?), militant anarchist and secretary of the Ivry-sur-Seine bourse.   In 1908 he was an unsuccessful candidate for undersecretary of the CGT.   He was involved for a time in editing a working-class newspaper.   After 1909 he developed a hostility to the direction the CGT was taking.   He eventually moved to the extreme right and became a royalist.

7. The Peasant Question: A Paradox

Although the libertarian element was very strong within the syndicalist movement, the hard line taken by anarchists on the question of collectivization was not so easy for revolutionary syndicalists to adopt. Anarchists thought in terms of future apocalypses; syndicalists had to concern themselves with immediate economic and organizational demands. The anarchist message reflected the assumption that the audience was an unconscious mass. The union members who helped shape syndicalism's position on the peasant question were frequently men from the provinces with strong rural ties and/or peasant backgrounds. They knew from experience that the peasantry was neither a mass, nor collectively mute. Most important, anarchist populism remained squarely positioned in the realm of theory. For syndicalists, the exigencies of left-wing politics dictated that the peasant question be framed with very definite goals in mind.

In the beginning the formulation of syndicalism's rural offensive was largely conditioned by the struggle to remain autonomous from the party socialists. Later it became a rallying point between the CGT and the FBT. Syndicalists were also aware that the influence of the countryside was increasing, and they feared the manipulation of the peasantry by politicians of both the right and left. Irrespective of the political issues, however, the peasant problem was one that would have to be addressed by the unions. Syndicalists knew that what happened to the industrial worker was as much determined by rural activity as by capitalist machinations.

Before industrialization, town and country workers might remain distinct entities, united only in a common concern for bountiful harvests. With the advent of machines, peasant influx to the factories became an added factor, along with food prices, directly affecting the city workers' economic well-being. Increasingly, the rural population figured into the working-class struggle. Peasant ignorance nourished the Church. Politicians scrambled with one another to court the country with material favors in order to maintain themselves in power; so peasant greed

buttressed the state. But when workers sought by collective
effort to use direct action to alleviate their sufferings,
they were dispatched by guns placed by the government in the
hands of peasant soldiers. Unionists became increasingly
aware that the course of the social revolution rested upon
the ability to win the peasantry over to syndicalism. That
goal was severely hampered by the fact that revolutionary
syndicalism, unlike party socialism, possessed neither a
single overriding ideology nor a concrete political forum.
Without either of these, it was exceedingly difficult to
formulate a clearly defined policy capable of overcoming the
mutual suspicion existing between city and country.
Nevertheless, syndicalism's rural offensive was an important
weapon in the struggle for survival: of the worker, the
unions, and of the socialist revolution.

GUESDIST POPULISM DESIGNED TO LEAD AT NANTES

     The discussion on the subject of the peasantry at the
Nantes congress of unions in 1894 provides a classic example
of the way in which syndicalists used the peasant question,
as they had often used the woman question, for purposes of
political expediency. The left was in disarray; a multitude
of sects were in contention. For those who had pressed for
the meeting, the congress was intended to provide the arena
for doing battle against the party socialists. As noted in
the first chapter, the major weapon was to be the issue of
the general strike, a principle gaining increasing
acceptance among anarchists, Allemanists, unionists, and
bourse activists. The vote on the general strike was
intended to serve as a shibboleth separating the issues of
economic activism from party opportunism. Although they had
opposed the convening of the congress, the Guesdists also
came prepared with a program that would serve as a rallying
point. Unlike the issue of the general strike, which was an
instrument of divisiveness between peasants and workers, the
Guesdists declared, the agrarian program adopted by the POF
was designed to be a positive platform on which to unite
city and country.
     Pelloutier opened the discussion on the peasant
question, the first order of business, by reading a petition
sent to the FBT from a group of farmworkers in the
Loire-Inférieure. The workers were trying to use all legal
means at their command to win a dispute with their employer.
They had sought the intervention of the Socialist Party
deputies; they were now appealing to the congress for a vote
of solidarity. The farmworkers' request provided the
occasion for all to wax eloquently on the theme of unity,
and on the fact that the traditional antagonisms existing
between agrarian and industrial workers were disappearing.
     All agreed that the workers in the factories and in the
fields were bound together in a commonality of suffering and
exploitation. The recognition of that unity, the delegates
contended, must serve as the stimulus for working together

to establish a just society based on collective ownership of property. The task would not be easy, noted Davin of Algeria.   Large proprietors had taken advantage of the 1884 law to unionize the countryside. Their program of mutual assistance was attracting a large following. Further, they had made their organizations centers for examining those questions in which the peasantry was interested: local concerns and the problems of agriculture in general.   There was also the question of the peasantry itself. Country folk were naturally suspicious. Unlike the city workers, peasants were not accustomed to meeting together to share their grievances and debate strategy. It was therefore incumbent upon the militant city worker, "the elect," according to Davin, to launch a propaganda offensive in the countryside. The organized workers must point out the disparity existing between the honest worker and the parasites who appropriated the peasant's labor and lived a life of ease. Militants must also preach the message that the solution to the desperate situation faced by peasant smallholders lay in collectivism. Collective exploitation would allow the farmer to realize more directly the benefits of his own labor because there would be no financial burdens for him to bear except nominal costs of operation.   A vigorous contact with the peasantry would make the agrarian laborer realize that the interests of all workers were the same: "to divest themselves of the hornets that live at their expense."(1)

The scandalous exploitation of the field hands was so flagrant that they were deserting the countryside to live in the city, declared Emile Noel of Bordeaux. The unions must recruit country workers, thereby convincing the peasantry that socialism "is not the bête-noire their bourgeois deputy or squire priest had made of it." But the farmers must be told the truth: the course of economic evolution would result in the disappearance of the small proprietor. The revolution could not be forestalled, Noel said.(2)

Victor Chiron presented a report on the "Travailleurs des campagnes," formulated by the Circle of Social Studies of Brest, of which he was a member. Because of the importance of the peasantry's social function and of the injustice and misery of their situation, the study group had undertaken an in-depth investigation of the special problems of the farmers. The guiding principle of the Brest group was that each person had a right to the exclusive use of the products of his labor, and that no one had the right to the fruits of another's labor. The best social organization was collectivism, which was not incompatible with individual property, because in each system the individual remained "absolute master of the equivalent of his work." Collective appropriation did not conflict with individual liberty, Chiron insisted, since that form of organization was intended "to rescue human individuality from the economic shackles inhibiting the free development" of every man. But since the social transformation could not occur all at once, Chiron concluded, his group called for the adoption of a

series of progressive reforms aimed at improving the lot of
the workers. The reforms suggested were virtually the   same
as those comprising the agrarian package of the POF.(3)

Delegates were in complete accord on the need for a
rural offensive and in support of a program of agrarian
reform and collective expropriation of the land. Martin of
the Ceramic Workers' Union suggested the ground might be
prepared for the peasants' acceptance of collectivism by a
vigorous campaign waged against the greatest curse in
society, the spirit of individualism.(4) Shoemaker Louis
Trévaux posited another way to achieve collectivism,
designed to benefit urban workers and farmers alike.   Young
people would be forced to attend agricultural school until
the ages of eighteen or twenty, after which they would be
given land to farm under the careful scrutiny of the farm
unions. The land parceled out to the young farmers would
have been expropriated in the same way as the land used by
the public utility companies, he declared.(5) The plan
offered something for everyone. Young people would be kept
on the farms and out of the job market; labor unions would
be assigned an important task in society; and collectivism
would be undertaken gradually but surely. Gabriel Farjat of
the Lyon <u>bourse</u> was less concerned about collectivism than
about articulating a program of practical agrarian reform.
His suggestions included the institution in the cantons of
free medical and pharmaceutical services, the creation of
hunting preserves, with the right to hunt extended to all,
and the indemnification of reservists called up by the
state.(6)

The resolution resulting from the lengthy debate on the
peasant question was submitted by Charles Brunellière,
representing naval rigging workers from Nantes. It noted
the deepening misery suffered by the farmers; it called for
an end to the competition between city and country induced
by the existing regime, and urged that a vigorous recruiting
campaign be carried out by the <u>bourses</u> and unions.   While
this general resolution, unanimously adopted by the
delegates, appears to have been nothing more than a bland
statement of principle and a call for solidarity, the
detailed reports submitted by the Marseille <u>bourse</u> and the
Dijon Fédération des Bourses, also adopted, were duplicates
of the agricultural program of the POF.(7)

The discussion of the peasant question at Nantes
illuminates the fact that the delegates were more concerned
about maintaining ideological integrity than in dealing with
the real problems of the countryside.   An economic
revolution was in the process of destroying the peasant's
way of life, one based on individualism and private
property, the delegates concluded. Although the capitalists
were the culprits, and the working class was equally
victimized by events with the peasantry, the conscious
workers would support a few interim economic reforms
intended to alleviate individual suffering, but not slow the
process.   The message of sympathy and the offer of
solidarity were hardly designed to comfort the farmer. Only

a few suggestions were made to cast their message in themes guaranteed to strike a responsive chord in the countryside. These included the expropriation of the large landowners and the reaffirmation of hunting privileges, part of the peasants' patrimony from the Revolution of 1789.

This apparent inability to speak to the needs of the peasantry demonstrated a general lack of understanding by the delegates of their rural constituency, to be sure. But more important, what the discussions reveal is that the peasant question was clearly intended to be a medium of the internal power struggle between economic and party socialists for control of the working-class movement. The theme of urban-rural harmony was regarded as a unifying one among the factions and a counter to the divisive issue of the general strike. As it turned out, Guesdists could take cold comfort in the professed accord on the agrarian question. During the ensuing bitter arguments over the issue of the general strike, the Guesdists attempted to use the peasant question as a defense against their attackers. The delegates had just committed themselves unreservedly to the task of rapprochement between town and country, noted the Guesdists. Yet they were now considering adopting a utopian scheme that would weaken the working-class movement by losing the support of the "pitchforks and scythes."(8) The tactic did not work. When the resolution in support of the general strike was passed, the Guesdists walked out of the meeting.

Throughout the convention, it was apparent that Pelloutier was angling for delegate support for FBT leadership of the working-class organization. His campaign was futile.(9) Following the Nantes meeting, Pelloutier turned his attention over the next few years until his death to strengthening the bourses and the FBT. Recruiting activity in the countryside was stepped up.(10) Pelloutier even supported the idea of changing the name of some member FBT unions to "Unions of Workers of the Soil and of the Supplementary Industries."(11) By placing the primary emphasis on farmworkers, Pelloutier hoped to attract large numbers of rural workers to the fold. His efforts in the countryside achieved some organizational success: while he lived the FBT was strong enough to maintain its autonomy as a parallel organization to the CGT.

THE RURAL OFFENSIVE AS THE MEANS TO SYNDICALIST UNITY

In the ensuing years the peasant question was frequently raised as a useful point of accord between the unions and the bourses. At the founding congress of the CGT in 1895, the agrarian question was the second item on the agenda. Its inclusion was guided less by the activities of the party socialists and more as a means of welding the bourse delegates to the new Confederation, particularly in the face of Pelloutier's boycott of the meeting.

Then in December 1899, as noted in an earlier chapter, an attempt was made at a General Congress of Socialists in Paris to weld all leftist groups, including corporate organizations such as the FBT, into a unified socialist party. The FBT declined the invitation and reasserted its autonomy within the CGT. Perhaps this overture, which pointed out the need to garner the support of the <u>bourse</u> members, prompted the Confederation to reexamine the peasant question at its 1900 congress. Delegates were also inspired by the need to increase union membership. Women were a hitherto untapped source of recruits. So too was the peasantry, as the FBT was demonstrating. In order to launch a successful rural offensive, a viable agrarian program was needed. In formulating that program, the CGT found itself on the horns of a dilemma. The Nantes program of 1894 was attractive to the peasantry, but it was the agrarian platform of the POF. A pro forma adoption would smack of "me-too-ism," and leave the CGT trailing in the shadow of the party socialists. With the political left again making forays on the unions, the need to delineate the differences between electoral and economic socialism became exceedingly important. The socialist politicians were opportunist and reformist, the syndicalists reasoned. The CGT must stand squarely on the side of revolution. The dilemma was that it was a communist revolution the unions were preaching, a message repulsive to the peasants. Further, unless the CGT could offer the rural population some hope of immediate economic reform, peasants would continue to remain aloof from revolutionary syndicalism. The obvious solution was for the CGT to concentrate its propaganda efforts on the agrarian proletariat--the landless peasant who worked for wages. As the delegates were to learn, the peasant question in France defied easy answers.

At Paris Paul Fribourg threw down the gauntlet. As an Allemanist he was frustrated by the fact that every time the left attempted to formulate propaganda for the countryside, it was confounded in its efforts, either by electoral preoccupations or by the inability to get past the question of the definition of small versus large proprietorship. Quantity of property was not an issue, Fribourg exclaimed; property ownership was. Distinction between ownership and nonownership was not a matter of contention, but an obvious fact. Syndicalism's task was to organize those farmworkers who owned nothing.(12)

Delegate Treich disagreed. The large proprietors were extending their grip on the smallholders by sponsoring agricultural exhibits and agrarian unions. These were the real enemies. In the Limousin, the small property holder was generally deeply in debt to the giant landlords. But although the small farmers were fearful of taking any action that might cut them off from future financing, the pettyholders regarded these giants as their enemies. This was a natural milieu for union organization, declared Treich. Syndicalism's task was to make propaganda, not employ grand formulas.(13)

The debate that followed centered on trying to reach an accord on these two positions. On the one hand, delegates argued that it was impossible to assess when a smallholder was a capitalist exploiter, and called for the exclusion of all property holders from the unions. On the other hand, numerous delegates argued that in the countryside the ownership of property was not an automatic equation with capitalism. Syndicalism should expand its power base by unionizing the smallholders as well as the propertyless farmworkers.

Delegate Bourguer, a weaver from Rheims, stated that the unions must stop haggling over the definition of property, since no one could adequately determine where an employer or a proprietor began or ended. The small-property farmer could not be classed as being truly exploited since, in Bourguer's opinion, it was too easy for even the marginal farmer to become an exploiter.(14) Delegate Paillot agreed that this was not the place to discuss the plight of the smallholders. If these people felt victimized by outside forces, they could form their own organizations of defense. If they were not careful, Paillot warned, syndicalists would soon find themselves arguing for the formation of unions for small merchants and industrialists.(15)

The decision to dismiss all property owners from union activity was not so simple, delegate Renier reminded the audience. He had been raised in a rural district in the Nord and was intimately aware of the problems occurring in the countryside. In the area where he grew up, farmers raised crops for the local distillery where his father was employed. In the early days, the large number of smallholders served as a buffer against the big landlords, so the lot of the farmhand was infinitely better than at present. Over the course of two decades, however, the distillery had centralized its holdings, and was now an immense farm owning more than two-thirds of the property in the area. Many of the small proprietors had become agrarian proletarians living a wretched existence because the large landowners, farmers, and sugar manufacturers could impose whatever conditions they wished on the smallholders who produced for them.(16)

Those who wished to include the peasant smallholder appeared to be in the majority. Another Allemanist, Albert Bourderon, spoke on the issue. He too had come from the land. He had worked with his father on a farm until the age of twenty-five. Then he became a cooper, but continued to work in the rural districts before coming to Paris. He knew that it was impossible to equate property ownership with exploitation. Too many peasants owned a hectare of land and a mortgaged shack. They worked for themselves during part of the year and then as day laborers on the sharecroppers' farms. These people were the true proletarians, Bourderon said, while the métayers and fermiers who harvested hundreds of sacks of wheat and employed three or four workers were not. The marginal farmer, like the day laborer, was as exploited as any industrial worker. The distinction between proletariat and proprietor must be based on the particular situation, Bourderon concluded, and must not be measured according to the simple distinctions holding sway in the city.(17) Carpenter Jean Voillot agreed. Smallholders in his province worked their plots of ground for seven or eight months a year just for the luxury of producing some carrots and cabbage. To earn the money to buy the wheat to make their bread, noted Voillot, these farmers then had to spend four months of every year chopping wood for wages. One could hardly call these people capitalists.(18)

Those arguing for the inclusion of the small peasant owner in the definition of exploited then took another tack, framing their position on the basis of what a strong syndicalist organization in the countryside would mean to the city workers. Bourderon reminded the delegates that it was the rural worker who competed with the city worker. The main reason for the rural exodus so devastating to the urban worker was the deep-seated belief that the city was the place to earn enough money to enable the landless farmer to return to the countryside and buy his little plot of land. Since childhood, declared Bourderon, the peasant was educated to the belief that land ownership was a worthy goal. The conscious workers must bring the true message of communism to their rural brethren.(19) Emile Pouget agreed that the work of reeducation was needed. But the task was difficult. The peasant was naturally mistrustful of anything that came from the city: merchants sold him adulterated goods; politicians sold him false promises; militants rebuked him for his longing for a plot of ground. The day the militants went to the country with nothing to sell the peasant except the message that there was a higher form of liberty, and that his individual property provided him with only a false freedom, then the peasant would easily accept the ideas of association and collectivism, said Pouget.(20)

The question of educating the countryside was a critical one, equal in importance to the issue of who might serve as worthy agents of propaganda to the rural masses. Numerous suggestions were offered. The unions could sponsor industrial fairs, said one delegate, at which the syndicalist message could be disseminated. Union members whose infants were wetnursed in the countryside might also have beneficial contacts, he pointed out. The military was another excellent medium for propaganda. Young union members might serve as hosts to soldiers stationed in their areas. Unionists in the reserve could also carry syndicalism to the peasants serving in their outfits.(21)

Several delegates even suggested the importance of small property holders in the union's propaganda offensive. Organization could occur only as long as there existed a certain degree of independence among the potential union members. Without the aid of enlightened spokesmen, most farmworkers would not even know when union meetings were being held. Delegate Mazas of Montpellier gave a more

pointed example of the importance of the smallholders to
unionism. A group of militants had gone into the smaller
communes preaching syndicalism. The results were positive:
the agricultural workers in his area received their first
pay raise in ten years. But after the harvest, some
unscrupulous employers attempted to lower their workers'
wages again. A "little strike" changed the proprietors'
minds. That strike would not have succeeded, Mazas
recounted, if the small proprietors had not served the
farmhands as intermediaries.(22)

The peasant question, as the delegates were learning,
offered no easy answers. Unable to arrive at a specific
definition of property holder, the Paris delegates agreed to
include in their definition of rural proletariat those
farmers who owned property but worked it themselves.(23)
Without the electoral experience as a device for raising
consciousness and counting their converts, the only medium
syndicalists had was their message. And that message had to
be broadcast as far as possible. The offer of union
membership and the promise to represent the agrarian
workers' cause had to be inclusive rather than exclusive.
With this realization, the Paris delegates accepted the fact
that they must pursue practical measures rather than employ
ideological formulas.

THE GENERAL STRIKE AND THE NEED FOR RURAL SUPPORT

After 1900 there was a strong drive within the FBT to
seek fusion with the CGT. Pelloutier died in 1901. The
party socialists seemed on the point of reaching a common
accord. The bulk of the CGT meeting at Lyon that year was
devoted to changing the Confederation's statutes in order to
allow the FBT to enter as an autonomous organization. The
fight over rules left no time to devote to the peasant
question. But at the next congress, held in Montpellier in
1902, delegates turned their attention to other matters, not
the least of which concerned the peasantry. The placing of
the peasant question on the CGT's agenda is not surprising,
given the fact that the congress was held in the center of
wine country. For the first time, farmworkers' unions were
represented at the congress. But from an organizational
standpoint, the attention paid to the peasant question
served many needs: membership rolls were still important; so
too was the need to cement the bonds of fusion with the FBT.
With Pelloutier gone, the FBT had voted to join the
Confederation. As a means, perhaps, of acknowledging
officially the importance of the FBT, the bourses were
assigned the job of handling agrarian affairs for the
Confederation. In addition, a new element had become
important at the congress: the general strike. A close
alliance with the rural organizations would provide a means
of convincing skeptics--both of the towns and the
countryside--that the general strike was not a utopian
scheme, but very much within the realm of practical

possibility. More pointed was the realization that the general strike would never succeed if the city workers had a hostile countryside behind them.

Members of the agrarian unions aggressively participated in the discussion, losing no time in stressing the need for solidarity. Describing himself as "a modest cultivator" and "a new recruit to the syndicalist army," Baptiste Milhaud brought salutations from the Syndicat des Cultivateurs de Mèze (Hérault). Peasants were finally becoming aware that they were being duped by the politicians and the large landowners, although propaganda was still needed to bring the peasants to unionism.(24) Delegate Charles Farras, a former farmworker who had been fired for his union activity, pointed out the increasing mutualism existing between city and country workers. Without the support of the industrial workers, the agrarian unions were helpless in their struggle for reform. He cited a recent example of a strike made by a group of workers against the imposition of a ten-hour day. The employer relented in the face of the harvesters' show of strength. But the owner well knew that because the workers were not firmly organized or affiliated with any outside power, when winter came he would be able to make good his threat to lower wages and recover his losses.(25)

The agrarian workers needed the power of the industrial unions, to be sure. But numerous delegates agreed with Farras and elaborated upon the importance of the peasantry to unionism's successful march toward revolution. Amédée Bousquet noted that the comrades who belonged to his foodworkers' union were nearly all drawn from the country proletariat. They had been "pushed onto the city's pavement by the imperious necessity to live," he explained, "but they had not lost their memories of their infancy nor forgotten the sufferings they had had to endure." Despite their separation from the centers of action, despite their sometime ignorance, the rural population was nevertheless a formidable force. "We should recall that in 1789 [the peasants] were the ones who burned the farms and chateaux," said Bousquet. With education and assistance from the CGT, the peasants would be ready to march with the city workers in the general strike.(26) Leatherworker Bourchet reported on the dangers inherent in neglecting the peasantry. The rightist unions were making strong advances in the countryside, he warned. In 1884 there were five such unions. In 1900 that figure had grown to 2,204, with over one-half million adherents.(27)

The need to root out reaction in the countryside was an important theme at the Montpellier congress. It was at this meeting that the principle of the general strike was adopted as the primary weapon in the revolutionary arsenal. Two lengthy presentations--one by Milhaud and the other by Bourchet--dealt with the nature of society following the revolution, a form of speculation seldom engaged in by syndicalists. To dwell on the particular attributes of post-revolutionary society had always been dismissed as

utopian   musings.   One   can only guess the reasons for this
deviation.   Was   it   to   provide   the   delegates   with   an
all-encompassing unity of vision?   Would that unity gain the
enthusiastic   support   of   all   for   the   general   strike as a
means by which to bring the future society into existence?
Perhaps.   The   more   prosaic   aspect   of   these   two
presentations,   however,   is   that   both   speakers   made   it
abundantly clear that the future could not be realized
without the support of the bourses and the peasantry.
     Milhaud's   report,   presented   on   behalf   of   his
agricultural workers, centered on two questions: how best to
organize the unions to replace the capitalist class, and how
to   assure   production, exchange, and consumption during and
after the revolution.   To prepare the   countryside   for   the
general   strike,   Milhaud   reported,   the   farm unions would have
to work closely with the bourses because of the need for the
professional   instruction   this   latter   organization   could
provide.   As for the future after the   revolution,   workers
need   have   nothing   to fear, Milhaud assured the delegates.
The soil was rich, the products of the fields and vines were
abundant.   With no monopolies or   famine,   the   prospect   of
economic   well-being   for   all   was   a   certainty.   The very
simplicity of life lent assurance to the fact that only   the
most   elemental   administrative machinery would be needed in
future   society.   Milhaud   could   foresee   only   two   such
organizations: a   Commission   of   Statistics   and   Labor
Allotment and   a   Study   Commission,   each   of   which   would
perform   functions   currently carried on by the bourses.(28)
The data presented by Bourchet in his report were   extremely
complex,   but   the   point was the same: both the bourses and
the peasantry were essential to the course of the revolution
and the establishment of a just society.(29)
     The resolutions passed by   the   delegates   after   such
voluminous   debate   on   the   peasant   question were standard.
The   issue   of   collectivization   was   muted,   although   the
delegates   vowed   that the CGT would dedicate itself anew to
the task of organizing the rural proletariat in   defense   of
its   demands.   One of the last proposed resolutions was that
offered by Lelorrain of the tobacco workers, who called   for
the   establishment   of   a   war   chest to carry out the rural
offensive.   To the penurious union members, the question   of
additional dues had an effect similar to baiting a bull with
a red cape.   After a brief discussion, the congress rejected
Lelorrain's   motion   and   adopted   the   one   of metallurgist
Eugène Reisz, which suggested that unions located   in   rural
areas   carry on the educational process by inviting peasants
to attend their meetings.   Then there would be no   special
propaganda   treasury   needed.(30)   Apparently   the   CGT   was
committed to the task of unionism in   the   countryside,   but
not if it were going to cost money!
     Despite the injunction made at Monpellier to place   the
peasant   question   on   the agenda of the following congress,
and in   the   face   of   the   violent   strike   activity   among
farmworkers   in   1904,   the   CGT gave no official attention to
the peasant question at its next congress.(31) Instead,   the

delegates to the Bourges congress of 1904 were too involved
in resolving the struggle between reformists and
revolutionaries, a fight in which the peasantry did not
figure. The degree to which the rural elements were
exempted from the larger issues of confederal organization
was revealed in the protest registered by Hippolyte Mauger
over the way the deliberations were going. A representative
of seven woodcutters' unions, Mauger declared his disgust
over the fact that the delegates were ignoring the important
issues. Peasant delegations had come to this congress to
make contact with their comrades in industry, he declared,
and to offer their collaboration on such vital questions as
the eight-hour day and retirement. The peasant question
demanded the attention of the unions. But for four or five
days, Mauger scolded, the delegates had engaged in "sterile
discussions" of a personal nature rather than of general
interest. He and his companions urged the assembly to
return to vital issues. After giving Mauger a round of
unanimous bravos, the delegates stopped haggling and took up
the question, not of the peasantry, but of the eight-hour
day.(32)

COMMUNIST HARMONY BETWEEN CITY AND COUNTRY WORKERS

With the left safely in control of the unions after
1904, delegates to the CGT congresses had virtually nothing
to say on the peasant question until the 1912 congress.(33)
In the interim, the issue continued to be addressed in La
Voix du Peuple. The most important series of articles to
appear in that paper was written by H. Beaujardin, a
collaborator on Emile Pouget's Père Peinard. The series,
entitled "Lettres d'un paysan," and running primarily during
the first half of 1901, contained a twofold message: to
point out the twin dangers of proprietary syndicalism and
party socialism, and to outline the natural revolutionary
tendencies already inherent in the peasantry.

The first article opened with a literary salute "in the
fraternal agape to the coming of a better world" designed to
cheer the hearts of those who labored in the vineyards. The
first year of the new century had been a good harvest year,
noted Beaujardin. It was time for the city and country
proletariat to fill their glasses and drink together often.
"After having clinked glasses with a comrade," said
Beaujardin, "one has more resources for the daily tasks and
future struggle. . . . The good juice of the vine sharpens
ideas and activates energy," Beaujardin counseled. That
energy must be turned toward the task of reaching common
accord. If times were bad in the city, they were likewise
bad in the country. If the city worker were out of work or
paid low wages, he could not buy the farmers' goods. If, on
the other hand, farmers could not sell their wheat, they
were unable to buy the manufactured goods produced in the
city. Therefore, all must drink together for "the day when
communist harmony replaces proprietary competition."

Workers of the factories and fields must depend upon one another for their liberation. The mixed syndicats may have brought some tangible monetary results for the peasantry, Beaujardin conceded, but one must not be beguiled by a few material benefits. These associations were under the control of large landowners, lawyers, and bureaucrats, and were ultraconservative organizations. Nor did the radical or socialist politicians hold the key to improving the peasant's lot. Thirty years of the Republic had brought no real advancement to the countryside, he noted. The few material benefits were paltry in the face of the multiplication of the bureaucracy and the intrusion of capitalism into the countryside. The social revolution could never be achieved by electoral combinations, Beaujardin asserted; it could come only by means of the general strike.

In this series Beaujardin constantly sought to articulate the revolution in the language of the countryside. To those who complained of peasant parochialism and of their independent nature, Beaujardin pointed out that these were virtues compatible with the success of revolution. After all, he reminded his readers, future society would be one based on the grouping of free individuals. Further, the commune in the countryside, like the syndicat, would become the foyer of a new life. In another article, Beaujardin implicitly hailed the general strike as the counterpart of the jacquerie, since the aim of both was to expropriate all privileges. He further noted that communalism was a natural mode of existence among the peasantry, and that the communal society of the future had its seeds in the agrarian past. Nor was the peasant's attachment to his individual holdings atavistic. The proprietary feelings held by the farmer was an indication to Beaujardin that the peasants wanted well-being and independence, which at this stage of evolution, they had come to associate with private property. Eventually the peasant would come to the realization that true well-being could only be achieved in communal possession.

In the final article of his series, Beaujardin responded to charges made by Jaurès, who had asserted that the syndicalists' reliance on the general strike was a chimera. One could overthrow governments, perhaps, but not make a spontaneous economic revolution, particularly when there were too many defenders of capitalism, such as the army, with which to contend. Most futile of all, Jaurès had concluded, was syndicalism's encouragement of the "morcellement" of power. Revolution can occur only when power is centralized, not dispersed and fragmented.

In answer to these assertions, Beaujardin pointed out that it was not necessary for revolutionary consciousness to permeate the masses before the new order could be brought forth. Even "the inert and unconscious" would support a revolution to improve their material existence. The old animosities between the city and country would disappear

once the peasantry saw the large numbers of
city-manufactured products made available to them. As for
the army, syndicalism was preparing the way for its
emasculation through propaganda. History has demonstrated,
Beaujardin pointed out, that the army is not always a
bastion of the status quo, but is often the force for
revolution. Jaurès' concept of power was also faulty, due
undoubtedly to his "political preoccupation." Centralization
of power might be useful in overthrowing a parliament or a
class, declared Beaujardin, struggles that change no basic
social relations. But centralization was useless for
carrying out a revolution that had nothing but a social
end. The dispersion of forces Jaurès had derided was just
what would make the general strike invincible, continued
Beaujardin, for it would carry out a revolution, not decided
in Paris, but involving the whole country. It was because
the impending revolution was unlike any other, concluded
Beaujardin, "that the general strike is necessary."(34)

Throughout the following few years, although the
articles appealing to the peasantry were few and far
between, the editors of La Voix du Peuple did not ignore the
countryside completely. Rather than publishing outright
propaganda pieces, such as those written by Beaujardin, the
pages of the CGT's paper were devoted to recording strike
activity and the growth of unions. Unlike the party
socialists and the syndicats agricoles of the right,
revolutionary syndicalism's channels of communication with
the countryside were limited to the bourses and a few
radical unions. Therefore, any proliferation of peasant
strikes and demonstrations, even if not directed by the CGT,
was regarded as a sign that syndicalism's message of direct
action was penetrating the countryside. In 1902 Pierre
Hervier asserted that union propaganda had produced "a
flourishing union" in the Cher.(35) The following year,
Louis Niel reported on the steady progress of peasant
syndicalism, noting that some meetings were attended by four
hundred people. This was an indication to Niel that the
message of unionism was being well-received by the
peasantry, particularly the farm women who were often the
first to suffer from the inadequacy of their husbands'
wages.(36)

The increase in strike activity, as noted in La Voix du
Peuple, was regarded as an optimistic sign to syndicalists.
In 1904 Charles Desplanques reported on a peasant revolt in
the Aude. After being fined 2,500 francs for taking lumber
from the forest of a large proprietor, the peasants of the
village armed themselves with their hunting rifles and kept
everyone from entering their commune. The rebellion was
finally mediated to a peaceful conclusion by the local
prefect and deputies. But as Desplanques joyfully pointed
out, the demonstration by these unorganized farmers was a
certain indication that the peasantry was "very close to the
ideal of liberty [already possessed] by organized
workers."(37) That same year Louis Niel reported that the
increase in peasant strike activity was a positive sign for

city workers, who had always feared that any effort on their part to realize a new social order might be checked by "the abstention of their peasant brothers." The rounds of strikes in the country should give the urban worker "courage and hope."(38)

In 1907 the editors reported on the peasant strikes in the Midi, in which one of the first to be killed was a militant of the Narbonne bourse. Despite the tragedy, it was evident that syndicalism had penetrated into the countryside: a regiment of the Seventeenth of the Line had crossed their rifles and refused to fire on the strikers. Those peasant soldiers, concluded the reporter, had received the union's message "that the bourgeoisie only maintain the army for war in the interior."(39) Two years later the recorded activity of another group of strikers again sounded the message of the mutual dependence existing between farmers and workers. Unionism had arrived in 1899 to Lavelanet, a town of forty factories, explained textile worker Delsaut, mostly making draperies and employing the majority of the town's 4,000 inhabitants. The unions had carried on a vigorous campaign against militarism and in support of the eight-hour day. The industrialists had ordered a lockout in order to squelch the growing militancy among the workers. Although this action occurred in midwinter, the unionists were not frightened because they knew they could call upon their peasant neighbors. The farmers opened their silos and advanced them 80,000 kilos of potatoes, thereby providing the strikers with the resources to hold out for six months. The workers were still on strike in April, when the bourgeoisie finally capitulated!(40)

THE DARKER SIDE OF THE PEASANT QUESTION

Despite these assertions of progress in the development of peasant consciousness and of the steady growth of mutual accord between factory worker and farmworker, it became increasingly apparent that the darker side of the peasant question nevertheless persisted. A growing number of syndicalists voiced despair over the fact that despite those decades of "going to the country," the returns seemed minuscule when compared to the efforts. Employer-employee unions continued to flourish, thereby guaranteeing the continuation of an entrenched conservatism among the peasantry and a deeper commitment to maintain the status quo.(41) Additionally, the Socialist Party's overtures in the countryside appeared to be reaping a rich harvest.(42) The socialist principle of collectivism, said Léopold Bernard in 1911, was interpreted by the peasantry to mean "the increase of the small proprietor at the expense of the large." To Bernard the SFIO's failure to correct the farmer's misunderstanding of the party program was being translated into party victories in the rural elections.(43)

Worse, socialism was a pernicious force that actually coopted peasant militancy, according to Victor Griffuelhes in his 1911 Voyages révolutionnaires. In the very heartland of revolutionary agrarian syndicalism--Montpellier, Béziers, and Narbonne--where the first agrarian syndicalist congress was held, where the first federation of agrarian syndicalists was formed, in an area where there were thousands of wage farmers, the population had become so victimized by "democratic fictions" and the "bavardage" of political promises that they were incapable of any long-term combat. "At Montpellier," Griffuelhes complained, "they are pawns, not combatants." "At Narbonne, the socialist municipality [was] more interested in administration than in labor action." In that city, the bourse du travail was located in the mairie. How could class war be waged effectively, Griffuelhes asked in disgust, when the workers "call the mayor comrade."(44)

The forces of reaction stubbornly persisted. The effect of the ducs' preachings in favor of traditionalism and the socialists' concurrence on the sanctity of the smallholder's land spelled the increase in superstition, big government, statism, and the enhancement of those atavistic virtues of materialism and competitiveness. However much attention they might devote to the Bourbonnais country workers, professed Léopold Bernard, the militants must realize that the Bourbon métayers had "only one dream: to be a proprietor."(45) The peasant's continued "passion for his little plot of ground," said Paul Ader, militant secretary of the Fédération Agricole du Midi in 1912, "will thwart all our action, it will ruin all our efforts, it will destroy all our work of social action."(46)

The peasant's passion for land ownership impeded the growth of the revolution. It also contributed to the terrible inflation plaguing industrial workers by 1910. High import duties on agricultural products, particularly wheat, were the result of politicians' efforts to curry favor with the peasantry. Rising food prices were not caused by bad harvests or grain shortages, explained Léon Jouhaux in La Voix du Peuple. High import duties meant that foreign grains were not competitive, and French farmers could speculate to their ease. While not wishing to see "a fratricidal struggle between the rural and urban populations, nor cities arrayed against the country," Jouhaux declared, nevertheless unionists must demand respite from "the caprices and exigencies" of the large and middle agriculturalists.(47) Delegates to the 1912 CGT congress at Le Havre also complained of the high cost of living. The major blame for inflation, they agreed, was the creation of international cartels and trusts. But the poor organization of the industrial and agrarian sectors at home was also a contributor. There were several courses open to them. They could tighten their belts or they could carry on an economic war against the farmers by boycotting high-priced foods.(48)

At the same time that party socialism and conservative

unionism seemed to be gaining ground, revolutionary syndicalism appeared to be losing the battle in the countryside. Before 1912 four federations of agricultural workers unions had adhered to the CGT, and three other large federations--the Horticulturists of the Midi, the Vineyard Workers of Champagne, and the Resin-Tappers and Agriculturists of the Landes--had tacitly united by voicing acceptance of CGT principles. Despite such victories, by 1913 membership in the militant rural unions was on the wane. Many of the 628 farmworkers' unions listed by the Labor Ministry at the end of 1912 were only paper organizations. In numerous others, only the secretaries were active.(49)

To a certain degree, the decline of radical agrarian unionism was due to factors outside the militants' control. The gradual easing of population pressures in the countryside because of declining birthrates and rural migration evident in the prewar years may have had a psychological effect in diluting labor militancy. Since there was no apparent increase in large-scale farming during this same period, according to Gordon Wright, the phenomenon of rural depopulation carried with it the prospect of land for the landless and increased holdings for those wishing to rise up the social and economic ladder.(50) The success or failure of rural strikes also played a part in diffusing agrarian militancy. As with his urban counterpart, during times of crisis the farmer was eager to associate to achieve his demands. After the strike was ended, however, either he could not afford union dues or he could see no tangible reason to continue to feed the union's treasury when the organization seemingly offered him nothing for his philanthropy. Of course, syndicalist leaders agreed with Augé-Laribé, who noted in 1907 that "if a lowering of wages provoked a new round of strikes, all the unions which today appear disunited would reform immediately."(51) That knowledge gave small comfort to the realization that the lack of revenue constituted a serious check to unionism's rural offensive.

Some of the inherent tendencies in syndicalism also mitigated against unionism's effective organizational growth among the peasantry. For one thing, syndicalism's antielectoral stand was often rejected by the peasantry. As Tony Judt notes in his study of the Var, voting was often the only avenue of protest for peasants and small-town artisans.(52) For another, the anarchist penchant for eschewing any structural force, preferring to rely instead on spontaneous organization, oftentimes prevented the militants from seizing the advantage. The strikes of 1904-1905 were clearly of an economic nature, noted Michel Augé-Laribé. Yet the local bourse generally waited to be called in by the peasant groups instead of taking advantage of the situation by leading the peasant movement. This lack of action caused Augé-Laribé to conjecture that the CGT had little understanding of rural strikes.(53)

Syndicalists often lost ground because of their

insistence on gaining support for things about which the peasantry cared little and understood less. A great deal of effort was expended to gain approval for the principle of the general strike at the Agricultural Workers' Congress at Narbonne in 1904. Undoubtedly the CGT representatives took pleasure in their victory, gained by changing the language of the resolution to read "general strike of the corporation, an economic and not a social strike" so as to appeal to the peasants' understanding of corporatism and to allay their suspicions against anything that smacked of social revolution. But one can only wonder about the efficacy of the syndicalist leaders' tactics among this group of farmworkers, unaligned with the CGT, who chose to demonstrate the degree of their radicalism by hanging a red flag in the meeting room and refusing to send a letter of condolence to Waldeck-Rousseau's widow!(54)

The commitment to the principle of collectivization, when it was discussed at all, was another barrier to the successful penetration of the countryside by anarchosyndicalism. Griffuelhes might insist in the CGT's 1912 Encyclopédie that syndicalism would not be moved to support a union of peasant proprietors and agrarian wage earners any more than it would countenance a union of petty shopkeepers and industrial workers.(55) But others rejected this hardline stance, suggesting a tactic of expediency in the battle for peasant hearts and minds. In 1908 a unionized teacher submitted an article to La Voix du Peuple reiterating the need to convince the peasantry to support the workers' movement. Effective propaganda would lessen the traditional hostility of the peasant toward the militant workers, whom the peasant regarded as "parasites and malcontents." Workers must understand that the peasant is not an idealist. "Exhortations to solidarity," the writer noted, were empty proclamations to the peasant. Syndicalism's tactic must be to show the concrete material gains to be derived from peasant support of unionism. Syndicalist's agrarian message, the writer suggested, must be:

> Brother peasant, we wish to free you, to liberate you. This land to which you are attached, we leave to you, to free you. The product of your labor will be integrally . . . left to your disposition, these machines which you envy, the industrial unions will place freely in your hands so that your creative work will cost less sweat. [The unions] will construct large farmhouses for you, ventilated, furnished to perfection with those things supplying health and well-being. As for the rapacious proprietor, he will no longer have the right and power to estrange you from the least portion of your profits.

By exalting unionism's "faith in holy labor" and proclaiming "their esteem for all producers"--and by apparently speaking to the stubborn materialism of the peasantry--the writer promised, the countryside would be theirs.(56)

THE QUESTION REMAINS A PARADOX

In attempting to resolve the peasant question, revolutionary syndicalists found themselves in the prewar years impaled with the party socialists on the horns of a dilemma. A stubborn insistence on remaining loyal to collectivism guaranteed that farmers would find little attraction for the left. Yet without peasant solidarity, the revolution would fail. That knowledge had caused party socialists to adopt some effective techniques to make their message more palatable. To win elections, they had softened the "maximalist" stance of no-nonsense expropriation by supporting a "minimalist" program of agrarian legislative reforms. Further, while the party center continued to espouse Marxian determinism, local chiefs were often able to make Marxian collectivism sound like Proudhonian mutualism.(57) On the practical level, the only way open for syndicalists to gain peasants' support was through direct action: encouraging unionism and strike activity. While this tactic was often successful-- both strikes and unions did increase--the method to achieve these ends was slow, difficult to control, and certainly not so flashy as the socialist and conservative politicians' promises for legislative reforms. Unless some improvement in the farmers' condition occurred, however, there would be little to stop the rural exodus to the cities. If farm incomes did not rise, disgruntled peasants would leave the land for the cities or the army--twin anathemas to the industrial worker. In addition, the drain of farmworkers impelled those who remained on the land to mechanize their production.(58) Mechanization increased the farmer's indebtedness and hence, his misery. But it also increased for the consumer the price of the farmer's products. It was a terrible irony syndicalists came to realize: the unions' intercession might bring greater well-being for the peasant; but his shorter work day and higher wages contributed to inflation and another round of labor violence in the cities.(59) In the early years of revolutionary syndicalism, the peasant question had been regarded as a practical response to reality: without peasant solidarity the revolution would fail; unless peasants kept out of the cities, workers' wages would fall. In terms of the organizational struggle, the attempts made to deal with the peasantry provided the syndicalists with a needed rallying point for the CGT's survival, both after the Guesdist walkout and in the light of Pelloutier's boycott of the organization. Further, the unions' rural offensive to gain support of the general strike bolstered syndicalism's radical and revolutionary posture, helped to delineate the movement from party socialism, and in that way, continued to attract to its folds dedicated militants interested in pursuing economic means to their liberation.

It became increasingly apparent that the ideological goal of collectivism could not be squared with the peasants' stubborn materialism. Syndicalism's response to the peasant question was the articulation of a triple agenda: to group rural workers around a program of immediate reform and distant social transformation; to work toward stemming the rural exodus by ameliorating the workers' condition in the countryside; and to prepare the entente for the future revolution.(60) Even with the attempt to mask collectivization in the rhetoric of "a distant social transformation," the CGT's rural offensive seemed impossible to implement, or worse, appeared to have opposite results.(61) The effort to group all the workers of the fields, the woods, and the vineyards around a single program was exceedingly difficult given the increasing diversity of this population.(62) The goal of improving the farmworkers' conditions so as to halt the rural exodus seemed fraught with complications for the urban consumer. The commitment to prepare the entente of all for the coming revolution was becoming to many an impossible task. With the realization that the peasant problem was not a question but a paradox, some expedient had to be found to bridge the gap between the city and the country.

An article by Gustave Hervé in a 1907 issue of La Guerre Sociale seemed to presage the tactic that the CGT would come to use increasingly. During times of unemployment, when the city worker begged in the country for a scrap of bread and a barn corner in which to sleep, the peasants always had exclaimed that the city workers were "sluggards" and malcontents. When the urban proletariat demanded an eight-hour day, the peasant always smugly asserted that he worked from sunup to sundown. When the workers resorted to violence, the peasant indignantly demanded that the government take strong action against these disturbers of the peace. "Now you are in misery and seek direct action," Hervé chided, "and they shoot you down as at Fourmies, Châlon, and Limoges." It was foolish for the farmers to believe that government could reform a society that was inherently evil. Why did the peasant continue to insist on the perpetuation of a system based on individualism and competition, a system that set apart the consumer and the producer, when each could work together to assure abundance for all. When the city workers begin the revolution, Hervé queried of his hypothetical peasant reader, will you be "inert, or will you leave your sons, who are at the barracks, to deal with the malefactors?"(63)

Syndicalists had tried to hold fast to the idea of the revolution occurring by the Marxian formula of capitalist concentration of industry and in the countryside. Not wishing to trust the revolution to chance, they sought to help it along by means of direct action. But propaganda

appealing to the concept of human solidarity was too
abstract for the unlettered and unsophisticated peasantry.
Attempts made at social education were often useless for
farmers who possessed only a rudimentary education. They
tended to be disinterested in reading at bourse libraries
and became restless during union-sponsored lectures.
Stirring oratory might inflame the peasant for the moment,
but he would quickly become disinterested when he understood
what commitment to revolution meant, or when his wife nagged
him for donating even a penny to the city slickers, who
would take his money and run.(64) Union rhetoric and
attempts at education were impractical when neither the
peasant nor the factory worker trusted each other.
Realistically, no grounds for trust existed, since each side
understood that any increase in the other's well-being would
be at its own expense. How then to design a campaign to
weld the disparate elements in the countryside with the
urban proletariat? The answer appears to have been arrived
at instinctively rather than consciously, the way so much of
revolutionary syndicalism's tactics were derived: by the
practical need to find the most effective way to address its
constituency. The bridge to the peasantry for
anarchosyndicalism lay in the use of antimilitarist
propaganda.

In the face of the increasing employment of the
military to suppress labor's demands, the advent of
universal military training which drew proportionately
larger numbers of peasants into the barracks, and the
escalating international tensions that bespoke the
eventuality of a capitalist imperialist war, the
syndicalists found the practical expedient they needed for
the inclusion of the country into their propaganda campaign.
In 1920 E. Martin Saint-Léon mused on the differences
existing between urban and rural syndicalism. Despite their
utterances regarding their alleged preference for pragmatic
action, Saint-Léon noted, urban unionists were more
ideological than were members of agrarian syndicats.
Farmers did not dream of changing the whole world, he
concluded; the dreams of their union leaders therefore were
less grandiose.(65) The increased use of antimilitarist
propaganda would certainly belie the notion that urban
unionists were awash in a sea of ideology.

Instead, antimilitarism was infinitely practical. It
pointed out to the peasantry the duplicity of the state,
thereby serving to check the statism and patriotism of both
the right and left. It was a practical and effective way to
appeal to the patriarchal nature of peasant society and to
bring women to union militancy. Those were mothers' boys
being taken away for cannon fodder; those were peasant sons
being forced to turn their rifles on their fathers and
brothers. The antimilitarist campaign struck a responsive
chord and awakened the long tradition of peasant opposition
to recruitment. Antimilitarism became a practical metaphor
for solidarity: unofficially, with the socialists, who after
1911 adopted a more overtly antimilitarist posture, and

between agrarian and urban workers, who were shot down by the same bullets and maimed by the same sabres.(66) The exploited of the town and country were joined in suffering against the same evil and in the interest of justice. Propaganda for an eight-hour day had little relevance to the farmer who worked his own land; the idea of the general strike was too abstract. Far from being ideological, the use of the tactic of antimilitarist propaganda by revolutionary syndicalists was a practical instrument--and seemingly the only available tactic--directed toward narrowing the chasm that traditionally had existed between the city and the country.

NOTES

1. 6(e) congrès national des syndicats de France: Compte rendu des travaux du congrès . . . (Nantes, 1894), pp. 52-53.

2. Ibid., pp. 102-103.

3. Ibid., pp. 54-57.

4. Ibid., p. 105.

5. Ibid., pp. 104-105.

6. Ibid., p. 100.

7. Ibid., p. 74.

8. Ibid., p. 40. See André May, Les origines du syndicalisme révolutionnaire (Paris, 1913), p. 84 for quote.

9. 6(e) congrès [Nantes, 1894], p. 52.

10. R. E. Matillon, Les syndicats ouvriers dans l'agriculture (Paris, 1908), pp. 22-24.

11. Fernand Pelloutier, Histoire des bourses du travail (Paris, 1902), pp. 204-214.

12. XI(e) congrès national corporatif (V(e) de la confédération générale du travail) . . . (Paris, 1900), p. 71.

13. Ibid., pp. 72-73. At the 1894 Nantes congress, Treich had spoken out in opposition to the general strike, fearing that its adoption as an instrument of direct action would repulse the agrarian segments of the population. See Sylvain Humbert, Le mouvement syndical (Paris, 1912), p. 23.

14. XI(e) congrès [Paris, 1900], p. 73.

15.   Ibid., p. 77.

16.   Ibid., pp. 77-78.

17.   Ibid., pp. 73-75.

18.   Ibid., p. 80.

19.   Ibid., pp. 73-74.

20.   Ibid., pp. 76-77.

21.   Ibid., p. 79.

22.   Ibid., p. 76.

23.   Ibid., p. 82.

24.   XIII(e) congrès national corporatif . . . Compte rendu officiel des travaux du congrès, publié par les soins de la commission d'organisation (Montpellier, 1902), pp. 204-205.

25.   Ibid., pp. 205-206.

26.   Ibid., p. 206.

27.   Ibid., pp. 208-209.

28.   Ibid., pp. 241-243.

29.   Ibid., pp. 223-231.

30.   Ibid., pp. 209-210.

31.   At these demonstrations, dragoons had to be called in. The result was a partial success. Workers received an eight-hour day and a higher ration of wine. In Confédération Générale du Travail. La confédération générale du travail et le mouvement syndical (Paris, 1925), p. 310. [Hereafter referred to as La CGT et le mouvement syndical.]

32.   XIV(e) congrès national corporatif (VIII(e) de la confédération) et conférence des bourses du travail, . . . Compte rendu des travaux (Bourges, 1904), pp. 202-204 for Mauger's comments.

33.   At Amiens in 1906 delegates were too concerned with adopting a modus vivendi by which unity could be achieved. The only reference to the agrarian issue occurred over a rather perfunctory issue concerning membership of those farm unions located too far from the union halls of the mother unions. XV(e) congrès national corporatif (IX(e) de la confédération) et conférence des bourses du

travail . . . Compte rendu des travaux (Amiens, 1906), p. 197.

34. La Voix du Peuple, 23 Dec. 1900, 6 Jan., 20 Jan., 3 Mar., 7 Jul., 18 Aug., 29 Sept. 1901.

35. Ibid., 9 Nov. 1902.

36. Ibid., 12 Apr. 1903.

37. Ibid., 10 Jan. 1904.

38. Ibid., 7 Feb. 1904.

39. Ibid., 30 June 1907.

40. Ibid., 11 Apr. 1909.

41. Statistics of the 1912 membership figures in the proprietary unions appear in an article on the subject by Léon de Seilhac in Victor Griffuelhes and Léon Jouhaux, eds., Encyclopédie du mouvement syndicalist (Paris, 1912), p. 45. They numbered 5,407 unions representing 912,944 men and 15,592 women.

42. The tenth legislative election was an indication to Amédée Dunois, writing on the agrarian question in Griffuelhes and Jouhaux, eds., Encyclopédie du mouvement syndicaliste, that the socialist program was propagating rapidly in the countryside. p. 34.

43. Léopold Bernard, Les idées révolutionnaires dans la campagne du bourbonnais (Paris, 1911), p. 30. Tony Judt would disagree that peasants voted socialist out of ignorance, at least in the Var. He claims that the collectivist implication of socialism was what made it attractive to many Varois peasants. Socialism in Provence 1871-1914. A Study in the Origins of the Modern French Left (Cambridge, 1979), p. 96.

44. Victor Griffuelhes, Voyage révolutionnaire (Paris, 1911), pp. 31-33.

45. Bernard, Les idées réevolutionnaires, p. 28. There were other groups springing up in the countryside that competed with revolutionary syndicalism for members. One such association formed during the peasant disorders in the Midi in 1907. It was led by Marcellin Albert, himself a vintner, who attracted crowds of up to one-half million with his harangues. Albert led a taxpayers' strike, resulting in the mass resignations of mayors and town councils in several hundred communes. When troops could not put down the rising violence, Albert was summoned to Paris and given a hundred franc note by Clemenceau to return home. While the bribe may have cooled Albert's evangelistic fervor, it apparently

did not squelch his desire for reform. Albert was subsequently instrumental in forming the Confédération Générale des Vignerons du Midi as a lobbying organization supporting vintners' interests. See Gordon Wright, Rural Revolution in France: The Peasantry in the Twentieth Century (Stanford, 1964), pp. 27-28.

46. Paul Ader, "Agricole du Midi," in Griffuelhes and Jouhaux, eds., Encyclopédie du mouvement syndicaliste, p. 37.

47. La Voix du Peuple, 12 May 1912.

48. XVIII(e) congress [Le Havre, 1912], reported in La CGT et le mouvement syndical, pp. 123-124.

49. Michel Auge-Laribé, Le paysan français après la guerre (Paris, 1923), p. 193. See also Le problème agraire du socialisme (Paris, 1907) by the same author, pp. 308-309 for the decrease in unionism. See for statistics on agrarian unions supportive of syndicalism: Confédération Générale du Travail. La confédération générale du travail et les terriens (Paris, 1919), pp. 12-14.

50. Wright, Rural Revolution in France, p. 16. Augé-Laribé notes that in 1923 the peasant hierarchy was still based on quantity of landholdings. Le paysan français après la guerre, pp. 190-191.

51. Augé-Laribé, Le problème agraire du socialisme, pp. 304 and 355 for quote.

52. Judt, Socialisme in Provence, p. 98.

53. Augé-Laribé, Le problème agraire du socialisme, p. 280.

54. M. Augé-Laribé, "Deuxième congrès des syndicats d'ouvriers agricoles," Annales du Musée Social, 9 (Sept. 1904): 394-401.

55. Griffuelhes and Jouhaux, eds., Encyclopédie du mouvement syndicaliste p. 19.

56. La Voix du Peuple, 27 Dec. 1908.

57. Judt., Socialism in Provence, p. 234. Philippe Gratton notes, on the other hand, that the leaders of agrarian unionism were far more radical than the masses they were seeking to represent. Les luttes des classes dans les campagnes (Paris, 1971), p. 306.

58. Georges Dupeux, French Society 1789-1970, Peter Wait, trans. (London, 1976), pp. 162-163.

59. André Marchal attributes the rise in labor violence to the increased cost of living. Le mouvement syndical en France (Paris, 1945), p. 150.

60. The CGT's program appears in the article by Amedée Dunois in Griffuelhes and Jouhaux, eds., Encyclopédie du mouvement syndicaliste, p. 34.

61. Augé-Laribé, Le paysan français après la guerre, p. 200.

62. Gratton, Les luttes des classes, p. 305.

63. La Guerre Sociale, the edition following that of 23 May 1907 in which neither the date nor the edition is readable. In that same issue Hervé observed that the 101st regiment, stationed at the Narbonne barracks in the Midi, had refused to march on their fathers and friends.

64. See Michel Bernard's assessment of the peasants in the Allier in La CGT et les terriens, pp. 31-34.

65. E. Martin Saint-Léon, Syndicalisme ouvrier et syndicalisme agricole (Paris, 1920), p. 146.

66. For a discussion of the response by international socialism and the question of antimilitarist activity see Georges Haupt, Socialism and the Great War: The Collapse of the Second International (Oxford, 1972).

PERSONS CITED

Ader, Paul (1877-1918), born in the Ariège, died at sea. A syndicalist of libertarian tendencies, and one interested in organizing the rural proletariat. He was involved in founding and leading an agricultural workers' federation in the Midi. Assisted at numerous CGT congresses, and edited two rural working-class newspapers. He also contributed to other radical papers. He directed all the large strikes in the Aude, Hérault, Gard, Pyrénées-Orientales, and Bouches-du-Rhône. He was an antimilitarist, a supporter of the general strike and sabotage, and he opposed the SFIO. Mobilized in 1914, Ader became a partisan of national defense.

Beaujardin, H (1866-1928), born in the Lot-et-Garonne. Wrote in numerous journals, particularly those aimed at rural propaganda. Collaborated on Père Peinard. He became a militant communist after 1920.

Bourderon, Albert (1858-1930), born in the Loiret, died at Paris. The son of a small proprietor, he worked as a domestique de ferme, and later as a cooper. In Paris he joined the Allemanists and ran in numerous municipal elections. He supported socialist unification, but was the founder and guiding light of the coopers' union and federation. He was an advocate of cooperatives, and founded a number of these organizations. He opposed the Union sacrée and went with Merrheim to Zimmerwald. Under the influence of Wilsonianism, he eventually slid toward the center. He voted to exclude the minority from the CGT in 1921, but remained on the left of the Confederation after the schism.

Bourguer (?-?), born in 1871 at Rheims. He was a weaver and militant anarchist. He was jailed and fined in 1892 for preaching insubordination to recruits. He attended CGT and FBT congresses. In 1907 he was condemned to hard labor for some crime, and he subsequently fled to the United States.

Bousquet, [Jean] Amédée (1867-1925), born in the Gironde, died in Paris. A baker and secretary of the Foodworkers' Union. He was first a Guesdist, then an Independent Socialist. Ran in numerous municipal elections. He campaigned against night work and participated in numerous CGT congresses. He was imprisoned for his strike activity, being charged over eight times during his lifetime for radicalism. In 1912 Bousquet became a baker in a cooperative bakery in the XVIII(e) arrondissement. He joined the CGTU in the last years of his life.

Brunellière, Charles (1847-1917), born and died at Nantes. He was the son of a tradesman. He left school at the age of fifteen to work in a grocery store, and later became a naval rigging maker. He created the Maritime Federation of Brittany. He married and fathered five children. His family often suffered as a result of his political activities. He joined the POF, although he was an antimilitarist. Brunellière collaborated on numerous socialist papers. An incredible organizer, he took a vital part in unionism and participated in all the municipal elections. He was also very active in organizing farmworkers. When war came, he supported the Union sacrée, believing that it was a vehicle for achieving unity of the leftist sects.

Chiron, Victor (1853-?), born in Deux-Sèvres, died in the Vendée. A watchmaker and militant socialist in Brest. He started a socialist group during his military service. He was involved in strike activity and demonstrations demanding amnesty for the Communards. He founded the Study Circle of Brest, which was the center of the avant-garde group in the region. He attended numerous bourses and CGT congresses. He was elected to the Municipal Council and edited several socialist newspapers.

Davin (?-?), lived in Algeria and was active in both the Confederal and Socialist Party congresses.

Desplanques, Charles (1877-?), born in the Department of the
Seine. He was a hairdresser, an anarchist, and held
numerous administrative posts in his union and federation.
He was elected undersecretary to Yvetot for the FBT.
Although imprisoned and fined for his antimilitarist
activties, he was mobilized during the war. After serving
as a hospital attendant, when the war ended, Desplanques was
no longer a militant unionist.

Farjat, Gabriel (1857-1930), born at Lyon, died at Paris.
He was born into a family of silk weavers. At eleven, he
began working with his father, but he continued his
education by reading. His knowledge made him a powerful
force in the Lyonnais socialist movement. He was one of the
founders of the POF, but he also participated in union and
bourse activities. Farjat worked on a Guesdist newspaper
after 1891. When the paper ceased publication, Farjat had
serious financial problems until he was admitted into the
union of the P.T.T.

Farras, Charles (1852-1929), born and died in the Hérault.
He was a militant republican, farmworker, member of the POF,
and founder of a farmworkers' union. Although fired for his
activities, he continued to direct strikes, write radical
tracts, and campaign against reactionaries in the municipal
government. After 1900 Farras became director of a bourse,
working to create various unions during his tenure of
office. After 1904 he withdrew from bourse and Socialist
Party activity.

Fribourg, Paul (1868-?), born in Paris. Railroad worker and
militant in the POSR. He supported the general strike and
participated in numerous CGT conferences.

Hervier, Pierre (1869-1952), born in the Cher. While
apprenticing as a linen weaver, he organized a union. After
fulfilling his military obligation, he became very involved
in syndicalism, particularly in antimilitarist activities.
Hervier participated in CGT congresses and organized the
woodcutters' union. He was a political socialist, and
served on the Municipal Council of Bourges. He supported
the government during the war, and the Third International
after the schism.

Lelorrain (?-?) belonged to the first bureau of the National
Federation of Tobacco Workers. He supported proportional
representation.

Mauger, Hippolyte (1857-1946), born and died in the Cher.
He was a woodcutter who entered into socialist activities at
a young age. He helped found a woodcutters' union. He was
finally elected as a Deputy, then a Senator from the Cher.
In parliament Mauger was always concerned with farm
problems. He defended the Union sacrée, and was excluded

from the SFIO in 1919 for his support of the Versailles Treaty.

Milhaud, Baptiste (?-?), he was a delegate to the CGT congresses and to the congress of the Fédération des Agricoles du Midi in 1903. During the 1904 strikes, Milhaud organized union propaganda. He was a bourse secretary from 1907 to 1913.

Noel, Emile, (1866-1938), born at Bordeaux, died at Tours. He was a son of an illiterate republican. At the age of ten he apprenticed to a lithographer, and joined the union at sixteen. In 1889 he ran unsuccessfully for the Municipal Council as a member of the POF. He was a bourse secretary. In 1891 Noel was fired from his job for his radical activities. He was very active in agrarian syndicalism, and formed numerous farm unions. He supported the general strike, cooperatives, and the UP's. During the war he was general secretary of the Freethinkers' Federation.

Reisz, Eugène (1863-1921), born and died in Paris. He was a militant socialist, an elected member of the Municipal Council, involved in a Paris cooperative, and a delegate to numerous CGT congresses. From 1904-1912 he was an administrator of a cooperative.

Trévaux, Louis (?-1908), shoemaker, socialist revolutionary from the Lorient, bourse manager, who participated in numerous CGT congresses.

Voillot, Jean (1874-1953), born at Nièvre. He entered his father's trade as a carpenter. He was an excellent orator and organizer. He advocated separation of syndicalism from party socialism, even though he was himself a member of the POF and later the SFIO. He later became a Deputy and Senator from the Rhone.

8. The Question of the State: "The Workers Have No Country"

To all who study the movement, revolutionary syndicalism is synonymous with two characteristics: direct action and antistatism. As noted in the second chapter, direct action was most consistently defined as apolitical and antigovernmental action. Electoral activity was regarded as a snare and a delusion, dulling the workers' revolutionary commitment and supporting a government of class bent only on the workers' exploitation. Direct action was advocated as a means by which the workers themselves could overthrow the oppressive class and its state. In that sense, antipatriotism and antimilitarism were expressed in forms of direct action having the same aim. Increasingly these two tactics, really one, came to compete in importance with the general strike. Together the two were regarded as being the most radical activities at the workers' disposal. It was not until 1900 that the FBT and the CGT took up the discussion of militarism. But beginning in 1904, antimilitarism was on the agenda of every CGT congress until the war.

Yet, despite the importance of antimilitarism and the years of antiwar propaganda carried on by the syndicalist movement, when the war came syndicalist leaders did not declare the general strike. Workers did not revolt, they mobilized. Notwithstanding the strongly antipatriotic stance taken by the workers' movement, the majority of unionists supported the Union sacrée. Critics consequently have charged that syndicalist actions in response to the war serve to indicate the impotence of the movement and its leaders, demonstrated in the inability to put into practice what it had for so long preached. CGT leaders have been assailed as demagogues, preaching violent overthrow of the government, but cowering under their blankets when the time came to take action. The antipatriotic, insurrectional talk had been only "a soufflé," Georges Dumoulin claimed.(1) Lacking substance, syndicalist propaganda never had penetrated the masses, who remained patriotic reactionaries and willing dupes of the capitalist imperialist government.

To assess these charges it is necessary to examine the

nature of syndicalism's antipatriotic and antimilitarist
posture and the movement's response to the war. By
analyzing the attitudes of the working class to the
"patrie," it becomes clear that as a result of economic
pressure and under the influence of revolutionary doctrines,
the workers' concept of the fatherland changed from a
metaphysical symbol identified with an historical patrimony,
to something concrete: an economic-political state and the
source of material well-being under the control of the
middle class. But bourgeois control was regarded as
temporary; therefore revolutionary activity was directed
toward capturing the state from the class enemy.
Antimilitarist sentiments and activity must also be
assessed. For syndicalists the use of antimilitarist
propaganda was clearly another form of direct action.
Antimilitary activity was revolutionary in that it was
directed to the overthrow of the exploitative state.
Syndicalism's antimilitarist program was also practically
aimed at building unionism. It was used to stifle reformist
voices within the ranks; it served as an effective
instrument in the rural offensive; and it offered a modus
vivendi between the competing theories of Marx and Proudhon
and between syndicalists and party socialists.

Finally, to understand anarchosyndicalism's attitude
toward the state, a brief look at syndicalist activity
during the war is in order. The conclusion drawn is that
this response did not constitute a failure of nerve and that
neither the leaders nor the movement was impotent.
Revolutionary propaganda had penetrated the masses. Largely
due to syndicalist activity the French worker in the years
before the war had come to regard the existing state as an
entity in the process of transformation, moving as a result
of working-class pressure toward its ultimate form: a regime
of economic liberty and equality. It was this patrie, with
its potential of ultimate social revolution, that had to be
protected against German barbarism. Given these perceptions
by the working class, anything contributing to the nation's
defeat constituted an antirevolutionary act. Under the
circumstances, a call for the general strike on the eve of
mobilization would have been regarded as a utopian action.
Instead, as will be demonstrated, syndicalism's response to
mobilization and war was consistent with its definition of
revolutionary action: the practical response to
possibilities inherent in the present.

THE INDISPENSABLE WORKERS' REPUBLIC

Antistatism was part of the revolutionary posture of
Marx and Proudhon. In the Manifesto, Marx and Engels had
declared that workers had no country, that class transcended
national frontiers. Proudhon's indictment of the state and
its government was based on his perception that the state
was force imposed on the individual. French radicals in the
First International were anarchist followers of Bakunin and

Proudhon.   Those   who formed the nucleus of the early labor
movement were the Communards, for whom not   even   government
amnesty   could   wipe   out the memory of the mur des fédérés.
The inheritance of French militancy was   one   in   which   the
nation state   was   synonymous   with force and the object of
working-class conquest.

Despite the antistatist inheritance, there was an early
tendency among French workers to regard the patrie as   being
the   vehicle   for   achieving   economic   reform.   They   were
supported   in   their   attitude   by   the   policies   of   the
government   during   its Opportunist stage, when efforts were
made to turn the working class into a bulwark of   the   Third
Republic.   Workers   frequently   regarded themselves as "the
sons of the Social   Contract,"   believing   they   had   earned
their   right   to   well-being because   it   was part of their
patrimony, given them by their forefathers, who   had   fought
in   the   wars   of   national   defense.(2) Striking workers in
Marseille in 1886 protested against the use of foreign labor
with stirring patriotic appeals: "You let the French die   of
famine to favor those who have hatred for the Patrie," their
placards   read.   Many workers regarded the state as a force
for justice, a mediator between employer and worker   in   the
interest   of   protecting republican order.   Having shared in
the triumph of the Republic,   workers   believed   they   would
share in its benefits.(3)

The   strikes   of   1878   to 1880, notes Michelle Perrot,
were usually demonstrations of "republican hope." Strikers
generally   seeking state intervention wrote letters, drafted
petitions, and even sent bouquets to   the   magistrates.   In
1890   a   group of striking weavers in Roanne appealed to the
municipal authorities to settle   the   strike,   stating that
because   the   sub-prefect--apparently   the   one in charge of
the negotiations--was a republican,   he   could   be   trusted.
During   workers'   demonstrations   the   "Carmagnole"   and the
"Marseillaise" were   often   sung.   Patriotism   was   also   a
strong   mitigating   force   against   strikes as well.   Higher
wages   would   make   French   goods   noncompetitive;   social
disturbances   would make France vulnerable to her neighbors:
these were the themes.(4) The eight-hour day would come when
France manufactured in eight hours what it   previously   took
twelve   hours   to   produce,   explained   a   member of L'Union
Prolétarienne. But workers must wait until such time as they
could compete effectively   with   Germany   and   England,   two
nations   possessing superior technology.(5) The feeling that
strikes   were   treasonous   helped   to   contribute   to   the
relatively   peaceful nature of working-class activity before
1880.(6)

Even among the early syndicalists and socialists   there
was   a   tendency to support the Republic. Fernand Pelloutier
remained a nationalist   and   a   republican   even   after   his
conversion   to anarchism, Jacques Julliard points out,
because Pelloutier believed the Republic was the only milieu
in which socialism could triumph.(7) Gustave Hervé, l'enfant
terrible of antimilitarism, who wrote under the   name   "Sans
Patrie," had   a peculiar attitude toward the Republic.   The

early articles written in his _Pioupiou de l'Yonne_ were both
pacifist and patriotic, urging conscripts always to defend
the republican patrie against foreign aggression.(8) Members
of the bourse remained similarly hopeful of the benefits of
republicanism, although this was the only course they could
follow perhaps, given the juridic nature of their existence.
At the 1893 inauguration of the Nîmes bourse, tailor
Victorien Bruguier declared that it would be "a feather in
the republican hat" if the state would grant such reforms as
were generally "prescribed by a monarchy." Workers must
remember that "the best of legislations concerning workers
[would] remain a dead letter so long as there was no state
to execute them." The role of the bourse, as envisioned by
Bruguier, was that of handmaiden to the state: it would
serve the workers as the Chamber of Commerce served the
employers.(9)

    The preservation of the Republic was a common theme in
the early stages of the workers' movement. In 1898 a report
at the Rennes congress of the CGT warned workers to remain
aloof in the Dreyfus affair. "Cosmopolitan Jewry" and
"clerical financiers" were working within the bowels of the
government to sap the Republic's strength. The manifesto
sounded the alarm:

> WORKERS!
>   The Republic, indispensable principle of future
> social emancipation, is in danger.
>
> SOCIALIST REVOLUTIONARIES!
>   Recall the memorable dates of 1793, 1830, 1848,
> 1871; be ready to defend the Republic and conquer
> our independence.
>
> SOLDIERS!
>   Don't forget you are the sons of workers; that
> tomorrow, in leaving the so-called national army,
> you return to the universal army of the Prole-
> tariat.
>
> PROLETARIAT!
>   The Republican army has no other rights than to
> defend the menaced liberty.
>
> LONG LIVE THE SOCIAL REVOLUTION!(10)

    Part of the reason for workers' passivity was that in
the early years, the power of the state had been sheathed
against them. In the 1882 strike at Montceau-les-Mines,
soldiers sent in to maintain order were perhaps relieved to
be coopted by labor's propaganda. The soldiers were treated
at the local café by the striking workers. Soon, not only
were the officers fraternizing with the striking workers,
but the enlisted men were also making professions of lasting
kinship with their officers!(11) An important reason for the
changing climate of working-class opinion toward the

republican state was the increasing use of government force.
In 1888 striking excavation workers at Corrèze experienced
the government's wrath in a violent confrontation, which
left six women mortally wounded and many injured. May Day
of 1890 brought on a "virtual mobilization" of government
forces, according to Perrot, although the Paris
demonstrations were relatively peaceful.(12) By the
following year, Perrot notes, workers no longer harbored the
illusion of a benign republicanism.(13)

STATE AGAINST PATRIE

Government repression of labor did not happen in a
vacuum. It was also helped along by the entrance of
Blanquists and anarchists into the labor movement.
Militancy did not happen in a vacuum either. Much of the
détente between workers and the state was the result of the
confusion within the left over the question of revolutionary
means. The schism between political and economic socialists
helped to clear up the confusion. Needing to win elections,
the party socialists muted their antistatism.(14) This
allowed the syndicalists to assume a more radical posture in
calling for the overthrow of the state. In addition, the
Dreyfus affair exposed the corruption of both the military
and the state. Responding to all of these factors--
anarchist militancy, socialist "opportunism," and government
repression--revolutionary syndicalism moved away from the
traditional posture of regarding the state as mediator in
workers' conflicts and donned the mantle of
Marxist-Proudhonist militant antistatism.

A good deal of printers' ink was spent by labor to
support Proudhon's contention that the bourgeois state was
immoral, unjust, and unnecessary. In a 1904 article in La
Voix du Peuple, Maurice Travaux railed against the vote in
parliament to increase the naval budget. What is the
patrie, asked Travaux: "It is pillage, theft, and
assassination to glorify war."(15) The state was a modern
fiction, according to Paul Louis in 1910. The Republic was
only seventy-five years old, yet the economic revolution was
posterior to the French Revolution. It was apparent to
Louis that democracy was impotent in the face of its
inability to achieve political equality in a society based
on economic inequality.(16)

To anarchosyndicalists the patrie was an economic
entity in which only producers could be citizens. This
conception was apparent to St. Cyr professor of Ethics, Jean
Taboreau, in 1912. The notion of the fatherland was
different for the worker than it was for the middle class.
Workers did not understand the arts and literature of their
country, which was their patrimony as citizens. Nor could
they identify the nation with their natal ground, since
workers typically had to leave their birthplaces to find
work elsewhere. The position of the proletariat, Taboreau
noted, was that it had no country because it owned nothing.

To defend the soil, therefore, would be to defend the soil of the possessing class.(17) Georges Yvetot bore out this observation in a 1913 article in La Voix du Peuple. The patrie, he said, "is our work [that] we do, the thoughts we think, that which elevates us, and all revolt against arbitrariness and tyranny."(18)

The equation of the fatherland with economic well-being and revolution was a constant theme in syndicalist literature. In 1908 the delegates to the CGT congress discussed patriotism. The convention followed in the wake of the use of martial force against the striking workers at Villeneuve-Saint-Georges. Recalling the words of the Manifesto, the resolution concluded with the reminder that the workers had no country.(19) At the 1907 regional meeting of the Auxerre bourse du travail delegate Ballin pointed out that patriotism was aimed at conserving the actual state of things in society. In France the good patriot was a Republican, and the antipatriot was the one aspiring for a better society.(20)

Socialists had only one country, declared Hervé, "the international Socialist Republic of their dreams; they have some compatriots: the socialists, the exploited, the oppressed, the rebellious of the entire world." That the bourgeois would love their country was natural, Hervé told the jurors during his 1905 trial for antimilitarist activity:

> For you and yours, the patrie is a good mother; she pampers you when you are infants; she gives you good instruction; she makes happy moments for you; she assures you of considerable work, well-paid; of long vacations, future security tomorrow and for your old age.
>
> You would be monsters of ingratitude, unnatural sons, if you were not ready to come to her defense when she calls.

But for the workers, concluded Hervé, the country is "a stepmother, a vixen who despises us."(21) "Vulgus" said it more succinctly in a 1905 article in La Guerre Sociale: "The rich have a country, the poor do not."(22)

Based as it was on economic exploitation and class domination, the state was a pernicious force hindering the growth of solidarity and encouraging murderous sentiments within the human heart. Delegates to the 1901 congress of the FBT agreed that the idea of the fatherland was a false principle. It had become "the pretext for periodic killings of men without hatred for one another."(23) The state sent its citizens to Madagascar, Tonkin, and China to exploit people in order to keep commerce wealthy and missionaries happily employed in soul saving, Hervé charged.(24) Visiting German delegate Joh von Sassenbach, speaking before the 1912 CGT congress at Le Havre, called for class unity. Workers knew very well that it would be foolish "to love the oppressing classes" of their own countries more than their "brothers in labor from the other side of the frontier."(25)

The word "patrie," wrote Yvetot in the Nouveau manuel du soldat in 1902, had been used to create illusions among their parents and grandparents that were transmitted to the present generation. "It is one of the words which are the most colored in human blood." Mothers rocked their babies to sleep singing patriotic songs; fathers amused their children with war stories; the first toys given a child were guns, flags, and soldiers. At school and in church, children were educated in the love of their country. But instead of wanting to develop human instincts, the state sought to instill in the human heart the brutal feelings of the warrior and murderer.(26) Why was this so? Amédée Bousquet at the 1910 CGT congress knew it was because their "government of stupid asses" was in constant fear of losing its power.(27)

As an instrument of the capitalist ruling class, the fatherland stood for repression of the French themselves. The patrie, asserted Victor Griffuelhes, "is that which gives me not enough to eat."(28) It is "the state incarnate," declared Dumoulin, whose centralization opposed "the free development of producers and consumers."(29) Patrie, concluded Yvetot, was "the meaningless words on the placards when candidates promise [us] the same reforms they promised our fathers and their fathers."(30) To Travaux the fatherland was the factory where workers passed their lives "joylessly and without profit, the barracks which raise our sons, the hospitals where we die, and the brothel where we take our daughters." Republicans liked to symbolize the patrie as having the traits of a Roman matron--an "antique Minerva," he concluded. But to us "she is like the modern version of the bloody Indian idol Kali."(31) Some syndicalists might preach reform of the state. Not Dumoulin. In 1913 he proclaimed: "I don't want to reinforce it, nor reform it, nor conquer it; I want to destroy it."(32)

ANTIMILITARISM AND THE CAMPAIGN FOR CONTROL OF THE YOUNG

Since anarchosyndicalists regarded the fatherland as being based on class domination, they were also opposed to the army upon which the state rested. Antimilitary sentiments had deep roots in French society. The peasants hated the army, as has been noted. Workers, too, harbored long-standing grudges against the military because soldiers traditionally had carried on some kind of productive activity in their spare time. Early workers' congresses usually called for suppression of all work in barracks, prisons, and convents because of the competition from these people "moonlighting" in their free time.(33) To these ongoing reasons for antimilitarist resentment were added others: the anarchists' aversion to any instrument of force, the republican government's growing commitment to put down workers' militancy, the disintegration of the

balance-of-power state system, and escalating world
tensions. The earliest antimilitarist activities were
inspired by a desire to spread unionism and to safeguard the
moral health of the working class.

As a result of the French defeat in the Franco-Prussian
War, in 1873 the government instituted universal military
training. For twenty years the army was popular with the
public as a whole. But in the midst of a period of
chauvinism and a desire for revenge, of which Boulangism was
a symptom, a growing disenchantment with militarism began to
occur. Antimilitarist sentiment was recorded first in
literature. Several important novels were written: Le
cavalier misérier and Sous' off', published in 1887,
followed by Abel Hermant. These novels took as their theme
the moral debasement of army life.(34) These literary works
both reflected and helped to effect a changing attitude
toward the military. Later the Dreyfus affair further
nudged along antimilitarist sentiments.

The Catholic church was the first to respond to the
issue of moral decay. Seeking to counter the allegedly
brutalizing effects of army life on the young, the church
established Catholic Circles to maintain contact with the
young recruits. When a young conscript left for the army,
the parish priest gave him a letter of introduction to the
regimental chaplain or alerted a priest in the town where
the new recruit would be stationed. The church also
provided the conscript with prayer books, pamphlets, and
manuals designed to sustain the young Christian in his faith
and provide him with some guidance on how to live a moral
life. Members of the Catholic Circles invited young
soldiers to their homes for dinner, and for religious study,
devotional exercises, or good Christian fun. If propaganda
were not enough, the church also established a "Sou du
soldat," paid for by parishioners, to provide the young
soldier with a small honorarium, which might be used to buy
special treats or to place in the collection plate on
Sunday.(35) The church's goal was undoubtedly threefold: to
sustain religious commitment among young men during a
critical period of their lives when delights of the flesh
rather than of the spirit beckoned; to preserve the
soldiers' souls from too many mortal sins; and to do battle
against the state--three years of army life was enough to
indoctrinate young men with the tenets of anticlerical
republicanism.

Syndicalism's aims for the young recruits paralleled
that of the church's: to preserve the moral health of the
youngster, the future worker; to dilute the state's
influence on him; and to educate the young recruit to the
goals of syndicalism and the class struggle. Regarding
themselves in combat with the church for control of the
young, syndicalists proceeded to adopt the church's tactics
in the early stages of their antimilitarist campaign.

As was the case with so many other campaigns, it was
the members of the bourses who provided the impetus for the
antimilitarist offensive. At the FBT congress held in Paris

in 1900, an important item on the agenda was the
relationship of the bourse to the worker-soldiers. The
delegate from Nîmes noted that young men going into the
service generally forgot about the unions in which they had
spent so little time before conscription. He suggested that
the syndicats give these recruits the opportunity to
continue their professional education and defend them
against the religious societies that were constantly
proselytizing. The delegate from Tours was shocked that
militants would consider imitating the congregations.
Instead, he suggested, they should invite soldiers to join
the young socialist organizations in the area. The
resolution following the discussion called for bourse
members to work actively to place young recruits from their
locales in contact with the bourses secretaries in the area
near the military garrisons.(36)

At the CGT meeting following the FBT congress that
year, the antimilitarist question also appeared on the
agenda. Again it was suggested that the unions take a leaf
from the Catholics' book. Before a soldier left his parish,
noted Vilde, he was given a letter putting him in touch with
the chaplain of the regiment. The workers' organizations
should do the same thing. Sanitation worker Jean-Baptiste
Sémanaz suggested that before they were inducted, soldiers
who were union members might be given a three- or four-franc
"subsidy." Meyer of the culinary workers thought five or ten
francs for "trinkets" might be more effective. "It would
have a good effect on the comrades who are ignorent of the
syndicalist idea," he declared, and would be good propaganda
among the soldiers of the entire regiment. Edouard Briat
suggested that the five or six thousand men drafted annually
should be called together by the unions before their
departure to the garrisons and be apprised of their rights.

The resolution following the discussion was the
beginning of unionism's official antimilitarist campaign, to
be aimed at the class of 1900. It called for the
organization of public meetings for the inductees. It voted
to send subsidies, in other words, a Sou du soldat, to reach
the young soldiers through the intermediaries of the bourse
or union secretaries in the garrison towns. The resolution
called for the invitation of the young draftees to "familial
festivals" organized in the towns in which they were
stationed.(37) The following year, at the behest of the FBT
delegates convened at Algeria, the CGT launched the more
radical phase of its antimilitarist campaign. A Manuel du
soldat was commissioned to be printed and circulated among
the military. The propaganda piece--clearly inflammatory in
nature--was also to be sold to the civilian population as a
way to enhance the Sou's treasury.(38)

In 1902 delegates to the FBT congress called for the
publication of another antimilitarist brochure and
encouraged all their member organizations to carry out
extensive antimilitarist propaganda. The resolution that
year, however, did grant full autonomy to each bourse in
determining the form and content of its particular

campaign.(39) The same year La Voix du Peuple took notice of the departure of the class of 1902 by reporting on the party organized by the Union des Syndicats de la Seine for the recruits. The party included dancing, elocutions, and orchestral performances. The aim of the affair had been to provide "a living reminder of solidarity" for the young men going to the barracks.(40)

The same paper carried another article mentioning that the editors had compiled a pamphlet for circulation among the military and urged the unions to use it. The gist of the message was that the soldiers should seek out a family of workers in their garrison cities to provide them with an acceptable familial relationship. They should visit the unions and the bourses, where they would be furnished with paper, stamps, professional courses, meetings, and lending libraries. The unionized soldiers should also invite their nonunion comrades to accompany them, since their friends would be treated hospitably and would want to return. The pamphlet closed with the injunction: "Remember what you were before being in the regiment. Dream of what you will be when you leave it."(41) In the following issue, an editorial called for the continued circulation of brochures in the barracks and propaganda visits to be carried out by union members.(42) Another notice reminded conscripts to get from their locals the names and addresses of comrades in the cities where they would be stationed.(43)

Delegates to the 1910 congress made the same appeals.(44) At the next congress at Le Havre in 1912, a Committee of the Bourses entered into the records another call directing soldiers' attention to the fact that they were welcome in the bourses, unions, and the maisons du peuple, and expressed hope that such visits would become more numerous. At the same congress some delegates spoke of the need for early antimilitarist education. Rimont of Bordeaux suggested that one could not ignore such training and then expect one's son to become an antimilitarist at the age of twenty. Delegates could no longer just "speak through their teeth" about militarism, he concluded; they must be committed to making propaganda at home as well as in their unions.(45)

In the years before the war, these devices constituted the basic tactics used by syndicalists in their campaign toward the military. It was a program, on the surface at least, benign in its intent, aimed as it was at neutralizing the church and the state's overtures, recruiting the young draftees to unionism, and protecting their moral health while serving in the military.

"A SCHOOL OF CRIME"

Stemming from the same literary milieu, and having adopted the same tactics as the Catholic church, not surprisingly, syndicalism's antimilitarist message had strong moral overtones. The unions had long campaigned to

outlaw   military   moonlighting.   Ultimately   they   were
successful. Now it seemed that soldiers had too much time
to waste.   During their years of inactivity young men lost
their productive tendencies, syndicalists charged.   They
became either mindless robots or murderous brutes in thrall
to their commanders. To escape boredom they too often gave
themselves over to a desultory life.
       A delegate to the 1901 FBT congress stated that
military service physically and morally corrupted young
people who were brought "into the place of vice and idiotic
discipline they call the barracks."(46) In 1912 Bousquet
charged that young soldiers were sent "to unspeakable
places, where they encounter pederasty and all the
vices."(47) Boucher de Perthes, writing in Le Libertaire in
1904, suggested that the single life of the barracks was
demoralizing.   Those years of "fickle love" rendered the
soldier "incapable of the faithful love and domestic joys"
awaiting him in the bosom of his family.(48) It was not just
working-class spokesmen who pointed out the horrors of army
life.   In his Manuel Yvetot was able to marshal numerous
testimonials,   even by the bourgeoisie. Three-time Minister
of War Freycinet had stated that since soldiers had so
little to do, "they were receptive to all occasions for
debauchery which the big cities offered." Edouard Drumont,
rightist editor of the Libre Parole, declared that all
recruits came back with syphilis, while conservative Deputy
Jules Delafasse concluded that military service brought the
majority of the young to sterility, a national threat in the
era of a German population explosion.(49)
       Worse, perhaps, than heightening the taste for sexual
perversion was the fact that military service encouraged
laziness. Delegate Granier of the Béziers bourse suggested
at the 1900 CGT congress that syndicalists should provide
professional courses for young soldiers during their
enlistment so they would return home "with a good and sane
notion of work."(50) Soldiers were parasites during their
time in the military because they were nonproducers,
declared Boucher de Perthes.   The soldier's father and
brother had to work for two while the young man was in the
army. This placed as great a strain on the family as having
to support one of its members during a long apprenticeship.
The only difference was that when a young man returned home
from the army, he had neither skills nor a desire to
work.(51) Also gone was his independent spirit. In the
barracks one learned "to obey the most idiotic,
contradictory, immoral orders," noted Yvetot. And if the
soldier refused, the firing squad was the reward for his
"gesture of dignity."(52)
       In 1912 delegates to the Le Havre congress heard
numerous protests against the passage of the infamous
Berry-Millerand Law which assigned stiff penalties against
soldiers for antimilitarist agitation, insubordination, and
radicalism. For any of these crimes the soldier was
consigned to duty with the Foreign Legion, the terrible
"Batt' d'Afr'" in Algeria. Delegate Bousquet made a lengthy

appeal for workers to protest this law, based on the fact that military service drained the soldier of his abilities to produce.

> Mothers, you who have nursed your infant to the strains of an ancient song, and you fathers, who return from your labor, passing your hand over the golden tresses of your child, whose simple smile comforts you, you who have sacrificed for him, you who have seen him grow, you other fathers and mothers who count on your child to help you when he reaches the age of twenty: they want to raise him for the eternal military carnival; they dress him in blue and red and make him fill the role of servant, of flunky. More serious, they make him forget his comrades in the workshop. They emasculate him of all his manly energies. They make of him a passive being, an inert being, without a conscience, like the flywheel on some kind of machine. They have inculcated in him the principles of passivity and obedience, and when they have sounded the quarry on the workers' backs, they will have made of him a soldier, a brute, an instrument of capitalists. One sees, oh abnormal spectacle, the capitalist class strong enough to defend its privileges through the people's children, dressed as soldiers.

The government was aware that in the barracks the young man became "a human tatter." Fathers must protest this dehumanization. Mothers must join the revolt. Recalling Roman history and the example of the Sabine women who threw themselves among the combattants, Bousquet called upon mothers to resist the continuation of this criminal practice: universal conscription.(53)

Appeals to women were a common device in the antimilitarist campaign. In his 1903 article in La Voix du Peuple, Amédée Bousquet again called upon women to join the antimilitarist legions. It was the mother who allowed her little boy to play with military toys. It was she who had unwittingly awakened in her son "feelings of murder and prepared him for the barracks." Mothers must teach their young "to hate war and to despise the military profession." Then when the rulers tried to claim their boys for their "school of crime," the mothers of France would show who was speaking.(54)

In his trial for antimilitarist activity in 1905, Gustave Hervé used the occasion to appeal above the heads of the jury to the mothers of France, who regardless of class, were united in their desire to keep their sons from being killed on the battlefield. If he were silenced in his antimilitary campaign, and a war should come, Hervé warned the jury, sons would fall "in the flower of their youth." Then they, the jury, would have to face the mothers, who

would remind them that the antimilitarists were courageous
men who had shown a way to prevent governments from
"unleashing war or massacring [their sons], and you
miserables had [them] thrown in prison." Hervé's defense was
so stirring that it brought "loud and repeated" applause
from the audience, causing the presiding judge to threaten
to clear the room.(55)

Military service not only emasculated the
worker-soldier, syndicalists claimed, it also brutalized
him. In his "Conseils de famille," railroad worker Paul
Fribourg declared in 1902 that the soldier learned the
métier of the brute, and that the best soldier was "a
machine for killing."(56) Boucher de Perthes expanded upon
the theme of brutalization. In the barracks young men
learned to destroy, not create. That the government needed
to teach destruction was an indication of the full extent of
its corruption.(57) A constant refrain was that when men
left the service they could only become policemen, working
to control the proletariat, or jaunes, replacing striking
workers. A cartoon appearing in one of the antimilitarist
issues of La Voix du Peuple graphically illustrated this
charge. In it was an obviously debauched, imbecilic-looking
young man lurching from the gates of the army post. An
equally dissolute captain asked the departing wretch: "What
are you going to do, now that you're free and have lost the
habit of working?" The departing soldier's answer was: "Get
a job as a cop so I can continue to live at the expense of
others."(58)

THE MANUEL AND THE SOU DU SOLDAT

Along with making direct contact with the recruits,
syndicalists continued to publish and circulate the Manuel
du soldat. By 1904, 20,000 of these pamphlets had been
distributed among the military and another 100,000 had been
commissioned by the CGT. In 1906 Amiens delegates heard the
report by Yvetot that over 200,000 Manuels had been sold.
By 1908 the Manuel was in its sixteenth printing and had
185,000 subscribers. In addition, another 20,000 brochures
of extracts from the Manuel were in circulation. The nature
of the work, combined with its successful circulation,
earned Yvetot--himself the son of a policeman--numerous
prison sentences.(59)

Less clearly successful was the device of the Sou du
soldat, although propaganda in support of this technique
continued to remain intense. In 1902 an article in La Voix
du Peuple urged workers to support the fund. The sons of
the bourgeoisie endured military service much better than
the workers' sons, the writer noted. Middle class youths
were treated less harshly by their commanders. Generally
they had business or family contacts in towns near the
barracks. Because they always had pocket money, they could
rent their own private quarters or have fun when they were
not on duty. It should no longer be the case that workers'

children must be confined to the barracks because they had neither contacts nor money. Alone and isolated, the young soldiers could too easily fall prey to the priests, who encouraged them to join the church, or the jaunes--that "hermaphrodite of the class." The Sou would provide the children of the poor with the same pleasures that middle-class sons enjoyed. It would furnish a monthly pension and further stimulate amicable relations between the soldiers and the local unionists.(60) In the 1903 edition of the Manuel, recruits were urged to accept the Sou, not to purchase alcohol, but as "a fraternal pledge of sympathy" uniting them with the comrades they had left behind.(61)

In 1912 La Voix du Peuple again appealed for funds. The Sou, noted the article, "comforts the slave who submits to the outrages of the galley; permits him to reflect on the role he is to play, and [allows him] to remain a man conscious of his acts and will." Young soldiers needed to be made aware that upon their discharge, they would join the ranks of the exploited. They must realize that if they carried out "a fratricidal gesture" while they were in the army, they would be working against their own emancipation. The Sou allowed the young soldiers to group into organizations they themselves had formed. In these groups the soldier-workers could talk freely, receive journals, and find "the moral comfort" needed after submitting to the brutalities and vexations of military life. Surely, concluded the article, the Sou might be considered as a downpayment on the future in that it worked to destroy useless militarism.(62)

How effectively workers supported or recruits took advantage of the fund is difficult to say, since there appears to have been no official accounting made of the treasury. By 1911, however, the Sûreté Générale--the state's criminal investigations department--regarded the plan as being successful, and noted that there had been good response by workers to Yvetot's appeals. The Sûreté stated in its reports that bourses and unions in numerous cities had Sou treasuries.(63) Still, the fund appears always to have suffered from a paucity of contributions, at least in the early stages. In 1902 La Voix du Peuple noted that perhaps raffle tickets might be sold to augment the treasury.(64) Delegates to the Amiens congress heard that the plan was not working well because of parochial concerns. There had been a suggestion that the Confederal Committee appoint a central organization to administer the fund; this plan was rejected. Local unions had built up their treasuries in order to aid their own hometown boys. Further, it was feared that a single bureau might not spend the money so wisely as all might wish. Also, many were afraid that a central administrative body might keep records too faithfully: those dossiers might be published, to the detriment of the contributors who could be prosecuted for antimilitarist activity.(65)

Subsequently this is precisely what happened. In March 1914 the government outlawed the Sou, much to the disgust of the editors of La Voix du Peuple, who charged that this action represented an example of injustice and government repression. Unionists regarded the Sou "as an act of solidarity, considered by the syndical organizations as being an absolute duty and right," the article declared. Catholics continued their program without any government restrictions; syndicalists demanded to be allowed to continue their work equally unhampered.(66)

"EPOCH OF BAYONETS"

Antimilitarist activity in the early stages of syndicalism was regarded as an appropriate form of direct action, that is, a positive activity carried on within the military designed to spread unionism and heighten morality. As the army was used increasingly against the workers themselves, syndicalist attitudes toward the military and the state hardened. In 1910 Amédée Bousquet, the secretary of the Foodworkers' Federation, recounted for the delegates of the CGT how, as a soldier in 1891, he had been forced to bake bread during the Parisian bakers' strike.(67) At the next congress, Bousquet noted again how his union was victimized by the army: bakers could not make a move without having soldiers sent in to replace them.(68)

Any workers' demonstration was threatened by the government's employment of troops. In the first May Day celebration in 1890, organized under the auspices of the Guesdists and supported by all the militants, massive numbers of troops were sent into Paris. The night before May 1, the major streets of Rivoli, Royale, Saint-Honoré, and Opéra were covered with a layer of fine gravel in order to mount a cavalry charge against the demonstrators. Troops were stationed in the basement of the Church of the Madeleine and in the train depots to prevent workers from flocking into the city. No violence occurred that day. But the government's demonstration of military might seemed to be a case of overkill, since the Guesdists' stated purpose for the May Day demonstrations was to present a petition to the Chamber.(69)

In the first years of the decade it seemed that the army would remain a benign, if annoying, force. Numerous examples of the military's support of the workers were cited. Soldiers had refused to march against the striking workers at Le Creusot. With increased propaganda by the militants, Louis Grandidier explained, the troops would soon become soldiers of the Revolution."(70) At the 1900 congress of the CGT, Briat was optimistic about the effects of antimilitarist propaganda. The regiment at Châlon-sur-Saône had refused to march against strikers. Troops in another strike were ordered by their sergeant to fire into the air and then let the workers pass.(71) The day was not too far off, declared Fribourg, when the army would throw its "instruments of massacre in the air and cry 'Vive la révolution sociale!'"(72)

Antimilitarist propaganda in the early years constantly enjoined soldiers to refuse to use force against their comrades. Because the army was composed of proletarians, stated a 1900 resolution of the CGT, it must remain aloof from labor disputes.(73) In his Manuel Yvetot urged young men to refuse to obey if their officers were going to make murderers of them. If sent into a strike, he said, "DO NOT FIRE! . . . Do not kill your brothers!"(74) In an open letter to a friend leaving for the service, anarchist Fred Pol offered a double enjoinder. In the event that the soldier might be called upon to use force against workers, Pol urged: "don't fire, my brother, or else--aim straight."(75)

As working-class militancy heightened, so too did government opposition, particularly as Clemenceau, "the strike breaker," gained increasing power within the government. After long years in eclipse as a viable means of publicizing workers' demands, the May Day demonstration experienced a resurgence of life in 1903. That year Hervé had been instrumental in organizing demonstrations against government intervention in the Russo-Japanese War. Seeing the potential of this tactic, the CGT linked May Day with its campaign for the eight-hour day. From 1903 to 1906, strikes in support of the eight-hour day quadrupled in number, according to the French Bureau of Labor Statistics.(76)

Concurrent with these strikes were the CGT-organized May Day demonstrations. Throughout 1904 May Day propaganda saturated the country. Over 150,000 May Day brochures were sold by the syndicalists that year. A song about May Day as the symbol of the struggle for the eight-hour day, set to the music of the "Internationale" and offered for one sou, sold over 400,000 copies. Posters announcing the demonstration and the demand were printed. La Voix du Peuple urged workers to "Stick them up all over. Yes, all over . . . . It is necessary that it become an obsession." Ultimately walls, fences, even café tables throughout France were plastered with over six million placards. The CGT campaign brought results, according to Maurice Dommanget, who made a study of May Day. By 1906 "a psychosis for the eight-hour day" had been created. In Béziers 15,000 fieldworkers paraded on the first of May. That day 40,000 were in the streets of Saint-Etienne. Factories throughout the country had to be closed. Two-thirds of the arsenal workers in Toulouse staged a one-day walkout. Declaring the demonstrations to be part of a "monarcho-anarchosyndicalist plot," the government of Sarrien-Clemenceau took extreme measures. Provincial bourses were closed. Fifty to sixty thousand troops were dispatched to Paris to keep order. All over France there were arrests, violence, and casualties. Once in power Clemenceau, the "number one cop," made certain that no similar show of force would take place. May Day of 1907 saw Paris again like an armed camp. The following year militants were so cowed by the government that Hervé disgustedly noted that not a single red flag was in evidence. In 1909, a year of high unemployment, Clemenceau again dispatched 20,000 troops to Paris to discourage any worker militancy. Demonstrations were squelched and the workers had to content themselves with issuing manifestos.(77)

The Clemenceau years of 1906 to 1909 were also years of strikes and shootings. The army intervened in the strike of shoeworkers at Raôn-l'Etape, leaving two dead. In 1908 troops fired into a crowd of striking excavation workers at Draveil and workers at Vigneaux and Villeneuve-Saint-Georges. In 1907 the casualty list among strikers totaled 9 dead and 167 wounded. In 1908 it was 10 dead and between 500 and 600 wounded.(78) To match the government's get-tough policy, syndicalism's antimilitarist campaign became increasingly radical, a fact that disturbed many in the CGT. Proponents of using extreme tactics soon found they had to defend themselves against members of their own rank-and-file with almost as much vigor as shown against the government.

One important reason for the aversion by some unionists to the adoption of a strong antimilitarist posture was the tendency on the part of the anarchists to preach desertion as a noble alternative to induction. At the 1901 Lyon congress of the CGT the decision was made to use the treasury of the Sou du soldat to aid draft resisters.(79) Many unionists believed that it was dangerous enough to assist conscientious objectors; it was quite another thing to preach desertion! This was clearly an option offered recruits in Yvetot's Manuel. Young men, it declared,

> If you think you cannot support the vexation, the
> insult, the imbecilities, the punishments and all
> the turpitude that awaits you in the army:
> DESERT! That would be better than serving at the
> amusement of the alcoholics' bureau, and for
> those insane fools who take control of you beyond
> your power in the military prisons.(80)

In 1902, the year when the syndicalists agreed to publish the Manuel, an article appeared in Le Libertaire penned by Pierre Monatte, which provided the anarchists' ethical stance for desertion. The government imprisoned soldiers in body and spirit. To escape that prison, and out of the felt need "to conserve moral propriety as a man," anarchists deserted from the army. Desertion was another form of propaganda by the deed, Monatte stated. The act of refusing to bear arms was a public demonstration that could not fail to cause discussion and reflection, and subsequently raise working-class consciousness. That was why, when it was "morally and materially possible" for anarchist conscripts to leave the barracks, Monatte declared, they should depart.(81)

Other radicals were more circumspect in their advice. In 1900 Fred Pol suggested that young conscripts practice passive resistance during their time of servitude. Do the job simply, he cautioned. If you are too angered, remain silent; direct that anger toward militarism. If things become too difficult, Pol counseled his young friends in the service, "swallow [your] spit; don't put it on the face of your commanding officer." The young soldiers must be careful, he noted, since they were "the combatants for the battle of tomorrow."(82) Gustave Hervé tendered the same advice in the 1903 edition of his Pioupiou de l'Yonne. He would never advise desertion because such an act would mean imprisonment for the conscript. Then the Socialist Party would be deprived of a valuable 'recruit. Instead, Hervé would counsel the soldier-worker to serve his time "with good humor, without letting all the drudgery fall on his neighbor." He must calmly, but indignantly, report all brutalities by his superiors to the leftist newspapers. He must discreetly and patiently propagate socialist and antimilitarist ideas. Above all, the conscript must demonstrate working-class solidarity, and if brought to a strike, fire his rifle into the air.(83)

DISSENSION WITHIN THE RANKS

Desertion was never officially linked with the antimilitarist campaign endorsed by the CGT, except insofar as it was offered in the Manuel as an acceptable alternative. But a series of events conspired to bring on a full-fledged rebellion against the continued support of antimilitarism by reformist elements in the Confederation. Although antimilitarist propaganda was adopted in 1900 as an acceptable activity, the implementation of this weapon, as with other forms of direct action, was left up to the individual to use how and when he saw fit. In the early congresses the general strike was not closely conjoined with the antimilitarist campaign. But by 1903 it was apparent that the CGT was bent on accelerating its antimilitarist activities and linking the general strike to the antimilitarist campaign.
In 1903 Yvetot wrote an article in La Voix du Peuple entitled "Syndicalisme-antimilitarisme," which was really a defense of the general strike. Unionism had evolved beyond the narrow constraints of the 1884 law; syndicalists should no longer attempt to hide its revolutionary ends. Strikes were increasing; so too was the use of the army against the workers. It was illogical, he said, to make union propaganda without making antimilitarist propaganda. Yet there were too many within the movement who sought to inhibit syndicalism's advance. Typographers and printers were opposed to a variety of syndicalist stands, Yvetot noted: the employment of women, the circulation of the Manuel, strict adherence to the 10 1/2-hour day, and the general strike. Their federations were very strong and rich, Yvetot added, but too many of their members were conservatives.(84) A few issues later metalworker Jean Latapie pointed out that the 1884 law allowed unions to defend the workers' economic interests. Well, it was in the

workers' economic interest to reveal to the world that the army supported capitalism.(85)

The following year the antimilitarists gained great propaganda mileage over the arrest, trial, and subsequent acquittal of Yvetot and Bousquet, who had been apprehended for distributing antimilitarist tracts in Troyes. They had been accused of "insulting the army and provoking disobedience," La Voix du Peuple reported on the trial. The deck had been stacked against the pair in that they were tried in the Aube, where juries allegedly were more supportive of the government's point of view. But the two had handled themselves well during the trial. To charges of inspiring disobedience among the military, the pair defended themselves by stressing the humanitarian aspects of their actions. Antimilitarist propaganda had been carried on, according to Yvetot, in order to prevent the recurrence of shootings, such as had taken place at Fourmies. Bousquet defended his penning of "Aux mères" by professing that the article's only objective had been to counsel mothers to raise their children to respect the value of human life. After five hours of deliberation the verdict rendered was "not guilty." At the news of the jury's decision, the article concluded, "A cry of 'vive le jury!' broke out from the back of the room."(86)

Apparently the reformists were not moved by this triumph or the fact that, thanks in part to Briand's brilliant defense, juries were constantly acquitting Hervé of any wrongdoing for his antimilitarist activity.(87) Rather, they were frightened by the growing specter of radicalism and militancy, which they feared would jeopardize all the gains made by unionism, and by the further fact that they were losing control of the workers' movement to the anarchist elements. At the Bourges congress in 1904, it was apparent to the reformists that syndicalism was wildly out of control. They had received a stinging defeat on the issue of proportional representation; the campaign for the eight-hour day was adopted, with May Day 1906 targeted as the last day "workers would agree to work more than eight hours"; and a commitment to undertake a vigorous campaign of antimilitarist propaganda was made.(88)

In the interim before the next congress, militancy increased. In 1906 there were 1,309 strikes, involving 438,460 strikers, with 9 1/2-million work days lost.(89) At the Amiens congress held that year, reformists were again defeated, and the Charter of Amiens, banishing politics from the official syndicalist program, was almost unanimously adopted. Less resounding a victory for the radicals was the vote on Yvetot's resolution demanding that antimilitarist and antipatriotic propaganda "become more intense and always more audacious." When the resolution came up for discussion, reformists used the antimilitarist question in an attempt to discredit the radicals. Taking the floor, Auguste Keufer declared that he was certain that no church "would presume to impose such dogma," and that none there that day, not even the anarchists, "could affirm the infallibility of their ideas." These revolutionaries demanded strict political neutrality; yet they did not respect their own injunctions. According to the anarchists, syndicalism had "an exclusively economic role to fill." Antimilitarist and antipatriotic action was hardly in the category of economic action. Furthermore, such a stance would be "a serious obstacle" to the development of unionism. Keufer ended his argument by calling for "absolute political and philosophical neutrality" in the dissemination of "libertarian, antimilitary [and] antipatriotic" ideas. The holding of these convictions must be left up to the dictates of the individual conscience, and the spreading of such propaganda should be carried on outside the syndicalist milieu. To Keufer, antimilitarist activity was a political act aimed against the Republic. But as delegate Philippe of Lille countered, antimilitarism had nothing to do with politics or ideology: it was a practical issue--workers were tired of having bayonets used against them. After lengthy debate, the Yvetot resolution passed, but only barely, with a vote of 388 to 310, with 63 abstentions.(90)

At the Marseille congress in 1908, reformists made another sally, only to be defeated once again. The time seemed optimum for them since Griffuelhes, Yvetot, and Pouget were all in prison at Corbeil for their participation in strikes. The absence of this important troika from the Confederal Committee meant that the revolutionary element lacked its most brilliant orators. In the two weeks preceding the congress, La Voix du Peuple carried on a vigorous campaign against militarism. The special issue of September 1908 was expressly devoted to "soldiers firing on workers." It was increasingly clear, noted the editors, that "War in the exterior [was] a pretext, a trick." Soldiers were really employed by the state to defeat the working class. Was it to make war on the striking Paris electricians that our soldiers were trained, the editors demanded to know? Should workers then wage war against soldiers? The answer to the latter query was in the negative. That would play into the hands of the exploiters, who were trying to create a chasm between the army and the workers. Instead, the militants must step up their propaganda among the soldiers. The Bastille would never have been taken, the writer noted, if the French Guard had not defected. We cannot "vanquish the army--but [we can] convince them."(91)

The following issue, which appeared the week before the opening of the Marseille congress, carried another sally against the reformists, this time penned by J. S. Boudoux of L'Union des Syndicats de Meurthe-et-Moselle. The CGT's stance was correct, he noted, because antimilitarism was not just an economic question; it was an ethical one: soldiers had the moral duty "to reject the role of jaune or assassin" imposed on them. They had as much right to refuse to march against their comrades, concluded Boudoux, as the Catholic officer who had recently refused to march against Catholic strikers.

Some said that in the interest of preserving union membership, syndicalists should remain neutral, and that they had no right to attack the sentiments of those who were patriotic. What nonsense, declared Boudoux. Workers did not join unions for patriotic or political reasons. They joined because they were exploited! Would antimilitarist activity damage unionism? He doubted it would. He and his union brethren never ceased their antimilitarist propaganda, he pointed out, and they lived in a frontier province where chauvinism was very strong. Yet their membership continued to climb. That was because their comrades had eyes to see French police fraternizing with German and Belgian police during a strike. Workers in Boudoux's union were aware that patriotism was nothing more than the defense of capitalism. As such, they regarded antimilitarist activities as "the defense of the class."(92)

In the face of these arguments, and of the reality of the violent suppression of strikes by the army, the reformists' defeat at Marseille was a foregone conclusion. For the last time before the outbreak of World War I they made an unsuccessful bid to gain proportional representation. On the question of antimilitarist propaganda, the reformists fared little better. Once again typographer Louis Niel warned that if they wished to give themselves over to antimilitarist propaganda, they would "violate [the Confederation's] statutes, shred its charter, and vitiate all its work, which is exclusively professional." The task confronting syndicalism, he declared, was already too enormous. Despite Niel's entreaties, the delegates maintained their antimilitarist posture. The right to strike would be just a sham, the resolution declared, if soldiers continued to massacre workers. The commitment to general strike in the event of war, so dear to radical hearts, passed by a hefty vote of 670 to 406.(93)

At the following congress of Toulouse the ground swell in support of antimilitarism continued to grow. That year, 1910, saw the outbreak of 1,501 strikes, with 4.8 million days lost. The antimilitarist resolution at the Toulouse congress was more complicated, consisting of a two-part motion: to continue antimilitarist activity and to fund that activity with a special "Caisse du sou du soldat." This last was the resolution of Raymond Péricat. Once more Niel railed against the fact that the CGT was ceasing to be strictly professional in order to be political. Yvetot defended the position by again reminding delegates that it was in their "corporate interest" not to have soldiers replacing workers or shooting them. Bousquet took the floor to bolster Yvetot's arguments: he had been present at the May Day demonstration in Dunkerque during the time the building trades were on strike. Saber blows rained. Soldiers did not ask the workers there if they were reformists or revolutionaries: they simply charged!

By the time Péricat rose to defend his resolution, feelings were running so high that he was frequently

interrupted by noisy outbursts from the audience. Reformist
Claude Liochon had asserted that antimilitarism was not a
syndical question. This was nonsense: workers were united
in solidarity. Every time strikers were cut down or fired
upon, the pain and suffering of the victims was shared by
all. The army was a nursery for jaunes, and workers must
destroy that nursery. If this is to be "an epoch of
bayonets," he continued, we cannot be interested in
respecting legality any more than the bourgeoisie respect
it. The government cared not at all for workers' liberty.
When they sent young workers to the regiment, they did not
first ask the young men if they were happy about being
drafted. Further, Péricat concluded, members of his
federation had acquitted themselves well. They had grown
from 9,000 members in 1897 to nearly 100,000. When
Liochon's group of typographers could boast of the same
success, he counseled, they would have the right to be more
critical.
    On the antimilitarist resolution, the reformists were
bested 430 to 900.(94) Their defeat was their swan song. By
the time of the next regular congress, held in Le Havre in
1912, the reformist "threat" was no more. The nature of the
antimilitarist campaign had moved away from being merely
antigovernmental; now it had become more closely identified
with antiwar activity, a campaign in which even the party
socialists were deeply involved. Given the temper of the
times, there was no way that any group of reformists could
have launched a successful assault on that.

SOME CONCLUSIONS ON THE NATURE OF ANTIMILITARISM

    There are some important insights to be gained into the
nature of revolutionary syndicalism's perceptions and
posture regarding antipatriotism and antimilitarism. The
party socialists were opposed to the bourgeois state, but
they carried on their revolution in the same electoral
arena. To them the state was not an enemy; it was a
political adversary that could be bested one vote at a time.
For them, practicing their tactic of burrowing from within,
the patrie and the state were unconsciously one. This was
not so with the syndicalists. Workers had long associated
the Republic with economic progress. When it became
increasingly apparent that the Republican state had not
shared its fruits with the workers, it was a natural
response for the workers to regard the state as their enemy.
The fatherland continued to exist; it was still identified
with material well-being; but it was held captive by the
bourgeoisie. The patrie had preceded the class, workers
believed; it would prevail in its most consummate actuality
once the enemy class was overthrown. The state would wither
away, as Marx had predicted, to bring forth the patrie of
the proletariat. Antipatriotism (read antistatism) was
therefore regarded by syndicalists as a practical, as well
as a revolutionary act.

Antimilitarism was equated with antipatriotism; not so much for the political socialists, except insofar as it meant voting in the Chamber against military expenditures. The path to revolution for them was to build the party. Overt antimilitarist activity would frighten away adherents; therefore such activity would be antirevolutionary in nature. It was not until 1912 and the realization that the Second International was impotent that the party adopted the tactic of a military strike, but only as an antiwar measure. For the revolutionary syndicalists, however, antimilitarism remained a constant tenet of unionism. But the content of the doctrine underwent a change based on the mandates of practical necessity.

Initially, antimilitarist activities were regarded as a means by which to heighten revolutionary consciousness and swell the ranks of syndicalism. Antimilitarism was directed to the task of preserving the younger generation of workers against the real enemies: the Jesuits and the agents of the bourgeois state, as well as against the morality-corrupting intangible enemies--sloth and hedonism. To the unionists, antimilitarism was a revolutionary act. It was also a practical action, not only to recruit young members, but also to effect peasant-worker solidarity. Further, when tied in with the general strike, the tactic of antimilitarism proved to be a successful way to separate revolutionary from reformist goals within the CGT. As workers' militancy increased, in tandem with government repression of labor activity, the antimilitarist offensive became an even more practical act of basic human survival. Syndicalist perceptions about antipatriotism and antimilitarist ideas were shaped initially by domestic realities and organizational concerns. With the onset of war, political forces began to hold sway; then the economic definitions were no longer valid. In 1914 the patrie became France, a political entity that must be defended. For syndicalists the revolutionary struggle was no longer exclusively economic; it became political as well.

NOTES

1. Georges Dumoulin, Les syndicats français et la guerre (Paris, 1921), p. 7. Roger Picard maintains that the interest of the leaders for organizational security had decreased their "spirit of initiative and risk." The result was that their revolutionary élan had been diluted by the time of the world crisis and the syndicalist movement was unable to respond actively to mobilization and the war. Le conflit des doctrines économiques en France à la veille de la guerre (New York, 1944), p. 152.

2. Michelle Perrot, Les ouvriers en grève, France 1871-1890, 2 vols. (Paris, 1974), vol. 1, pp. 197-198.

3. Ibid., vol. 2, pp. 701-702; vol. 1, p. 178.

4. Ibid., vol. 2, pp. 562, 701-702.

5. Françisque   Brunet,   A   mon   frère   l'ouvrier
(Bordeaux, n.d.).

6. Perrot, Les ouvriers en grève, vol. 2, p. 443.

7. Jacques   Julliard,   Fernand   Pelloutier   et   les
origines du syndicalisme d'action directe (Paris, 1971), pp.
27-29.

8. Gustave   Hervé, Mes   crimes,   ou onze ans de prison
pour délits de presse (Paris, 1912), p. 3.   Perhaps   Hervé's
commitment   to "republicanism"--with its changing definition
best   explains   his   actions.   Hervé   was   a   virulent
antimilitarist,   but   not   so   violent   an antipatriot. His
series in La Guerre Sociale against birth control has been
discussed in Chapter 3 of this work. A statistical analysis
had   led   Hervé   to   conclude that by 2112 there would be no
Frenchmen living in France if the   population   continued   to
decline   at   its   present   rate.   The French race would be
committing   suicide,   for   France   would   be   overrun   by
foreigners.   He called upon his   readers   in   the   name   of
protecting   the   "patrie   révolutionnaire"   and   of   "the
patriotism   of   free-thinking   socialists   and
internationalists" to save the race,   for   "après nous, le
déluge!" The   series   appeared   on   the following dates: 17
June, 24 June, 1 July, 15 July, 22 July 1914.

9. Victorien Bruguier in Souvenir   de   l'inauguration
de la nouvelle bourse du travail (Nîmes, 1893), p. 12.

10. X(e)   congrès   national   corporatif   (IV(e)   de   la
confédération générale   du travail) . . . Compte rendu des
travaux du congrès (Rennes, 1898), pp. 63-64.

11. Perrot, Les ouvriers en grève, vol. 2, p. 696.

12. Ibid.,   vol.   2, pp. 696-698. Since   the men were
peasants,   they had their wives   with   them   in   the   strike,
Perrot   points   out.   Hence, the female mortality. The May
Day 1890 demonstration is discussed later in this chapter.

13. Ibid., vol. 2, p. 698.

14. For a discussion of the antimilitarist   debate   in
the Second International and among French socialists, see L.
Gravereaux,   Les   discussions   sur le patriotisme et le
militarisme dans les congrès socialistes (Paris, 1913).

15. La Voix du Peuple, 3 Apr. 1904.

16. Paul Louis, Le syndicalisme contre l'état   (Paris,
1910), p. 68.

17.   Jean Taboreau, Le sophisme antipatriotique (Paris, 1912), pp. 7-8. It must be noted that Taboreau's book was intended to serve as a reply to the syndicalists' allegedly incorrect and unethical stance.

18.   La Voix du Peuple, 25 Dec. 1913.

19.   Gravereaux, Discussions sur le patriotisme, pp. 132-140.

20.   Bourse Régional du Travail, Compte rendu du congrès régional corporatif (Auxerre, 1907), p. 8.

21.   Hervé, Mes crimes, pp. 67-69.

22.   La Guerre Sociale, 2 July 1905.

23.   Gravereaux, Discussions sur le patriotisme, pp. 120-122; quote of Rennes delegate appears on p. 121.

24.   Hervé, Mes crimes, p. 35. This was part of his "Address to Conscripts" appearing in Pioupiou de l'Yonne in 1901.

25.   XVIII(e) congrès national corporatif (XII(e) de la C.G.T.) . . . Compte rendu des travaux (Le Havre, 1912), p. 2.

26.   [Georges Yvetot], Nouveau manuel du soldat (Paris, 1903), pp. 3-5. The tract was written by Yvetot, but a commission of the FBT was listed as the author. This was apparently for legal reasons: the supposition that the law would take the position that if all were guilty, then none were. The court was not fooled and members of the FBT were arrested for the publication and distribution of the Manuel.

27.   XVII(e) congrès national corporatif (XI(e) de la confédération) . . . Compte rendu des travaux [1910] (Toulouse, 1911), p. 191.

28.   Griffuelhes quoted in Taboreau, Le sophisme antipatriotique, p. 9.

29.   La Voix du Peuple, 3 March 1913.

30.   Manuel, pp. 6-7.

31.   La Voix du Peuple, 3 Apr. 1904.

32.   Ibid., 3 Mar. 1913.

33.   See IX(e) congrès de la fédération nationale des bourses du travail . . . Compte rendu des travaux du congrès (Toulouse, 1897), p. 117.

34. Jean-Jacques Becker, Le Carnet B: Les pouvoirs publics et l'antimilitarisme avant la guerre de 1914 (Paris, 1973), pp. 13-14.

35. The information on the church's activities was expressed by delegates of the CGT congresses. Also in ibid., p. 23.

36. Gravereaux, Discussions sur le patriotisme, p. 120.

37. XI(e) congrès national corporatif (V(e) de la confédération générale du travail) . . . (Paris, 1900), pp. 84-87.

38. Robert Brécy, Le mouvement syndical en France 1871-1921: Essai bibliographique (Paris, 1963), p. 58.

39. Gravereaux, Discussions sur le patriotisme, p. 122.

40. La Voix du Peuple, 9 Nov. 1902.

41. Ibid., 13 Apr. 1902.

42. Ibid., 20 Apr. 1902.

43. Ibid., 31 Jan. 1904.

44. Jouhaux's resolution at the 1910 Toulouse congress of the CGT in Gravereaux, Discussions sur le patriotisme, p. 141.

45. XVIII(e) congrès [Le Havre, 1912], p. 189; discussion also noted on pp. 71-73.

46. Gravereaux, Discussions sur le patriotisme, p. 120.

47. XVIII(e) congrès [Le Havre, 1912], p. 186.

48. La Voix du Peuple, Jan. 1904. This was a special military issue.

49. Manuel, pp. 10-14. One can only ponder the ramifications of these numerous testimonials concerning the degeneracy of army veterans, particularly in a nation that had universal conscription, and particularly, as Jean-Jacques Becker notes, where so many workers were themselves former soldiers. Le Carnet B, p. 176.

50. XI(e) congrès [Paris, 1900] p. 84. The cost of the military was extremely high. Yvetot calculated that the military budget of one billion francs annually could provide 5,000 francs to each family in France for one year. Manuel, p. 17.

51. La Voix du Peuple, Jan. 1904 (military issue).

52. Yvetot in Manuel, pp. 7-8.

53   XVIII(e) congrès [Le Havre, 1912], p. 186.

54. La Voix du Peuple, Jan. 1903 (military issue).

55. Hervé, Mes crimes, pp. 92-95.

56. La Voix du Peuple, Jan. 1902 (military issue).

57. Ibid., Jan. 1904 (military issue).

58. Ibid., Feb. 1909 (military issue).

59. For statistics see Gravereaux, Discussions sur le patriotisme, p. 124. Report appears in Confédération Générale du Travail, Rapports des comités et des commissions pour l'exercise 1904-1906 (Paris, 1906), p. 51. See Becker, Le Carnet B, pp. 69-71.

60. La Voix du Peuple, 20 Apr. 1902.

61. Manuel, p. 32.

62. La Voix du Peuple, 21 Sept. 1912.

63. Becker, Le Carnet B, p. 27.

64. La Voix du Peuple, 20 Apr. 1902.

65. Rapports des comités [Amiens, 1906], p. 50.

66. La Voix du Peuple, 18 Mar. 1914.

67. XVII(e) congrès [Toulouse, 1910], p. 194.

68. XVIII(e) congrès [Le Havre, 1912], p. 186.

69. Maurice Dommanget, Histoire du Premier Mai (Paris, 1953), pp. 122-124.

70. Le Libertaire, 19 Aug. 1900. In 1906 Grandidier, Hervé, Almeréyda, and Yvetot were given prison sentences for their participation in antimilitarist activities. Announced in ibid., 6 Jan. 1906.

71. XI(e) congrès [Paris, 1900], p. 83.

72. Ibid. La Voix du Peuple, 1 Dec. 1901, recorded another similar example. At a strike in Le Havre, four soldiers of the 129th regiment, speaking in the name of 704 of their comrades, declared they would raise their rifles in

the air rather than fire.

73. Gravereaux, Discussions sur le patriotisme, p. 118.

74. Manuel, p. 32.

75. Le Libertaire, 21 Oct. 1900.

76. Dommanget, Histoire du Premier Mai, p. 223.

77. Ibid., pp. 206-219 for discussion of the eight-hour campaign.

78. Confédération Générale du Travail, La confédération générale du travail et le mouvement syndical (Paris, 1925), p. 102. Hereafter cited as La CGT et le mouvement syndical. See also Becker, Le Carnet B, p. 25.

79. Reported in La CGT et le mouvement syndical, p. 82.

80. Manuel, pp. 29-30.

81. Le Libertaire, 11 Oct. 1902.

82. Ibid., 21 Oct. 1900.

83. Hervé, Mes crimes, pp. 38-42.

84. La Voix du Peuple, 4 Jan. 1903.

85. Ibid., Jan. 1903 military issue.

86. Ibid., 31 Jan. 1904.

87. For a time Hervé was able to escape prison not only because of Briand's "magistral" pleading in his behalf, but also because he was always being tried before republican juries in the Yonne, a region that was saturated with his doctrines. Hervé, Mes crimes, p. 37. Hervé was dismissed from his professorship at the Lycée de Sens, however.

88. Brécy, Le mouvement syndical, p. 62.

89. Roger Picard, Le mouvement syndical durant la guerre (Paris, 1928), p. 41.

90. XV(e) congrès national corporatif (IX(e) de la confédération) . . . Compte rendu des travaux (Amiens, 1906), pp. 156-175. Quotes appear on pp. 156, 157, 174. The vote recorded in the proceedings of the congress is listed here. It conflicts with Brécy's tally in Le mouvement syndical. He records it as being 484 to 300. (P. 65.)

91. Ibid., p. 69 for data on the imprisonment of the militants. Quote appears in La Voix du Peuple, Sept. 1908 (military issue).

92. La Voix du Peuple, 27 Sept. 1908.

93. For statistics see Brécy, Le mouvement syndical, p. 69. For the resolutions see, La CGT et le mouvement syndical, pp. 102-104. For Niel's remark see Gravereaux, Discussions sur le patriotisme, pp. 132-133.

94. See Picard, Le mouvement syndical, p. 41 for statistics. For discussion, see XVII(e) congrès [Toulouse, 1910], pp. 191-193, 225, 227.

PERSONS CITED

Boudoux, J. E. (1881-1936), born at Saint-Etienne; real name Jean Sellenet. Married; a forger by profession. He deserted the army in 1904 and hid under his assumed name of Boudoux. The following year he was involved in strikes in Lunéville and Longwy. That year he was arrested for his desertion, then amnestied. Thereafter, he was involved in numerous strikes and antimilitarist demonstrations, for which he finally served a prison term. After prison, he became an officer in a union of workers in the Meurthe-et-Moselle. He contributed to working-class publications and assisted at CGT congresses. He was expelled from the Confederation later on charges that he was a police spy. He was mobilized during the war and earned the Croix de guerre for saving his commander's life. At war's end, he continued his militancy. He worked on Le Libertaire, and joined the CGTU. In 1936 he was killed in Spain fighting against Franco.

Bruguier, Victorien (1858-1944), a tailor by profession, he founded the Nîmes bourse and was an officer in the Clothing Workers' Federation. He was involved in the FBT, and was elected as a socialist to the Nîmes Municipal Council. Interested in public education, Bruguier worked for free public education for children, construction of bourses, and vocational training for workers. He was married and the father of two sons.

Liochon, Claude (1880-1941), born and died in the Seine-et-Oise. He was a typographer who joined the reformist wing of the CGT after his military service. He attended numerous CGT congresses and was opposed to the Confederation's antimilitarist line. He was mobilized in 1914, wounded, and returned to civilian life profoundly pacifistic. He succeeded Keufer in 1919 as head of the Fédération du Livre, leaving the Socialist Party out of respect for syndicalism's stand on political activism. His penchant for peace later inclined him toward collaboration with Vichy.

Monatte, Pierre (1881-1960), born in the Haute-Loire, died
in Paris. His father managed a blacksmith shop, his mother
was a lacemaker. Monatte received his bachelor's degree and
taught in the Nord. During this period he became involved
with militant syndicalists and anarchists, and was
subsequently fired for his political activities. He
migrated to Paris, founded a union of librarians, and became
a proofreader, a profession he would exercise until 1952.
He was arrested and imprisoned in 1905 for his union
activity. In 1908 he fled to Switzerland to escape arrest
as one of those involved in the strike at Villeneuve-
Saint-Georges. On his return to Paris, Monatte worked as a
librarian for the CGT, until he opened his own journal, La
Vie Ouvrière, although the paper was always in debt. He
opposed the Union sacrée, and was critical of the CGT
majority. He supported the Third International.

Péricat, Raymond (1873-1957), born in the Seine-et-Marne.
He was a plasterworker, involved in his first strike in
1888. After his military service, he became a secretary in
the Building Workers' Federation. He went into exile for a
time after being involved in demonstrations in Draveil in
1908. Upon his return, Péricat joined the SFIO, and spent
the next few years traveling throughout France participating
in strikes, demonstrations, and workers' meetings. He was
in charge of propaganda in Algeria for the CGT after 1912.
It was on his inspiration tht the CGT initiated the Sou du
soldat. On 31 July 1914 he called for a general strike, and
was the only one on the Confederal Committee to do so.

Philippe (?-?), represented a union of employees of commerce
from Lille at the 1906 CGT congress. He believed that
political and economic activity should be carried on by the
workers.

Sémanaz, Jean-Baptiste (1874-1914), born at Lyon, died in
the Nord. At fifteen, he joined a union of municipal
workers. In 1900 he attended both the socialist and the CGT
congresses as a representative of sewer workers. He was
elected mayor of Le Pré-Saint-Gervais. Sémanaz was gravely
wounded at the Somme and died en route to the hospital.

9. The Question of the State: ... Unless It Is the *Patrie* in Danger!

In the early stages of the syndicalist movement, antimilitarist and antigovernmental activity was regarded as a form of direct action leading to social revolution. International peace was seen as a necessary subordinate to the course of the class revolution. Under the twin terrors of the escalating diplomatic tensions abroad and the increasing use of government force at home, antimilitarist sentiment and activities proliferated. Although the intent of this work is to deal with revolutionary syndicalism from its inception to the war, some comments are in order regarding the movement's seeming about-face with regard to its long-held views on the question of antimilitarism and antistatism. The reader is reminded that these remarks are intended to address the thesis that syndicalism was directed toward practical revolution, and are in no way meant to constitute an in-depth study of anarchosyndicalism and the war. Such a work, which calls for greater insights into the motives of the individuals involved, and a more diligent effort to separate interpretation from interpretation-become-history, requires a larger arena for exposition, and thus lies outside the purview of this examination.

The bulk of criticism made against syndicalism tends to fall within two large categories: that the war was a catalyst revealing an inherent weakness within the workers' movement, and/or that syndicalist leaders betrayed the workers and supported the Government of National Defense to achieve their own personal advantage. As noted in the previous chapter, this study argues to the contrary: syndicalism did not capitulate to expediency or abandon its revolutionary tactic of direct action.(1) Concerns for the security of the movement did not dampen its revolutionary resolve.(2) Nor did the leaders of the CGT "renege on the idea of revolutionary action" with the advent of war.(3) Rather, this study concludes that syndicalists responded to the national crisis in a manner consistent with the movement's definition of revolution and with the means to carry it out.

SYNDICALIST RESPONSE TO INTERNATIONAL TENSIONS

From the inception of the organized labor movement, the CGT had declared itself in favor of international accord. The first few issues of La Voix du Peuple dutifully reported all antiwar demonstrations in England and on the continent.(4) Contributors to the working-class papers insisted that wars were the bourgeois governments' means to extend their control over the people, to command obedience, and to suppress all individual expression. Further, as Constant Martin wrote in Le Libertaire in 1897, war was "the grand aborter of revolution." Evil statesmen manipulated events to bring on war so people's attention would turn "from social questions . . . to bulletins from the battlefield."(5)

Throughout the crisis of the Russo-Japanese War, labor militants charged that the French government was angling to become involved in order to protect French capitalists' investments in Russia on the one hand, and to diffuse working-class militancy at home on the other. In 1904 Raymond Dubéros alerted readers of La Voix du Peuple to the anti-Japanese propaganda campaign being carried on by the bourgeois press. Even songwriters had been enlisted. He cited a then-current satirical song: "The war has begun/ the Japanese maggots/ are going to receive a good spanking." The press was rallying Frenchmen to the aid of their "good friend the Tsar" by telling people that if Russia fell before the yellow peril, there would be nothing to prevent Germans from streaming westward. Workers must not be deceived by this scare talk, Dubéros noted, for what was really in the offing was a capitalist-imperialist war.(6)

The bourgeois-controlled state's true objective was not lost on members of the CGT at their 1904 meeting in Bourges. Pro-Russian propaganda was a sham designed to gain public support for French intervention against the Japanese. Syndicalists were not beguiled. True to his profession, Spirus-Gay of the Union of Lyric Artists offered a lofty pronouncement for the delegates' approval. Even if antimilitarism were not a professional concern, he declared, the congress must assert its "reprobation against war, this ignoble vestige of barbarian epochs, this cowardly and cruel means of servitude of man by man." Delegates opted for a less fanciful statement: they agreed that the proletariat must save "all its energy for the real syndicalist battle" against capitalism.(7)

The Moroccan crisis the following year provoked another wave of antimilitarism. The "Lesson to Remember," according to D. Sieruin, was that most of those patriots now pressing for conflict were really too old and infirm to fight. They would remain comfortably at home. Every time someone shouts "Down with Berlin!" said Sieruin, workers should answer that they would leave for the front if the warmongers marched in the first ranks. That would turn all the national hotheads into pacifists in a hurry. The real cause of the Moroccan crisis was the bourgeoisie's fear that the workers were shedding their "religious and economic tutelage." No French soldier had fired at a foreigner in thirty-five years, although numerous rounds had been expended against French strikers. The best tactic for workers to adopt, concluded Sieruin, was to remain calm in the face of the bourgeois saber rattlers.(8)

On trial for his antimilitarism in 1905, Hervé asked if the prospect of being swallowed up by the Kaiser was such a horrible fate. French liberties would not end; the "maternal language" would not be snuffed out. Universal suffrage existed in Germany; unions had double the membership of their French counterpart; their public meetings were more numerous; their socialist papers were "more red" than those of the French left's. The Germans could not suppress political liberties--the French were better conspirators than the Germans and would resort to all manner of clandestine activity. As for the language, concluded Hervé, after a century of occupation, the Russians had not been able to erase the Polish language.(9) In other words, the French would remain French even in the face of German domination!

Despite Hervé's blandishments, delegates at Amiens in 1906 were very much concerned about the crisis abroad and at home. In each war between nations or colonies, their resolution stated, "the working class is duped and sacrificed to the class of bourgeois parasites." Workers would not be fooled by cries of saving national honor, knowing that the phrase was invented by financiers to lead the proletariat to massacre. The Algeciras conference and the settlement from that meeting had occurred only because the leaders of all the governments knew that the workers wanted "Peace at Any Price." This, their manifesto, was to serve as a call for "War on War."(10)

The idea that the European proletariat was a potent force for peace was an ongoing theme in the congresses and in the working-class press as the simmering Moroccan crisis gave way to the Balkan explosions. In 1908 A. Luquet called for more vigorous peace demonstrations. The North African crisis was designed to increase the profits of the Krupps and the Schneiders. But capitalists must not be deceived. Workers had the power to change the course of history. Fashoda represented "the rapprochement, the exchange of visits between English and French workers [which had largely] stopped that war between the two countries." French workers must declare their "indissoluble fraternity" with the German proletariat. They must also impress upon those who were searching for an excuse for "fratricidal butchery" to keep in mind that if war could suppress revolution, it might also precipitate revolution.(11)

In a 1908 article in _La Guerre Sociale_ the editors noted that the antimilitarist campaign was reaping a rich harvest. Recent statistics published by the Minister of War documented a rise in incidences of insubordination and desertion in the armed forces between 1904 and 1907 equivalent to three infantry divisions. "Poor France!" the editor clucked. "If this continues, there won't even be a cat to defend your honor and your patrimony of glory and liberty."(12)

In 1912, in the face of the Balkan War crisis abroad and the move to pass the three-year conscription law at home, unionists stepped up their antimilitarist-antipatriotic campaign. The Young Syndicalists of the Seine issued a manifesto charging that it was not the Germans but their own bosses who were the real enemies of the workers.(13) Another article in La Voix du Peuple called on women to work against war by preventing their husbands from leaving for the front. If blood were to be spilled, the writer said, it must be for revolution, not war. "In place of making soldiers," women must "make men."(14)

Direct action included deeds as well as words. Syndicalists believed theirs was the only voice of protest being raised against war and militarism, since it appeared that other leftists were content to give only lip service to the cause of peace. The Second International was impotent: members were too involved in purging anarchists, silencing Hervéists, and being solicitous of Germans. The French party socialists were too preoccupied with achieving détente among the numerous schools and leaders within political socialism.(15) But during the Moroccan crisis of 1905, when socialists remained mute, Griffuelhes went to Berlin to convince Germans to join the French in antiwar demonstrations. The Germans refused.(16) In 1908 the German left was again called upon to make parallel demonstrations with French and English workers. Once more citing the illegality of such actions, the Germans opted instead for the convening of "study sessions" in Berlin. Despite the fact that the CGT had voted at Amiens to stop sending delegates to the Second International because of international socialism's puny stand on militarism, forty-five French unionists traveled to Berlin to coordinate some form of demonstration.(17) In 1910, when the delegates of the Second International agreed to turn over the responsibility of deciding antiwar tactics to a specially created bureau, 20,000 syndicalists turned out at the congress of Toulouse to protest against war.(18) Delegates at the 1912 congress of the CGT at Le Havre called for demonstrations to be carried out in France and Germany. Deeming this "a material impossibility," the Germans again refused.(19)

In the wake of the Agadir crisis in 1911, the syndicalists were able to generate tremendous protest activity by combining the issue of inflation with that of peace. Workers were urged by Jouhaux and Yvetot in an article in La Voix du Peuple "to demonstrate the possibilities of using the general strike to elevate workers' consciousness" on the issues.(20) Conferences were staged in bourses throughout the country during that year, and French union delegates again journeyed to Berlin to demonstrate proletarian solidarity.(21) A special congress

of bourses was convened to confirm once more the use of the
general strike to avert war. Delegates agreed to refuse to
recognize the state's right "to dispose of the working
class."(22)   In   1912,   when   Hervé   was   chiding   the
International to muster up at least "a platonic
demonstration" supporting peace, over 10,000 workers
demonstrated at the special peace congress convened in
Paris.(23) Young Syndicalists held their meeting on 1
September 1912 and agreed "to disrupt mobilization."(24) May
Day demonstrations revived that year, as Frenchmen protested
war and the Three Year Law.(25) On 23 November an enormous
peace demonstration was staged at the Aéro-Park in Paris,
organized by the unions.   It attracted 60,000 people by
syndicalist count and 20,000 by police estimates.(26) The
unions called for a show of force in December, with a
twenty-four-hour general strike. Government repression
deflected some of the strike's impact, yet approximately
80,000 French workers, by police estimates, were involved in
these demonstrations.(27) In July 1913 delegates met from
all over Europe at the Salle Wagram in Paris for another
"belle journée internationale" against the outbreak of
war.(28)

GOVERNMENT CRACKDOWN ON ANTIMILITARISM

     The question to be asked is just how effective
syndicalist antimilitary activity was. Jean-Jacques Becker,
author of a study on the Carnet B, declares that the
workers' movement was in a period of eclipse in the
immediate prewar years. He points to the numerous checks on
strike activity and the weakening of the Sou du soldat
movement as being evidence of this decline. Becker also
cites Jacques Julliard's conclusion that the years 1904-1914
witnessed a "cease fire" sentiment on the part of the
leaders of the CGT, and a backing away from violent
antimilitarist activity.(29) If this is true, it was a
reality not shared either by syndicalists or the government.
Demonstrations and propaganda increased during those years,
as has been noted.   Insofar as the French government was
concerned, syndicalist antimilitarism appeared to be
dangerously successful. The Sûreté Générale expressed
concern over the positive response to the Sou du soldat, and
was equally impressed with the effectiveness of the
Manuel.(30) On the basis of that perceived success, the
government prosecuted Yvetot for his part in antimilitarist
propaganda.(31) Other forms of harassment were in evidence.
In 1906 Yvetot reported that circulation of La Voix du
Peuple had dropped from 85,000 to 6,300 subscribers in one
year because of the post office's sabotage of the paper.
Under government directive, he alleged, the post office
either destroyed or held up the paper.(32) Beginning in
1907, there was increasing talk in the Chamber to dissolve
the CGT.(33) In 1909 Millerand called for the suppression of
political dissenters in the interest of the nation.(34)

The years 1910 to 1914 were years of intense chauvinism in France. The cabinet was extremely nationalistic. Deputies demanded the increase in military strength. Between 1910 and 1912 the doctrine of the offensive and of guerre à outrance was developed within the French general staff. Every crisis abroad was regarded as another skirmish in the war of revenge against Germany. The Balkan wars were seen as another arena for trouncing the Germans. Nationalist sentiment was heightened, with the press gleefully reporting that "it is our cannon that sounded there," and that the Balkans were "the pupils of the French army."(35)

In this climate of ultranationalism, the government was moved to take action against the enemies of the country. The campaign of repression saw the implementation of the Berry-Millerand Act, passed unanimously in 1911, and modified the following year. By its stipulations, soldiers could be consigned to the infamous Batt' d'Afr' in Algeria for antimilitary activity. The law also included prison terms for any civilian who preached insubordination or defamed the military. The latter was defined as anything from insulting the army to carrying out "provocative addresses." The law's supporters received a boost from data released by War Minister Adolphe Messimy, who spoke on the effectiveness of syndicalists' antipatriotic and antimilitaristic activities. In the decade between 1890 and 1900, he noted, desertions had numbered 1,900; insubordinate acts, 4,000. Incidences in these two categories had risen steadily, so that in 1911, 80,000 men were defaulting in some way on their military obligation. The previous year Briand had denounced the "insidious doctors of pacifism." In concurrence with the Berry-Millerand Law and Briand's diatribe against antimilitarism, the government increased its repression. There was a sharp rise in arrests and surveillance of pacifists and union members, and the suppression of antiwar meetings and demonstrations.(36)

The antimilitarist Fédération des Syndicats d'Instituteurs was dissolved in 1912. So too was the Chambre Syndicale de la Maçonnerie de la Pierre, less because of its antimilitarism than from the government's concern for that union's rapid growth and vigorous strike activity, fearing that the increase in antimilitarist propaganda was closely linked with syndicalist strength.(37) In 1913 the Three-Year Law, dubbed by many of its supporters as "the law of national health," was passed, again without opposition from socialist deputies.(38) So too was legislation declaring the bourses off limits to the military. A young recruit was made an example of for reading leftist literature. Protest demonstrations were staged in numerous forts throughout France. Sanctions against these protests created more furor and more repression.(39) On 26 May 1913 there were forced searches of the homes of hundreds of union members carried on throughout France. On 1 July that year the police launched dawn raids on union headquarters, arresting twenty leaders, eighteen of whom were directors of the CGT. They were tried and sentenced for the crime "of exciting the military to disobedience." Yvetot was given a five-month prison sentence for his participation. On 13 July the CGT was almost dissolved by the government for circulating the _Sou_ to the military.(40)

By the following year, the names of unionists had swelled the roster on the _Carnet B_. This list, begun in the late nineteenth century as a directive to the police and prefects in France to keep a close eye on foreigners or spies, now contained about 2,500 names, 1,500 of whom were French citizens. Of that number, most were workers, and many were involved in unionism or with the _bourses_. Evidently, the government feared mobilization would be sabotaged by this unionist fifth column in its midst. These "traitors" were not wild-eyed anarchists, however. Instead, notes Becker, they were generally "workers of rank, well-established in life and in their professional life, having a well-defined family situation, a known domicile, a stable job and profession [and were] men whose links with the world of work were narrow and direct."(41)

Certainly the state's fears seemed to have been born out by union activity during the first half of 1914. Despite their knowledge of the _Carnet B_ and in the face of government repression, in January, 9,000 delegates again met in Paris to demand peace and an end to the Three-Year Law. In March Yvetot was sentenced to one year in prison and fined 100 francs. May Day activity that year increased inordinately, and perhaps helped cow the government. After 1 May, there were no more arrests, even though from January to July, strike activity escalated. The jail sentences handed down for those already convicted, however, totaled 167 months.(42)

SUBMERGED BY EVENTS

In light of this prewar antimilitarist activity, what was syndicalism's response during the July crisis and the war years? The general strike was never implemented to prevent the declaration of war. To understand why, one must document the daily activities of the leftists beginning on 25 July when Austria and Serbia broke diplomatic relations. That day Jouhaux and Dumoulin were in Brussels attending the Congress of Belgian Unions. That afternoon, over a cup of coffee, Jouhaux asked Karl Legien what the German working class would do in case of mobilization. Legien responded simply: "they would march."(43) Feeling uneasy about events, the pair returned to Paris the next day. That day's edition of _La Bataille Syndicaliste_ carried an article written by Jouhaux, expressing accord with Jaurès' antiwar utterances and stating that workers were responsible for peace and must be ready to impose it.(44)

On 27 July the Union des Syndicats de la Seine issued a manifesto calling for the increase in agitation to keep the governments of Europe from being drawn into the abyss. That day the editors of La Bataille Syndicaliste urged Parisians to demonstrate in front of the offices of Le Matin, a newspaper well-known for its chauvinist stance. The manifesto calling for the demonstration was phrased in the most graphic terms. Readers were reminded of the barbarity of the Balkan wars: women violated, young and old mutilated, the plundering and burning of villages, the cadavers "abandoned to the crows and the wolves. These cadavers will be yours tomorrow!" All must demonstrate, the paper declared. "It is the last hope remaining to us to stop the catastrophe." That night an enormous demonstration occurred in Paris.(45)

On 28 July representatives of the CGT and the Socialist Party agreed to form a Comité d'Action to collaborate on convening a giant meeting slated for the following day at the Salle Wagram. The CGT then issued its own manifesto. Austria carried a heavy responsibility before history, it said, but the responsibility of the other European nations would be no less great if the workers throughout the world did not act to stop the conflict. "The CGT firmly believes that the popular will can stop the frightening cataclysm which will be a European War," it concluded.(46)

That militants were in complete disarray at that moment was indicated by the contents of the 28 July edition of Hervé's La Guerre Sociale. It is a masterpiece of confused signals, connoting not just Hervé's befuddlement, but the confusion of the left as well. Its headline proclaimed, "Down With War!" An article written by Hervé, "Au bord de l'abîme," wondered where "the beautiful dream" of the general strike was. It urged that it would be far better for the French to break the defensive alliance with the Tsar than to risk an offensive war against Austria. In another article, "Governants imbécile," unsigned, but undoubtedly penned by Hervé, the government was taken to task for not allowing demonstrations. But the paper also ran the last installment of Hervé's diatribe against neo-Malthusianism under the title "Les consequences économiques désastreuses de la population."(47)

On 29 July the joint demonstration planned by syndicalists and socialists was forbidden by the government. Crowds converged anyway. That evening syndicalist leaders met in the office of Jaurès' newspaper, L'Humanité, to decide with Socialist Party heads on the proper course of action. Syndicalists wanted to initiate immediate demonstrations, but deferred to the socialists, who urged that the demonstrations be forestalled until 9 August, when the Second International planned to meet in Paris. By waiting, Jaurès affirmed, the acts would take on more of "an international character."(48)

On 30 July Tsar Nicholas II ordered mobilization. The following day the German government proclaimed that the threat of war existed. Back in Paris that day, Jouhaux sent a telegram to Legien at Berlin. The CGT was against the war. Would the international proletariat intervene by pressuring governments to localize the conflict? Peace remained possible as long as workers organized internationally and opposed the conflagration. Jouhaux further advised Legien that peaceful demonstrations were in the process of being undertaken in France. He called on the German workers also to work against the war. The telegram received no response.(49)

That morning, War Minister Messimy brought in an order for the signature of Malvy, Minister of the Interior, calling for the arrest of those listed on the <u>Carnet</u> B. Malvy suggested that mass arrests during a national crisis would throw the country into disarray. When Messimy left, Malvy telephoned the prefects, urging them to keep close surveillance of those listed on the <u>Carnet B</u>, but only to take individual measures against the anarchists. Malvy's order drew a query from a provincial prefect: how could one tell the difference between anarchists and others? Perplexed by the whole question, Malvy sought guidance from Clemenceau. Later, while under the sentence of banishment for not having implemented the arrests, Malvy wrote that during his interview with Clemenceau, it became apparent that the latter was quite willing to see three thousand workers jailed. "My friend," Clemenceau warned the Interior Minister, "you will be the ultimate criminal if you do not leave my office instantly and sign the arrest order." But Malvy persisted in his cautious attitude. Shortly after midnight, after learning the Confederal Committee of the CGT had agreed not to implement the general strike, Malvy sent another telegram of advice, urging that the authorities have confidence "for political reasons," in all those listed on the <u>Carnet B</u>, and to arrest only foreigners engaged in sabotage.(50)

That same day, 31 July, Jaurès chided the French government for being "the vassal of Russia." Although the state was impotent in the face of the crisis, he declared publicly, the workers would continue to carry out autonomous action to prevent war. Later, while taking coffee at his usual place, Jaurès was killed by a deranged patriot. That night frenzied crowds surged through the streets of Paris. They were shocked by Jaurès' assassination, hysterical at the threat of German invasion, exhilarated over mobilization against an old enemy, and anxious about declaring the general strike and/or the revolution.(51) The headlines in Hervé's <u>La Guerre Sociale</u>, now a daily broadside, screamed "La Patrie en Danger!" If war were to break out, Hervé insisted, it was the fault of the military aristocracy who governed in Clemenceau's name. But as soldiers moved to the frontier to face the Austrian and Prussian military caste, they must be assured that "no one will shoot them in the back." With the militarists purged from the Second International, that group would now become the embodiment of the "Marseillaise" sung by their fathers 120 years ago. "Socialist friends, syndicalist friends, anarchist friends, who are not just the avant-garde, idealists of humanity [Hervé called], who are also the nerve and conscience of the

French army, the patrie is in danger!   The Patrie of the
Revolution is in danger!"(52)

On 2 August the French government ordered mobilization.
The following day the CGT issued its manifesto, signed by
the Confederal Committee. If they had not gained all they
had hoped, it was because "they had been submerged by
events." The CGT deplored the "FAIT ACCOMPLI," the manifesto
asserted, but workers must preserve humanity from the
horrors of war and remain attached to the cause of
syndicalism, "which must transcend and survive the crisis
that presents itself." The same day, La Bataille
Syndicaliste carried an article praising the government for
having "confidence in the French people and particularly the
working class," and thanked it for not implementing the
Carnet B. That afternoon the Socialist Party leaders met in
Paris and agreed that the invasion of neutral Luxembourg
compelled the French to go to war. Socialists must fight to
defend French culture and freedom.(53)

Meanwhile, the French government acted to create a
Comité de Secours National (CSN), naming to this group
important representatives from all segments of society:
labor, industry, and the church. At the government's
invitation, both Jouhaux and Bled agreed to serve. On 4
April the president urged a commitment by all to "holy
union." The names of the members of the CSN were printed on
beautiful white posters and pasted up all over Paris.(54)
That day Jaurès was buried. As the secretary general of the
CGT, Jouhaux was called upon to speak at the grave. A
special edition of La Voix du Peuple, not in print since the
13 July issue, published the full text of Jouhaux's elegy to
Jaurès, which was a mixture of revolutionary exhortation and
patriotic élan. He mentioned Jaurès' belief that the
workers of all nations had the duty to save humanity. He
would have said, had his life not been snuffed out, Jouhaux
declared, "you have defended the international cause and
that of civilization, of which France is the cradle."
Socialists and syndicalists had always sought to generalize
those popular rights that the French had so painfully
gained. Jaurès had fortified them all in their passionate
action for peace. It was not Jaurès' fault or theirs if
peace had not triumphed. In the name of those patriots,
such as himself, who were leaving for the front, Jouhaux
denounced "the savage imperialism that had given rise to
this horrible drama." He closed by proclaiming undying faith
in the Second International and its resolve to conquer all
liberties in order to bestow them on others.(55)

AN ABDICATION OF LEADERSHIP

Throughout the war, the CGT assisted the Government of
National Defense by serving with representatives from all
sectors on various labor commissions. Syndicalist leaders
also participated in interallied conferences in the course
of the war. In 1915 and 1916 the CGT leaders, meeting with

representatives from other allied nations, called for construction of a United States of Europe after the hostilities ended, and demanded that workers' clauses be included in the peace treaty. In 1918 the CGT, and particularly Jouhaux, was instrumental in the reconstitution of the Second International with a meeting at Amsterdam. Jouhaux was named vice-president of that organization.(56) These activities provided grist for the mill of opprobrium directed against the CGT leadership starting in the second year of the war.

Commencing on May Day 1915 protestors in the metalworkers' union began their offensive: the war was not a proletarian conflict; workers must abstain from participating in any government action. The Union sacrée was denounced as a "bourgeois trick and a betrayal of unionism." Special rancour was reserved for the CGT's alleged cooperation with the government. In their paper the following year, the metalworkers charged that Jouhaux's participation on mixed commissions constituted class collaboration.(57) By 1917, after the Zimmerwald and Kienthal meetings, the minority had formed itself into a Committee for Syndicalist Defense (CDS). That year saw the proliferation of labor unrest caused by a series of factors: workers' fears of automation; their hatred of war profiteering; concern over the competition for their jobs from women, young men, and foreigners; and a galloping inflation. A manifesto signed by Raymond Péricat for the CDS chided the CGT's leaders for being "valets and lackies of the government." The CGT had done nothing to support May Day, to ease the cost of living, or to counter the allegation that the strikes carried on that year had been paid for by German money, Péricat charged.(58)

Perhaps the most concerted criticism of CGT leadership came from Georges Dumoulin, although his charges underwent considerable modification as he moved from the position of being with the minority to standing with the majority.(59) Dumoulin had been with Jouhaux in Brussels during the July crisis and the meeting with Legien. His position of importance as an editor on La Voix du Peuple and as undersecretary of the CGT, however, had not protected him from being mobilized on 2 August. He was sent to Boulogne-sur-Mer, where he continued to write and receive visits from his militant CGT friends and from other dignitaries, such as Léon Trotsky and Charles Malato. After seeing some action at Verdun, in January 1917, Dumoulin was reassigned to the mines at Roche-la-Molière. During that year he was involved in strike activity with the miners, and he voiced his support of the Zimmerwaldian position. That year also, Dumoulin penned a brochure entitled Les syndicalistes française et la guerre, which placed him squarely in the minority camp.(60)

The actions of the Confederation's leaders during the July crisis, he charged, had been guided by cowardice. Jouhaux had always made much of the meeting with Legien, but Legien's speculation about the German workers was not the reason Jouhaux and the others had not called for the general strike. They had really feared being sent to a concentration camp if they had. Without any mandate from the CGT, Jouhaux and Griffuelhes had accepted the phony title of "National Commissar" and fled with the Socialist Party leaders to Bordeaux because they feared being taken hostage of the Germans in the event that Paris fell. Fear for their lives, Dumoulin charged, had caused the leaders to act only "by the necessities of the moment." And all their actions had been incorrect. Their first manifesto on the war, charging Austria with responsibility, had only provided the occasion for the French proletariat "to have faith in the occult work of diplomacy." The flight to Bordeaux, Dumoulin said, had constituted an abdication of the leadership's responsibilities. The leaders had not supported the Zimmerwald congress for the revival of internationalism, noted Dumoulin. Instead the Confederation's elite had gone to London to participate in a congress that was only "a war machine." It was in London that Jouhaux, wining and dining with capitalists and reviewing the British fleet, had discovered a new working-class politics that would "deliver the working class to the reigning bourgeois order."(61)

The fault of the Confederation's misdirection, however, did not lie with its leaders, but with the rank and file who were an immoral mass of drunks and hedonists.(62) What could one expect, Dumoulin continued, from "an ignorant proletariat that cannot read, do not want to read, or read only smut." What can be said for militants who prefer "to play cards interminably at the homes of their bistro friends." The Paris bourse was frequented by "drunks" and "high-livers" whose only purpose was to entertain administrators who had adopted the language of the "gros fonctionnaire." Such a degenerate membership could hardly impose a proper attitude on its leadership. Further, the majority in the Confederation had become "a bloc of corruption" composed of "fatalists, tartars," and workers so deeply in debt that they were afraid to risk their material well-being to take a courageous stand.

In such a milieu, any action against the war was impossible. In the prewar years, the antimilitarist propaganda, "more noisy than profound," according to Dumoulin, had tricked them. All had been blinded by syndicalism's success and "the applause at meetings." The leaders had assumed the masses were behind "those who did not wish to be less revolutionary than Yvetot." They had thought it enough to hate the barracks. They had waved their antimilitarist flags as if "to conjure away evil and frighten the bad genies." But the externals had blinded them from the realization that they had not truly instructed the proletariat to hate th state of things to which that class had to submit.

Union sacrée was possible, continued Dumoulin, "Because capitalism [has not been judged] guilty by the masses of exploited." Further, the order for insurrection at the time

of mobilization could never have occurred--not just because
of the ignorance of the working class, but because it was
organizationally impossible: federal secretaries could not
order the bourses to do anything! Now, he noted, the
Confederation was reflecting only the materialistic desires
of the rank and file and fighting only for bread-and-butter
issues. The CGT, Dumoulin noted, had become "a syndicalism
of order" with "Taylorist arms and Germanic bellies."(63)

THE MINORITY'S CRITIQUE OF "SOCIAL OPPORTUNISM"

Certainly for many, the CGT leaders' wartime activities
constituted a negation of the principles upon which
syndicalism stood. Direct action in terms of a military
strike never occurred. The leadership's apparent acceptance
of the Union sacrée seems to have flown in the face of
syndicalism's long-standing position regarding parliamentary
participation. The publication of the CGT's minimum program
at the end of 1918, with its emphasis on the desire to work
for immediate economic reforms, seemed to prove the charge
that the movement's leaders had abandoned revolution.(64)
When compared with the bolshevik example, French syndicalism
appeared to have been coopted by the bourgeoisie insofar as
many radicals were concerned. It was not just that the
Russian situation provided a stunning example for
comparison. A growing amount of criticism heaped on the
CGT, as well as the heightened violence within the movement,
came from the fact that after 1917, the minority critique of
the Confederation tended to be less centered on the CGT's
collaboration with the government during the war than on its
alleged timidity to support the Russian Revolution.
At the May 1918 meeting of the CGT at Versailles, it
was quite apparent that the minority was willing to do
violence to anyone who dared criticize Russia. Delegate
LeGuennic found that out when he publicly rejected the idea
of the dictatorship of the proletariat and received an
inkstand in the face.(65) The minority's resolution at the
1919 Lyon Congress of the CGT stated that the union's
leadership had led the workers to war. But worse, it had
made of the French proletariat "an international gendarmerie
and strangler of liberty" by not vigorously supporting the
Russian Revolution and its extension "to all countries,
wherein resides the hope of all the martyrized
proletarians." The Russian workers had no confidence in
those who had created "international federations to betray
the interests of the working class." The resolution
concluded with a demand that must have been the ultimate
insult to the old-guard revolutionaries and advocates of
direct action in attendance: the French Socialist Party--the
political socialists--it declared, must seek to organize
revolutionary elements in place of the CGT and its "social
traitors." A few weeks later, demonstrators celebrated the
Russian Revolution in a series of events that was
punctuated by violence and street brawls.(66)

During 1920 a propaganda offensive was launched by the pro-bolsheviks. That year, and until the spring of 1920, there were waves of strikes in France, carried on almost outside of the CGT's purview.(67) Criticism against the CGT and its leaders reached a crescendo of ill will. In 1919 Henri Guilbeaux called Jouhaux a traitor for having spoken before a banquet of industrialists in 1916, and further charged that socialist and syndicalist bosses had squelched the spontaneous demonstrations carried on following Jaurès' death.(68) Writing a few years later, Edouard Berth, now a supporter of Lenin and the Third International, saw method in Jouhaux's actions: he had joined the government because he nursed a secret wish to become Labor Minister. Jouhaux was "the red prefect of a Bonapartist Republic." Under him, the CGT had become "a kind of social gendarmerie, as the church in the hands of Napoleon had become a sacred gendarmerie." By his support of the Second International rather than the Third, Berth continued, Jouhaux had reentered "the bosom of bourgeois Europe."(69)

The most violent abuse against syndicalism came from the Russian bolsheviks, whose circulars and articles in the western newspapers called for war on the social traitors. Typical of the genre was a letter appearing in a November 1920 issue of the London Daily Herald, signed by the Russian leaders and some of the French minoritaires, reproaching the Second International for being a congress of jaunes who had betrayed the working class. The syndicalists and other leftists who had supported the government had become the "guard dogs of capitalism." Take care, the majority was warned: "you have only a short time to live."(70)

In July 1920 the Third International declared war on independent syndicalism. Although the Socialist Party was not able to stave off schism that year at their Congress of Tours, the CGT was able to avert the crisis, at least temporarily.(71) SFIO General Secretary Ludovich Frossard, recently returned from Moscow, addressed the 1920 Confederal congress at Orléans. He sought support for the minority position within the CGT and called for a fusion of socialists and syndicalists to make the revolution. He also made a stirring defense of Leninism and the Russian Revolution, which if vanquished, would lead "to a night of sinister reaction in the world" and compromise the workers' liberation. His oration, punctuated by great applause, terminated in the singing of the "Internationale" from the delegates of "the Mountain" seated in the upper banques of the conference hall. Frossard's call for unity did not mask the fact that minority leaders intended to effect "a syndicalist renaissance" by throwing out the old leaders and committing unionism unreservedly to the Third International under Moscow's direction. In numerous sessions, carried on in an atmosphere supercharged by catcalls, harangues, and insults, Griffuelhes, Merrheim, and Jouhaux defended their actions and the decisions of the Confederal Committee during and after the war. Their testimonies were so effective that the majority position was subsequently supported.(72)

But the inevitable could only be postponed, not diffused. In 1921 the CGT convened a special congress, again to address the minority's charges. The session opened with scuffles, verbal insults, and gunfire, which wounded several delegates, and closed with a shaky victory by the majority. The resolution determining the issue between the two factions was the one citing the Amiens' Charter disavowing permanent liaisons with any group connected to a political party. Following the meeting, the minority reunited in congress in the same city. Taking a page from the bolshevik's book, they declared themselves the representatives of the proletarian majority, and voted to adopt as their emblem the logo of the CGT.(73)

TRANSPORTED BY EVENTS

The censure by the minority followers of the Third International and the reproach of those who remained with the majority are important in assessing syndicalism's actions during the war and to the schism. Central to this discussion is the fact that these charges have become an integral part of the litany of criticism coloring the perception of syndicalism from its inception to World War I, and as such, must be addressed here. To some, such as Dumoulin, the weak link in the Confederation was its leaders' fears for their own safety. This was the reason the general strike was never called, the revolution was never made, and the war was not averted. Later Dumoulin would write in a gentler vein: "Fear is neither syndicalist, nor socialist, nor any other 'ist. It is human."(74)

But fear seems to have been a fact of life with which most militants dealt on a daily basis. Some of these people had served time in prison for their activities. The rest were acutely aware that their actions could land them in jail. The years immediately preceding the war served to remind them of the government's power. Yet while government persecution increased, so did antimilitarist activities. During the war, regardless of their cooperation with the government, the unions' leaders were never trusted. They continued to be spied upon and followed. The government's attitude was apparent by the fact that in 1917, in an attempt to mask its own ruinous conduct of the war, a scapegoat was found in the person of Malvy, and by extension, of the left in general. Charges of treason were leveled against the wartime Interior Minister for having been sympathetic to workers and for not having prosecuted the pacifists.(75)

Perhaps fear of being thrown into a concentration camp had caused the Confederation's leaders to hesitate in calling a general strike. But there is a valid body of evidence to show that they were aware before mobilization occurred that the government would not implement the _Carnet B_. Dumoulin later recalled that they had known by the evening of 31 July that they were safe.(76) Jouhaux confessed in 1918 that he had received word of Malvy's designs by someone in the Interior Ministry before his decision had become public.(77) Malvy himself later wrote that his intention to refuse to sign the order in advance of mobilization had been relayed to representatives of the left.(78)

What of the charge that Jouhaux's speech at Jaurès' funeral had been intended to whip up working-class support of the war? Jouhaux later recalled that he had had no idea of what he was going to say until he arrived at the funeral: he had spoken from emotion rather than from design. Naturally the bourgeois press had emphasized the patriotic rather than the internationalist aspects of his speech, Jouhaux declared. But barring his seeing every editor to explain what he had meant, there was little he could do.(79) Further, since all who had presented eulogies that day were awash in patriotic sentimentality, Jouhaux could scarcely have done otherwise.(80)

Did the Bordeaux flight reveal that the working-class leaders were crass opportunists, wanting nothing more than to be accepted into the bourgeois-capitalist establishment? Jouhaux later defended his evacuation and his short-lived acceptance of the position of National Commissar. In that capacity he was to visit all the provinces under government auspices. Jouhaux perceived this as an opportunity to revive syndicalist spirits, he said. Unionism was in complete disarray: workers had been mobilized; meetings were forbidden by the government during the siege; in the first year of the war, unemployment was astronomical due to the closure of many shops and industries formerly engaged in producing peacetime luxury items. When he realized he would be allowed only to preach the government's propaganda line, he then refused to participate.(81)

If personal desires for safety and security were not the primary motives in the leaders' failure to call the general strike, what was? Simply the demands of practical necessity, based on existing factors: the long-time realization that the Second International was nothing more than a talk shop and an arena for the Germans to show off their organizational power and wealth; the long-held belief that the German left would not or could not take any reciprocal action to prevent war; and the increasing awareness of the depth of patriotic sentiments existing among the French masses. Syndicalist leaders had always known the Second International was impotent: they knew the French party socialists were equally unprepared. With Jaurès' death, no effort was made by that group to declare an insurrectional strike to avert war.

Critics charged that the leaders of the CGT were anti-German and supported the war because they wanted to purge the Second International of the Germans' influence.(82) That may have been true. But more to the point, the German left's commitment to peace and internationalism had always been shaky. Such suspicions were less the result of organizational jealousies than of

history: when the German socialists had been called upon to
join the French and/or the British in mutual and concerted
demonstrations for peace, they had refused. Based on that
experience, there was no reason for Jouhaux or Dumoulin to
suspect that Legien was muttering into his coffee cup when
he told them the German socialists and unionists would pick
up their guns and march to the front. On that basis, for
the leaders to have unleashed a general strike in France
knowing such actions would not be reciprocated in Germany,
at the very moment when German soldiers were on their way to
the frontier, would have been insane. They would have been
"duped--and defeated," Merrheim reflected. More practical,
he recalled at the Lyon congress of the CGT, if the
Confederal leaders had declared the general strike, "the
working class of Paris . . . would not have waited for the
police; they would have shot us on the spot."(83)
     In the waning days before mobilization, the depth of
French chauvinism had become patently apparent. From its
inception, syndicalism had sought to build a transforming
paradigm of revolution. But the period of heightened
nationalism in the prewar years had either excited a
resurgence of patriotism among the masses, or simply
cultivated those emotions already there. The Austrian
declaration of war on Serbia was met by cheering crowds of
French patriots demonstrating in the streets on the night of
26 July, shouting "Hooray for the army, hooray for the war,
on to Berlin."(84) When the order of mobilization came,
Dumoulin recalled, soldiers gleefully departed for the front
in a high state of exhilaration. They were singing
patriotic songs, he remembered, shouting nationalist
slogans, and leaving their graffiti wherever they stopped:
"War on William," "Hooray for German whores."(85) If the
Confederation's leaders harbored grudges against the
Germans, so too did the French masses.
     What of the CGT leaders' collaboration with the wartime
government? To have remained aloof would have been
impractical. Anarchosyndicalism had always sought
improvements for workers as a condition of revolution. The
war aggravated the workers' plight and threatened to erase
all the gains previously made; thus union protection was
even more necessary than it had been before the national
crisis. The CGT's representation on the various commissions
was a positive benefit to the workers. From that forum the
unionists were able to fight against lower wages; they
worked to get employment and financial assistance to wives
of the mobilized workers; they established soup kitchens,
assisted in the relocation of refugees, evacuees, and
orphans; and pressured for unemployment relief and dependent
allowances. CGT representatives made reports and
recommended legislation on a host of matters, from factory
safety legislation to demands for government subsidy of
staple items.(86) Did this participation mean that the
revolutionary syndicalists had been coopted by the
government? Jouhaux answered these charges in 1919. What he
had done during the war, he insisted, had had nothing to do

with ideology. He had merely been carrying out "a human politics," dedicated not by issues of class struggle or class collaboration, but by "simply human" impulses.(87)

As to their participation on the arbitration boards during the 1917-1918 strikes, Jouhaux asserted that the CGT's presence on the arbitration commissions was not intended to diffuse working-class militancy, but to wrest whatever benefits they could for the strikers.(88) Since union activism always had been designed to force concessions, either on the local or national level--in the workshop or from parliament--such participation remained clearly in the realm of acceptable direct action. The union leadership did not capitulate to passivity during the war. When circumstances dictated, the CGT could, and did, demonstrate its militancy. The May Day 1919 demonstration under CGT auspices was particularly violent, leaving in its wake two dead and 428 wounded.(89)

The issue of the CGT's participation in the interallied congresses rather than in the Zimmerwald and Kienthal conferences was evidence to many of syndicalism's inherently reformist nature and of the abdication of union leadership. The invitation to participate in a Socialist International Conference to establish international relations and to work toward ending the war was not accepted by either the French Socialist Party or the CGT. The Zimmerwald conference, which drew only enough delegates to fit into four carriages, Trotsky later recalled, was attended by two members of the French minority, Merrheim and Bourderon, neither of whom carried mandates from either the SFIO or the Confederal Committee.(90) Merrheim later remembered, however, that he had spent more time at Zimmerwald arguing with Lenin against the bolshevik's demand that the war be converted into a revolutionary civil war, and that a Third International be formed, than in working toward any viable solution for ending the war. The Merrheim-Bourderon resolution calling for a peace without victory was accepted by the delegates over that presented by the "Zimmerwaldian Left" headed by Lenin.(91)

When a second congress was convened in Kienthal in April 1916, Bourderon and Merrheim again planned to represent the French minority, but were unable to do so when their passports were refused by the government. Although Merrheim remained an adversary of the Union sacrée and a propagandist for Zimmerwaldian principles during the war, he constantly rejected the viability of the Leninist plan to foment revolution in the midst of war. "Even if I had been shot upon my return from Zimmerwald," a martyr to the call for a general strike in the name of peace, he affirmed in 1919, "the masses would not have arisen." They were too weighed down with general preoccupations on the war and by the propaganda fed them by the press.(92) Although on opposite sides of the fence with Merrheim and the minority in the CGT on the issue of collaboration with the government, the majority members of the Confederal Committee, nevertheless, supported by their participation in

the interallied congresses throughout the war the same
principles Merrheim and the "Zimmerwaldians of the right"
had also accepted: peace without victory, self-determination
for all people, and a call to organize a permanent
international organization. The fact that they were united
in principle is evidenced by the fact that in 1917 and 1918
syndicalist delegates were able to agree on "a resolution of
unanimity" which claimed that the principles of Wilson and
those of the Russian Revolution were the same as those of
the French working class.(93)

In 1922 Jouhaux defended revolutionary syndicalism
against the charges of opportunism. Syndicalism, he
declared, was not only a doctrine, it was "a movement of
realizations," each of which carried the working class
further along toward the ideal end.(94) Throughout its
history syndicalism had been impelled by three concerns: to
advance the cause of democratic revolution by improving the
workers' condition, by raising class consciousness, and by
surviving as an organization. This goal remained the
objective of union leadership during the July crisis and
after. What of the means to achieve that goal? For
syndicalists, the use of direct action had always been
grounded in reality. Its objectives were manifold: either
to gain small victories leading to the complete
restructuring of society, or to remind the bourgeois
government that the latter could no longer carry on domestic
or international policies in a vacuum--working men and
women, unionized or not, were a powerful force with which to
be reckoned. During the war the syndicalist leaders
continued to maintain the same posture and make claims on
the government when and where it could. The unions
protested against profiteering and demanded the government
make its war aims public. Jouhaux insisted before a group
of parliamentary leftists in 1918 that diplomacy be based
"on the wishes of the people and not on the pretensions of
some personalities." The hour had come, he said, to give the
people its say in public affairs. That day Merrheim ended
his speech before the same body with a subtle threat: if the
government ignored the workers, they might refuse to fight
for that government tomorrow.(95)

In the years before July 1914 the general strike was
regarded by syndicalists as a practical instrument with
which to threaten the capitalist warlords. The July Days
only demonstrated that this weapon was no longer relevant to
the needs of the moment. All--bourgeois and
proletariat--were indeed overcome by events. By the first
of August, with the Germans on the march, the general strike
had become a chimera: an aborted general strike declared on
the day of mobilization would have rendered syndicalism as
enemies of the people; it might have caused the fall of
France; and it certainly would have left the working class
without an official organ of representation, thereby
jeopardizing all the gains made by French labor. Further,
the insurrectional strike would not have halted the war; it
would not have precipitated the revolution; its only success

might have been in upholding an ideal. But French syndicalism had never been committed to utopian visions or Pyrrhic victories. As the war wearied along, the idea of the general strike became a panacea for those expressing a longing for peace. In the hands of the minoritaires the general strike was fashioned into a weapon to be used against the "reformist" leaders who allegedly had failed to prevent war and initiate the workers' revolution. The bolshevik example of 1917 only seemed to prove the efficacy of the argument of the power of the workers in revolt. But 1914 France was not 1917 Russia. Indeed, Red October would not itself have become a reality without the decisions made during the July Days.

In 1918 Jouhaux noted that at the present moment, syndicalists could not be content "just to throw formulas across space."(96) But revolutionary syndicalism had never been committed to upholding formulas. The general strike, as previously noted, was never regarded as all-inclusive of direct action; it was only a particular form of direct action. With military insurrection deemed impractical, syndicalist leadership seized the moment, as it had always done, to work within the bounds of reality to keep syndicalism alive, to further the workers' well-being, and to press for a future based on international solidarity and the absence of class distinctions. By encouraging and participating in strikes, by collecting data or drawing up guidelines, by recommending legislation, by assisting in the relief of refugees or soldiers' families, by serving on peace commissions, revolutionary syndicalists continued to carry on direct action. And it is essential to note that all their activities were carried out outside the parliamentary arena. As a result of syndicalist action, French labor made its greatest advances--and this during a time of national crisis.(97)

The commitment to direct action was the primary reason for the stance the majority would take on the question of participation in international organizations. Historically, the CGT had been only tacitly supportive of the Second International, largely because syndicalists regarded that organization as merely a forum for politicians and intellectuals. In the hands of the party socialists, the Second International had been a dismal failure in furthering the workers' cause and in advancing international solidarity. But a reconstituted Second International could be a practical revolutionary tool, syndicalists like Jouhaux came to believe, if it could be made to serve as an effective international arena for publicizing, and with luck realizing, proletarian demands. This perception was the basis for supporting the League of Nations. After 1919, when Jouhaux and others of the majority became disillusioned with the League, now "crippled," they believed, by the European allies--and particularly by Clemenceau--they nevertheless remained steadfast to the Wilsonian ideal of general disarmament and of a great society of nations.(98)

The commitment to make this ideal a lasting reality was

the reason for rejecting the Third International, which seemed to the CGT majority to be both superfluous and disruptive of working-class unity. As it became apparent that a third international organization seemed concerned only with preserving bolshevik Russia, many syndicalists became more opposed to its creation. The CGT had been steadfast in its support of the bolshevik revolution and in opposition to the allied intervention and the cordon sanitaire. But the Third International was seen by many in the majority as an instrument of Russian domination; and the French leaders in the CGT simply refused to play Jonah to the Russian whale. Many unionists were angered by the bolshevik's diatribes against them, confused by their acerbic condemnation of both the Amsterdam International and the League, and were repulsed by Lenin's dictatorship of the proletariat, which appeared to be nothing more than political totalitarianism in disguise. Other syndicalists were equally offended by what appeared to be Moscow's increasing interference in the internal affairs of French unionism, as witnessed by the Twenty-One Conditions, and horrified at the bolshevik's mandate to reorganize the unions under the direction of the French Communist Party.(99) If the Third International were going to be merely a replay of the Second, with the Russians now assuming the place previously occupied by the Germans, then it seemed to the majority of syndicalists that there was no reason to endure the long train ride to Moscow.

If the idea of direct action as being prescribed by the reality of the moment rendered the tactics of antimilitarism irrelevant in 1914, so too did the changing conceptions of the fatherland make antipatriotism unnecessary. Syndicalism had always been committed to wresting from the bourgeois interests the well-being with which the fatherland was equated. When the Germans mobilized, the patrie was in danger: workers must rally to preserve the gains made against the bourgeois captives that would have been lost before the advancing Teutonic hordes. If much of the left's defense of the fatherland during the war, couched as it was in the romantic phrases of the French Revolution, appears to be evidence of the inherent chauvinism and nationalism of the French worker, one must also keep in mind that the patrie had long remained a symbol of morality and justice whose contents could and would be defined by present realities. To the men of '89, justice was rendered as a regime of "liberty, equality, and fraternity," political in nature. To the syndicalists, the patrie morale had to evolve into a state of economic liberty and equality. Only then, they believed, could the worker control the instruments of production, reap the benefit of his labor, and be truly morally responsible for his own actions. What the experience of 1914-1918 demonstrated was that only when this regime of economic liberty and equality was internationalized could true human solidarity and justice triumph, and a peace based on fraternity and altruism become a permanent reality.

Did the war expose a fatal flaw that had always existed in syndicalism? The conclusion to be drawn from this study is no. The war did not render the movement impotent; revolutionary syndicalism survived not only the war, but the schism as well, albeit in a largely different form from that which it had held during the heroic period of its organizational existence. In fact, war and schism actually strengthened the movement: the CGT's membership base was broadened as larger segments of the working population were encompassed into its folds. The Confederation's organizational structure was revamped so as to guarantee greater input from the provinces and more efficiency and continuity of operation. Such changes were the hallmark of a modern industrial working-class organization.

The French economy had been jerked into the twentieth century by the war. Responding to the new realities, revolutionary syndicalism moved beyond its narrow base of artisanal and anarchist elements to become a more viable representative of the working class. That survival was based on the movement's ability to adapt once more to the imperatives dictated by the necessities of the moment. For syndicalists, the revolution had always been carried on within the context of what was practically possible. Given that tradition, revolutionary syndicalists before and after the war might be faulted for their lack of idealism, but they can never be charged with behaving in a way that was inconsistent with their long-standing preference for practical revolution.

NOTES

1. The claim of Pierre Monatte, critic of the wartime CGT leadership and member of the Communist Party following the schism. Trois scissions syndicales (Paris, 1958), p. 142.

2. Jean Brécot [Gaston Monmousseau] charged the CGT and its leaders with having come under the feudal domination of the government by 1914. La grande grève de mai 1920 et la lutte actuelle des fonctionnaires (Paris, n.d.), p. 1. Henri Barbusse claimed that the organization was too concerned about money and power and had "the soul of the nouveaux riches." La lueur dans l'abîme (Paris, 1920), p. 136. Both Monmousseau and Barbusse were supporters of the Third International.

3. Louis Bouët, Le syndicalisme dans l'enseignement (Saumur, 1924), p. 24.

4. La Voix du Peuple, May Day issue, 16 June 1901.

5. Le Libertaire, 22 Apr. 1897.

6. La Voix du Peuple, 28 Feb. 1904, 6 Mar. 1904.

7. Discussions relating to antimilitarism at the Bourges congress of the CGT in 1904 in L. Gravereaux, _Les discussions sur le patriotisme et le militarism dans les congrès socialistes_ (Paris, 1913), pp. 123-126.

8. _La Voix du Peuple_, 10 Oct. 1905.

9. Gustave Hervé, _Mes crimes, ou onze ans de prison pour délits de presse_ (Paris, 1912), pp. 72-75.

10. Confédération Générale du Travail, _Rapports des comités et des commissions pour l'exercise 1904-06, presentés au XV(e) congrès corporatif, Amiens 8-13 octobre 1906_ (Paris, 1906), pp. 10-12.

11. _La Voix du Peuple_, 2 Aug. 1908. In the same issue the editors protested against "the premeditated massacre" at Villeneuve-Saint-Georges.

12. _La Guerre Sociale_, 8 Apr. 1908.

13. Comité d'Entente des Jeunesses Syndicalistes de la Seine, _La Loi Millerand_ (Paris, n.d. [1911]).

14. _La Voix du Peuple_, 16 Dec. 1912. On 19 and 20 May 1917 the women of Saint-Etienne reputedly did stop their men from being mobilized by lying on the railroad tracks. Reported by André Marty in a propaganda piece supporting the pro-Third International position in the CGT. _La révolte de la Mer Noire_ (Paris, 1949), p. 113.

15. Georges Haupt notes that after 1913, following the apparent settlement of the Balkan crisis and because of international socialism's increasing organizational success, the International Socialist Bureau (ISB), the directing arm of the Second International, used antimilitarism not as an antiwar device, but as a common denominator to achieve détente among the fragmented socialist factions within the International. _Socialism and the Great War: The Collapse of the Second International_ (Oxford, 1972), pp. 131-132.

16. Jean-Jacques Becker, _Le Carnet B: Les pouvoirs publics et l'antimilitarisme avant la guerre de 1914_ (Paris, 1973), p. 51. See _Rapports des comitées_ [Amiens, 1906], p. 11. The Germans said the SPD would be outlawed by the government if the organization called for any such demonstrations.

17. Legien was secretary of the German Labor Confederation. He had suggested that the International was no place to take up the question of military insurrection. At the Amiens congress of the CGT, Pouget reported on this statement, declaring that if those questions were not to be placed before that international body, there was no point in

sending delegates to its meetings. The Delesalle-Pouget
resolution to suspend relations with the International
secretariat was approved 815 to 106. See Rapports des
comités [Amiens, 1906], pp. 7-8; Léon Jouhaux, Le
syndicalisme francais contre la guerre (Paris, 1913), p. 50.

18. Gravereaux, Les discussions sur le patriotisme,
pp. 108, 209-210. For an estimate of the number of
demonstrators at Toulouse see Victor Griffuelhes and Léon
Jouhaux, eds., Encyclopédie du mouvement syndicaliste
(Paris, 1912), p. 10.

19. XVIII(e) congrès national corporatif . . . Comte
rendu des travaux (Le Havre, 1912), pp. 15-16.

20. La Voix du Peuple, 15 Oct. 1911.

21. Brécy, Robert, Le mouvement syndical en France
1871-1921: Essai bibliographique (Paris, 1969), p. 76.
Police estimate that 20,000 attended the meeting; Becker, Le
Carnet B, p. 53.

22. La Voix du Peuple, 15 Oct. 1911.

23. XVIII(e) congrès [Le Havre, 1912], pp. 13-16

24. La Guerre Sociale, 30 Oct. 1912. See La Voix du
Peuple, 1 Dec. 1912 for figures on the number of
demonstrators. Between 10,000 and 12,000 Parisian workers
demonstrated outside the city hall to protest the trial and
sentencing of three directors of the Chambre Syndicale de la
Maçonnerie de la Pierre in 1912, according to Becker, Le
Carnet B, p. 30.

25. Maurice Dommanget, Histoire du Premier Mai (Paris,
1953), pp. 38-39.

26. La Voix du Peuple, 25 Nov. 1912.

27. Becker, Le Carnet B, p. 57.

28. Dommanget, Histoire du Premier Mai, p. 39.

29. Becker, Le Carnet B, p. 80; citing Julliard on
page 16.

30. Ibid., p. 26.

31. Ibid., pp. 41-42, 44.

32. Rapports des comités [Amiens, 1906], p. 65.

33. Sylvain Humbert, Le mouvement syndical (Paris,
1912), p. 69. During this period Briand supported the
suppression of the Sou, but not of the unions. Ibid. In

1911 he became more militant, calling for the surveillance of the bourses in order to combat antimilitarism and antipatriotism. Becker, Le Carnet B, p. 83. For a discussion of the Radical Party's disillusionment with unionism see Judith F. Stone, The Search for Social Peace. Reform Legislation in France, 1890-1914 (New York, 1985), p. 166.

34. Becker, Le Carnet B., p. 85. There were always threats to the unions and bourses. Police invaded the Paris bourse on Bastille Day 1901 because there were red flags flying from the windows of the building. La Voix du Peuple, 14 July 1901. Delegate Chareille noted at the Le Havre congress that in 1908, fourteen of his comrades had spent almost one month in prison for singing the "Internationale." XVIII(e) congrès [Le Havre, 1912], p. 35.

35. Georges Michon, La préparation à la guerre. Le Lois de Trois Ans 1910-1914 (Paris, 1935), pp. 96-98; quote on p. 115.

36. Becker, Le Carnet B, pp, 37-38, 176-177. Briand's quote is in Michon, La préparation à la guerre, p. 87.

37. Becker, Le Carnet B, pp. 27-34.

38. Michon, La préparation à la guerre, p. 176.

39. Becker, Le Carnet B., pp. 40-44, 91.

40. Ibid., p. 40.

41. Ibid., pp. 105, 128; quote on p. 178.

42. Ibid., pp. 42-43, 45-46. The existence of the Carnet B was exposed in La Guerre Sociale in a series of articles running in the first part of 1912. See the following issues: 26 Feb. 1912, 13 Mar. 1912. For strike information see Roger Picard, Le mouvement syndical durant la guerre (Paris, 1928), p. 45.

43. Confédération Générale du Travail, La Confédération générale du travail et le mouvement syndical (Paris, 1925), pp. 133-134. Hereafter referred to as La CGT et le mouvement syndical. For coverage of the CGT and the war see the following: Annie Kriegel, Aux origines du communisme français, 1914-1920: Contribution à l'histoire du mouvement ouvrier français, 2 vols. (Paris, 1964); Maurice Labi, La grande division des travailleurs: Première scission de la C.G.T. 1914-1921 (Paris, 1964); Robert Wohl, French Communism in the Making, 1914-1924 (Stanford, 1966). It was no secret among French leftists that the German workers were nationalists first. An article appeared in Le Temps on 9 May 1901 reporting Marcel Sembat's discussion with his German friend Edouard Lockroy, who told Sembat:

> Our socialist workers declare themselves
> internationalists, but they consider themselves
> the masters and they regard the socialists of
> other nations as disciples, or better, as
> schoolchildren. [Lockroy's emphasis] At bottom,
> they remain patriots and Germans. If again, once
> more, Germany--be it to attack or defend--calls
> [the workers] to the flag, they will be the first
> to take a gun and make a profession of soldiering.

Reported in Georges Goyau, L'idée de patrie et l'humanitarianism (Paris, 1902), p. 362.

44. Picard, Le mouvement syndical, p. 49. For an account of the socialists' response to the war see L. Gravereaux, Les discussions sur le patriotisme, Haupt, Socialism and the Great War, Jack D. Ellis, The French Socialists and the Problem of Peace, 1904-1914 (Chicago, 1967).

45. Michon, La préparation à la guerre, p. 98. See also La CGT et le mouvement syndical.

46. René Modiano and Alfred Rosmer, Union sacrée 1914-193... (Paris, n.d.), pp. 10-11.

47. La Guerre Sociale, 28 July 1914.

48. La CGT et le mouvement syndical, pp. 134-135; Brécy, Le mouvement syndical en France, p. 84.

49. La CGT et le mouvement syndical, pp. 135-137. This telegram was the object of much confusion and criticism. Picard says it was sent after Jouhaux's return to Paris on 30 July: Le mouvement syndical, pp. 49-50. Bourderon claimed that Jouhaux's emphasis on receiving no word from Legien as the excuse for the Confederal Committee not to call for military insurrection was a flimsy one. The Committee had met until 10:00 PM the night of the thirty-first, he later recalled, so that the telegram could not have been dispatched until the following day. By that time, as everyone knew, the borders were closed and Legien could not have received Jouhaux's appeal, much less responded. See footnote 1 in Brécy, Le mouvement syndical en France, p. 84.

50. Modiano and Rosmer, Union sacrée, pp. 11-13; L.-J. Malvy, Mon crime (Paris, 1921), pp. 35-39. Malvy was not arrested, he was "tried" in the Senate and banished from France on 6 August 1918.

51. Modiano and Rosmer, Union sacrée, p. 11.

52. La Guerre Sociale, 31 July 1914.

53.   Quoted in Modiano and Rosmer, *Union sacrée*, pp. 15-16.

54.   Ibid., p. 19.

55.   Le droit au bonheur: *Jean Jaurès défenseur de la classe ouvrière: estrait de ses oeuvres et notes dactylographiques*, *discours prononcé à sa mort par Jouhaux, Vaillant* (Paris, n. d.). La *Voix du Peuple*, 4 Aug. 1914. Jouhaux's reference to his mobilization is confusing, since he was never mobilized. He may have believed he would be: he was thirty-five years old at the time. Critics of his actions claim his reference to the call-up was a ploy to identify the CGT with supporting the war.

56.   Picard, *Le mouvement syndical*, pp. 56-62, 155-160, 202. See also Léon Jouhaux, *L'organisation internationale du travail* (Paris, 1921), p. 9.

57.   Picard, *Le mouvement syndical*, pp. 62, 149.

58.   Raymond Péricat, *Lettre ouverte: Défense syndicaliste à l'Union des Syndicats de la Seine: Maîtres valets expulsés!* (Paris, 1917), pp. 7, 11, 13. For information on the inflation see Yves Merlin, *Les conflits collectifs de travail pendant la guerre 1914-1918* (Paris, 1928), pp. 33, 41-51.

59.   For a discussion of the reasons for Dumoulin's move from radical to *minoritaire* to his move back to the majority see the article by Peter M. Arum, "Du syndicalisme révolutionnaire au réformisme: Georges Dumoulin 1903-1923," *Le Mouvement Social* 87 (April-June 1974): 35-61. Dumoulin's disillusionment with the minority position, according to Arum, was based on the same concerns voiced by others who remained with the majority: his fear that schism would weaken the working-class movement and his revulsion over the bolshevik's tactics of infiltration.

60.   Georges Dumoulin in *Les syndicalistes français et la guerre* (Paris, 1918). Dumoulin continued to remain critical of the CGT's support of the war, but by 1918 he had moved back into the position of majority, again becoming undersecretary of the Confederation that year. At the 1920 Orléans congress, Dumoulin chastised the minority for blindly following Moscow's directives. Reported in Pierre Paraf, *Les formes actuelles du syndicalisme en France* (Paris, 1923), p. 212. The following year he authored another tract attempting to justify why he had sided with the minority during the war. In this work his criticism was definitely tempered. The CGT had been powerless to lead because it had had to broker all the workers' demands; as a result, its revolutionary potential was nil.

61.   Dumoulin, Les syndicalistes français [1918], pp. 14-18.   See also Paraf, Les formes actuelles, p. 136.

62.   Dumoulin continued to criticize the alleged immorality of the working class and its leaders.   In a March 1918 edition of Information Ouvrière et Sociale, the CGT's wartime newspaper, Dumoulin submitted an article on unionism and the war.   He said the class was demoralized because of "bad habits, errors, corruptions" that had "stifled the class instinct."   This was why they had gone off to war rather than take a moral stand in opposition to the carnage. When he wrote this article he was a member of the CGT majority.   Ibid., 24 Mar. 1918.

63.   Dumoulin, Les syndicalistes française [1918], pp. 12-15, 21-26.

64.   For an exposition of the minimum program of the CGT see Picard, Le mouvement syndical, pp. 187-191.

65.   Ibid., p. 160.

66.   Paraf, Les formes actuelles, pp. 173-174.

67.   The literature on the strikes of 1920 is vast and extremely partisan.   The most succinct treatments in English are Wohl, French Communism in the Making, pp. 161-168; and Val R. Lorwin, The French Labor Movement (Cambridge, Mass., 1954), pp. 54-55.

68.   Henri Guilbeaux, Le mouvement socialiste et syndicaliste français pendant la guerre (Esquisse historique) 1914-1918, preface by N. Lenin (Petrograd, 1919), pp. 6, 25.

69.   Edouard Berth, Les derniers aspects du socialisme (Paris, 1923), see pp. 4, 10, 21-22.   Berth declared the Versailles Treaty was "the charter of plutocracy," ibid., p. 29.

70.   Quoted in Maurice Labi, La grande division, p. 186.

71.   For an account of these events see Annie Kriegel, ed., Le congrès de Tours (Decembre 1920). Naissance du parti communiste français (Paris, 1973).

72.   Paraf, Les formes actuelles, p. 211.   See also L. O. Frossard, Socialisme et syndicalisme (Paris, 1920), which is his speech before the 1920 Orléans congress in separately published form; pp. 22-24 for quotes.   It might be noted that the anarchists within the CGT, then aligned with the minority, insisted that Frossard speak to the assemblage.   Labi, La grande division, p. 177.

73.   Le CGT et le mouvement syndical, pp. 221-226.

74.   Dumoulin quoted in Picard, Le mouvement syndical, p. 8.

75.   Malvy, Mon crime, p. 83.

76.   Dumoulin, Les syndicalistes français, pp. 14-15 of the revised edition of that published in 1918. The reissued version is dated 1921.

77.   XIX(e) congrès national corporatif (XIII(e) de la C.G.T.) . . . Compte rendu des travaux [1918], (Paris, 1919), pp. 222-223.

78.   Malvy, Mon crime, pp. 38-39.

79.   XIV(e) congrès de la C.G.T. (Lyons, 1919), pp. 228-229.

80.   See Vaillant's discourse in Le droit au bonheur, p. 8.

81.   Jouhaux at XIV(e) congrès [Lyon, 1919], pp. 229-230. Picard notes that the "commissars" never exercised their function under the government directive because such action would have been--and was--suspected by the militants. Later the CGT did organize a propaganda campaign and sent delegates to visit all the departmental unions and many bourses. Picard, Le mouvement syndical, pp. 54-55.

82.   Dumoulin, Les syndicalistes français, p. 19 of the 1918 edition.

83.   Merrheim reported in Picard, Le mouvement syndical, p. 50. Jouhaux said basically the same thing at the Lyon congress. XIV(e) congrès [Lyon, 1919], p. 222.

84.   Modiano and Rosmer, Union sacrée, p. 7.

85.   Dumoulin, Les syndicalistes français, 1918 edition, p. 19.

86.   Picard, Le mouvement syndical, pp. 55-60.

87.   Paraf, Les formes actuelles, p. 176.

88.   Jouhaux at the XIX(e) congrès [Paris, 1918], pp. 227-230. Minister of the Interior Malvy often mediated these disputes. Several workers claimed that he was generally impartial in these conflicts, wishing to resolve the problems in the best interest of the nation. His impartiality was a factor in bringing on his five-year banishment from the country. Paraf, Les formes actuelles, p. 154.

89.   Dommanget, Histoire du Premier Mai, pp. 66-67.

90.   Brécy, Le mouvement syndical en France, p. 91.

91.   Labi, La grande division, p. 64.

92.   Merrheim at the XIV(e) congrès [Lyon, 1919], p. 173.

93.   Merrheim noted that the resolution of the Zimmerwaldian majority called for peace, fraternity, socialism, and peace without victory. He maintained that he continued to uphold these tenets. Ibid., pp. 174-182. See also Pierre Miquel, La paix de Versailles et l'opinion publique française (Paris, 1972), particularly the chapter entitled "L'illusion Wilsonienne de la gauche," beginning on p. 95. For an exposition of the effect of Wilson-Leninist philosophies see Arno J. Mayer, Political Origins of the New Diplomacy, 1917-1918 (New Haven, 1959).

94.   Léon Jouhaux, Réponse à des calomnies: Discours prononcé par Jouhaux à la conférence de Douai, 12 Mar. 1922 (Lille, 1922), p. 20.

95.   Confédération Générale du Travail, La leçon des faits (Paris, 1918), p. 7 for quote.

96.   XIX(e) congrès [Paris, 1918], p. 221.

97.   See Paul Louis, Histoire de la classe ouvrière en France de la Révolution à nos jours (Paris, 1927), pp. 376-377 for workers' legislation passed from 1919 to 1926.

98.   See Jouhaux's support of Wilsonianism at the XIX(e) congrès [Paris, 1918], p. 234.

99.   Paraf points out that after the war, Moscow was officially represented at every C.G.T. congress. The representatives of the Third International and of the bolshevik line never missed a chance to support the minority position and discredit CGT leaders. This shocked many members, who opposed the work of "these foreign comrades." The Russians were denounced for their "imperialist aims" and their pretentions to interfere with the hegemony of the French proletariat. Les formes actuelles, p. 207. The report given to the delegates to the 1923 Lille congress of the CGT was that the divisiveness existing within the left had been the work of "the men paid by Moscow." The resolution called for workers to do something for the poor Russian population suffering from the barbarity of bolshevism. Confédération Générale du Travail, VII(e) congrès corporatif, tenu à Lille . . . Compte rendu des travaux, (Lille, 1923), pp. 10, 20-21.

PERSONS CITED

<u>Dubéros</u>, <u>Raymond</u> (1881-?), a hairdresser who joined the socialists when he was eighteen. He served as secretary to the Union des Syndicats de la Seine from 1904-1908. He also served one year in prison for signing an antimilitarist tract. He withdrew from union activities after his marriage.

<u>Guilbeaux</u>, <u>Henri</u> <u>Emile</u> (1884-1938), born at Verviers in Belgium of a French father. He was not a syndicalist, although he contributed to anarchist journals. In 1915 he was mobilized, but fled to Geneva.

<u>LeGuennic</u> (?-?), was born in Brittany into a very religious family. He was schooled in the seminary until the age of fifteen. He joined the railroad workers' federation, and attended numerous CGT congresses. He was in rebellion against all forms of authority, and was finally excluded from union membership for not carrying out the wishes of his union's rank and file. He opposed reformism, and was instrumental in bringing the state rail workers into strike in 1910. He was also a secretary in the <u>bourse</u> at Alais (Gard).

10. The Revolution Reconsidered: A Final Assessment

This study has examined the labor movement in France from its inception to World War I. It has focused on four questions: the unions' response to women workers, peasants, direct action, and the state. The conclusion drawn is that through the period studied, syndicalism was a working-class movement practically aimed at achieving a thoroughgoing social change based on the ideological inheritance from the past and the economic, social, and political realities of the present.

The French revolutionary inheritance was rich, but oddly dualistic.(1) It glorified the centralization of political power and praised the state as an instrument of economic reform. The legacy also carried within it an anti-Jacobin strain, which aimed at political diffusion and placed the locus of reform in the will of the individual. The philosophers of the eighteenth century had insisted that man was rational and innately good, and social institutions were anachronistic and unnatural. The Enlightenment provided certainty for radical change: once artificial barriers were overturned, reasonable men would live forever in a just and natural order.

The Revolution of 1789 was both a practicum for testing the Enlightenment faith in the individual and the culmination of a process of political centralization begun two hundred years before. The king was overthrown, the absolutist state was seized in the name of the people, and the centralization process was accelerated. If the Revolution was a political success, it was a moral failure. When the social institutions were swept away, the people were revealed as being neither noble nor rational. They were merely brutes incapable of living under a reasonable order. The Revolution did not establish social justice. It created a centralized state that became a more effective instrument of popular terror than it had ever been under the kings. Three times during the nineteenth century the power of the state was challenged. Each time bloodshed and failure was the result. The Enlightenment idea of individual emancipation and the establishment of a moral and just society remained a promise unfulfilled.

The unfinished social revolution remained the legacy

for nineteenth-century philosophers, who sought to understand why the Revolution had degenerated. They found their answer by separating society into political and economic realms. The Revolution of 1789, they agreed, had been the work of the bourgeoisie, an economic class whose power had increased with commercial and industrial expansion. The Revolution had been directed toward gaining control of the monarchical state from a political class whose authority rested on historical fiction rather than on economic realities. The object of the revolution was to use political power to impose an economic tyranny on the producers so the possessing class could increase its wealth. It had been a political revolution for economic ends. If the Revolution had degenerated into barbarism, it was because the bourgeois class, which had gained control, was corrupt, and the producers were in disarray.

Bourgeois ethics were based on the law of the jungle. The middle class was parasitic and exploitative, living off the labor of the producers. A just society could be established only by ethical men. Who were these moral agents? Nineteenth-century theorists provided several suggestions. Utopian Socialists hearkened back to the Enlightenment in their conclusion that only reasonable men could establish a rational society. Others disagreed. Intellectuals could not bring about lasting change; nineteenth-century society was materialistic, not idealistic. The only true revolutionaries were the producers themselves. In this conclusion, both Marx and the anarchists concurred. Their major point of disagreement was based on different interpretations of how the industrial revolution had affected the producers. For Marx the proletariat, a new class of producers spawned by capitalist exploitation, was the natural medium of revolution. Anarchists believed that those uncorrupted by industrialism were the elect. To some it was the peasant still in a state of nature; to others, it was the artisan alone who possessed the necessary social virtues needed to overcome the atomism of bourgeois society.

Anarchists and Marxists assigned the carrying out of revolution to an economic class. But each disagreed on the mechanism by which this revolution would be achieved. For Marx the social revolution was inevitable. The political state reflected economic realities. Economic concentration and political centralization were conjoined. Industrialism had given birth to a new social class; capitalist exploitation guaranteed that this class would be revolutionary. No longer willing to submit to economic degradation, the proletariat would use the political state to gain control of the riches industrialism could generate. The bourgeoisie had used the state to expropriate the political class; the proletariat would use the state to expropriate the economic class. The political party would serve as the vehicle for challenging the bourgeoisie. As capitalist competition accelerated, the exploitation of workers would increase. Deepening misery would develop class consciousness and increase the power of the working-class party in parliament. The weight of proletarian numbers would guarantee victory to the masses. The expropriation of political power would parallel the expropriation of the means of economic production. The political state would give way to the state of economic well-being and social justice.

In seeking to use the Jacobin state to carry out the revolution, Marx represented one strain of the French intellectual legacy. The anarchists represented the other. Marx emphasized state centralization; the anarchists looked to the individual will, which must be protected from moral suffocation. Marx preached the inevitability of the coming revolution, finding certainty in analyses of historical trends and economic data. Anarchists trusted neither to chance nor to historical determinism. For them the revolution could only be achieved by the individual acting ethically within his economic milieu. Anarchists and Marxists agreed that the social revolution depended upon moral agents working to achieve a just order. But to anarchists, the battle for control of a political state was a dangerous diversion. The state was a leviathan against which the individual will would feel intimidated and powerless. It was an immoral creation that would corrupt those who attempted to battle with it on its own terms. As the product of an exploitative class, the state was a parasite. Producers would expend their strength without ever really attacking the evil host. For anarchists there was no need to be sidetracked from the moral struggle by the charade of politics.

EMPHASIS ON INDIVIDUAL WILL AND ACTION

It was the anarchist route to revolution—individualistic and antistatist—which French revolutionary syndicalists chose. Marx had said that a change in the economic structure would result in political and ideological change. Syndicalists agreed. But they chose the union rather than the party as their vehicle for revolution. In France the political process led to confusion and political cooptation consonant with economic domination by the middle class. As instruments of the parliamentary process, parties were large brokerages designed to mediate and subvert individual demands. Syndicalism was not interested in strengthening the center; it sought to diffuse power and encourage individualism.

For syndicalists the bourses and unions were natural economic units. Unions had a continuity with the past. Workers grouped together by profession represented the traditional corporate organizations destroyed by the Revolution. The bourses organized workers by locale, thereby reflecting French parochialism and also providing an important point of reference in areas undergoing social and economic change. Together bourses and unions represented

elemental economic groupings of producers united by their
work and the customs they shared. They were also social
communities for the skilled and unskilled and for the
farmers and industrial proletariat. The bourses and unions
were also regarded as revolutionary units, where communalism
replaced selfishness, and where the spirit of brotherhood
flowed into the creation of class consciousness. Further,
in a society that was an economic mosaic, the unions and
bourses were organic units capable of responding naturally
to the pace and variety of economic change. Reflecting
local and individual needs, these small working-class units
were designed to serve as the construction blocks of an
enormous bastion of workers' strength, which would wrest
economic advantages against employers on the one hand, and
cow the political state on the other.

In this revolutionary edifice, the emphasis on
individual rights and responsibilities was constantly
maintained. Stearns makes much of the spontaneous nature of
working-class action, and the fact that so much of it was
directed toward limited and traditional goals. From this he
concludes that syndicalism was incapable of undertaking
modern forms of protest. But syndicalists intended that the
union structure would be one in which individuals could work
to achieve the most personal or local demands, such as
getting a manager fired, or a dismissed comrade
rehired.(2) The maintenance of professional integrity was
a right carried over from the artisanal period and
sanctioned by the Waldeck-Rousseau Law. But in this
structure, insofar as syndicalist theory was concerned, each
man's individual act benefited all. French history had
clearly demonstrated that a lasting society of justice could
not be obtained by mass action or by violence and bloodshed.
The industrial revolution had provided the employer with an
overweening power against the producers. Capitalist profits
were derived from the value stolen from the individual's
labor. The worker had the moral duty and the legal right to
protect himself against further theft. The action of a
single producer seeking to take back from the exploiter the
value of his labor represented a powerful attack upon the
entire capitalist structure. Direct action in the economic
realm was a revolutionary act: deprived of that upon which
it depended for its survival, the capitalist parasite would
eventually wither and die. Individual action in the
economic realm, therefore, was a way to carry out a
revolution that was moral, legal, and superior to bombs and
barricades.

Morality was a constant theme in the labor movement.
Only just men could create a just universe. Society must be
based on the ethics of labor and a reflection of the virtues
of the producer. But the workers lived in an immoral world
constructed by the bourgeoisie. Capitalism had taken away
from the worker his means of self-determination, and had
subjected him and his family to disgusting material
conditions. Syndicalism preached the need for the producer
to work toward his own moral emancipation by means of direct

action.   Acting   together   the   producers would then demand
from the capitalist   exploiter   and   his   state   reforms   to
improve the workers' material condition.   These reforms were
never   regarded   by   syndicalists   as   palliatives.   Reforms
would reduce capitalist profits and give back to the   worker
a   larger   share   of   the   value of his production.   Reforms
would also increase individual   morality   so   necessary   for
revolution.   More free time would allow the worker to enjoy
his family; fewer working hours would preserve his strength,
and he would not have to seek   energy   from   cheap   alcohol.
Higher wages would mean that his wife could stay at home and
be   the   moral   guardian   of   the family; or at least, better
working conditions would check   the   dehumanization   of   the
worker   and   his laboring wife.   Syndicalism's antipatriotic
stand also had moral goals.   The   state   was   unethical,   so
could only teach injustice.   It fostered militarism.   In the
barracks   young   men   were   corrupted   and   ruined as future
producers.   The state led youths to war,   the   most   heinous
act of brutality.
    The union as a moral instrument of class revolution had
to   be   preserved.   Throughout syndicalism's history leaders
of the movement fought to maintain the union   of   individual
producers   in   the   face   of   its   étatiste   enemies: party
socialists, conservative politicians,   the   Catholic   church,
and   the   landowning   aristocrats.   The society of producers
was   fragmented.   To   survive,   the   unions   had   to   be
inclusionary   rather than exclusionary.   Direct action was a
practical way to build   unionism: it   appealed   to   a   wide
variety   of   philosophical   schools;   it   could be adapted to
individual   consciences and the needs   of   the   moment.   The
constant   reference to individual action was seen as the way
to   keep   the   individual   from   being   subsumed   by   the
organizational   structure.   The emphasis on the spontaneity
of direct action was   not   an   indication   of   syndicalism's
backwardness.   It   was a perfect reflection of the localist
and individualist   nature   of   French   society   and   of   the
weakness   of the early syndicalist movement, which possessed
few organizers and fewer funds.   Strikes already in progress
could be directed at critical   junctures   by   a   handful   of
militants   who   knew   how   to seize every advantage to build
unionism.   Further, the   emphasis   on   spontaneity   and   the
loosely   organized   structure   of   syndicalism   meant   that
failures of the small locals to achieve their demands   would
not   do   irreparable   damage   to   the   reputation   of   the
Confederal organization as a whole.
    Of paramount importance to a   better   understanding   of
revolutionary   syndicalism   is   the   fact   that while in the
early days of unionism there was a   greater   stress   on   the
spontaneous nature of direct action, as the power of the CGT
grew,   the definition of direct action became more concrete,
finally   centering   on   its   two   chief   instruments   of
revolution: the general strike and antimilitarist activity.
As has been noted in this work, the general strike was never
clearly defined by syndicalists as to its nature or purpose.
Such   ambiguity   did   not   make   the   general   strike   a

metaphysical act; only an individual one. For the artisanal
element within unionism, the general strike was reminiscent
of the guilds and compagnonnages. But the general strike
was also regarded as providing a modern form of protest by
building working-class solidarity among industrial workers
of varying skills and employment. Further, as the economy
centralized, the general strike became a practical way to
attack a society increasingly dependent upon a few key
industries for its survival. Antimilitarist activity became
the other important weapon in syndicalism's arsenal. By
appealing to the basic human emotions of parental love and
the traditional peasants' hatred of conscription, it was a
means to attract women and peasants to unionism.
Antimilitarist propaganda was also a means to attack the
capitalist state in the same way that the general strike was
intended to be an assault on the capitalist employer, both
of which were immoral and unjust.

The fact that working-class actions came increasingly
to be directed away from spontaneous and localized
demonstrations toward participation in general strikes and
antimilitarist activity is a clear indication of the role of
the CGT in organizing and leading the French workers.
Stearns therefore errs in his conclusion that syndicalism
had little effect on the working-class population and that
its leaders were never representative of the needs and
desires of the workers.(3) To illustrate his point,
Stearns makes much of the fact that French workers seemed
not to have heeded the antipolitical injunctions of the
syndicalists.(4) Unfortunately, Stearns and other critics
demonstrate a lack of understanding regarding the nature of
direct action. As has been noted, the majority of
syndicalists were also party socialists who had agreed to
banish partisan politics from the union halls and stressed
the fact that economic action was superior to the indirect
action of electoral activity. Syndicalist leaders were
always directed toward dealing with the realities of the
French economic, political, and social order. As practical
revolutionaries, they were always reflective of and united
with the working class as a whole.

To achieve the revolution, union membership had to be
increased and syndicalist independence maintained. The
position of syndicalism on the woman question was designed
not only to heighten the morality of the individual, but
also to gain women supporters of unionism. Syndicalist
populism was designed to educate the peasantry to the idea
that morcellation meant economic serfdom, while collectivism
would bring material benefits for all. Direct action was a
means of building solidarity between town and country
workers, and unionists involved themselves deeply in
directing strikes and demonstrations in the countryside in
order to punctuate the call for workers unity. The stand on
the peasant question was also intended to appeal to
followers of Proudhon and Bakunin, and to bourses members
with their strong grassroots concerns. Antimilitarist
activity and support of working women were also intended to

silence the reformists, who the anarchosyndicalists believed were bent on capturing unionism and delivering it into the hands of the party socialists.

The revolutionary syndicalist movement offered workers the means to achieve a social revolution based on the possibilities inherent in the French situation. Marx's concept of revolution reflected the need to group individuals in a society fragmented by the growth of the middle class and industrialism. For Marx, the phenomenon of common suffering would develop the class consciousness necessary to overthrow the bourgeois exploiters. Syndicalists sought the same revolutionary end, but rejected the Marxian notion of immiserization, which they believed would only further dehumanize and fragment the producing class. Instead, they believed that individuals fighting in common to achieve material well-being would grow as moral human beings, would increase the strength of unions, and would build working-class consciousness, while all the while whittling away at capitalism both from without and within. For Marx, the revolution was inevitable and the worker was determined by history. For the syndicalists, the individual must continue to exercise his free will, because neither chance, history, nor the electoral process could be trusted. Both sought moral regeneration in a morally unjust world. But syndicalists chose to carry out their revolution based on the exigencies of the French milieu. Thus, in their ability to adapt the goal of revolution to the French experience, the revolutionary syndicalists anticipated both Lenin and Mao, each of whom were also geniuses at translating the proletarian revolution into the people's vernacular.

NOTES

1. In his study on Sorel, John Stanley takes note of another dualism in the French inheritance. The political system witnessed a high degree of state centralization and bureaucratization on the one hand, becoming unusually repressive in putting down labor disorders; but, on the other hand, the French economy remained stubbornly decentralized, which meant that union victories against the smaller business and industrial units ought to have been easier. Sorel misread this dualism, Stanley claims, believing that France was to be "the harbinger of a new historical tendency toward decentralization and local control rather than centralization." Both Sorel and Fernand Pelloutier regarded the FBT as the perfect organization to reflect the economic and political tradition in France. The bourses were localist, worker-directed, and were to be the incubators of French socialism. It was on this basis that Sorel's Reflections on Violence was posited. As we have seen, the FBT was eventually subsumed by the CGT. The French economy did undergo increasing centralization. The CGT, representing the French experience, also witnessed a

degree of centralization and more control over the working
class. See Stanley's The Sociology of Virtue: The Political
and Social heories of Georges Sorel (Berkeley, 1981); pp.
218-230; p. 219 for quote.

2. Peter Stearns, Revolutionary Syndicalism and French
Labor: A Cause Without Rebels (New Brunswick, 1971), pp. 56,
61-62.

3. Ibid., p. 102.

4. Ibid., p. 4.

Selected Bibliography

1. PERIODICALS

Bulletin Officiel de la Bourse du Travail, 1887–1888.

Information Ouvrière et Sociale, 1918–1920.

La Guerre Sociale, 1906–1915.

La Voix du Peuple, 1900–1914.

Le Libertaire, 1885–1907.

Le Mouvement Socialiste, 1899–1914.

Travailleur de la Terre, n. d.

2. CONGRESSES OF THE CGT AND FBT

IX(e) congrès de la fédération nationale des bourses du travail, tenu à Toulouse les 15, 16, 17 et 18 septembre 1897. Compte rendu des travaux du congrès. Toulouse: Imp. Berthoumieu, 1897.

X(e) congrès national corporatif (IV(e) de la confédération générale du travail) tenu à Rennes les 26, 27, 28, 29, 30 septembre et 1(er) octobre 1898. Compte rendu des travaux du congrès. Rennes: Imp. des Arts et Manufactures, 1898.

XI(e) congrès national corporatif (V(e) de la confédération générale du travail) tenu à la bourse du travail de Paris les 10, 11, 12, 13, 14 septembre 1900. Compte rendu des travaux du congrès, publié par les soins de la commission d'organisation. Paris: Imp. Nouvelle, 1900.

Dixième congrès national des bourses du travail de France et des colonies tenu à Alger les 15, 16, 17 et 18 septembre 1902. Alger: Adolphe Jourdan, 1902.

XIII(e)   congrès national corporatif, tenu à Montpellier les 22, 23, 24, 25, 26 et 27 septembre 1902 dans la Salle des Concerts du Grand Théâtre, sous les auspices de la bourse du travail de Montpellier. Compte rendu officiel des travaux du congrès, publié par les soins de la commission d'organisation. Montpellier: Impr. Delord-Boehm et Martial, 1902.

XIV(e)   congrès national corporatif (VIII(e) de la confédération) et conférence des bourses du travail, tenu à Bourges du 12 au 20 septembre 1904. Compte rendu des travaux. Bourges: Impr. Ouvrière du Centre, 1904.

XV(e)   congrès national corporatif (IX(e) de la confédération) et 2(e) conférence des bourses du travail, tenu à Amiens du 8 au 16 octobre 1906. Compte rendu des travaux. Amiens: Impr. du Progrès de la Somme, 1906.

XVII(e)   congrès national corporatif (XI(e) de la Confédération) et 4(e) conférence des bourses du travail ou unions de syndicats, tenus à Toulouse du 3 au 10 octobre 1910. Compte rendu des travaux. Toulouse: Imprimerie Ouvrière, 1911.

XVIII(e)   congrès national corporatif (XII(e) de la C.G.T.) et 5(e) conférence des bourses du travail ou unions de syndicats tenus au Havre du 16 au 23 Septembre 1912. Compte rendu des travaux. Le Havre: Imprimerie de L'Union (Société Coop) [1912].

XIX(e)   congrès national corporatif (XIII(e) de la C.G.T.) tenu à Paris, maison des syndicats, du 15 au 18 juillet 1918. Compte rendu des travaux. Paris: Impr. Nouvelle, 1919.

XXI(e)   congrès national corporatif (XV(e) de la C.G.T.), tenu à Orléans du 27 septembre au 2 octobre 1920. Compte rendu des travaux. Villeneuve-Saint-Georges: L'Union Typographique [1920].

3. REGIONAL AND TRADE UNION CONGRESSES

Séances du congrès ouvrier socialiste de France, troisième session tenue à Marseille du 20 au 31 octobre 1879. Marseille: Imp. Doucet, 1879.

Congrès ouvrier régional de Bordeaux: extrait des procès verbaux et résolutions prises sur les questions

contenues dans le program. Bordeaux: Imprimerie
Commerciale Auguste Bord, 1880.

Congrès   corporatifs nationaux et internationaux de la
chapellerie. Lyon: n. p.

Congrès national des syndicats ouvriers tenu à Lyon en
octobre 1886. Compte rendu officielle. Lyon: Imp.
Nouvelle, 1887.

Société générale des chapeliers de France. Congrès national
et international tenu à Paris, les 13, 14, 15, et
16 juillet, 1889. Paris: Imp. du Prolétariat 1889.

Compte rendu du congrès national et international des
ouvriers travaillant ou employant le cuir et la
peaux [1900]. Paris: Imp. Ouvrière, 1901.

Bourse du Travail du Toulon. Compte rendu du 1(er) congrès
régional. Toulon: Petit Var, 1904.

Deuxième congrès national et troisième congrès national de
la fédération nationale des travailleurs de
l'alimentation. Compte rendu des travaux des deux
congrès. Paris: Imp. Le Papier, 1904.

Compte rendu du neuvième congrès national de la fédération
des travailleurs du livre. Paris: Imp. nouvelle,
1905.

Bourse   Régionale du Travail. Compte rendu du congrès
régional corporatif. Auxerre: L'Universelle,
1907.

Compte rendu officiel des travaux du sixième congrès de la
fédération des travailleurs de l'habillement.
Grenoble: n. p. 1906.

Fédération des syndicats ouvriers de la chapellerie:
treizième congrès national et sixième congrès
international. Paris: Maison des Fédérations,
1906.

Cinquième congrès de la fédération nationale des cuirs et
peaux. Paris: Maison des Fédérations, 1907.

Cinquième congrès national des syndicats et groupes
corporatifs ouvriers de France. Compte rendu
recueille dans les archives de la bourse du
travail de Marseille. Paris: Rivière, 1909.

Sixième congrès de la fédération nationale des cuirs et
peaux. Paris: Maison des Fédérations, 1909.

Compte rendu du douzième congrès national ouvrier de l'industrie textile [Roubaix]. Lille: Imp. Dhoossche, 1911.

Compte rendu du septième congrès national de la fédération nationale des cuirs et peaux. Paris: Maison des Fédérations, 1911.

Fédération nationale des ouvriers et ouvrières des tabacs. Congrès national annuel, 19-24 juin 1911. Paris: Imprimerie Le Papier, 1912.

Fédération nationale des syndicats de l'industrie du sciage et féconnage mécanique du bois. Paris: Imp. Nouvelle, 1918.

VII(e) congrès corporatif, tenu à Lille 20 mai 1923. Compte rendu des travaux. Lille: Union Départementale des Syndicats Ouvriers du Nord, 1923.

Compte rendu du dixième congrès national de la fédération française des travailleurs du livre. Paris: Imp. Nouvelle, n. d.

Compte rendu du premier congrès national de la fédération nationale des travailleurs de l'industrie de la bijouterie-orfévrerie-horlogerie. Paris: Maison des Fédérations, n. d.

Quatrième congrès national de la fédération nationale des cuirs et peaux. Puteaux: La Cootypographie, n. d.

4. OTHER CONGRESSES

6(e) congrès national des syndicats de France. Compte rendu des travaux du congrès tenu à Nantes du 17 au 22 septembre 1894. Publié par les soins de la commission d'organisation. Nantes: Impr. Schwab et Fils, 1894.

Union Centrale des Syndicats des Agriculteurs de France. XVII(e) congrès national des syndicats agricoles, Nancy, juin 1909. Paris: n. p. [1909].

5. OTHER SOURCES

Agulhon, Maurice. Une ville ouvrière au temps du socialisme utopique: Toulon de 1815-1851. Paris: Mouton, 1970.

Arum, Peter M. "Du syndicalisme révolutionnaire au réformisme: Georges Dumoulin 1903-1925," Le Mouvement Social 87 (Apr.-June 1974): 35-61.

Audiganne, Armand. Mémoire d'un ouvrier de Paris. Paris: Charpentier, 1875.

Augé-Laribé, M[ichel]. "Deuxième congrès des syndicats d'ouvrier agricole," Le Musée Social: Mémoires et Documents. Paris: Arthur Rousseau, 1905.

_____. Grande ou petite propriété. Montpellier: Imp. G. Fermin, Montane et Ricardi, 1902.

_____. Le paysan français après la guerre. Paris: Librairie Garnier Frères, 1923.

_____. Le problème agraire du socialisme. Paris: V. Giard & E. Brière, 1907.

_____. La révolution agricole. Paris: Albin Michel, 1955.

_____. Syndicats et cooperatives agricoles. Paris: Armand Colin, 1926.

Barbusse, Henri. La lueur dans l'abîme. Paris: Editions Clarté, 1920.

Barthous, Louis. L'action syndicale. Paris: Arthur Rousseau, 1904.

Baumal, Francis. Le féminisme au temps de Molière. Paris: La Renaissance du Livre, n. d.

Bebel, August. Women and Socialism. Meta L. Stern (Hite), trans. New York: The Socialist Literature Company, 1910.

Becker, Jean-Jacques. Le Carnet B: Les pouvoirs publics et l'antimilitarisme avant la guerre de 1914. Paris: Klincksieck, 1973.

_____. 1914: Comment les français sont entrés dans la guerre; contribution à l'étude de l'opinion publique printemps-été 1914. Paris: Presses de la Fondation Nationale des Sciences Politiques, 1977.

Bernard, Léopold. Les idées révolutionnaires dans la campagne du bourbonnais. n. p., 1911.

Berth, E[douard]. "Le centenaire de Proudhon," Le Mouvement Socialiste (1 Jan. 1909): 49-55.

_____ . Les derniers aspects du socialisme. Paris: Marcel Rivière, 1923.

Berthold, Aimé. P.-J. Proudhon et la propriété: Un socialisme pour les paysans. Paris: V. Giard & E. Brière, 1910.

Besse, Auguste. Education sociale. Les lois sociales et le syndicalisme. Paris & Cahors: Imp. Typographique A. Coulslant, 1908.

Blanquart, Louisette. Femmes: L'Age politique. Paris: Editions Sociales, 1974.

Blum, Léon. Les congrès ouvriers et socialistes français. 2 vols. Paris: Societe Nouvelle de Librairie et d'Editions, 1901.

Bouët, Louis. Le syndicalisme dans l'enseignement. Saumur: Librairie de l'Ecole Emancipée, 1924.

Bouglé, C[élestin]. Syndicalisme et démocratie. Paris: Edouard Cornély et Cie., 1908.

Bourdeau, Jean. L'evolution du socialisme. Paris: Félix Alcan, 1901.

Bourse du Travail de Nîmes. Souvenir de l'inauguration de la nouvelle bourse du travail. Nîmes: Roger et Laporie, 1893.

Boxer, Marilyn Jacoby. "Socialism Faces Feminism in France: 1879-1913." (Ph.D. Dissertation: University of California, Riverside, 1975.)

Boxer, Marilyn J[acoby] and Jean H. Quataert, eds. Socialist Women, European Feminism in the Nineteenth and Early Twentieth Centuries. New York: Elsevier, 1978.

Branca, Patricia. Women in Europe Since 1750. London: Croom Helm, 1978.

Brécot, Jean [Gaston Monmousseau]. La grande grève de mai 1920 et la lutte actuelle des fonctionnaires. Paris: n. p., n. d.

Brécy, Robert. La grève générale en France. Paris: EDI, 1969.

_____. Le mouvement syndical en France 1871-1921: Essai bibliographique. Paris: Mouton, 1963.

Brogan, D. W. The Development of Modern France 1870-1939. London: Hamilton, 1940.

_____. Proudhon. London: Hamish Hamilton, 1934.

Brunet, Françisque. A mon frère l'ouvrier. Bordeaux: L'Union Prolétarienne, n.d.

Cazalis, Jules. Syndicalisme ouvrier et evolution sociale. Paris: Marcel Rivière, 1925.

Cerez, Jane. La condition sociale de la femme de 1804 à l'heure présente. Paris: Librairie General de Droit & de Jurisprudence, 1940.

Challaye, Félicien. Syndicalisme révolutionnaire et syndicalisme réformiste. Paris: Félix Alcan, 1909.

Champion, Armand. Propos syndicalistes et révolutionnaires. Paris: Vendome: Imp. Ouvrière, 1911.

Chaysson, Emile. "Le rôle de la femme dans la mutualité," Le Musée Social: Mémoires et Documents. Paris: Arthur Rousseau, 1905.

Choppé, Albert. Le label. Paris: V. Giard & E. Brière, 1908.

Clark, Marjorie Ruth. A History of the French Labor Movement (1910-1928). Berkeley: University of California, 1930.

Clay, Arthur. Syndicalism and Labour. London: John Murray, 1912.

Comité de syndicaliste aux organisations syndicales à leur militants. Paris: Section du Comité pour la Réprise des Relations Internationales, n. d.

Comité d'Entente des Jeunesses Syndicalistes de la Seine. La Loi Millerand. Paris: La Vie Ouvrière [1911].

"La Commission." Syndicalisme et néo-malthusianisme. Lille: M. Dhoossche, 1911.

Compère-Morel [Constant Adéodat]. Le programme socialiste de réformes agraires. Paris: Marcel Rivière, 1919.

_____. La question agraire et le socialisme en France. Paris: Marcel Rivière, 1912.

Confédération Générale du Travail. La confédération generale du travail et le mouvement syndical. Paris: n. p., 1925.

_____. La crise du syndicalisme et l'action de la C.G.T. Lille: n. p., 1921.

_____. La leçon des faits. Paris: Siège de la Confédération Générale du Travail, 1916.

_____. Rapports des comités et des commissions pour l'exercise 1904-06. Paris: Maison des Fédérations, 1906.

Coornaert, Emile. Les compagnonnages en France du moyen âge à nos jours. Paris: Les Editions Ouvrières, 1966.

Coulet, Elie. Le mouvement syndical et coopératif dans l'agriculture. Montpellier: Camille Coulet, 1898.

Courtin, André. Les congrès nationaux des syndicats agricoles. Paris: Lib. Agricole de la Maison Rustique, 1920.

Danrez, Arthur. Verités syndicales. Paris: Imp. Ouvrière Oyannoux, 1908.

Daudé-Bancel, A. Le mouvement ouvrier français et la guerre. Paris: Marcel Rivière, 1915.

Delesalle, Paul. La grève. Paris: Bureau des Temps Nouveaux, 1900.

_____. L'action syndicale et les anarchistes. Paris: Bureau des Temps Nouveaux, 1901.

_____. Les bourses du travail et la C.G.T. Paris: Marcel Rivière, n. d.

_____. Les deux méthodes du syndicalisme. Paris: La Cootypographie, Société Ouvrière d'Imprimerie, 1903.

Demartial, G. La guerre de 1914: Le mobilisation des consciences. Paris: Les Editions Riedir, 1922.

Dolléans, Edouard. La caractère religieux du socialisme. Paris: L. Larose et L. Tenin, 1906.

_____. Féminisme et le mouvement ouvrier: George Sand. Paris: Les Editions Ouvriers, 1951.

_____. Histoire du mouvement ouvrier. 3 vols. Paris: Librairie Armand Colin, 1967.

_____. Proudhon. Paris: Gallinard, 1948.

Dolléans, Edouard, and Michel Crozier. Mouvement ouvrier et socialiste: Chronologie et Bibliographie 1750-1918. Paris: Les Editions Ouvriers, 1950.

Dommanget, Maurice. Histoire du Premier Mai. Paris: Société Universitaire d'Editions et de Librairie, 1953.

Dovring, Folke. Land and Labour in Europe in the 20(th) Century: A Comparative Survey of Recent Agrarian History. The Hague: International Publications Service, 1960.

Le droit à bonheur: Jean Jaurès défenseur de la class ouvrière: extrait de ses oeuvres et notes dactylographique, discours prononcé à sa mort par Jouhaux, Vaillant, Paris: n. p., [1914].

Dufour. Le syndicalisme et la prochaine révolution. Paris: n. p., 1913.

Dumoulin, Georges. Les syndicalistes français et la guerre. Paris: Editions de l'Avenir International, 1918.

_____. Les syndicats français et la guerre. Paris: Editions du Syndicat Textile de Vienne (Sère), 1921.

Dupeux, Georges. French Society 1789-1970. Peter Wait, trans. London: Methuen, 1976.

Duveau, Georges. La vie ouvrière en France sous le Second Empire. Paris: Librairie Gallinard, 1946.

Earl, E. M., ed. Modern France. Princeton: Princeton University Press, 1951.

Elliott, W. Y. The Pragmatic Revolt in Politics. New York: Macmillan, 1928.

Ellis, Jack D. The French Socialists and the Problem of the Peace 1904-1914. Chicago: Loyola University, 1967.

Escarra, Edouard. Nationalisation du sol et socialisme
     (Etude d'histoire des doctrines économiques).
     Paris: Imp. Henri Jouve, 1904.

Esquerre, Albert. Le néo-syndicalisme et la myth de la
     grève générale. Bordeaux: Barthélemy et Clèdes,
     1913.

Fagniez, Gustave. La femme et la société française dans la
     premier moitié du XVIII(e) siècle. Paris:
     J. Gambes, 1929.

Febvre, Lucien. Une question d'influence: Proudhon et le
     syndicalisme contemporain. Paris: Libraire de
     Pages Libres, 1919.

Fédération des bourses du travail de France et des
     colonies. Brochure de propagande syndicale.
     Paris: Imp. Nouvelle, 1902.

Feuer, Lewis, ed. Marx & Engels: Basic Writings on
     Politics & Philosophy. Garden City: Doubleday &
     Co., 1959.

Fleming, Marie. The Anarchist Way to Socialism: Elisée
     Réclus and Nineteenth-Century European Anarchism.
     London: Croom Helm, 1979.

Foreman, Ann. Femininity as Alienation. London: Pluto
     Press, 1977.

Franck, Charles. Les bourses du travail et la C.G.T. Paris:
     Giard et Brière, 1910.

Frois, Marcel. La santé et le travail des femmes pendant la
     guerre. Paris: Les Presses Universitaires de
     France, n. d.

Frossard, L.-O. Socialisme et syndicalisme. Paris: Librairie
     du Parti Socialiste et de L'Humanité, 1920.

Gailhard-Bancel, H[yacinthe] de. Quinze anneés d'action
     syndicale. Paris: La Muelle et Poisson, 1900.

Garmy, René. Histoire du mouvement syndical en France.
     2 vols. Paris: Bureau d'Edition, 1933-1934.

Gatti, G. Le socialisme et l'agriculture. Paris: V. Giard
     et E. Briere, 1902.

Georges, Bernard, and Denise Tintant. Léon Jouhaux: Cinquant
     ans de syndicalisme. 2 vols. Paris: Presses
     Universitaires de France, 1962.

Ghesquière [Henri], and [Adéodat] Compère-Morel. L'action syndicale. Lille: M. Doossche, 1911.

Godfrey, E. Drexel, Jr. Fate of the Non-Communist Left. New York: Random House, 1955.

Goetz-Girey, Robert. La pensée syndicale française: Militants et théoriciens. Paris: Armand Colin, 1948.

Goguel-Nyegaard, François. Géographie des élections françaises de 1870 à 1951. Paris: Armand Colin, 1951.

Goldberg, Harvey. "Jaurès and the Formulation of a Socialist Peasant Policy," International Review of Social History. 153 (1957): 372-391.

Goyard, L. La crise du petit commerce et le syndicalisme. Paris: V. Giard et E. Brière, 1911.

Goyau, Georges. L'idée de patrie et l'humanitarianisme. Paris: Perrin, 1902.

Gratton, Philippe. Les luttes de classes dans les campagnes. Paris: Anthropos, 1971.

_____. "Mouvement et physionomie des grèves agricoles en France de 1890 à 1935," Le Mouvement Social 71 (Apr. - June 1970): 3-38.

Gravereaux, L. Les discussions sur le patriotisme et le militarisme dans les congrès socialistes. Paris: G. Dussardier et P. Frank, 1913.

Griffuelhes, Victor. L'action syndicaliste. Paris: Marcel Rivière, 1908.

_____. Voyage révolutionnaire. Paris: Marcel Rivière, 1911.

Griffuelhes, V[ictor], et al. Syndicat et syndicalisme. Paris: La Publication Sociale, n. d.

Griffuelhes, Victor, and Léon Jouhaux, eds. Encyclopédie du mouvement syndicaliste. Paris: Marcel Rivière, 1912.

Gros, Gaston. Le contrat collectif et le syndicalisme. Paris: Comité Executif du Parti Républican Radical-Radical-Socialiste, 1910.

Guérin, Joseph. Le syndicalisme et la propriété. Paris: Pierre Roger, n. d.

Guesde, Jules, and Paul Lafargue. Le programme du parti ouvrier. Lille: Imp. Ouvrière, 1897.

Guieysse, Charles. Les universités populaires et le mouvement ouvrier. Paris: Cahiers de la Quinzaine, n.d.

Guilbeaux, Henri. Le mouvement socialiste et syndicaliste française pendant la guerre (Esquisse historique) 1914-1918. Preface by N. Lenin. Petrograd: Editions de l'Internationale Communiste, 1919.

Guilbert, Madeleine. Les femmes et l'organisation syndical avant 1914. Paris: Editions du Centre National de la Récherche Scientifique, 1966.

_____. Les fonctions des femmes dans l'industrie. Paris: Mouton, 1966.

Hanagan, Michael P. The Logic of Solidarity: Artisans and Industrial Workers in Three French Towns 1871-1914. Urbana: University of Illinois, 1980.

Haupt, Georges. Socialism and the Great War: The Collapse of the Second International. Oxford: Oxford University, 1972.

Hervé, Gustave. Après la Marne. Paris: Bibliothèque des Ouvrages Documentaires, 1915.

_____. L'internationalisme. Paris: V. Giard & E. Brière, 1910.

_____. Mes crimes, ou onze ans de prison pour délits de presse. Paris: Editions de La Guerre Sociale, 1912.

Hoffman, Robert, ed. Anarchism. New York: Atherton, 1970.

Humbert, Sylvain. Le mouvement syndical. Paris: Marcel Rivière, 1912.

Humphrey, Richard. Georges Sorel: Prophet Without Honor. Cambridge: Harvard University, 1952.

Hunter, Neil. Peasantry and Crisis in France. London: Victor Gollancz, 1938.

Jacob, B. Devoirs (conférences de morale individuelle et de morale sociale). Paris: Edouard Cornély, 1910.

Janey, Charles. Evolution de l'idée syndicale. Toulouse: Edouard Prévat, 1904.

Jean, O. Le syndicalisme: Son origine, son organisation,
        son but, son rôle social. Paris: Action
        Populaire, 1922.

Joll, James. The Anarchists. New York: Grosset & Dunlap,
        1964.

Joran, Raymond. L'organisation syndicale dans l'industrie du
        bâtiment. Paris: Arthur Savaété, 1914.

Jouhaux, Germaine. Rapports sur la condition du travail au
        point de vue féminin. Paris: Editions de l'Union
        des Syndicats Confédérés de la Région Parisienne,
        1926.

Jouhaux, Léon. L'organisation internationale du travail.
        Paris: n. p. 1921.

_____. Réponse à des calomnies: discours prononcé par
        Jouhaux à la conférence de Douai, 12 Mar. 1922.
        Lille: M. Dhoossche, 1922.

_____. Le syndicalisme français contre la guerre.
        Paris: Marcel Rivière, 1913.

Judt, Tony. Socialism in Provence 1871-1914. A Study in
        the Origins of the Modern French Left. Cambridge:
        Cambridge University, 1979.

Julliard, Jacques. Fernand Pelloutier et les origines du
        syndicalisme d'action directe. Paris: Editions du
        Seuil, 1971.

Kemp, Tom. Economic Forces in French History. London:
        Dennis Dobson, 1971.

Keufer, Auguste. La crise syndicaliste. Aurillac:
        Imprimerie, 1910.

Klein, Alexandre. Les théories agraires du collectivisme.
        Paris: V. Giard & E. Brière, 1906.

Kriegel, Annie. Aux origines du communisme français, 1914-
        1920: Contribution à l'histoire du mouvement
        ouvrier français. Paris: Flammarion, 1964.

_____. Le congrès du Tours (Décembre 1920). Naissance
        du parti communiste français. Paris: Gallimard,
        1973.

_____. La croissance de la C.G.T. 1918-1921: Essai
        statistique. Paris: Mouton, 1966.

_____. Le pain et les roses. Paris: Presses
        Universitaires de France, 1968.

Krimerman, Leonard   I.,   and Lewis Perry, eds. Patterns of
        Anarchy. Garden City: Doubleday, 1966.

Kritsky, Mademoiselle. L'évolution   du   syndicalisme   en
        France. Paris: V. Giard & E. Brière.

Kropotkin, Peter. The Conquest of Bread. New York: New York
        University, 1972.

Labi, Maurice. La grande division des travailleurs. Paris:
        Les Editions Ouvrières, 1964.

Lafargue, Paul. La question de la femme. Paris: L'Oeuvre
        Nouvelle, 1904.

Lagardelle, Hubert, et al. Syndicalisme et socialisme.
        Paris: Marcel Rivière, 1908.

Lefranc, Georges. Le syndicalisme en France. Paris: Presses
        Universitaires de France, 1957.

Lequin, Yves. La formation de la classe ouvrière régionale.
        vol. 1. Lyon: Presses Universitaires de Lyon, 1977.

Leroy, Maxime. Les techniques nouvelles du syndicalisme.
        Paris: Librairie Garnier Frères, 1921.

Levey, Jules. "The Sorelian Syndicalists: Edouard Berth,
        Georges Valois, and Hubert Lagardelle." Ph.D.
        Dissertation, Columbia University, 1967.

Lichtheim, George. Marxism. New York: Praeger, 1965.

_____. A Short History of Socialism. New York: Praeger,
        1971.

Lorwin, Val R. The French Labor Movement. Cambridge:
        Harvard University, 1954.

Lougee, Carolyn C. Le Paradis des Femmes: Women, Salons,
        and Social Stratification in Seventeenth-Century
        France. Princeton: Princeton University, 1976.

Louis, Paul. "L'état présent du syndicalisme mondial," Le
        Musée Social: Annales. Paris: Arthur Rousseau,
        1913.

_____. Histoire de la classe ouvrière en France de la
        révolution à nos jours. Paris: Marcel Rivière,
        1927.

_____. Le syndicalisme contre l'état. Paris: Félix
        Alcan et Guillarimin Réunies, 1910.

Maitron, Jean. Dictionnaire biographique du mouvement ouvrier français, vols. 10-15. Paris: Editions Ouvrières, 1964.

_____. Histoire du mouvement anarchiste en France 1880-1914. Paris: Société Universitaire d'Editions et de Librairie, 1955.

_____. "La personnalité du militant ouvrier français dans la seconde moitié du XIX(e) siècle," Le Mouvement Social 33-34 (Oct. 1960-1961): 67-86.

_____. Ravachol et les anarchistes. France: Collection Archives, 1964.

Malvy, L.-J. Mon crime. Paris: Ernest Flammarion, 1921.

Marchal, André. Le mouvement syndical en France. Paris: Bourrelier, 1945.

Marty, André. La révolte de la Mer Noire. Paris: Editions Sociales, 1949.

Matillon, R. E. Les syndicats ouvriers dans l'agriculture. Paris: Bonvalot-P. Jouve, 1908.

May, André. Les origines du syndicalisme révolutionnaire. Paris: Jouve & Cie., 1913.

Mayer, Arno. Political Origins of the New Diplomacy, 1917-1918. New Haven: Yale University, 1959.

Mazgaj, Paul. The Action Française and Revolutionary Syndicalism. Chapel Hill: University of North Carolina, 1979.

McMillan, James F. Housewife or Harlot. New York: St. Martin's, 1981.

Merlin, Yves. Les conflits collectifs de travail pendant la guerre 1914-1918. Paris: Imp. du Nord Maritime, 1928.

Meyers, Louis. La crise du syndicalisme. Paris: Au Sillon, 1909.

Michon, Georges. La préparation à la guerre: La Loi de Trois Ans 1910-1914. Paris: Marcel Rivière, 1935.

Miquel, Pierre. La paix de Versailles et l'opinion publique française. Paris: Flammarion, 1972.

Mitchell, Harvey, and Stearns, Peter N. The European Labor Movement, the Working Classes, and the Origins of Social Democracy 1890-1914. Itasca: F. E. Peacock Publishers, 1971.

Mitrany, David. Marx Against the Peasant: A Study of Social Dogmatism. Chapel Hill: University of North Carolina Press, 1957.

Modiano, René, and Alfred Rosmer, Union sacrée 1914-193... Paris: Sparticus Cahiers Mensuels, n.d.

Monatte, Pierre. Trois scissions syndicales. Paris: Les Editions Ouvrières, 1958.

Montreuil, Jean. Histoire du mouvement ouvrier en France. Paris: Aubier, 1947.

Moreau, Georges. Essai sur les théories et l'histoire du syndicalisme ouvrier en France. Paris: Marcel Rivière, 1925.

Moss, Bernard H. The Origins of the French Labor Movement. Berkeley: University of California, 1976.

Noland, Aaron. The Founding of the French Socialist Party 1893-1905. Cambridge: Harvard University Press, 1956.

Paraf, Pierre. Les formes actuelles du syndicalisme en France. Paris: Editions de la Vie Universitaire, 1923.

Pawlowski, Auguste. Les syndicats féminins et les syndicats mixtes en France. Paris: Félix Alcan, 1912.

Pelissonnier, Georges. Etude sur le socialisme agraire en France. Dijon: Librairie L. Vernot, 1902.

Pelloutier, Fernand. Histoire des bourses du travail. Paris: Schleicher Frères, 1902.

Pelloutier, Fernand, and Maurice. La vie ouvrière en France. Paris: Schleicher Frères, 1900.

Péricat, Raymond. Lettre ouverte: défense syndicaliste à l'union des syndicats de la Seine: maîtres valets expulsés! Paris: 1928.

Perrot, Michelle. Les ouvriers en grève, France 1871-90. 2 vols. Paris: Mouton, 1974.

Picard, Roger. Le conflit des doctrines économiques en France à la veille de la guerre. New York: Brentano's, 1944.

_____. Le mouvement syndical durant la guerre. Paris: Les Presses Universitaires de France, 1928.

Pierrot, M. Socialisme et syndicalisme. Paris: Les Temps Nouveaux, 1913.

Pinchbeck, Ivy. Women Workers and the Industrial Revolution, 1750-1850. London: Frank Cass, 1969.

Prestwich, P. E. "French Workers and the Temperance Movement." International Review of Social History 25 (1980):35-52.

_____. "Temperance in France: The Curious Case of Absinth." Historical Reflections 6 (Winter 1979): 301-319.

Price, Roger. An Economic History of Modern France. London: St. Martin's Press, 1981.

Proudhon, Pierre-Joseph. La pornocratie: Ou les femmes dans les temps modernes. Paris: Libraires Internationales, 1875.

Prugnaud, Louis. Les étapes du syndicalisme agricole en France. Paris: Éditions de l'Epi, 1957.

Réclus, Elisée. A mon frère, le paysan. Saint-Josse-ten-Noode: D. Villeval, n. d.

Renard, Georges F., and G. Weulersse. Life and Work in Modern Europe, Fifteenth to Eighteenth Centuries. Margaret Richards, trans. New York: Barnes & Noble, 1968.

Rennes, J[acques]. Syndicalisme français. Paris: Marcel Rivière, 1948.

Ridley, Frederick F. Revolutionary Syndicalism in France. Cambridge, 1970.

Rocker, Rudolph. Anarcho-Syndicalism: Theory and Practice. London: Secher and Warburg, 1938.

Ronsin, Francis. La grève des ventres: Propagande néo-malthusienne et baisse de la natalité en France 19(me)-20(me) siècles. Paris: Éditions Aubier Montaigne, 1980.

Rosmer, Alfred. Le mouvement ouvrier pendant la première guerre mondiale. vol. 2. De Zimmerwald à la Révolution Russe. Paris: Mouton, 1959.

Sagaret, Jules. Le syndicalisme intellectuel: Son rôle politique et social. Paris: Libraire Plon, 1922.

Saint-Léon, E. Le compagnonnage. Paris: Armand Colin, 1901.

_____. Syndicalisme ouvrière et syndicalisme agricole. Paris: P. Payot, 1920.

_____. Le syndicalisme révolutionnaire et la C.G.T. Lyon: Chronique du Sud-Est, 1909.

Saulière, André. La grève générale: De Robert Owen à la doctrine syndicaliste. Bordeaux: Imp. de l'Academie et des Facultés, 1913.

Schirmacker, Mademoiselle. "Le travail des femmes en France." Le Musée Social: Mémoires et Documents. Paris: Arthur Rousseau, 1902.

Scott, Joan W. The Glassworkers of Carmaux. Cambridge: Harvard University, 1974.

Scott, John Waugh. Syndicalism and Philosophic Realism. London: A. & C. Black, 1919.

Séailles, Gabriel, introduction. Société des Universités Populaires. Les universités populaires: Paris-Banlieu 1900-1901. Paris: Impr. de Surèsmes, n. d.

Seilhac, Léon. Les congrès ouvriers en France de 1876 à 1897. Paris: Armand Colin, 1899.

Sévérat, J. B. Le mouvement syndical, vol. 7 of Encyclopédie socialiste, syndicale, et coopérative de l'internationale ouvrière 1912-1913. Paris: Aristide Quillet, 1912-1913.

Shorter, Edward, and Charles Tilly. Strikes in France 1930-1968. Cambridge: Harvard University, 1974.

Soltau, Roger. French Political Thought in the Nineteenth Century. New Haven: Yale University, 1931.

Sorel, Georges. Lettres à Paul Delesalle, 1914-1921. Paris: Editions Bernard Grasset, 1947.

Souvarine, Boris. La troisième internationale. Paris: Editions "Clarté," 1919.

Sowerwine, Charles. "Le groupe féministe socialiste 1899-1902," Le Mouvement Social, 90 (Jan.-Mar. 1975): 87-120.

_____. "Workers and Women in France Before 1914: The Debate Over the Couriau Affair," Journal of Modern History 55 (Sept. 1983): 411-440.

Spengler, Joseph J. France Faces Depopulation. Durham: Duke University, 1938.

Stafford, David. From Anarchism to Reformism: A Study of the Political Activities of Paul Brousse Within the First International and the French Socialist Movement, 1870-90. Toronto: University of Toronto Press, 1971.

Stanley, John. The Sociology of Virtue: The Political and Social Theories of Georges Sorel. Berkeley: University of California, 1981.

Stanton, Theodore, ed. The Woman Question in Europe. New York: G. P. Putnam's Sons, 1884.

Stearns, Peter. Revolutionary Syndicalism and French Labor: A Cause Without Rebels. New Brunswick: Rutgers University, 1971.

Stone, Judith F. The Search for Social Peace: Reform Legislation in France 1890-1914. New York: State University of New York Press 1985.

Le syndicalisme contre l'état. Paris: Félix Alcan et Guillarimin Réunies, 1910.

Syndicalisme et néo-malthusiennisme. Lille: M. Dhoossche, 1911.

Taboreau, Jean. Le sophisme antipatriotique. Paris: Henri Charles-Lavauzelle, 1912.

Tavernier, Yves. Le syndicalisme paysan, FNSEA, CNJA. Paris: A. Collin, 1969.

Thibert, Marguerite. Le féminisme dans le socialisme français de 1830 à 1850. Paris: Marcel Giard, 1926.

Thomas, Edith. Pauline Roland: Socialisme et féminisme au XIX(e) siècle. Paris: Marcel Rivière, 1956.

_____. The Women Incendiaries. James & Starr, trans. New York: George Braziller, 1966.

Tilly, Charles, Louise, and Richard. The Rebellious Century.
        Cambridge: Harvard University, 1975.

Toussaint, Adrien. L'union centrale des syndicats agricoles.
        Paris: Payot, 1920.

Trebilcock, Clive. The Industrialization of the Continental
        Powers 1780-1914. London and New York: Longman,
        1981.

Université populaire, Histoire de douze ans (1898-1910),
        preface by Gabriel Eailles. Paris: Imp. la
        Coopération du Livre, 1910.

Les universités populaires 1900-1901: Departéments. Paris:
        Cahiers de la Quinzane, n. d.

Les universités populaires 1900-1901: Paris et banlieu.
        Paris: Cahiers de la Quinzane, n.d.

Vaillant, Edouard. Cherté de la vie et nationalisation du
        sol. Paris: Marcel Rivière, 1914.

Vandervelde, Emile. Le socialisme agraire ouvrier ou
        collectivisme et l'evolution agricole. Paris:
        V. Giard & E. Brière, 1908.

Vincent, K. Steven. Pierre-Joseph Proudhon and the Rise of
        French Republican Socialism. New York: Oxford
        University, 1984.

Vral, André (Abbé). Les pages de l'ouvrier. Paris: Chez
        l'Auteur, 1908.

Weber, Eugen. Peasants Into Frenchmen: The Modernization
        of Rural France 1870-1914. Stanford: Stanford
        University Press, 1976.

Weil, Georges. Histoire du mouvement social en France.
        Paris: Alcan, 1924.

Willard, Claude. Le mouvement socialiste en France 1893-
        1905. Paris: Éditions Sociales, 1965.

Wohl, Robert. French Communism in the Making, 1914-1924.
        Stanford: Stanford University, 1966.

Woodcock, George. Anarchism: A History of Libertarian
        Ideas and Movements. Cleveland and New York:
        World Publishing Co., 1962.

Wright, Gordon. Rural Revolution in France: The Peasantry
        in the Twentieth Century. Stanford: Stanford
        University, 1964.

[Yvetot, Georges]. Nouveau manuel du soldat. Paris:
        Federation des Bourses du Travail de France et des
        Colonies, 1903.

Index

About the Author

BARBARA MITCHELL is Professor of History at Chaffey College. Her articles have appeared in *Proceedings of the Western Society for French History*.

DATE DUE